The Reformation in England

Volume Two

William Tyndale. Before he left Gloucestershire for London and subsequent exile, an old man warned him, "Do you not know that the Pope is very Antichrist of whom the Scripture speaks? But beware what you say . . . that knowledge may cost you your life." So it proved; "the Apostle of England", as Foxe calls him, was executed at Vilvorde on October 6th, 1536, but not before his New Testament had spread divine truth throughout the nation.

[Frontispiece

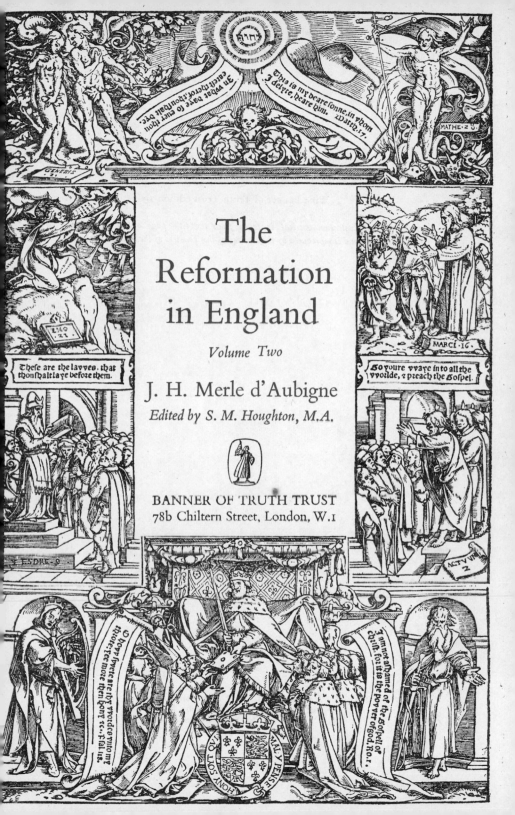

The Reformation in England

Volume Two

J. H. Merle d'Aubigne

Edited by S. M. Houghton, M.A.

BANNER OF TRUTH TRUST
78b Chiltern Street, London, W.1

First published in 1866–78 as Books VI, VIII, and XV of
The History of the Reformation in Europe in the Time of Calvin

First Banner of Truth Trust edition 1963

*The illustration overleaf is taken from the title page of the Coverdale
Bible, and is reproduced by the courtesy of the Trustees of the British Museum*

*This book is set in 11 on 12 point Baskerville
and printed in Great Britain by Billing and
Sons Limited, Guildford and London*

Contents

BOOK ONE

England Begins to Cast off the Papacy

v

CHAPTER TWO

The Church Becomes a Department of State
(CHRISTMAS 1533 TO JUNE 1534)

The King's Proceedings against Catherine—The Monks and the Priests
renounce the Pope—Preparations of Charles V against Henry—Henry
prepares to resist him—The Two Chiefs of the Anti-Roman Party—The
Orator of the Reformation—The King abolishes the Authority of the Pope—
The Sheriffs ordered to see the Proclamation carried out—The Church, a
Department of the State—Authority in the Church—Form which the Church
might have assumed—Various Systems   *Page* 179

CHAPTER THREE

Tyndale and his Enemies
(1534 TO AUGUST 1535)

Tyndale translates the Old Testament at Antwerp—His Charity and Zeal
—Joye pretends to correct his Version—Tyndale's noble Protest—Anne
protects the Friends of the Gospel—Her Message in Harman's Favour—
Discontent of the King—Plot against Tyndale—Snares laid for him—
Stratagem—Attempt at Bribery—Recourse to the Imperial Government
—Tyndale's House surrounded—The Traitor—Tyndale's Arrest—His
Imprisonment in the Castle of Vilvorde—The Life of the Reformers:
Apologies for the Reformation   *Page* 188

CHAPTER FOUR

Henry VIII as King-Pontiff
(1534—1535)

Opposition of certain Priests—Mental Restrictions—Fanatical Monks and
timid Monks—Agitation of Sir Thomas More—More and Fisher refuse to
take the Oath—They are taken to the Tower—The Carthusians required to
swear—Paul III desires to bring back England—Henry rejects the Papacy—
Severe Laws concerning his Primacy—The King not the Head of the Church
                                                                Page 200

CHAPTER FIVE

Henry Destroys his Opponents
(1534—1535)

Frankness and Misery of Sir Thomas More—Confusion in England—
Character of Cranmer—Cranmer's Work—The Bible to be translated into
English—Cranmer's Joy—Failure of the Translation by the Bishops—
Popish and seditious Preachers—The King orders the Carthusians to reject
the Pope—The Carthusians resolve to die—Threats of Revolt—Incompatibility of Popery and Liberty—The Carthusians are condemned—Execution
of the Three Priors—Henry strikes on all sides   *Page* 208

Contents   xiii

BOOK THREE

Reformation, Reaction, Relief

Illustrations

BOOK ONE

England Begins to Cast off the Papacy

CHAPTER ONE

The Nation and its Parties

(Autumn 1529)

ENGLAND, during the period of which we are about to treat, began to separate from the pope and to reform her Church. The fall of Wolsey divides the old times from the new.

The level of the laity was gradually rising. A certain amount of instruction was given to the children of the poor; the universities were frequented by the upper classes, and the king was probably the most learned prince in Christendom. At the same time the clerical level was falling. The clergy had been weakened and corrupted by its triumphs, and the English, awakening with the age and opening their eyes at last, were disgusted with the pride, ignorance, and disorders of the priests.

While France, flattered by Rome calling her its eldest daughter, desired even when reforming her doctrine to preserve union with the papacy, the Anglo-Saxon race, jealous of their liberties, desired to form a Church at once national and independent, yet remaining faithful to the doctrines of Catholicism. Henry VIII is the personification of that tendency, which did not disappear with him, and of which it would not be difficult to discover traces even in later days.

Other elements calculated to produce a better reformation existed at that time in England. The Holy Scriptures, translated, studied, circulated, and preached since the fourteenth century by Wycliffe and his disciples, became in the sixteenth century, by the publication of Erasmus' Testament and the translations of Tyndale and Coverdale, the powerful instrument of a real evangelical revival, and created the scriptural reformation.

These early developments did not proceed from Calvin,

3

he was too young at that time; but Tyndale, Fryth, Latimer, and the other evangelists of the reign of Henry VIII, taught by the same Word as the reformer of Geneva, were his brethren and his precursors. Somewhat later, his books and his letters to Edward VI, to the regent, to the primate, to Sir William Cecil and others, exercised an indisputable influence over the reformation of England. We find in those letters proofs of the esteem which the most intelligent persons of the kingdom felt for that simple and strong man, whom even non-protestant voices in France have declared to be "the greatest Christian of his age."

A religious reformation may be of two kinds: internal or evangelical, external or legal. The evangelical reformation began at Oxford and Cambridge almost at the same time as in Germany. The legal reformation was making a beginning at Westminster and Whitehall. Students, priests, and laymen, moved by inspiration from on high, had inaugurated the first; Henry VIII and his parliament were about to inaugurate the second, with hands occasionally somewhat rough. England began with the spiritual reformation, but the other had its motives too. Those who are charmed by the reformation of Germany sometimes affect contempt for that of England. "A king impelled by his passions was its author," they say. We have placed the scriptural part of this great transformation in the first rank; but we confess that for it to lay hold upon the people in the sixteenth century, it was necessary, as the prophet declared, that kings should be its nursing-fathers, and queens its nursing-mothers. If diverse reforms were necessary, if by the side of German cordiality, Swiss simplicity and other characteristics, God willed to found a protestantism possessing a strong hand and an outstretched arm; if a nation was to exist which with great freedom and power should carry the Gospel to the ends of the world, special tools were required to form that robust organization, and the leaders of the people—the commons, lords, and king—were each to play their part. France had nothing like this: both princes and parliaments opposed the reform; and thence partly arises the difference between those two great nations, for France had in Calvin a mightier reformer than any of those whom England possessed. But let us not forget that we are speaking of the sixteenth century. Since then the work has advanced; important changes have been wrought in Christendom; political society is growing daily more distinct from religious society, and more independent; and we willingly say with Pascal, "Glorious is the state of the Church when it is supported by God alone!"

Two opposing elements—the reforming liberalism of the people, and the almost absolute power of the king—combined in England to accomplish the legal reformation. In that singular island these two rival forces were often seen acting together; the liberalism of the nation gaining certain victories, the despotism of the prince gaining others; king and people agreeing to make mutual concessions. In the midst of these compromises, the little evangelical flock, which had no voice in such matters, religiously preserved the treasure entrusted to it: the Word of God, truth, liberty, and Christian virtue. From all these elements sprang the Church of England. A strange Church some call it. Strange indeed, for there is none which corresponds so imperfectly in theory with the ideal of the Church, and, perhaps, none whose members work out with more power and grandeur the ends for which Christ has formed His kingdom.

Scarcely had Henry VIII refused to go to Rome to plead his cause, when he issued writs for a new parliament (25th September, 1529). Wolsey's unpopularity had hitherto prevented its meeting: now the force of circumstances constrained the king to summon it. When he was on the eve of separating from the pope, he felt the necessity of leaning on the people. Liberty is always the gainer where a country performs an act of independence with regard to Rome. It was natural that in England, possessing as it did from of old time a body of elected representatives, the king should seek the nation's co-operation in the work of reform: and certainly the house of commons gained power and prestige during this period. At the same time, the whole kingdom being astir, the different parties became more distinct.

The papal party was alarmed. Fisher, bishop of Rochester, already very uneasy, became disturbed at seeing laymen called upon to give their advice on religious matters. Men's minds were in a ferment in the bishop's palace, the rural parsonage, and the monk's cell. The partisans of Rome met and consulted about what was to be done, and retired from their conferences foreseeing and imagining nothing but defeat. Du Bellay, at that time bishop of Bayonne, and afterwards of Paris, envoy from the King of France, and eye-witness of all this agitation, wrote to Montmorency (Grand-master of France): "I fancy that in this parliament the priests will have a terrible fright." Ambitious ecclesiastics were beginning to understand that the clerical character, hitherto so favourable to their advancement in a political career, would now be an obstacle to them. "Alas!" exclaimed one of them, "we must off with our frocks."

Such of the clergy, however, as determined to remain faithful to Rome gradually roused themselves. A prelate put himself at their head. Fisher, bishop of Rochester, was learned, intelligent, bold, and slightly fanatical; but his convictions were sincere, and he was determined to sacrifice everything for the maintenance of Roman Catholicism in England. Though discontented with the path upon which his august pupil King Henry had entered, he did not despair of the future, and candidly applied to the papacy our Saviour's words: *The gates of hell shall not prevail against it.*

A recent act of the king's increased Fisher's hopes: Sir Thomas More had been appointed chancellor. The Bishop of Rochester regretted indeed that the king had not given that office to an ecclesiastic, as was customary; but he thought to himself that a layman wholly devoted to the Church, as the new chancellor was, might possibly in those strange times be more useful to it than a priest. With Fisher in the Church, and More in the State (for Sir Thomas, in spite of his gentle *Utopia*, was more papistical and more violent than Wolsey), had the papacy anything to fear? The whole Romish party rallied round these two men, and with them prepared to fight against the Reformation.

Opposed to this hierarchical party was the political party, in whose eyes the king's will was the supreme rule. The dukes of Norfolk and Suffolk, president and vice-president of the Council, Sir William Fitz-William, Comptroller of the Household, and those who agreed with them, were opposed to the ecclesiastical domination, not from the love of true religion,

but because they believed the prerogatives of the State were
endangered by the ambition of the priests, or else because,
seeking honour and power for themselves, they were impatient
at always encountering insatiable clerics on their path.

Between these two parties a third appeared, on whom the
bishops and nobles looked with disdain, but with whom the
victory was to rest at last. In the towns and villages of England,
and especially in London, were to be found many lowly men,
animated with a new life—poor artisans, weavers, cobblers,
painters, shopkeepers—who believed in the Word of God
and had received moral liberty from it. During the day they
toiled at their respective occupations; but at night they stole
along some narrow lane, slipped into a court, and ascended
to some upper room in which other persons had already
assembled. There they read the Scriptures and prayed. At
times even during the day, they might be seen carrying to
well-disposed citizens certain books strictly prohibited by the
late cardinal. Organized under the name of "The Society
of Christian Brethren," they had a central committee in
London and missionaries everywhere, who distributed the
Holy Scriptures and explained their lessons in simple language.
Several priests, both in the city and country, belonged to their
society.

This Christian brotherhood exercised a powerful influence
over the people, and was beginning to substitute the spiritual
and life-giving principles of the Gospel for the legal and
theocratic ideas of popery. These pious men required a moral
regeneration in their hearers, and entreated them to enter,
through faith in the Saviour, into an intimate relation with
God, without having recourse to the mediation of the clergy;
and many of those who listened to them, enraptured at hearing
of truth, grace, morality, liberty, and of the Word of God,
took the teachings to heart. Thus began a new era. It has
been asserted that the Reformation entered England by a
back-door. Not so; it was the true door these missionaries
opened, having even prior to the rupture with Rome preached
the doctrine of Christ. Idly do men speak of Henry's passions,
the intrigues of his courtiers, the parade of his ambassadors,
the skill of his ministers, the complaisance of the clergy, and
the vacillations of parliament: we too shall speak of these

things; but above them all there was something else, something better—the thirst exhibited in this island for the Word of God, and the internal transformation accomplished in the convictions of a great number of its inhabitants. This it was that worked such a powerful revolution in English society.

In the interval between the issuing of the writs and the meeting of parliament, the most antagonistic opinions came out. Conversation everywhere turned on present and future events, and there was a general feeling that the country was on the eve of great changes. The members of parliament who arrived in London gathered round the same table to discuss the questions of the day. The great lords gave sumptuous banquets, at which the guests talked about the abuses of the Church, of the approaching session of parliament, and of what might result from it. One would mention some striking instance of the avarice of the priests; another slyly called to mind the strange privilege which permitted them to commit with impunity certain sins which they punished severely in others. "There are, even in London, houses of ill-fame for the use of priests, monks, and canons." "And," added others, "they would force us to take such men as these for our guides to heaven." Du Bellay, the French ambassador, a man of letters, who, although a bishop, had attached Rabelais to his person in the capacity of secretary, was frequently invited to parties given by the great lords. He lent an attentive ear, and was astonished at the witty and often very biting remarks uttered by the guests against the disorders of the priests. One day a voice exclaimed: "Since Wolsey has fallen, we must forthwith regulate the condition of the Church and of its ministers. We will seize their property." Du Bellay on his return home did not fail to communicate these things to Montmorency: "I have no need," he says, "to write this strange language in cipher; for the noble lords utter it at open table. I think they will do something to be talked about."

The leading members of the commons held more serious meetings with one another. They said they had spoken enough, and that now they must act. They specified the abuses they would claim to have redressed, and prepared petitions for reform to be presented to the king.

Before long the movement descended from the sphere of the nobility to that of the people: a sphere always important, and particularly when a social revolution is in progress. Petty tradesmen and artisans spoke more energetically than the lords. They did more than speak. The apparitor of the Bishop of London having entered the shop of a mercer in the ward of St. Bride, and left a summons on the counter calling upon him to pay a certain clerical tax, the indignant tradesman took up his yard-measure, whereupon the officer drew his sword, and then, either from fear or an evil conscience, ran away. The mercer followed him, assaulted him in the street, and broke his head. The London shopkeepers did not yet quite understand the representative system; they used their staves when they should have waited for the speeches of the members of parliament.

The king tolerated this agitation because it forwarded his purposes. There were advisers who insinuated that it was dangerous to give free course to the passions of the people; and that the English, combining great physical strength with a decided character, might go too far in the way of reform, if their prince gave them the rein. But Henry VIII, possessing an energetic will, thought it would be easy for him to check the popular ebullition whenever he pleased. When Jupiter frowned, all Olympus trembled.

CHAPTER TWO

Parliament and its Grievances

(November 1529)

ON the morning of the 3rd of November, Henry went in his barge to the palace of Bridewell; and, having put on the magnificent robes employed on great ceremonies, and followed by the lords of his train, he proceeded to the Blackfriars church, in which the members of the new parliament had assembled. After hearing the mass of the Holy Ghost, king, lords, and commons met in parliament; when, as soon as the king had taken his seat on the throne, the new chancellor, Sir Thomas More, explained the reason of their being summoned. Thomas Audley, chancellor of the Duchy of Lancaster, was appointed Speaker of the lower house.

Generally speaking, parliament confined itself to passing the resolutions of the government. The Great Charter had, indeed, been long in existence, but until now it had been little more than a dead letter. The Reformation gave it life. "Christ brings us out of bondage into liberty by means of the Gospel," said Calvin. This emancipation, which was essentially spiritual, soon extended to other spheres, and gave an impulse to liberty throughout all Christendom. Even in England such an impulse was needed. Under the Plantagenets and the Tudors the constitutional machine existed, but it worked only as it was directed by the strong hand of the master. Without the Reformation, England might have slumbered long.

The impulse given by religious truth to the latent liberties of the people was felt for the first time in the parliament of 1529. The representatives shared the lively feelings of their constituents, and took their seats with the firm resolve to introduce the necessary reforms in the affairs of both Church and State. Indeed, on the very first day several members pointed out the abuses of the clerical domination, and proposed to lay the desires of the people before the king.

The Commons might of their own accord have applied to the task, and by proposing rash changes have given the Reform a character of violence that might have worked confusion in the State; but they preferred petitioning the king to take the necessary measures to carry out the wishes of the nation; and accordingly a petition respectfully worded, but in clear and strong language, was agreed to. The Reformation began in England, as in Switzerland and in Germany, with personal conversions. The individual was reformed first; but it was necessary for the people to reform afterwards, and the measures requisite to success could not be taken in the sixteenth century without the participation of the governing powers. Freely therefore and nobly a whole nation was about to express to their ruler their grievances and wishes.

On one of the first days of the session, the Speaker and certain members who had been ordered to accompany him proceeded to the palace. "Your Highness," they began, "of late much discord, variance, and debate hath arisen and more and more daily is likely to increase and ensue amongst your subjects, to the great inquietation, vexation, and breach of your peace, of which the chief causes followingly do ensue."

This opening could not fail to excite the king's attention, and the Speaker of the House of Commons began boldly to unroll the long list of the grievances of England. "First, the prelates of your most excellent realm, and the clergy of the same, have in their convocations made many and divers laws without your most royal assent, and without the assent of any of your lay subjects.

"And also many of your said subjects, and specially those that be of the poorest sort, be daily called before the said spiritual ordinaries or their commissaries, on the accusement of light and indiscreet persons, and be excommunicated and put to excessive and impostable charges.

"The prelates suffer the priests to exact divers sums of money for the sacraments, and sometimes deny the same without the money be first paid.

"Also the said spiritual ordinaries do daily confer and give sundry benefices unto certain young folks, calling them their nephews or kinsfolk, being in their minority and within

age, not apt nor able to serve the cure of any such benefice
. . . whereby the said ordinaries accumulate to themselves
large sums of money, and the poor silly souls of your people
perish without doctrine or any good teaching.

"Also a great number of holydays be kept throughout this
your realm, upon the which many great, abominable, and
execrable vices, idle and wanton sports be used, which holydays might by your Majesty be made fewer in number.

"And also the said spiritual ordinaries commit divers of
your subjects to ward, before they know either the cause of
their imprisonment, or the name of their accuser."

Thus far the Commons had confined themselves to questions
that had been discussed more than once; they feared to touch
upon the subject of heresy before the Defender of the [Roman]
Faith. But there were evangelical men among their number
who had been eye-witnesses of the sufferings of the reformed.
At the peril, therefore, of offending the king, the Speaker
boldly took up the defence of the pretended heretics.

"If heresy be ordinarily laid unto the charge of the person
accused, the said ordinaries put to them such subtle interro-
gatories concerning the high mysteries of our faith, as are
able quickly to trap a simple unlearned layman. And if any
heresy be so confessed in word, yet never committed in thought
or deed, they put the said person to make his purgation. And
if the party so accused deny the accusation, witnesses of little
truth or credence are brought forth for the same, and deliver
the party so accused to secular hands."

The Speaker was not satisfied with merely pointing out
the disease: "We most humbly beseech your Grace, in whom
the only remedy resteth, of your goodness to consent, so that
besides the fervent love your Highness shall thereby engender
in the hearts of all your Commons towards your Grace, ye
shall do the most princely feat, and show the most charitable
precedent that ever did sovereign lord upon his subjects."

The king listened to the petition with his characteristic
dignity, and also with a certain kindliness. He recognized
the just demands in the petition of the Commons, and saw
how far they would support the religious independence to
which he aspired. Still, unwilling to take the part of heresy,
he selected only the most crying abuses, and desired his

faithful Commons to take their correction upon themselves. He then sent the petition to the bishops, requiring them to answer the charges brought against them, and added that henceforward his consent would be necessary to give the force of law to the acts of Convocation.

This royal communication was a thunderbolt to the prelates. What! the bishops, the successors of the apostles, accused by the representatives of the nation, and requested by the king to justify themselves like criminals! . . . Had the Commons of England forgotten what a priest was? These proud ecclesiastics thought only of the indelible virtues which, in their view, ordination had conferred upon them, and shut their eyes to the vices of their fallible human nature. We can understand their emotion, their embarrassment, and their anger. The Reformation which had made the tour of the Continent was at the gates of England; the king was knocking at their doors. What was to be done? they could not tell. They assembled, and read the petition again and again. The Archbishop of Canterbury, and the bishops of London, Lincoln, St. Asaph, and Rochester carped at it and replied to it. They would willingly have thrown it into the fire— the best of answers in their opinion; but the king was waiting, and the Archbishop of Canterbury was commissioned to enlighten him.

Warham did not belong to the most fanatical party; he was a prudent man, and the wish for reform had hardly taken shape in England when, being uneasy and timid, he had hastened to give a certain satisfaction to his flock by reforming abuses which he had sanctioned for thirty years. But he was a priest, a Romish priest; he represented an inflexible hierarchy. Strengthened by the clamours of his colleagues, he resolved to utter the famous *non possumus*, less powerful, however, in England than in Rome.

"Sire," he said, "your Majesty's Commons reproach us with uncharitable behaviour. . . . On the contrary, we love them with hearty affection, and have only exercised the spiritual jurisdiction of the Church upon persons infected with the pestilent poison of heresy. To have peace with such had been against the Gospel of our Saviour Christ, wherein he saith, *I came not to send peace, but a sword.*

"Your Grace's Commons complain that the clergy daily do make laws repugnant to the statutes of your realm. We take our authority from the Scriptures of God, and shall always diligently apply to conform our statutes thereto; and we pray that your Highness will, with the assent of your people, temper your Grace's laws accordingly; whereby shall ensue a most sure and hearty conjunction and agreement.

"They accuse us of committing to prison before conviction such as be suspected of heresy. . . . Truth it is that certain apostates, friars, monks, lewd priests, bankrupt merchants, vagabonds, and idle fellows of corrupt intent have embraced the abominable opinions lately sprung up in Germany; and by them some have been seduced in simplicity and ignorance. Against these, if judgment has been exercised according to the laws of the Church, we be without blame.

"They complain that two witnesses be admitted, be they never so defamed, to vex and trouble your subjects to the peril of their lives, shames, costs, and expenses. . . . To this we reply, the judge must esteem the quality of the witness, but in heresy no exception is necessary to be considered, if their tale be likely. This is the universal law of Christendom, and hath universally done good.

"They say that we give benefices to our nephews and kinsfolk, being in young age or infants, and that we take the profit of such benefices for the time of the minority of our said kinsfolk. If it be done to our own use and profit, it is not well; but if it be bestowed to the bringing up and use of the same parties, or applied to the maintenance of God's service, we do not see but that it may be allowed."

As for the irregular lives of the priests, the prelates remarked that they were condemned by the laws of the Church, and consequently there was nothing to be said on that point.

Lastly, the bishops seized the opportunity of taking the offensive: "We entreat your Grace to repress heresy. This we beg of you, lowly upon our knees, so entirely as we can."

Such was the brief of Roman Catholicism in England. Its defence would have sufficed to condemn it.

CHAPTER THREE

Early Reforms

(End of 1529)

THE answer of the bishops was criticized in the royal residence, in the House of Commons, at the meetings of the burgesses, in the streets of the capital, and in the provinces, everywhere exciting a lively indignation. "What!" said they, "the bishops accuse the most pious and active Christians of England—men like Bilney, Fryth, Tyndale, and Latimer—of that idleness and irregularity of which their monks and priests are continually showing us examples. To no purpose have the Commons indisputably proved their grievances, if the bishops reply to notorious facts by putting forward their scholastic system. We condemn their practice, and they take shelter behind their theories; as if the reproach laid against them was not precisely that their lives are in opposition to their laws. 'The fault is not in the Church,' they say. But it is its ministers that we accuse."

The indignant parliament boldly took up the axe, attacked the tree, and cut off the withered and rotten branches. One bill followed another, irritating the clergy, but filling the people with joy. When the legacy dues were under discussion, one of the members drew a touching picture of the avarice and cruelty of the priests. "They have no compassion," he said; "the children of the dead should all die of hunger and go begging, rather than they would of charity give to them the silly cow which the dead man owed, if he had only one." There was a movement of indignation in the house, and they forbade the clergy to take any mortuary fees when the effects were small.

"And that is not all," said another; "the clergy monopolise large tracts of land, and the poor are compelled to pay an extravagant price for whatever they buy. They are everything in the world but preachers of God's Word and shepherds of souls. They buy and sell wool, cloth, and other merchandise; they keep tanneries and breweries. . . . How can they attend to their spiritual duties in the midst of such occupations?" The clergy were consequently prohibited from holding large estates or carrying on the business of merchant, tanner, brewer, etc. At the same time plurality of benefices (some ignorant priests holding as many as ten or twelve) was forbidden, and residence was enforced. The Commons further enacted that any one seeking a dispensation for non-residence (even were the application made to the pope himself) should be liable to a heavy fine.

The clergy saw at last that they must reform. They forbade priests from keeping shops and taverns, playing at dice or other games of chance, passing through towns and villages with hawks and hounds, being present at unbecoming entertainments, and spending the night in suspected houses. Convocation proceeded to enact severe penalties against these disorders, doubling them for adultery, and tripling them for incest. The laity asked how it was that the Church had waited so long before coming to this resolution; and whether these scandals had become criminal only because the Commons condemned them?

But the bishops who reformed the lower clergy did not intend to resign their own privileges. One day when a bill relating to wills was laid before the upper house, the Archbishop of Canterbury and all the other prelates frowned, murmured, and looked uneasily around them. They exclaimed that the Commons were heretics and schismatics, and almost called them infidels and atheists. In all places, good men required that morality should again be united with religion, and that piety should not be made to consist merely in certain ceremonies, but in the awakening of the conscience, a lively faith, and holy conduct. The bishops, not discerning that God's work was then being accomplished in the world, determined to maintain the ancient order of things at all risks.

Their efforts had some chance of success, for the House of Lords was essentially conservative. The Bishop of Rochester, a sincere but narrow-minded man, presuming on the respect inspired by his age and character, boldly came forward as the defender of the Church. "My lords," he said, "these bills have no other object than the destruction of the Church; and if the Church goes down, all the glory of the kingdom will fall with it. Remember what happened to the Bohemians. Like them, our Commons cry out, 'Down with the Church!' Whence cometh that cry? Simply from lack of faith. . . . My lords, save the country, save the Church."

This speech made the Commons very indignant; some members thought the bishop denied that they were Christians. They sent thirty of their leading men to the king. "Sire," said the Speaker, "it is an attaint upon the honour of your Majesty to calumniate before the upper house those whom your subjects have elected. They are accused of lack of faith, that is to say, they are no better than Turks, Saracens, and heathens. Be pleased to call before you the bishop who has insulted your Commons."

The king made a gracious reply, and immediately sent one of his officers to invite the Archbishop of Canterbury, the Bishop of Rochester, and six other prelates to appear before him. They came quite uneasy as to what the prince might have to say to them. They knew that, like all the Plantagenets, Henry VIII would not suffer his clergy to resist him. Immediately the king informed them of the complaint made by the Commons their hearts sank and they lost courage. They thought only how to escape the prince's anger, and the most venerated among them, Fisher, asserted that when speaking about "lack of faith," he had not thought of the Commons of England, but of the Bohemians only. The other prelates confirmed this inadmissible interpretation. This was a graver fault than the fault itself, and the unbecoming evasion was a defeat to the clerical party from which they never recovered. The king allowed the excuse, but he afterwards made the bishops feel the little esteem he entertained for them. As for the House of Commons, it loudly expressed the disdain aroused in them by the bishop's subterfuge.

One chance of safety still remained to them. Mixed committees of the two houses examined the resolutions of the Commons. The peers, especially the ecclesiastical peers, opposed the reform by appealing to usage. "Usage!" ironically observed a Gray's Inn lawyer; "the usage hath ever been of thieves to rob on Shooter's Hill, *ergo* it is lawful and ought to be kept up!" This remark sorely irritated the prelates; "What! our acts are compared to robberies!" But the lawyer, addressing the Archbishop of Canterbury, seriously endeavoured to prove to him that the exactions of the clergy in the matter of probates and mortuaries were open robbery. The temporal lords gradually adopted the opinions of the Commons.

In the midst of these debates, the king did not lose sight of his own interests. Six years before, he had raised a loan among his subjects; he thought parliament ought to relieve him of this debt. This demand was opposed by the members most devoted to the principle of the Reformation; John Petit, in particular, the friend of Bilney and Tyndale, said in parliament: "I give the king all I lent him; but I cannot give him what others have lent him." Henry was not however discouraged, and finally obtained the act required.

The king soon showed that he was pleased with the Commons. Two bills met with a stern opposition from the Lords; they were those abolishing pluralism and non-residence. These two customs were so convenient and advantageous that the clergy determined not to give them up. Henry, seeing that the two houses would never agree, resolved to cut the difficulty. At his desire eight members from each met one afternoon in the Star Chamber. There was an animated discussion; but the lay lords, who were in the conference, taking part with the Commons, the bishops were forced to yield. The two bills passed the Lords the next day, and received the king's assent. After this triumph the king adjourned parliament in the middle of December.

The different reforms that had been carried through were important, but they were not the Reformation. Many abuses were corrected, but the doctrines remained unaltered; the power of the clergy was restricted, but the authority of Christ was not increased; the dry branches of the tree had been lopped off, but a scion calculated to bear good fruit had not been grafted on the wild stock. Had matters stopped here, England might perhaps have obtained a Church with morals less repulsive, but not with a holy doctrine and a new life. But the Reformation was not contented with more decorous forms; it required a second creation.

At the same time parliament had taken a great stride towards the revolution that was to transform the Church. A new power had taken its place in the world: the laity had triumphed over the clergy. No doubt there were upright catholics who gave their assent to the laws passed in 1529; but these laws were nevertheless a product of the Reformation. This it was that had inspired the laity with that new energy, parliament with that bold action, and given the liberties of the nation that impulse which they had lacked hitherto. The joy was great throughout the kingdom; and while the king removed to Greenwich to keep Christmas there "with great plenty of viands, and disguisings and interludes," the members of the Commons were welcomed in the towns and villages with great rejoicings. In the people's eyes their representatives were like soldiers who had just gained a brilliant victory. The clergy, alone in all England, were downcast and exasperated. On returning to their residences the bishops could not conceal their anguish at the danger to the Church. The priests, who had been the first victims offered up on the altar of reform, bent their heads. But if the clergy foresaw days of mourning, the laity hailed with joy the glorious era of the liberties of the people, and of the greatness of England. The friends of the Reformation went further still: they believed that the Gospel would work a complete change in the world, and talked, as Tyndale informs us, "as though the golden age would come again."

CHAPTER FOUR

Anne Boleyn's Father Meets the Emperor and the Pope

(Winter 1530)

BEFORE such glorious hopes could be realized, it was necessary to emancipate Great Britain from the yoke of Romish supremacy. This was the end to which all generous minds aspired; but would the king assist them?

Henry VIII united strength of body with strength of will: both were marked on his manly form. Lively, active, eager, vehement, impatient, and voluptuous—whatever he was, he was with his whole soul. He was at first all heart for the Church of Rome; he went barefoot on pilgrimages, wrote against Luther, and flattered the pope. But before long he grew tired of Rome without desiring the Reformation: profoundly selfish, he cared for himself alone. If the papal domination offended him, evangelical liberty annoyed him. He meant to remain master in his own house, the only master, and master of all. Even without the divorce, Henry would possibly have separated from Rome. Rather than endure any contradiction, he put to death friends and enemies, bishops and missionaries, ministers of state and favourites—even his wives. Such was the prince whom the Reformation found king of England.

History would be unjust, however, were it to maintain that passion alone urged him to action. The question of the succession to the throne had for a century filled the country with confusion and blood. This Henry could not forget. Would the struggles of the Two Roses be renewed after his death, occasioning perhaps the destruction of an ancient monarchy? If Mary, a princess of delicate health, should die, Scotland, France, the party of the White Rose, the Duke of Suffolk, whose wife was Henry's sister, might drag the kingdom into endless wars. And even if Mary's days were prolonged, her title to the crown might be disputed, no female sovereign having as yet sat upon the throne. Another train of ideas also occupied the king's mind. He enquired sincerely whether his marriage with the widow of his brother was lawful. Even before its consummation, as we have seen, he had felt doubts about it. But even his defenders, if there are any, must acknowledge that one circumstance contributed at this time to give unusual force to these scruples: his love for Anne Boleyn.

Catholic writers imagine that this guilty motive was the only one: it is a mistake, for the two former indisputably occupied Henry's mind. As for parliament and people, the king's love for Anne Boleyn affected them very little: it was the reason of state which made them regard the divorce as just and necessary.

A congress was at that time sitting at Bologna with great pomp. On the 5th of November 1530, Charles V, having arrived from Spain, had entered the city, attended by a magnificent suite, and followed by 20,000 soldiers. He was covered with gold, and shone with grace and majesty. The pope waited for him in front of the church of San Petronio, seated on a throne and wearing the triple crown. The Emperor, master of Italy, which his soldiers had reduced to the last desolation, fell prostrate before the pontiff, but lately his prisoner. The union of these two monarchs, both enemies of Henry VIII, seemed destined to ruin the King of England and thwart his great affair.

And yet not long before, an ambassador from Charles V had been received at Whitehall: it was Master Eustace Chapuys. He came to solicit aid against the Turks. Henry caught at the chance: he imagined the moment to be favourable, and that he ought to despatch an embassy to the head of the Empire and the head of the Church. He sent for the Earl of Wiltshire, Anne Boleyn's father; Edward Lee, afterwards archbishop of York; John Stokesley, afterwards bishop of London, and some others. He told them that the Emperor desired his alliance, and commissioned them to proceed to Italy and explain to Charles V the serious motives that induced him to separate from Catherine. "If he persists in his opposition to the divorce," continued Henry, "threaten him, but in covert terms. If the threats prove useless, tell him plainly that, in accord with my friends, I will do all I can to restore peace to my troubled conscience." He added with more calmness: "I am resolved to fear God rather than man, and to place full reliance on comfort from the Saviour." Was Henry sincere when he spoke thus? No one can doubt of his sensuality, his scholastic catholicism, and his cruel violence: must we also believe in his hypocrisy? He was no doubt under a delusion, and deceived himself on the state of his soul.

An important member was added to the deputation. One day when the king was occupied with this affair, Thomas Cranmer appeared at the door of his room with a manuscript in his hand. Cranmer had a fine understanding, a warm heart, a character perhaps too weak,[1] but extensive learning. Captivated by the Holy Scriptures, he desired to seek for truth nowhere else. He had suggested a new point of view to Henry VIII. "The essential thing," he said, "is to know what the Word of God teaches on the matter in question." "Show me that," exclaimed the king. Cranmer brought him his treatise, in which he proved that the Word of God is above all human jurisdiction, and that it forbids marriage with a brother's widow. Henry took the work in his hand, read it again and again, and praised its excellence. A bright idea occurred to him. "Are you strong enough to maintain before the bishop of Rome the propositions laid down in this treatise?" said the king. Cranmer was timid, but convinced and devoted. "Yes," he made answer, "with God's grace, and if your Majesty commands it." "Marry, then!" exclaimed Henry with delight, "I will send you." Cranmer departed with the others in January 1530.

While Henry's ambassadors were journeying slowly, Charles V, more exasperated than ever against the divorce, endeavoured to gain the pope. Clement VII, who was a clever man, and possessed a certain kindly humour, but was at heart

[1] G. W. Bromiley argues that Cranmer was more than a weak puppet and that he influenced the King behind the scenes: *Thomas Cranmer, Theologian* (Lutterworth Press, 1956); *Thomas Cranmer, Archbishop and Martyr* (Church Book Room Press, 1956).]

cunning, false, and cowardly, amused the puissant Emperor
with words. When he learnt that the King of England was
sending an embassy to him, he gave way to the keenest sorrow.
What was he to do? which way could he turn? To irritate
the Emperor was dangerous; to separate England from Rome
would be to endure a great loss. Caught between Charles V
and Henry VIII, he groaned aloud: he paced up and down
his chamber gesticulating; then suddenly stopping, sank into a
chair and burst into tears. Nothing succeeded with him: it
was, he thought, as if he had been bewitched. What need
was there for the King of England to send him an embassy?
Had not Clement told Henry through the Bishop of Tarbes:
"I am content the marriage should take place, provided it
be without my authorization." It was of no use: the pope
asked him to do without the papacy, and the king would
only act with it. He was more popish than the pope.

To add to his misfortunes, Charles began to press the
pontiff more seriously, and yielding to his importunities,
Clement drew up a brief on the 7th of March, in which he
commanded Henry "to receive Catherine with love, and to
treat her in all things with the affection of a husband." But
the brief was scarcely written when the arrival of the English
embassy was announced. The pope in alarm immediately
put the document back into his portfolio, promising himself
that it would be long before he published it.

As soon as the English envoys had taken up their quarters
at Bologna, the ambassadors of France called to pay their
respects. De Gramont, bishop of Tarbes, was overflowing
with politeness, especially to the Earl of Wiltshire. "I have
shown much honour to M. de Rochford," he wrote to his
master on the 28th of March. "I went out to meet him. I
have visited him often at his lodging. I have fêted him, and
offered him my solicitations and services, telling him that
such were your orders." Not thus did Clement VII act: the
arrival of the Earl of Wiltshire and his colleagues was a
cause of alarm to him. Yet he must make up his mind to
receive them: he appointed the day and the hour for the
audience.

Henry VIII desired that his representatives should appear
with great pomp, and accordingly the ambassador and his

colleagues went to great expense with that intent. Wiltshire entered first into the audience-hall: being father of Anne Boleyn, he had been appointed by the king as the man in all England most interested in the success of his plans. But Henry had calculated badly: the personal interest which the earl felt in the divorce made him odious both to Charles and Clement. The pope, wearing his pontifical robes, was seated on the throne, surrounded by his cardinals. The ambassadors approached, made the customary salutations, and stood before him. The pontiff, wishing to show his kindly feelings towards the envoys of the *"Defender of the Faith,"* put out his slipper according to custom, presenting it graciously to the kisses of the proud Englishmen. The revolt was about to begin. The earl, remaining motionless, refused to kiss his holiness's slipper. But that was not all: a fine spaniel, with long silky hair, which Wiltshire had brought from England, had followed him to the episcopal palace. When the bishop of Rome put out his foot, the dog did what other dogs would have done under similar circumstances: he flew at the foot, and caught the pope by the great toe. Clement hastily drew it back. The sublime borders on the ridiculous: the ambassadors, bursting with laughter, raised their arms and hid their faces behind their long rich sleeves. "That dog was a *protestant*," said a reverend father. "Whatever he was," said an Englishman, "he taught us that a pope's foot was more meet to be bitten by dogs than kissed by Christian men." The pope, recovering from his emotion, prepared to listen, and the earl, regaining his seriousness, explained to the pontiff that as Holy Scripture forbade a man to marry his brother's wife, Henry VIII required him to annul as unlawful his union with Catherine of Aragon. As Clement did not seem convinced, the ambassador skilfully insinuated that the king might possibly declare himself independent of Rome, and place the English Church under the direction of a patriarch. "The example," added the ambassador, "will not fail to be imitated by other kingdoms of Christendom."

The agitated pope promised not to remove the suit to Rome, provided the king would give up the idea of reforming England. Then, putting on a most gracious air, he proposed to introduce the ambassador to Charles V. This was giving

Wiltshire the chance of receiving a harsh rebuff. The earl saw it; but his duty obliging him to confer with the Emperor, he accepted the offer.

The father of Anne Boleyn proceeded to an audience with the nephew of Catherine of Aragon. Representatives of two women whose rival causes agitated Europe, these two men could not meet without a collision. True, the earl flattered himself that as it was Charles' interest to detach Henry from Francis I, that phlegmatic and politic prince would certainly not sacrifice the gravest interests of his reign for a matter of sentiment; but he was deceived. The Emperor received him with a calm and reserved air, but unaccompanied by any kindly demonstration. The ambassador skilfully began by speaking of the Turkish war; then ingeniously passing to the condition of the kingdom of England, he pointed out the reasons of state which rendered the divorce necessary. Here Charles stopped him short: "Sir Count, you are not to be trusted in this matter; you are a party to it; let your colleagues speak." The earl replied with respectful coldness: "Sire, I do not speak here as a father, but as my master's servant, and I am commissioned to inform you that his conscience condemns a union contrary to the law of God." He then offered Charles the immediate restitution of Catherine's dowry. The Emperor coldly replied that he would support his aunt in her rights, and then abruptly turning his back on the ambassador, refused to hear him any longer.

Thus did Charles, who had been all his life a crafty politician, place in this matter the cause of justice above the interests of his ambition. Perhaps he might lose an important ally; it mattered not; before everything he would protect a woman unworthily treated. On this occasion we feel more sympathy for Charles than for Henry. The indignant Emperor hastily quitted Bologna on the 22nd or 24th of February.

The earl hastened to his friend M. de Gramont, and, relating how he had been treated, proposed that the kings of France and England should unite in the closest bonds. He added that Henry could not accept Clement as his judge, since he had himself declared that he was ignorant of the law of God. "England," he said, "will be quiet for three or four months. Sitting in the ball-room, she will watch the dancers, and will form her resolution according as they dance well or ill." A rule of policy that has often been followed.

Gramont was prepared to make common cause with Henry against the Emperor; but, like his master, he could not make up his mind to do without the pope. He strove to induce Clement to join the two kings and abandon Charles; or else —he insinuated in his turn—England would separate from the Romish Church. This was to incur the risk of losing Western Europe, and accordingly the pope answered with much concern: "I will do what you ask." There was, however, a reserve; namely, that the steps taken overtly by the pope would absolutely decide nothing.

Clement once more received the ambassador of Henry VIII. The earl carried with him the book wherein Cranmer proved that the pope cannot dispense any one from obeying the law of God, and presented it to the pope. The latter took it and glanced over it, his looks showing that a prison could not have been more disagreeable to him than this impertinent volume. The Earl of Wiltshire soon discovered that there was nothing for him to do in Italy. Charles V, usually so reserved, had made the bitterest remarks before his departure. His chancellor, with an air of triumph, enumerated to the English ambassador all the divines of Italy and France who were opposed to the king's wishes. The pope seemed to be a puppet which the Emperor moved as he liked; and the cardinals had but one idea, that of exalting the Romish power. Wearied and disgusted, the earl departed for France and England with the greater portion of his colleagues.

Cranmer was left behind. Having been sent to show Clement that Holy Scripture is above all Roman pontiffs, and speaks in a language quite opposed to that of the popes, he had asked more than once for an audience at which to discharge his mission. The wily pontiff had replied that he would hear him at Rome, believing he was thus putting him off until the Greek calends. But Clement was deceived: the English doctor, determining to do his duty, refused to depart for London with the rest of the embassy, and repaired to the metropolis of Catholicism.

CHAPTER FIVE

Oxford and Cambridge Debate
the Divorce
(Winter 1530)

A T the same time that Henry sent ambassadors to Italy to obtain the pope's consent, he invited all the universities of Christendom to declare that the question of divorce was of divine right, and that the pope had nothing to say about it. It was his opinion that the universal voice of the Church ought to decide, and not the voice of one man.

First he attempted to canvass Cambridge, and as he wanted a skilful man for that purpose, he applied to Wolsey's old servant, Stephen Gardiner, an intelligent, active, wily churchman and a good catholic. One thing alone was superior to his catholicism—his desire to win the king's favour. He aspired to rise like the cardinal to the summit of greatness. Henry named the chief almoner, Edward Fox, as his colleague.

Arriving at Cambridge one Saturday about noon in the latter half of February, the royal commissioners held a conference in the evening with the vice-chancellor (Dr. Buckmaster), Dr. Edmunds, and other influential men who had resolved to go with the court. But these doctors, members of the political party, soon found themselves checked by an embarrassing support on which they had not calculated: it was that of the friends of the Gospel. They had been convinced by the writing which Cranmer had published on the divorce. Gardiner and the members of the conference, hearing of the assistance which the evangelicals desired to give them, were annoyed at first. On the other hand, the champions of the court of Rome, alarmed at the alliance of the two parties who were opposed to them, began that very night to visit college after college, leaving no stone unturned that the peril might be averted. Gardiner, uneasy at their zeal, wrote to

Henry VIII: "As we assembled they assembled; as we made friends they made friends." Dr. Watson, Dr. Tomson, and other papal supporters at one time shouted very loudly, at another spoke in whispers. They said that Anne Boleyn was a heretic, that her marriage with Henry would hand England over to Luther; and they related to those whom they desired to gain—wrote Gardiner to the king—"many fables, too tedious to repeat to your Grace." These "fables" would not only have bored Henry, but greatly irritated him.

The vice-chancellor, flattering himself that he had a majority, notwithstanding these clamours, called a meeting of the doctors, bachelors of divinity, and masters of arts, for Sunday afternoon. About two hundred persons assembled, and the three parties were distinctly marked out. The most numerous and the most excited were those who held for the pope against the king. The evangelicals were in a minority, but were quite as decided as their adversaries, and much calmer. The politicians, uneasy at seeing the friends of Latimer and Cranmer disposed to vote with them, would have, however, to accept of their support, if they wished to gain the victory. They resolved to seize the opportunity offered them. "Most learned senators," said the vice-chancellor, "I have called you together because the great love which the king bears you engages me to consult your wisdom." Thereupon Gardiner and Fox handed in the letter which Henry had given them, and the vice-chancellor read it to the meeting. In it the king set forth his hopes of seeing the doctors unanimous to do what was agreeable to him. The deliberations commenced, and the question of a rupture with Rome soon began to appear distinctly beneath the question of the divorce. Edmunds spoke for the king, Tomson for the pope. There was an interchange of antagonistic opinions, and a disorder of ideas among many; the speakers grew warm; one voice drowned another, and the confusion became extreme.

The vice-chancellor, desirous of putting an end to the clamour, proposed referring the matter to a committee, whose decision should be regarded as that of the whole university, which was agreed to. Then seeing more clearly that the royal cause could not succeed without the help of the evangelical party, he proposed some of its leaders—Doctors Salcot, Reps,

Crome, Shaxton, and Latimer—as members of the committee. On hearing these names, there was an explosion of murmurs in the meeting. Salcot, abbot of St. Benet's, was particularly offensive to the doctors of the Romish party. "We protest," they said, "against the presence in the committee of those who have approved of Cranmer's book, and thus declared their opinion already." "When any matter is talked of all over the kingdom," answered Gardiner, "there is not a sensible man who does not tell his friends what he thinks about it." The whole afternoon was spent in lively altercation. The vice-chancellor, wishing to bring it to an end, said: "Gentlemen, it is getting late, and I invite every one to take his seat, and declare his mind by a secret vote." It was useless; no one took his seat; the confusion, reproaches, and declamations continued. At dark, the vice-chancellor adjourned the meeting until the next day. The doctors separated in great excitement, but with different feelings. While the politicians saw nothing else to discuss but the question of the king's marriage, the evangelicals and the papists considered that the real question was this: Which shall rule in England—the Reformation or Popery?

The next day, the names of the members of the proposed committee having been put to the vote, the meeting was found to be divided into two equal parties. In order to obtain a majority Gardiner undertook to get some of his adversaries out of the way. Going up and down the Senate-house, he began to whisper in the ears of some of the less decided; and inspiring them either with hope or fear, he prevailed upon several to leave the meeting.

The grace was then put to the vote a third time and passed. Gardiner triumphed. Returning to his room, he sent the list to the king. Sixteen of the committee, indicated by the letter A, were favourable to his Majesty. "As for the twelve others," he wrote, "we hope to win most of them by *good means*." The committee met and considered the royal demand. They carefully examined the passages of Holy Scripture, the explanations of translators, and gave their opinion. Then followed the public discussion. Gardiner was not without fear: as there might be skilful assailants and awkward defenders, he looked out for men qualified to defend the royal cause worthily. It was a remarkable circumstance that, passing over the traditional doctors, he added to the defence —of which he and Fox were the leaders—two evangelical doctors, Salcot, abbot of St. Benet's, and Reps. He reserved to his colleague and himself the political part of the question; but notwithstanding all his catholicism, he desired that the scriptural reasons should be placed foremost. The discussion was conducted with great thoroughness, and the victory remained with the king's champions.

On the 9th of March, the doctors, professors, and masters having met after vespers in the priory hall, the vice-chancellor said: "It has appeared to us as most certain, most in accord with Holy Scriptures, and most conformable to the opinions of commentators, that it is contrary to divine and natural law for a man to marry the widow of his brother dying childless." Thus the Scriptures were really, if not explicitly, declared by the university of Cambridge to be the supreme and only rule of Christians, and the contrary decisions of Rome were held to be not binding. The Word of God was avenged of the long contempt it had endured, and after having been long put below the pope's word, was now restored to its lawful place. In this matter Cambridge was right.

It was necessary to try Oxford next. Here the opposition was stronger, and the popish party looked forward to a victory. Longland, bishop of Lincoln and chancellor of the university, was commissioned by Henry to undertake the matter, Doctor Bell, and afterwards Edward Fox, the chief almoner, being joined with him. The king, uneasy at the results of the negotiation, and wishing for a favourable decision at any cost, gave Longland a letter for the university, through every word of which an undisguised despotism was visible. "We will and command you," he said, "that ye, not leaning to wilful and sinister opinions of your own several minds, considering that we be your sovereign liege lord, and totally giving your affections to the true overtures of divine learning in this behalf, do show and declare your true and just learning in the said cause. . . . And we, for your so doing, shall be to you and to our university there so good and gracious a lord for the same, as ye shall perceive it well done in your well fortune to come. And in case you do not uprightly handle yourselves herein, we shall so quickly and sharply look to your unnatural misdemeanour herein, that it shall not be to your quietness and ease hereafter. . . . Accommodate yourselves to the mere truth; assuring you that those who do shall be esteemed and set forth, and the contrary neglected and little set by . . . . We doubt not that your resolution shall be our high contentation and pleasure."

This royal missive caused a great commotion in the university. Some slavishly bent their heads, for the king spoke rod in hand. Others declared themselves convinced by the political reasons, and said that Henry must have an heir whose right to the throne could not be disputed. And, lastly, some were convinced that Holy Scripture was favourable to the royal cause. All men of age and learning, as well as all who had either capacity or ambition, declared in favour of the divorce. Nevertheless a formidable opposition soon showed itself.

The younger members of the Senate were enthusiastic for Catherine, the Church, and the pope. Their theological education was imperfect; they could not go to the bottom of the question, but they judged by the heart. To see a Catholic lady oppressed, to see Rome despised, inflamed their anger; and if the elder members maintained that their view was the more reasonable, the younger ones believed theirs to be the more noble. Unhappily, when the choice lies between the useful and the generous, the useful commonly triumphs. Still, the young doctors were not prepared to yield. They said— and they were not wrong—that religion and morality ought not to be sacrificed to reasons of state, or to the passions of princes. And seeing the spectre of Reform hidden behind that of the divorce, they regarded themselves as called upon to save the Church. "Alas!" said the royal delegates, the Bishop of Lincoln and Dr. Bell, "alas! we are in continual perplexity, and we cannot foresee with any certainty what will be the issue of this business."

They agreed with the heads of houses that, in order to prepare the university, three public disputations should be solemnly held in the divinity schools. By this means they hoped to gain time. "Such disputations," they said, "are a very honourable means of amusing the multitude until we are sure of the consent of the majority." The discussions took place, and the younger masters, arranging each day what was to be done or said, gave utterance to all the warmth of their feelings.

When the news of these animated discussions reached Henry, his displeasure broke out, and those immediately around him fanned his indignation. "A great part of the youth of our university," said the king, "with contentious and factious manners, daily combine together." . . . The courtiers, instead of moderating, excited his anger. Every day, they told him, these young men, regardless of their duty towards their sovereign, and not conforming to the opinions of the most virtuous and learned men of the university, meet together to deliberate and oppose his Majesty's views, "Has it ever been seen," exclaimed the king, "that such a number of right small learning should stay their seniors in so weighty a cause?" Henry, in exasperation, wrote to the heads of the houses: "It is not good to stir a hornet's nest." This threat excited the younger party still more: if the term "hornet" amused some, it irritated others. In hot weather, the hornet (the king) chases the weaker insects; but the noise he makes in flying forewarns them, and the little ones escape him. Henry could not hide his vexation; he feared lest the little flies should prove stronger than the big hornet. He was uneasy in his castle of Windsor; and the insolent opposition of Oxford pursued him wherever he turned his steps—on the terrace, in the wide park, and even in the royal chapel. "What!" he exclaimed, "shall this university dare show itself more unkind and wilful than all other universities, abroad or at home?" Cambridge had recognized the king's right, and Oxford refused.

Wishing to end the matter, Henry summoned High-Almoner Fox to Windsor, and ordered him to repeat at Oxford the victory he had gained at Cambridge. He then dictated to his secretary a letter to the recalcitrants: "We cannot a little marvel that you, neither having respect to our estate, being your prince and sovereign lord, nor yet remembering such benefits as we have always showed unto you, have hitherto refused the accomplishment of our desire. Permit no longer the private suffrages of light and wilful heads to prevail over the learned. By your diligence redeem the errors and delays past.

"Given under our signet, at our castle of Windsor."

Fox was entrusted with this letter.

The Lord High-Almoner and the Bishop of Lincoln immediately called together the younger masters of the university, and declared that a longer resistance might lead to their ruin. But the youth of Oxford were not to be overawed by threats of violence. Lincoln had hardly finished, when several masters of arts protested loudly, some even spoke "very wickedly." Not permitting himself to be checked by such rebellion, the bishop ordered the poll to be taken; twenty-seven voted for the king, and twenty-two against. The royal commissioners were not yet satisfied; they assembled all the faculties, and invited the members to give their opinion in turn. This intimidated many, and only eight or ten had courage enough to declare their opposition frankly. The bishop, encouraged by such a result, ordered that the final vote should be taken by ballot. Secrecy emboldened many of those who had not dared to speak; and while thirty-one voted in favour of the divorce, twenty-five opposed it. That was of little consequence, as the two prelates had the majority. They immediately drew up the statute in the name of the university, and sent it to the king; after which the bishop, proud of his success, celebrated a solemn mass of the Holy Ghost. The Holy Ghost had not, however, been much attended to in the business. Some had obeyed the prince, others the pope; and if we desire to find those who obeyed Christ, we must look for them elsewhere.

The university of Cambridge was the first to send in its submission to Henry. The Sunday before Easter (1530), Vice-Chancellor Buckmaster arrived at Windsor in the forenoon. The court was at chapel, where Latimer, recently appointed one of the king's chaplains, was preaching. The vice chancellor came in during the service and heard part of the sermon. Latimer was a very different man from Henry's servile courtiers. He did not fear even to attack such of his colleagues as did not do their duty: "That is no godly preacher that will hold his peace, and not strike you with his sword that you smoke again. . . . Chaplains will not do their duties, but rather flatter. But what shall follow? They shall have God's curse upon their heads for their labour. The minister must reprove without fearing any man, even if he be threatened with death." Latimer was particularly bold in all that concerned the errors of Rome, which Henry VIII desired to maintain in the English Church. "Wicked persons," he said, "men, who despise God, call out, We are christened, therefore we are saved. Make no mistake, to be christened and not obey God's commandments is to be worse than the Turks! Regeneration cometh from the Word of God; it is by hearing and believing this Word that we are born again."

Thus spoke one of the fathers of the English Reformation: such is the real doctrine of the Church of England; the contrary doctrine is a mere relic of popery.

As the congregation were leaving the chapel, the vice-chancellor spoke to the secretary (Cromwell) and the provost, and told them the occasion of his visit. The king sent a message that he would receive the deputation after evening service. Desirous of giving a certain distinction to the decision of the universities, Henry ordered all the court to assemble in the audience-chamber. The vice-chancellor presented the letter to the king, who was much pleased with it. "Thanks, Mr. Vice-Chancellor," he said, "I very much approve the way in which you have managed this matter. I shall give your university tokens of my satisfaction. . . . You heard Mr. Latimer's sermon," he added, which he greatly praised and then withdrew. The Duke of Norfolk, going up to the vice-chancellor, told him that the king desired to see him the following day.

The next day, Dr. Buckmaster, faithful to the appointment, waited all the morning; but the king had changed his mind, and sent orders to the deputy from Cambridge that he might depart as soon as he pleased. The message had scarcely been delivered before the king entered the gallery. An idea which quite engrossed his mind urged him on: he wanted to speak with the doctor about the principle put forward by Cranmer. Henry detained Buckmaster from one o'clock until six, repeating in every possible form, "Can the pope grant a dispensation when the law of God has spoken?" He even displayed much ill-humour before the vice-chancellor, because this point had not been decided at Cambridge. At last he quitted the gallery; and, to counterbalance the sharpness of his reproaches, he spoke very graciously to the doctor, who hurried away as fast as he could.

CHAPTER SIX

Henry Appeals to Foreign Opinion

(January to September 1530)

THE king did not limit himself to asking the opinions of England: he appealed to the universal teaching of the Church, represented according to his views by the universities and not by the pope. The element of individual conviction, so strongly marked in Tyndale, Fryth, and Latimer, was wanting in the official reformation that proceeded from the prince. To know what Scripture said, Henry was about to send delegates to Paris, Bologna, Padua, and Wittenberg: he would have sent even to the East, if such a journey had been easy. That false catholicism which looked for the interpretation of the Bible to churches and declining schools where traditionalism, ritualism, and hierarchism were magnified, was a counterfeit popery. Happily the supreme voice of the Word of God surmounted this fatal tendency in England.

Henry VIII, full of confidence in the friendship of the King of France, applied first to the university of Paris; but Dr. Pedro Garray, a Spanish priest, as ignorant as he was fanatical (according to the English agents), eagerly took up the cause of Catherine of Aragon. Aided by the impetuous Beda, he obtained an opinion adverse to Henry's wishes.

When he heard of it, the alarmed prince summoned Du Bellay, the French ambassador, to the palace, gave him for Francis I a famous diamond fleur-de-lis valued at £10,000 sterling, also the acknowledgments for 100,000 livres which Francis owed Henry for war expenses, and added a gift of 400,000 crowns for the ransom of the king's sons. Unable to resist such strong arguments, Francis charged Du Bellay to represent to the faculty of Paris "the great scruples of Henry's conscience"; whereupon the Sorbonne deliberated, and several doctors exclaimed that it would be an attaint upon the pope's honour to suppose him capable of refusing con-

35

solation to the wounded conscience of a Christian. During these debates, the secretary took the names, received the votes, and entered them on the minutes. A fiery papist, observing that the majority would be against the Roman opinion, jumped up, sprang upon the secretary, snatched the list from his hands, and tore it up. All started from their seats, and "there was great disorder and tumult." They all spoke together, each trying to assert his own opinion; but as no one could make himself heard amid the general clamour, the doctors hurried out of the room in a great rage. "Beda acted like one possessed," wrote Du Bellay.

Meanwhile the ambassadors of the King of England were walking up and down an adjoining gallery, waiting for the division. Attracted by the shouts, they ran forward, and seeing the strange spectacle presented by the theologians, and "hearing the language they used to one another," they retired in great irritation. Du Bellay, who had at heart the alliance of the two countries, conjured Francis I to put an end to such "impertinences." The president of the parlement of Paris consequently ordered Beda to appear before him, and told him that it was not for a person of his sort to meddle with the affairs of princes, and that if he did not cease his opposition, he would be punished in a way he would not soon forget. The Sorbonne profited by the lesson given to the most influential of its members, and on the 2nd of July declared in favour of the divorce by a large majority. The universities of Orleans, Angers, and Bourges had already done so, and that of Toulouse did the same shortly after. Henry VIII had France and England with him.

This was not enough: he must have Italy also. He filled that peninsula with his agents, who had orders to obtain from the bishops and universities the declaration refused by the pope. A rich and powerful despot is never in want of devoted men to carry out his designs.

The university of Bologna, in the states of the Church, was, after Paris, the most important in the Catholic world. A monk was in great repute there at this time. Noble by birth and an eloquent preacher, Battista Pallavicini was one of those independent thinkers often met with in Italy. The English agents applied to him; he declared that he and his colleagues were ready to prove the unlawfulness of Henry's marriage, and when Stokesley spoke of remuneration, they replied: "No, no! what we have received freely, we give freely." Henry's agents could not contain themselves for joy: the university of the pope declares against the pope! Those among them who had an inkling for the Reformation were especially delighted. On the 10th June the eloquent monk appeared before the ambassadors with the judgment of the faculty, which surpassed all they had imagined. Henry's marriage was declared "horrible, execrable, detestable, abominable for a Christian and even for an infidel, forbidden by divine and human law under pain of the severest punishment. . . . The holy father, who can do almost everything," innocently continued the university, "has not the right to permit such a union." The universities of Padua and Ferrara hastened to add their votes to those of Bologna, and declared the marriage with a brother's widow to be "null, detestable, profane, and abominable." Henry was conqueror all along the line. He had with him that universal consent which, according to certain illustrious doctors, is the very essence of Catholicism. Crooke, one of Henry's agents, and a distinguished Greek scholar, who discharged his mission with indefatigable ardour, exclaimed that "the just cause of the king was approved by all the doctors of Italy."

In the midst of this harmony of catholicity, there was one exception of which no one had dreamt. That divorce which, according to the frivolous language of a certain party, was the cause of the Reformation in England, found opponents among the fathers and the children of the Reformation. Henry's envoys were staggered. "My fidelity bindeth me to advertise your Highness," wrote Crooke to the king, "that all Lutherans be utterly against your Highness in this cause, and have letted [hindered] as much with their wretched poor malice, without reason or authority, as they could and might, as well here as in Padua and Ferrara, where be no small companies of them." The Swiss and German reformers having been summoned to give an opinion on this point, Luther, Œcolampadius, Zwingli, Bucer, Grynæus, and even Calvin,[1] all expressed the same opinion. "Certainly," said

[1] Calvin's letter or dissertation (*Calvini Epistolæ*, p. 384) harmonizes the

Luther, "the king has sinned by marrying his brother's wife; that sin belongs to the past; let repentance, therefore, blot it out, as it must blot out all our past sins. But the marriage must not be dissolved; such a great sin, which is future, must not be permitted. There are thousands of marriages in the world in which sin has a part, and yet we may not dissolve them. *A man shall cleave unto his wife, and they shall be one flesh.* This law is superior to the other, and overrules the lesser one." The collective opinion of the Lutheran doctors was in conformity with the just and Christian sentiments of Luther. Thus (we repeat) the event which, according to Catholic writers, was the cause of the religious transformation of England, was approved by the Romanists and condemned by the evangelicals. Besides, the latter knew very well that a Reformation must proceed, not from a divorce or a marriage, not from diplomatic negotiations or university statutes, but from the power of the Word of God and the free conviction of Christians.

While these matters were going on, Cranmer was at Rome, asking the pope for that discussion which the pontiff had promised him at their conference in Bologna. Clement VII had never intended to grant it: he had thought that, once at Rome, it would be easy to elude his promise; it was that which occupied his attention just now. Among the means which popes have sometimes employed in their difficulties with kings, one of the most common was to gain the agents of those princes. It was the first employed by Clement; he nominated Cranmer Grand Penitentiary for all the states of the King of England, some even say for all the Catholic world. It was little more than a title, and "was only to stay his stomach for that time, in hope of a more plentiful feast hereafter, if he had been pleased to take his repast on any popish preferment." But Cranmer was influenced by purer motives; and without refusing the title the pope gave him— since, having the task of winning him to the king's side, he would thus have compromised his mission—he made no account of it, and showed all the more zeal for the accomplishment of his charge.

---

apparently contradictory passages of Leviticus and Deuteronomy; but I much doubt if it belongs to this period.

The embassy had not succeeded, and they were getting uneasy about it in England. Some of the pope's best friends could not understand his blindness. The two archbishops, the dukes of Norfolk and Suffolk, the marquises of Dorset and Exeter, thirteen earls, four bishops, twenty-five barons, twenty-two abbots, and eleven members of the Lower House determined to send an address to Clement VII. "Most blessed father," they began, "the king, who is our head and the life of us all, has ever stood by the see of Rome amidst the attacks of your many and powerful enemies, and yet he alone is to reap no benefit from his labours. . . . Meanwhile we perceive a flood of miseries impending over the commonwealth. If your Holiness, who ought to be our father, have determined to leave us as orphans, we shall seek our remedy elsewhere. . . . He that is sick will by any means be rid of his distemper; and there is hope in the exchange of miseries, when, if we cannot obtain what is good, we may obtain a lesser evil. . . . We beseech your Holiness to consider with yourself: you profess that on earth you are Christ's vicar. Endeavour then to show yourself so to be by pronouncing your sentence to the glory and praise of God." Clement gained time: he remained two months and a half without answering, thinking about the matter, turning it over and over in his mind. The great difficulty was to harmonize the will of Henry VIII, who desired another wife, and that of Charles V, who insisted that he ought to keep the old one. . . . There was only one mode of satisfying both these princes at once, and that was by the king's having the two wives together. Wolsey had already entertained this idea. More than two years before, the pope had hinted as much to Da Casale: "Let him take another wife," he had said, speaking of Henry. Clement now recurred to it, and having sent privately for Da Casale, he said to him: "This is what we have hit upon: we permit his Majesty to have two wives." The infallible pontiff proposed bigamy to a king. Da Casale was still more astonished than he had been at the time of Clement's first communication. "Holy father," he said to the pope, "I doubt whether such a mode will satisfy his Majesty, for he desires above all things to have the burden removed from his conscience."

This guilty proposal led to nothing; the king, sure of the

lords and of the people, advanced rapidly in the path of independence. The day after that on which the pope authorized him to take two wives, Henry issued a bold proclamation, pronouncing against all who should ask for or bring in a papal bull contrary to the royal prerogative "imprisonment and further punishment of their bodies according to his Majesty's good pleasure." Clement, becoming alarmed, replied to the address: "We desire as much as you do that the king should have male children; but, alas! we are not God to give him sons."

Men were beginning to stifle under these manœuvres and tergiversations of the papacy: they called for air, and some went so far as to say that if air was not given them, they must snap their fetters and break open the doors.

CHAPTER SEVEN

Latimer at Court

(January to September 1530)

ENRY, seeing that he could not obtain what he asked from the pope, drew nearer the evangelical party in his kingdom. In the ranks of the Reformation he found intelligent, pious, bold, and eloquent men, who possessed the confidence of a portion of the people. Why should not the prince try to conciliate them? They protest against the authority of the pope: good! he will relieve them from it; but on one condition, however—that if they reject the papal jurisdiction they recognize his own.

The first of the evangelical leaders whom Henry tried to gain was Latimer. He had placed him, as we have seen, on the list of his chaplains. "Beware of contradicting the king," said a courtier to him one day, mistrusting his frankness. "Speak as he speaks, and instead of presuming to lead him, strive to follow him." "Away with your counsel!" replied Latimer; "shall I say as he says? Say what your conscience bids you. . . . Still, I know that prudence is necessary. The drop of rain maketh a hole in the stone, not by violence, but by oft falling. Likewise a prince must be won by a little and a little."

This conversation was not useless to the chaplain, who set to work seriously amid all the tumult of the court. He studied the Holy Scriptures and the Fathers, and frankly proclaimed the truth from the pulpit. But he had no private conversation with the king, who filled him with a certain fear. The thought that he did not speak to Henry about the state of his soul troubled him. One day, in the month of November, the chaplain was in his room, and in the volume of St. Augustine which lay before him he read these words: "He who for fear of any power *hides the truth*, provokes the wrath of God to come upon him, for he fears men more than God." At another time, while studying St. Chrysostom, these words struck

41

him: "He is not only a traitor to the truth who openly for truth teaches a lie; but he also who *does not pronounce and show the truth* that he knoweth." These two sentences sank deeply into his heart. "They made me sore afraid," he continued, "troubled and vexed me grievously in my conscience." He resolved to declare what God had taught him in Scripture. His frankness might cost him his life (lives were lost easily in Henry's time); it mattered not. "I had rather suffer extreme punishment," he said, "than be a traitor unto the truth."

Latimer reflected that the ecclesiastical law, which for ages had been the very essence of religion, must give way to evangelical faith—that the form must yield to the life. The members of the Church (calling themselves regenerate by baptism) used to attend catechism, be confirmed, join in worship, and take part in the communion without any real individual transformation; and then finally rest all together in the churchyard. But the Church, in Latimer's opinion, ought to begin with the conversion of its members. Lively stones are needed to build up the temple of God. Christian individualism, which Rome opposed from her theocratic point of view, was about to be revived in Christian society.

The noble Latimer formed the resolution to make the king understand that all real reformation must begin at home. This was no trifling matter. Henry, who was a man of varied information and lively understanding, but also imperious, passionate, fiery, and obstinate, knew no other rule than the promptings of his strong nature; and although quite prepared to separate from the pope, he detested all innovations in doctrine. Latimer did not allow himself to be stopped by such obstacles, and resolved to attack this difficult position openly.

"Your Grace," he wrote to Henry, "I must show forth such things as I have learned in Scripture, or else deny Jesus Christ. The which denying ought more to be dreaded than the loss of all temporal goods, honour, promotion, fame, prison, slander, hurts, banishment, and all manner of torments and cruelties, yea, and death itself, be it never so shameful and painful. . . . There is as great distance between you and me as between God and man; for you are here to me and to all your subjects in God's stead; and so I should quake to speak to your Grace. But as you are a mortal man having in you the corrupt nature of Adam, so you have no less need of the merits of Christ's passion for your salvation than I and others of your subjects have."

Latimer feared to see a Church founded under Henry's patronage, which would seek after riches, power, and pomp; and he was not mistaken. "Our Saviour's life was very poor. In how vile and abject a place was the mother of Jesus Christ brought to bed! And according to this beginning was the process and end of His life in this world. . . . But this He did to show us that his followers and vicars should not regard the treasures of this world. . . . Your Grace may see what means and craft the clergy imagine to break and withstand the acts which were made in the last parliament against their superfluities."

Latimer desired to make the king understand who were the true Christians. "Our Saviour showed his disciples," continued he, "that they should be brought before kings. Wherefore take this for a sure conclusion, that where the Word of God is truly preached, there is persecution as well of the hearers as of the teachers; and where quietness and rest in worldly pleasure, there is not the truth."

Latimer next proceeded to declare what would give real riches to England. "Your Grace promised by your last proclamation that we should have the Scripture in English. Let not the wickedness of worldly men divert you from your godly purpose and promise. There are prelates who, under pretence of insurrection and heresy, hinder the Gospel of Christ from having free course. . . . They would send a thousand men to hell ere they send one to God."

Latimer had reserved for the last the appeal he had determined to make to his master's conscience: "I pray to God that your Grace may do what God commandeth, and not what seemeth good in your own sight; that you may be found one of the members of His Church, and a faithful minister of His gifts, and not," he added, showing contempt for a title of which Henry was very proud, "and not a defender of His faith; for He will not have it defended by man's power, but by His Word only.

"Wherefore, gracious king, remember yourself. Have pity

on your soul, and think that the day is even at hand when you shall give account of your office, and of the blood that hath been shed with your sword. In the which day that your Grace may stand steadfastly, and not be ashamed, but be clear and ready in your reckoning, and to have (as they say) your *quietus est* sealed with the blood of our Saviour Christ, which only serveth at that day, is my daily prayer to Him that suffered death for our sins, which also prayeth to His Father for grace for us continually."[1]

Thus wrote the bold chaplain. Such a letter from Latimer to Henry VIII deserves to be pointed out. The king does not appear to have been offended at it: he was an absolute prince, but there was occasionally some generosity in his character. He therefore continued to extend his kindness to Latimer, but did not answer his appeal.

Latimer preached frequently before the court and in the city. Many noble lords and old families still clung to the prejudices of the middle ages; but some had a certain liking for the Reformation, and listened to the chaplain's preaching, which was so superior to ordinary sermons. His art of oratory was summed up in one precept: "Christ is the preacher of all preachers." "Christ," he exclaimed, "took upon Him our sins: not the work of sin—not to do it—not to commit it, but to purge it, to bear the stipend [wages] of it, and that way He was the greatest sinner of the world.[2] . . . It is much like as if I owed another man £20,000, and must pay it out of hand, or else go to the dungeon of Ludgate; and when I am going to prison, one of my friends should come and ask, Whither goeth this man? I will answer for him; I will pay all for him. Such a part played our Saviour Christ with us."

Preaching before a king, he declared[3] that the authority of Holy Scripture was above all the powers of the earth. "God," he said, "is great, eternal, almighty, everlasting; and the Scripture, because of Him, is also great, eternal, most mighty, and holy. . . . There is no king, emperor, magistrate, or ruler, but is bound to give credence unto God's holy

---

[1] Latimer, *Remains* (Parker Society), pp. 297–309.

[2] Ibid., p. 223.

[3] Ibid., p. 85 (First Sermon preached before King Edward VI, 8th March, 1549).

Word." He was cautious not to put "the two swords" into the same hand. "In this world God hath two swords," he said; "the temporal sword resteth in the hands of kings, whereunto all subjects—as well the clergy as the laity—be subject. The spiritual sword is in the hands of the ministers and preachers of God's Word to correct and reprove. Make not a mingle-mangle of them. To God give thy soul, thy faith; . . . to the king, tribute and reverence. Therefore let the preacher amend with the spiritual sword, fearing no man, though death should ensue." Such language astonished the court. "Were you at the sermon to-day?" said one of his hearers to a zealous courtier one day. "Yes," replied the latter. "And how did you like the new chaplain?" "Oh, even as I liked him always—a seditious fellow."

Latimer did not permit himself to be intimidated. Firm in doctrine, he was at the same time eminently practical. He was a moralist; and this may explain how he was able to remain any time at court. Men of the world, who soon grow impatient when you preach to them of the cross, repentance, and change of heart, cannot help approving of those who insist on certain rules of conduct. King Henry found it convenient to keep a great number of horses in abbeys founded for the support of the poor. One day when Latimer was preaching before him, he said, "A prince ought not to prefer his horses above poor men. Abbeys were ordained for the comfort of the poor, and not for kings' horses to be kept in them."

There was a dead silence in the congregation—no one dared turn his eyes towards Henry—and many showed symptoms of anger. The chaplain had hardly left the pulpit, when a gentleman of the court, the lord-chamberlain apparently, went up to him and asked, "What hast thou to do with the king's horses? They are the maintenances and part of a king's honour, and also of his realm; wherefore, in speaking against them, ye are against the king's honour." "To take away the right of the poor," answered Latimer, "is against the honour of the king. . . . God is the grand-master of the king's house, and will take account of every one that beareth rule therein."

Thus the Reformation undertook to re-establish the rule of

conscience even in the courts of princes. Latimer knowing, like Calvin, that "the ears of the princes of this world are accustomed to be pampered and flattered," armed himself with invincible courage.

The murmurs grew louder. While the old chaplains let things take their course, the other wanted to restore morality among Christians. The Reformer was alive to the accusations brought against him, for his was not a heart of steel. Reproaches and calumnies appeared to him sometimes like those impetuous winds which force the husbandman to fly hurriedly for shelter to some covered place. "O Lord!" he exclaimed on one occasion, "these people pinch me; nay, they have a full bite at me." He would have desired to flee away to the wilderness, but he called to mind what had been done to his Master; "I comfort myself," he said, "that Christ Himself was noted to be a stirrer up of the people against the emperor and was content to be called seditious."

The priests, delighted that Latimer censured the king, resolved to take advantage of it to ruin him. One day, when there was a grand reception, and the king was surrounded by his councillors and courtiers, a monk slipped into the midst of the crowd, and, falling on his knees before the monarch, said, "Sire, your new chaplain preaches sedition." Henry turned to Latimer: "What say you to that, sir?" The chaplain bent his knee before the prince; and, turning to his accusers, said to them, "Would you have me preach nothing concerning a king in the king's sermon? Have you any commission to appoint me what I shall preach?" His friends trembled lest he should be arrested. "Your Grace," he continued, "I put myself in your hands: appoint other doctors to preach in my place before your Majesty. There are many more worthy of the room than I am. If it be your Grace's pleasure, I could be content to be their servant, and bear their books after them. But if your Grace allow me for a preacher, I would desire you give me leave to discharge my conscience. Permit me to frame my teaching for my audience."

Henry, who always liked Latimer, took his part, and the chaplain retired with a low bow. When he left the audience, his friends, who had watched this scene with the keenest emotion, surrounded him, saying, with tears in their eyes, "We were convinced that you would sleep to-night in the Tower." "*The king's heart is in the hand of the Lord,*" he answered, calmly.

The evangelical Reformers of England nobly maintained their independence in the presence of a catholic and despotic king. Firmly convinced, free, strong men, they yielded neither to the seductions of the court nor to those of Rome. We shall see still more striking examples of their resolution, bequeathed by them to their successors.

CHAPTER EIGHT

The King Seeks Tyndale

(January to May 1531)

HENRY VIII, finding that he wanted men like Latimer to resist the pope, sought to win over others of the same stamp. He found one, whose lofty range he understood immediately. Thomas Cromwell had laid before him a book then very eagerly read all over England, namely, the *Practice of Prelates*. It was found in the houses not only of the citizens of London, but of the farmers of Essex, Suffolk, and other counties. The king read it quite as eagerly as his subjects. Nothing interested him like the history of the slow but formidable progress of the priesthood and prelacy. One parable in particular struck him, in which the oak represented royalty, and the ivy the papacy. "First, the ivy springeth out of the earth, and then awhile creepeth along by the ground till it find a great tree. There it joineth itself beneath alow unto the body of the tree, and creepeth up a little and a little, fair and softly. And at the beginning, while it is yet thin and small, that the burden is not perceived, it seemeth glorious to garnish the tree in the winter, and to bear off the tempests of the weather. But in the mean season it thrusteth roots into the bark of the tree to hold fast withal; and ceaseth not to climb up till it be at the top and above all. And then it sendeth its branches along by the branches of the tree, and overgroweth all, and waxeth great, heavy, and thick; and sucketh the moisture so sore out of the tree and his branches, that it choaketh and stifleth them. And then the foul stinking ivy waxeth mighty in the stump of the tree, and becometh a seat and a nest for all unclean birds and for blind owls, which hawk in the dark and dare not come at the light. Even so the Bishop of Rome, now called pope, at the beginning crept along upon the earth. . . . He crept up and fastened his roots in the heart of the emperor, and by subtilty climbed above the emperor, and subdued him, and made him stoop unto his feet and kiss them another while. Yea, when he had put the crown on the emperor's head, he smote it off with his feet again, saying that he had might to make emperors and to put them down again."[1]

Henry would willingly have clapped his hand on his sword to demand satisfaction of the pope for this outrage. The book was by Tyndale. Laying it down, the king reflected on what he had just read, and thought to himself that the author had some striking ideas "on the accursed power of the pope," and that he was besides gifted with talent and zeal, and might render excellent service towards abolishing the papacy in England.

Tyndale, from the time of his conversion at Oxford, set Christ above everything: he boldly threw off the yoke of human traditions, and would take no other guide but Scripture only. Full of imagination and eloquence, active and ready to endure fatigue, he exposed himself to every danger in the fulfilment of his mission. Henry ordered Stephen Vaughan, one of his agents, then at Antwerp, to try to find the Reformer in Brabant, Flanders, on the banks of the Rhine, in Holland . . . wherever he might chance to be; to offer him a safe-conduct under the sign-manual, to prevail on him to return to England, and to add the most gracious promises in behalf of his Majesty.

To gain over Tyndale seemed even more important than to have gained Latimer. Vaughan immediately undertook to seek him in Antwerp, where he was said to be, but could not find him. "He is at Marburg," said one; "at Frankfort," said another; "at Hamburg," declared a third. Tyndale was invisible now as before. To make more certain, Vaughan determined to write three letters directed to those three places, conjuring him to return to England. "I have great hopes," said the English agent to his friends, "of having done something that will please his Majesty." Tyndale, the most scriptural of English reformers, the most inflexible in his faith, labouring at the Reformation with the cordial approbation of the monarch, would truly have been something extraordinary.

[1] Tyndale, *Expositions and The Practice of Prelates* (Parker Society), p. 270.

Scarcely had the three letters been despatched when Vaughan heard of the ignominious chastisement inflicted by Sir Thomas More on Tyndale's brother. Was it by such indignities that Henry expected to attract the Reformer? Vaughan, much annoyed, wrote to the king (26th January, 1531) that this event would make Tyndale think they wanted to entrap him, and he gave up looking for him.

Three months later (17th April), as Vaughan was busy copying one of Tyndale's manuscripts in order to send it to Henry (it was his answer to the *Dialogue* of Sir Thomas More), a man knocked at his door. "Some one, who calls himself a friend of yours, desires very much to speak with you," said the stranger, "and begs you to follow me."—"Who is this friend? where is he?" asked Vaughan.—"I do not know him," replied the messenger, "but come along, and you will see for yourself." Vaughan doubted whether it was prudent to follow this person to a strange place. He made up his mind, however, to accompany him. The agent of Henry VIII and the messenger threaded the streets of Antwerp, went out of the city, and at last reached a lonely field, by the side of which the Scheldt flowed sluggishly through the level country. As he advanced, Vaughan saw a man of noble bearing awaiting him. "Do you not recognize me?" he asked Vaughan. "I cannot call to mind your features," answered the latter. "My name is Tyndale," said the stranger. "Tyndale!" exclaimed Vaughan with delight. "Tyndale! what a happy meeting!"

Tyndale, who had heard of Henry's new plans, had no confidence either in the prince or in his pretended Reformation. The king's endless negotiations with the pope, his worldliness, his amours, his persecution of evangelical Christians, and especially the ignominious punishment inflicted on John Tyndale: all these matters disgusted him. However, having been informed of the nature of Vaughan's mission, he desired to turn it to advantage by addressing a few warnings to the prince. "I have written certain books," he said, "to warn his Majesty of the subtle demeanour of the clergy of his realm towards his person, in which doing I showed the heart of a true subject; to the intent that his Grace might prepare remedies against their subtle dreams. An exile from my native country, I suffer hunger, thirst, cold, absence of friends, everywhere encompassed with great danger; in innumerable hard and sharp fightings, I do not feel their asperity, by reason that I hope with my labours to do honour to God, true service to my prince, and pleasure to his commons."

"Cheer up," said Vaughan, "your exile, poverty, fightings, all are at an end; you can return to England." . . . "What matters it," said Tyndale, "if my exile finishes, so long as the Bible is banished? Has the king forgotten that God has commanded His Word to be spread throughout the world? If it continues to be forbidden to his subjects, very death were more pleasant to me than life."

Vaughan did not consider himself worsted. The messenger, who remained at a distance and could hear nothing, was astonished at seeing the two men in that solitary field conversing together so long, and with so much animation. "Tell me what guarantees you desire," said Vaughan: "the king will grant them you." "Of course the king would give me a safe-conduct," answered Tyndale, "but the clergy would persuade him that promises made to heretics are not binding." Night was coming on, Henry's agent might have had Tyndale followed and seized. The idea occurred to Vaughan, but he rejected it. Tyndale began, however, to feel himself ill at ease. "Farewell," he said, "you shall see me again before long, or hear news of me." He then departed, walking away from Antwerp. Vaughan, who re-entered the city, was surprised to see Tyndale make for the open country. He supposed it to be a stratagem, and once more doubted whether he ought not to have seized the Reformer to please his master. "I might have failed of my purpose," he said; besides it was now too late, for Tyndale had disappeared.

As soon as Vaughan reached home he hastened to send to London an account of this singular conference. Cromwell immediately proceeded to court and laid before the king the envoy's letter and the Reformer's book. "Good!" said Henry, "as soon as I have leisure I will read them both." He did so, and was exasperated against Tyndale, who refused his invitation, mistrusted his word, and even dared to give him advice. In his passion the king in all probability tore off the latter part of Vaughan's letter, flung it in the fire, and entirely gave up his idea of bringing the Reformer into

England to make use of him against the pope, fearing that such a torch would set the whole kingdom in a blaze. He thought only how he could seize him and punish him for his arrogance.

He sent for Cromwell; before him on the table lay the treatise by Tyndale, which Vaughan had copied and sent. "These pages," said Henry to his minister, while pointing to the manuscript, "these pages are the work of a visionary: they are full of lies, sedition, and calumny. Vaughan shows too much affection for Tyndale. Let him beware of inviting him to come into the kingdom. He is a perverse and hardened character who cannot be changed. I am too happy that he is out of England."

Cromwell retired in vexation. He wrote to Vaughan, but the king found the letter too weak, and Cromwell had to correct it, to make it harmonize with the wrath of the prince.[1] An ambitious man, he bent before the obstinate will of his master; but the loss of Tyndale seemed irreparable. Accordingly, while informing Vaughan of the king's anger, he added that if wholesome reflection should bring Tyndale to reason, the king was "*so inclined to mercy, pity, and compassion,*" that he would doubtless see him with pleasure. Vaughan, whose heart Tyndale had gained, began to hunt after him again, and had a second interview with him. He gave him Cromwell's letter to read, and when the Reformer came to the words we have just quoted about Henry's compassion, his eyes filled with tears. "What gracious words!" he exclaimed. "Yes," said Vaughan, "they have such sweetness, that they would break the hardest heart in the world." Tyndale, deeply moved, tried to find some mode of fulfilling his duty towards God and towards the king. "If his Majesty," he said, "would condescend to permit only a bare text of the Scriptures to circulate among the people, as they do in the states of the Emperor and in other Christian countries, I would bind myself never to write again; I would throw myself at his feet, offering my body as a sacrifice, ready to submit if necessary to torture and to death."

---

[1] The corrections are still to be seen in the original draft, and are indicated in the biographical notice of Tyndale printed in *Doctrinal Treatises, etc.* (Parker Society).

But a gulf lay between the monarch and the Reformer. Henry VIII saw the seeds of heresy in the Scriptures; and Tyndale rejected every reformation which they wished to carry out by proscribing the Bible. "Heresy springeth not from the Scriptures," he said, "no more than darkness from the sun." Tyndale disappeared again, and the name of his hiding-place is unknown.

The King of England was not discouraged by the check he had received. He wanted men possessed of talent and zeal, men resolved to attack the pope. Cambridge had given England a teacher who might be placed beside, and perhaps even above, Latimer and Tyndale; this was John Fryth. He thirsted for the truth; he sought God, and was determined to give himself wholly to Jesus Christ. One day Cromwell said to the king, "What a pity it is, your Highness, that a man so distinguished as Fryth in letters and sciences, should be among the sectarians!" Like Tyndale, he had quitted England. Cromwell, with Henry's consent, wrote to Vaughan: "His Majesty strongly desires the reconciliation of Fryth, who (he firmly believes) is not so far advanced as Tyndale in the evil way. Always full of mercy, the king is ready to receive him to favour; try to attract him charitably, politically." Vaughan immediately began his inquiries; it was May 1531, but the first news he received was that Fryth, a minister of the Gospel, was just married in Holland. "This marriage," he wrote to the king, "may by chance hinder my persuasion." This was not all; Fryth was boldly printing, at Amsterdam, Tyndale's answer to Sir Thomas More. Henry was forced to give him up, as he had given up his friend. He succeeded with none but Latimer, and even the chaplain told him many harsh truths. There was a decided incompatibility between the spiritual reform and the political reform; the work of God refused to ally itself with the work of the throne. The Christian faith and the visible Church are two distinct things. Some (and among them the Reformers) require Christianity—a living Christianity; others (and it was the case of Henry and his prelates) look for the Church and its hierarchy, and care little whether a living faith be found there or not. This is a capital error. Real religion must exist first; and then this religion must produce a true religious society. Tyndale, Fryth, and their friends desired to begin with religion; Henry and his followers with an ecclesiastical society, hostile to faith. The king and the reformers could not, therefore, come to an understanding. Henry, profoundly hurt by the boldness of those evangelical men, swore that as they would not have peace they should have war, . . . war to the knife.

CHAPTER NINE

The King of England—"Head of the Church"

(January to March 1531)

HENRY VIII desired to introduce great changes into the ecclesiastical corporation of his kingdom. His royal power had much to bear from the power of the clergy. It was the same in all Catholic monarchies; but England had more to complain of than others. Of the three estates, Clergy, Nobility, and Commons, the first was the most powerful. The nobility had been weakened by the civil wars; the commons had long been without authority and energy; the prelates thus occupied the first rank, so that in 1529 an archbishop and cardinal (Wolsey) was the most powerful man in England, not even the king excepted. Henry had felt the yoke, and wished to free himself, not only from the domination of the pope, but also from the influence of the higher clergy. If he had only intended to be avenged of the pontiff, it would have been enough to allow the Reformation to act; when a mighty wind blows from heaven, it sweeps away all the contrivances of men. But Henry was deficient neither in prudence nor calculation. He feared lest a diversity of doctrine should engender disturbances in his kingdom. He wished to free himself from the pope and the prelates, without throwing himself into the arms of Tyndale or of Latimer.

Kings and people had observed that the domination of the papacy, and its authority over the clergy, were an insurmountable obstacle to the autonomy of the State. As far back as 1268, St. Louis had declared that France owed allegiance to God alone; and other princes had followed his example. Henry VIII determined to do more—to break the chains which bound the clergy to the Romish throne, and fasten them to the crown. The power of England, delivered from the papacy, which had been its canker-worm, would then be developed with freedom and energy, and would

place the country in the foremost rank among nations. The
renovating spirit of the age was favourable to Henry's plans;
without delay he must put into execution the bold plan
which Cromwell had unrolled before his eyes in Whitehall
Park. Henry concentrated upon having himself recognized
as head of the Church.

This important revolution could not be accomplished by
a simple act of royal authority—in England particularly,
where constitutional principles already possessed an in-
contestable influence. It was necessary to prevail upon the
clergy to cross the Rubicon by emancipating themselves
from Rome. But how to bring it about? This was the subject
of the meditations of the sagacious Cromwell, who, gradually
rising in the king's confidence to the place formerly held by
Wolsey, made a different use of it. Urged by ambition,
possessing an energetic character, a sound judgment, un-
shaken firmness, no obstacle could arrest his activity. He
sought how he could give the king the spiritual sceptre, and
this was the plan on which he fixed. The kings of England
had been known occasionally to revive old laws fallen into
desuetude, and visit with heavy penalties those who had
violated them. Cromwell represented to the king that the
statutes made punishable any man who should recognize a
dignity established by the pope in the English Church; that
Wolsey, by exercising the functions of papal legate, had en-
croached upon the rights of the Crown and been condemned,
which was but justice; while the members of the clergy—who
had recognized the unlawful jurisdiction of the pretended
legate—had thereby become as guilty as he had been. "The
statute of *Præmunire*," he said, "condemns them as well as
their chief." Henry, who listened attentively, found that the
expedient of his Secretary of State was in conformity with
the letter of the law, and that it put all the clergy in his
power. He did not hesitate to give full power to his ministers.
Under such a state of things there was not one innocent
person in England; the two houses of parliament, the privy
council, all the nation must be brought to the bar. Henry,
full of "condescension," was pleased to confine himself to the
clergy.

The convocation of the province of Canterbury having

met on the 7th of January, 1531, Cromwell entered the hall
and quietly took his seat among the bishops; then rising, he
informed them that their property and benefices were to be
confiscated for the good of his Majesty, because they had
submitted to the unconstitutional power of the cardinal.
What terrible news! It was a thunderbolt to those selfish
prelates; they were amazed. At length some of them plucked
up a little courage. "The king himself had sanctioned the
authority of the cardinal-legate," they said. "We merely
obeyed his supreme will. Our resistance to his Majesty's
proclamations would infallibly have ruined us."—"That is of
no consequence," was the reply; "there was the law: you
should obey the constitution of the country even at the peril
of your lives." The terrified bishops laid at the foot of the
throne a magnificent sum by which they hoped to redeem
their offences and their benefices. But that was not what
Henry desired: he pretended to set little store by their money.
The threat of confiscation must constrain them to pay a
ransom of still greater value. "My lords," said Cromwell,
"in a petition that some of you presented to the pope not
long ago, you called the king your *soul* and your *head*. Come,
then, expressly recognize the supremacy of the king over the
Church, and his Majesty, of his great goodness, will grant
you your pardon." What a demand! The distracted clergy
assembled, and a deliberation of extreme importance began.
"The words in the address to the pope," said some, "were
a mere form, and had not the meaning ascribed to them."
—"The king being unable to untie the Gordian knot at
Rome," said others, alluding to the divorce, "intends to cut
it with his sword."—"The secular power," exclaimed the
most zealous, "has no voice in ecclesiastical matters. To
recognize the king as head of the Church would be to overthrow the catholic faith. . . . The head of the Church is the
pope." The debate lasted three days, and as Henry's ministers
pointed to the theocratic government of Israel, a priest
exclaimed: "We oppose the New Testament to the Old;
according to the gospel, Christ is head of the Church." When
this was told the king, he said: "Very well, I consent. If
you declare me *head of the Church* you may add *under God*."
In this way the papal claims were compromised all the

more. "We will expose ourselves to everything," they said, "rather than dethrone the Roman pontiff."

The bishops of Lincoln and Exeter were deputed to beseech the king to withdraw his demand: they could not so much as obtain an audience. Henry had made up his mind: the priests must yield. The only means of their obtaining pardon (they were told) was by their renouncing the papal supremacy. The bishops made a fresh attempt to satisfy both the requirements of the king and those of their own conscience. "Shrink before the clergy and they are lions," the courtiers said; "withstand them and they are sheep."—"Your fate is in your own hands. If you refuse the king's demand, the disgrace of Wolsey may show you what you may expect." Archbishop Warham, president of the convocation, a prudent man, far advanced in years and near his end, tried to hit upon some compromise. The great movements which agitated the Church all over Europe disturbed him. He had in times past complained to the king of Wolsey's usurpations, and was not far from recognizing the royal supremacy. He proposed to insert a simple clause in the act conferring the required jurisdiction on the king, namely, *Quantum per legem Christi licet* (so far as the law of Christ permits). "You have played me a shrewd turn," exclaimed the King. "I thought to have made fools of those prelates, and now you have so ordered the business that they are likely to make a fool of me. Go to them again, and let me have the business passed without any *quantums* or *tantums*. . . . So far as the law of Christ permits! Such a reserve would make one believe that my authority was disputable."

Henry's ministers ventured on this occasion to resist him: they showed him that this clause would prevent an immediate rupture with Rome, and it might be repealed hereafter. He yielded at last, and the archbishop submitted the clause with the amendment to convocation. It was a solemn moment for England. The bishops were convinced that the king was asking them to do what was wrong, the end of which would be a rupture with Rome. In the time of Hildebrand the prelates would have answered "No," and found a sympathetic support in the laity. But things had changed; the people were weary of the long domination of the priests. The primate, desirous of ending the matter, said to his colleagues: "Do you recognize the king as sole protector of the Church and clergy of England, and, so far as is allowed by the law of Christ, also as your supreme head?" All remained speechless. "Will you let me know your opinions?" resumed the archbishop. There was a dead silence. "Whoever is silent seems to consent," said the primate."—"Then we are all silent," answered one of the members. Were these words inspired by courage or by cowardice? Were they an assent or a protest? We cannot say. In this matter we cannot side either with the king or with the priests. The heart of man easily takes the part of those who are oppressed; but here the oppressed were also oppressors. Convocation next gave its support to the opinion of the universities respecting the divorce, and thus Henry gained his first victory.

For breach of præmunire the Convocation of Canterbury was permitted by the king to purchase his pardon by rendering to the royal exchequer a hundred thousand pounds sterling, an enormous sum for those times. This was in February, 1531. Later in the year the Convocation of York followed suit with a payment of a little less than nineteen thousand pounds. Thus at one stroke the clergy of England were deprived of both riches and honour.

Animated discussion took place in the northern Convocation. "If you proclaim the king supreme head," said bishop Tunstall, "it can only be in temporal matters."—"Indeed!" retorted Henry's minister, "is an act of convocation necessary to determine that the king reigns?"—"If spiritual things are meant," answered the bishop, "I withdraw from convocation that I may not withdraw from the Church."

"My lords," said Henry, "no one disputes your right to preach and administer the sacraments. Did not Paul submit to Cæsar's tribunal, and our Saviour himself to Pilate's?" Henry's ecclesiastical theories prevailed also at York. A great revolution was effected in England, and fresh compromises were to consolidate it.

The king, having obtained what he desired, condescended in his great mercy to pardon the clergy for their unpardonable offence of having recognized Wolsey as papal legate. At the request of the Commons this amnesty was extended to all

England. The nation, which at first saw nothing in this affair but an act enfranchising themselves from the usurped power of the popes, showed their gratitude to Henry; but there was a reverse to the medal. If the pope was despoiled, the king was invested. Was not the function ascribed to him contrary to the Gospel? Would not this act impress upon the Anglican Reformation a territorial and aristocratic character, which would introduce into the Reformed Church the world with all its splendour and wealth? If the royal pre-eminence endows the Anglican Church with the pomps of worship, of classical studies, of high dignities, will it not also carry along with it luxury, sinecures, and worldliness among the prelates? Shall we not see the royal authority pronounce on questions of dogma, and declare the most sacred doctrines indifferent? A little later an attempt was made to limit the power of the king in religious matters. "We give not to our princes the ministry of God's Word or the sacraments," says the thirty-seventh Article of Religion.

CHAPTER TEN

The King Puts Catherine Away

(March to June 1531)

THE king, having obtained so important a concession from the clergy, turned to his parliament to ask a service of another kind—one in his eyes still more urgent. On the 30th of March, 1531, the session being about to terminate, Sir Thomas More, the chancellor, went to the House of Commons, and submitted to them the decision of the various universities on the king's marriage and the power of the pope. The Commons looked at the affair essentially from a political point of view; they did not understand that because the king had lived twenty years with the queen, he ought not to be separated from her. The documents placed before their eyes "made them detest the marriage" of Henry and Catherine. The chancellor desired the members to report in their respective counties and towns that the king had not asked for this divorce of his own will or pleasure, but "only for the discharge of his conscience and surety of the succession of his crown." "Enlighten the people," he said, "and preserve peace in the nation with the sentiments of loyalty due to the monarch."

The king hastened to use the powers which universities, clergy, and parliament had placed in his hands. Immediately after the prorogation, certain lords went down to Greenwich and laid before the queen the decisions which condemned her marriage, and urged her to accept the arbitration of four bishops and four lay peers. Catherine replied sadly but firmly: "I pray you, tell the king I say I am his lawful wife, and in that point I will abide until the court of Rome determine to the contrary."

The divorce which, notwithstanding Catherine's refusal, was approaching, caused great agitation among the people, and the members of parliament had some trouble to preserve

order, as Sir Thomas More had desired them. Priests proclaimed from their pulpits the downfall of the Church and the
coming of Anti-christ; the mendicant friars scattered discontent
in every house which they entered, the most fanatical of them
not fearing to insinuate that the wrath of God would soon
hurl the impious prince from his throne. In towns and villages,
in castles and alehouses, men talked of nothing but the divorce
and the primacy claimed by the king. Women standing at
their doors, men gathering round the blacksmith's forge,
spoke more or less disrespectfully of parliament, the bishops,
the dangers of the Romish Church, and the prospects of the
Reformation. If a few friends met at night around the hearth,
they told strange tales to one another. The king, queen, pope,
devil, saints, Cromwell, and the higher clergy formed the
subject of their conversation. The gipsies at that time strolling
through the country added to the confusion. Sometimes they
would appear in the midst of these animated discussions, and
prophesy lamentable events, at times calling up the dead to
make them speak of the future. The terrible calamities they
predicted froze their hearers with affright, and their sinister
prophecies were the cause of disorders and even of crimes.
Accordingly an act was passed pronouncing the penalty of
banishment against them.

An unfortunate event tended still more to strike men's
imaginations. It was reported that the bishop of Rochester,
that prelate so terrible to the reformers and so good to the
poor, had narrowly escaped being poisoned by his cook.
Seventeen persons were taken ill after eating porridge at the
episcopal palace; one of the bishop's gentlemen died, as well
as a poor woman to whom the remains of the food had been
given. It was maliciously remarked that the bishop was the
only one who frankly opposed the divorce and the royal
supremacy. Calumny even aimed at the throne. When Henry
heard of this, he resolved to make short work of all such
nonsense; he ordered the offence to be deemed as high-
treason, and the wretched cook was taken to Smithfield, there
to be boiled to death. This was a variation of the penalty
pronounced upon the evangelicals. Such was the cruel justice
of the sixteenth century.

While the universities, parliament, convocation, and the

nation appeared to support Henry VIII, one voice was
raised against the divorce. It was that of a young man,
brought up by the king, and that voice moved him deeply.
There still remained in England some scions of the house of
York, and among them a nephew of that unhappy Warwick
whom Henry VII had cruelly put to death. Warwick's sister,
Margaret, had been married to Sir Richard Pole, a knight of
Buckinghamshire. In 1505 she was left a widow with two
daughters and three sons—the youngest, Reginald, became
a favourite with Henry VIII, who destined him for the
archiepiscopal see of Canterbury. "Your kindnesses are such,"
said Pole to him, "that a king could grant no more, even to
a son." But Reginald, to whom his mother had told the story
of the execution of the unhappy Warwick, had contracted
an invincible hatred against the Tudors. Accordingly, in
despite of certain evangelical tendencies, Pole seeing Henry
separating from the pope, resolved to throw himself into the
arms of the pontiff. Reginald, invested with the Roman
purple, rose to be president of the council and primate of all
England under Queen Mary. Elegant in his manners, with a
fine intellect, and sincere in his religious convictions, he was
selfish, irritable, and ambitious: desires of elevation and
revenge led a noble nature astray. If the branch of which he was
the representative was ever to recover the crown, it could only
be by the help of the Roman pontiffs: henceforward their
cause was his. Loaded with benefits by Henry VIII, he was
incessantly pursued by the recollection of the rights of Rome
and of the White Rose; and he went so far as to insult before
all Europe the prince who had been his first friend.

At this time Pole was living at a house in the country
which Henry had given him. One day he received at this
charming retreat a communication from the duke of Norfolk.
"The king destines you for the highest honours of the English
Church," wrote this nobleman, "and offers you at once the
important sees of York and Winchester, left vacant by the
death of Cardinal Wolsey." At the same time the duke asked
Pole's opinion about the divorce. Reginald's brothers, and
particularly the eldest, Lord Montague, entreated him to
answer as all the catholic world had answered, and not
irritate a prince whose anger would ruin them all. The blood

D(II)

of Warwick and the king's revolt against Rome induced
Pole to reject with horror all the honours which Henry
offered; and yet that prince was his benefactor. He fancied
he had discovered a middle course which would permit him
to satisfy alike his conscience and his king.

He went to Whitehall, where Henry received him like a
friend. Pole hesitated in distress she wished to let the king
know his thoughts, but the word; would not come to his lips.
At last, encouraged by the prince's affability, he summoned
up his resolution, and in a voice trembling with emotion,
said: "You must not separate from the queen." Henry had
expected something different. Was it thus that his kindnesses
were to be repaid? His eyes flashed with anger, and he laid
his hand on his sword. Pole humbled himself: "If I possess
any knowledge, to whom do I owe it, unless to your Majesty?
In listening to me, you are listening to your own pupil." The
king recovered himself, and said, "I will consider your
opinion, and send you my answer." Pole withdrew. "He
put me in such a passion," said the king to one of his gentlemen, "that I nearly struck him. . . . But there is something in
the man that wins my heart."

Montague and Reginald's other brother again conjured
him to accept the high position which the king reserved for
him; but his soul revolted at being subordinate to a Tudor.
He therefore wrote a memoir, which he presented to Henry,
and in which he entreated him implicitly to submit the
divorce question to the court of Rome. "How could I speak
against your marriage with the queen?" he said. "Should I
not accuse your Majesty of having lived for more than twenty
years in an unlawful union? By the divorce, you will array
all the powers against you—the pope, the Emperor; and as
for the French . . . we can never find in our hearts to trust
them. You are at this moment on the verge of an abyss. . . .
One step more, and all is over. There is only one way of
safety left your Grace, and that is submission to the pope."

Henry was moved. The boldness with which this young
nobleman dared accuse him irritated his pride; still his
friendship prevailed, and he forgave it. Pole received the
permission he had asked to leave England, and to continue
to draw his revenues as Dean of Exeter.

Reginald Pole was, as it were, the last link that united the royal pair. Thus far the king had continued to show the queen every respect; their mutual affection seemed the same, only they occupied separate rooms. Henry now decided to take an important step. On the 14th of July, 1531, a new deputation entered the queen's apartment at Windsor, one of whom informed her that as her marriage with Prince Arthur had been duly consummated she could not be the wife of her husband's brother. Then after reproaching her with having, contrary to the laws of England and the dignity of the crown, cited his Majesty before the pope's tribunal, he desired her to choose for her residence either the castle of Oking or of Estamsteed, or the monastery of Bisham. Catherine remained calm, and replied: "Wheresoever I retire, nothing can deprive me of the title which belongs to me. I shall always be his Majesty's wife." She left Windsor the same day, and removed to the More in Hertfordshire, a splendid mansion which Wolsey had surrounded with beautiful gardens; then to Estamsteed, and finally to Ampthill in Bedfordshire. The king never saw her again; but all the papists and discontented rallied round her. She entered into correspondence with the sovereigns of Europe, and became the centre of a party opposed to the emancipation of England.

CHAPTER ELEVEN

"Not Sparing the Flock"

(September 1531 to 1532)

As Henry, by breaking with Catherine, had broken with the pope, he felt the necessity of uniting more closely with his clergy. Wishing to proceed to the establishment of his new dignity, he required bishops, and particularly dexterous bishops. He therefore made Edward Lee archbishop of York, and Stephen Gardiner bishop of Winchester; and these two men, devoted to scholastic doctrines, ambitious and servile, were commissioned to inaugurate the new ecclesiastical monarchy of the king of England. Although the pope had hastened to send off their bulls, they declared they held their dignity "immediately and only" of the king, and began without delay to organize a strange league. If the king needed the bishops against the pope, the bishops needed the king against the reformers. It was not long before this alliance received its baptism of blood.

But before proceeding so far, the prelates deliberated about the means of raising the £119,000 they had bound themselves to pay the king. Each wished to make his own share as small as possible, and throw the largest part of the burden upon his colleagues. The bishops determined to place it in great measure on the shoulders of the parochial clergy.

Stokesley, bishop of London, began the battle. An able, greedy, violent man, and jealous of his prerogatives, he called a meeting of six or eight priests on whom he believed he could depend, in order to draw up with their assistance such resolutions as he could afterwards impose more easily upon their brethren. These picked ecclesiastics were desired to meet on the 1st of September, 1531, in the chapter-house of St. Paul's.

The bishop's plan had got wind, and excited general indignation in the city. Was it just that the victims should pay the fine? Some of the laity, delighted at seeing the clergy quarrelling, sought to fan the flame instead of extinguishing it.

When the 1st of September arrived the bishop entered the chapter-house with his officers, where the conference with the priests was to be held. Presently an unusual noise was heard round St. Paul's: not only the six or eight priests, but six hundred, accompanied by a great number of citizens and common people, made their appearance. The crowd swayed to and fro before the cathedral gates, shouting and clamouring to be admitted into the chapter-house on the same footing as the select few. What was to be done? The prelate's councillors advised him to add a few of the less violent priests to those he had already chosen. Stokesley adopted their advice, hoping that the gates and bolts would be strong enough to keep out the rest. Accordingly he drew up a list of new members, and one of his officers, going out to the angry crowd, read the names of those whom the bishop had selected. The latter came forward, not without trouble; but at the same time the excluded priests made a vigorous attempt to enter. There was a fierce struggle of men pushing and shouting, but the bishop's officials having passed in quickly, those who had been nominated hurriedly closed the doors. So far the victory seemed to rest with the bishop, and he was about to speak, when the uproar became deafening. The priests outside, exasperated because their financial matters were to be settled without them, protested that they ought to hold their own purse-strings. Laying hands on whatever they could find, and aided by the laity, they began to batter the door of the chapter-house. They succeeded: the door gave way, and all, priests and citizens, rushed in together. The bishop's officials tried in vain to stop them; they were roughly pushed aside. Their gowns were torn, their faces streamed with perspiration, their features were disfigured, and some even were wounded. The furious priests entered the room at last, storming and shouting. It was more like a pack of hounds rushing on a stag than the reverend clergy of the metropolis of England appearing before their bishop. The prelate, who had tact, showed no anger, but sought rather to calm the rioters. "My brethren," he said, "I marvel not a little why ye be so heady. Ye know not what shall be

said to you, therefore I pray you hear me patiently. Ye all
know that we be men frail of condition, and by our lack of
wisdom have misdemeaned ourselves towards the king and
fallen in a *præmunire*, by reason whereof all our lands, goods,
and chattels were to him forfeit, and our bodies ready to be
imprisoned. Yet his Grace of his great clemency is pleased to
pardon us, and to accept of a little instead of the whole of our
benefices, to be paid in five years. I exhort you to bear your
parts towards payment of this sum granted."

This was just what the priests did not want. They thought
it strange to be asked for money for an offence they had not
committed. "My lord," answered one, "we have never
offended against the *præmunire*, we have never meddled with
cardinal's faculties. Let the bishops and abbots pay; they
committed the offence, and they have good places."—"My
lord," added another, "twenty nobles[1] a year is but a bare
living for a priest, and yet it is all we have. Everything is
now so dear that poverty compels us to say 'No.' Having
no need of the king's pardon we have no desire to pay."
These words were drowned in applause. "No," exclaimed
the crowd, which was getting noisy again, "we will pay
nothing." The bishop's officers grew angry and came to
high words; the priests returned abuse for abuse; and the
citizens, delighted to see their "masters" quarrelling, fanned
the strife. From words they soon came to blows. The episcopal
ushers, who tried to restore order, were "buffeted and stricken,"
and even the bishop's life was in danger. At last the meeting
broke up in great confusion. Stokesley hastened to complain
to the chancellor, Sir Thomas More, who, being a great
friend of the prelate's, sent fifteen priests and five laymen to
prison. They deserved it, no doubt; but the bishops, who, to
spare their superfluity, robbed poor curates of their necessaries,
were more guilty still.

Such was the unity that existed between the bishops and
the priests of England at the very time the Reformation was
appearing at the doors. The prelates understood the danger
to which they were exposed through that evangelical doctrine,
the source of light and life. They knew that all their ecclesiastical pretensions would crumble away before the breath

[1] The noble was worth six shillings and eightpence.

of the divine Word. Accordingly, not content with robbing of their little substance the poor pastors to whom they should have been as fathers, they determined to deprive those whom they called *heretics*, not only of their money, but of their liberty and life. Would Henry permit this?

The king did not wish to withdraw England from the papal jurisdiction without the assent of the clergy. If he did so of his own authority, the priests would rise against him and compare him to Luther. There were at that time three great parties in Christendom: the evangelical, the catholic, and the popish. Henry purposed to overthrow popery, but without going so far as evangelicalism: he desired to remain in catholicism. One means occurred of satisfying the clergy. Although they were fanatical partisans of the Church, they had sacrificed the pope; they now imagined that, by sacrificing a few heretics, they would atone for their cowardly submission. In a later age Louis XIV did the same to make up for errors of another kind. The provincial synod of Canterbury met and addressed the king: "Your Highness one time defended the Church with your pen, when you were only a member of it; now that you are its supreme head, your Majesty should crush its enemies, and so shall your merits exceed all praise."

In order to prove that he was not another Luther, Henry VIII consented to hand over the disciples of that heretic to the priests; and gave them authority to imprison and burn them, provided they would aid the king to resume the power usurped by the pope. The bishops immediately began to hunt down the friends of the Gospel.

A will had given rise to much talk in the county of Gloucester. William Tracy, a gentleman of irreproachable conduct and "full of good works, equally generous to the clergy and the laity," had died praying God to save his soul through the merits of Jesus Christ, but leaving no money to the priests for masses. The primate of England had his bones dug up and burnt.[1] But this was not enough: they must also burn the living.

[1] [The "testament and last will" of William Tracy is worthy of notice as showing how far Reformed doctrine had penetrated into England by the year 1530. Tracy belonged to Toddington, eight miles south of Evesham, and was at one time High Sheriff of his county. His will ran as follows: "First and before all other things, I commit myself to God

and to His mercy, believing, without any doubt or mistrust, that by His grace, and the merits of Jesus Christ, and by the virtue of His passion and of His resurrection, I have and shall have remission of all my sins, and resurrection of body and soul, according as it is written, I believe that my Redeemer liveth, and that in the last day I shall rise out of the earth, and in my flesh shall see my Saviour: this my hope is laid up in my bosom. And touching the wealth of my soul, the faith that I have taken and rehearsed is sufficient (as I suppose) without any other man's works or merits. My ground of belief is, that there is but one God and one Mediator between God and man, which is Jesus Christ; so that I accept none in heaven or in earth to be mediator between me and God, but only Jesus Christ: and therefore will I bestow no part of my goods for that intent that any man should say or do to help my soul: for therein I trust only to the promises of Christ: 'He that believeth and is baptized shall be saved, and he that believeth not shall be damned.' As touching the burying of my body, it availeth me not whatsoever be done thereto; for . . . the funeral pomps are rather the solace of them that live, than the wealth and comfort of them that are dead. And touching the distribution of my temporal goods, my purpose is, by the grace of God, to bestow them to be accepted as the fruits of faith; so that I do not suppose that my merit shall be by the good bestowing of them, but my merit is the faith of Jesus Christ only, by whom such works are good . . . and ever we should consider that true saying, that a good work maketh not a good man, but a good man maketh a good work; for faith maketh a man both good and righteous; for a righteous man liveth by faith, and whatsoever springeth not of faith is sin. Witness mine own hand the tenth of October in the twenty-second year of the reign of King Henry the Eighth."

It was for such a clear testimony as this that the dead body of this worthy successor of Wycliffe was exhumed and burnt nearly two years after his death. The will was likewise condemned under the common seal of the University of Oxford on the 28th January, 1531.]

CHAPTER TWELVE

The Martyrs

(1531)

THE first blows were aimed at the court-chaplain. The bishops, finding it dangerous to have such a man near the king, would have liked (Latimer tells us) to place him on burning coals. But Henry loved him, the blow failed, and the priests had to turn to those who were not so well favoured at court.

Thomas Bilney, whose conversion had begun the Reformation in England, had been compelled to do penance at St. Paul's Cross; but from that time he became the prey of the direst terror. His backsliding had manifested the weakness of his faith. Bilney possessed a sincere and lively piety, but a judgment less sound than many of his friends. He had not got rid of certain scruples which in Luther and Calvin had yielded to the supreme authority of God's Word. In his opinion none but priests consecrated by bishops had the power to bind and loose. This mixture of truth and error had caused his fall. Such sincere but imperfectly enlightened persons are always to be met with—persons who, agitated by the scruples of their conscience, waver between Rome and the Word of God.

At last faith gained the upper hand in Bilney. Leaving his Cambridge friends, he had gone into the Eastern counties to meet his martyrdom. One day, arriving at a hermitage in the vicinity of Norwich, where a pious woman[1] dwelt, his words converted her to Christ. He then began to preach "openly in the fields" to great crowds. His voice was heard in all the county; weeping over his former fall, he said: "That doctrine which I once abjured is the truth. Let my example be a lesson to all who hear me."

Before long he turned his steps in the direction of London,

[1] [Described by John Foxe as "an anachoress."]

and, stopping at Ipswich, was not content to preach the Gospel only, but violently attacked the errors of Rome before an astonished audience. Some friars had crept among his hearers, and Bilney perceiving them called out: "*The Lamb of God taketh away the sins of the world*. If the bishop of Rome dares say that the hood of St. Francis saves, he blasphemes the blood of the Saviour." John Huggen, one of the friars, immediately made a note of the words. Bilney continued: "To invoke the saints and not Christ, is to put the head under the feet and the feet above the head." Richard Seman took down these words. "Men will come after me," continued Bilney, "who will teach the same faith and manner of living that I do, the true gospel of our Saviour, and will disentangle you from the errors in which deceivers have bound you so long." Friar Julles hastened to write down the bold prediction.

Latimer, surrounded by the favours of the king and the luxury of the great, watched his friend from afar. He called to mind their walks in the fields round Cambridge, their serious conversation as they climbed the hill afterwards called after them "the heretics' hill," and the visits they had paid together to the poor and to the prisoners. Latimer had seen Bilney very recently at Cambridge in fear and anguish, and had tried in vain to restore him to peace. "He now rejoiced that God had endued him with such strength of faith, that he was ready to be burnt for Christ's sake."

Bilney, drawing still nearer to London, arrived at Greenwich about the middle of July. He procured some New Testaments, and hiding them carefully under his clothes, called upon a humble Christian named Lawrence Staples. Taking them "out of his sleeves," he desired Staples to distribute them among his friends. Then, as if impelled by a thirst for martyrdom, and saying that "he would go up to Jerusalem," he turned again toward Norwich, whose bishop Richard Nix, a blind octogenarian, was in the front rank of the persecutors. Arriving at the solitary place where the pious "anachoress" lived, he left one of the precious volumes with her. This visit cost Bilney his life. The poor solitary read the New Testament, and lent it to the people who came to see her. The bishop, hearing of it, informed Sir Thomas More, who had Bilney arrested, brought to London, and shut up in the Tower.

Bilney began to breathe again: a load was taken off him; he was about to suffer the penalty his fall deserved. In the room next to his was John Petit, a member of parliament of some eloquence, who had distributed his books and his alms in England and beyond the seas. Philips, the under-gaoler of the Tower, who was a good man, told the two prisoners that only a wooden partition separated them, which was a source of great joy to both. He would often remove a panel, and permit them to converse and take their frugal meals together.

This happiness did not last long. Bilney's trial was to take place at Norwich, where he had been captured: the aged bishop Nix wanted to make an example in his diocese. A crowd of monks and friars—Augustins, Dominicans, Franciscans, and Carmelites—visited the prison of the evangelist to convert him. Dr. Call, provincial of the Franciscans, having consented that the prisoner should make use of Scripture, was shaken in his faith; but, on the other hand, Stokes, an Augustin and a determined papist, repeated to Bilney: "If you die in your opinions, you will be lost."

The trial commenced, and the witnesses gave their evidence. "He said," deposed William Cade, "that the Jews and Saracens would have been converted long since, if the idolatry of the Christians had not disgusted them with Christianity."—"I heard him say," added Richard Neale: "down with your gods of gold, silver, and stone."—"He stated," resumed Cade, "that the priests take away the offerings from the saints and hang them about their women's necks; and then, if the offerings do not prove fine enough, they are put upon the images again."

Every one foresaw the end of this piteous trial. One of Bilney's friends endeavoured to save him. Latimer took the matter into the pulpit, and conjured the judges to decide according to justice. Although Bilney's name was not uttered, they all knew who was meant. The bishop of London went and complained to the king that his chaplain had the audacity to defend the heretic against the bishop and his judges. Said Latimer later: "It might have become a preacher to say as I said, though Bilney had never been born." The chaplain escaped once more, thanks to the favour he enjoyed with Henry.

Bilney was condemned, and after being degraded by the priests, was handed over to the two sheriffs of Norwich, one of whom, having great respect for his virtues, begged pardon for discharging his duty. The prudent bishop wrote to the chancellor, asking for an order to burn the heretic. "Burn him first," rudely answered More, "and then ask me for a bill of indemnity."

A few of Bilney's friends went to Norwich to bid him farewell: among them was Matthew Parker, later archbishop of Canterbury. It was in the evening, and Bilney was taking his last meal. On the table stood some frugal fare (ale brew), and on his countenance beamed the joy that filled his soul. "I am surprised," said one of his friends, "that you can eat so cheerfully."—"I only follow the example of the husbandmen of the country," answered Bilney, "who having a ruinous house to dwell in, yet bestow cost so long as they may hold it up and so do I now with this ruinous house of my body." With these words he rose from the table, and sat down near his friends, one of whom said to him: "To-morrow the fire will make you feel its devouring fierceness, but the comfort of God's Holy Spirit will cool it for your everlasting refreshing." Bilney, appearing to reflect upon what had been said, stretched out his hand towards the lamp that was burning on the table and placed his finger in the flame. "What are you doing?" they exclaimed.—"Nothing," he replied; "I am only trying my flesh; to-morrow God's rods shall burn my whole body in the fire." And still keeping his finger in the flame, as if he were making a curious experiment, he continued: "I feel that fire by God's ordinance is naturally hot; but yet I am persuaded, by God's Holy Word and the experience of the martyrs, that when the flames consume me, I shall not feel them. Howsoever this stubble of my body shall be wasted by it, a pain for the time is followed by joy unspeakable." He then withdrew his finger, the first joint of which was burnt. He added, "*When thou walkest through the fire, thou shalt not be burned.*"[1] These words remained imprinted on the hearts of

---

[1] Isaiah 43. 2. In Bilney's Bible, which is preserved in the library of Corpus Christi College, Cambridge, this passage (verses 1–3) is marked in the margin with a pen. [The book also contains many annotations in Bilney's own hand.]

some who heard them, until the day of their death, says a chronicler.

Beyond the city gate—that known as the *Bishop's gate*—was a low valley, called the *Lollards' Pit*: it was surrounded by rising ground, forming a sort of amphitheatre. On Saturday, the 19th of August, a body of javelin-men came to fetch Bilney, who met them at the prison gate. One of his friends approaching and exhorting him to be firm, Bilney replied: "When the sailor goes on board his ship and launches out into the stormy sea, he is tossed to and fro by the waves; but the hope of reaching a peaceful haven makes him bear the danger. My voyage is beginning, but whatever storms I shall feel, my ship will soon reach the port."

Bilney passed through the streets of Norwich in the midst of a dense crowd: his demeanour was grave, his features calm. His head had been shaved, and he wore a layman's gown. Dr. Warner, one of his friends, accompanied him; another distributed liberal alms all along the route. The procession descended into the Lollards' Pit, while the spectators covered the surrounding slopes. On arriving at the place of punishment, Bilney fell on his knees and prayed, and then rising up, warmly embraced the stake and kissed it. Turning his eyes towards heaven, he next repeated the Apostles' Creed, and when he confessed the incarnation and crucifixion of the Saviour his emotion was such that even the spectators were moved. Recovering himself, he took off his gown, and ascended the pile, reciting the hundred and forty-third psalm. Thrice he repeated the second verse: "*Enter not into judgment with thy servant, for in thy sight shall no man living be justified.*" And then he added: "*I stretch forth my hands unto thee; my soul thirsteth after thee.*" Turning towards the officers, he said: "Are you ready?" —"Yes," was their reply. Bilney placed himself against the post, and held up the chain which bound him to it. His friend Warner, with eyes filled with tears, took a last farewell. Bilney smiled kindly at him and said: "Doctor, *pasce gregem tuum* (feed your flock), that when the Lord cometh He may find you so doing." Several monks who had given evidence against him, perceiving the emotion of the spectators, began to tremble, and whispered to the martyr: "These people will believe that we are the cause of your death, and will withhold their alms." Upon which Bilney said to them: "Good folks, be not angry against these men for my sake; as though they be the authors of my death, *it is not they*." He knew that his death proceeded from the will of God. The torch was applied to the pile: the fire smouldered for a few minutes, and then suddenly burning up fiercely, the martyr was heard to utter the name of Jesus several times, and sometimes the word "Credo" ("I believe"). A strong wind which blew the flames on one side prolonged his agony; thrice they seemed to retire from him, and thrice they returned, until at length, the whole pile being kindled, he expired.

A strange revolution took place in men's minds after this death: they praised Bilney, and even his persecutors acknowledged his virtues. The bishop of Norwich was heard to exclaim, "I fear I have burnt Abel and let Cain go." Latimer was inconsolable; twenty years later he still lamented his friend, and one day preaching before Edward VI he called to mind that Bilney was always doing good, even to his enemies, and styled him "that blessed martyr of God."

One martyrdom was not sufficient for the enemies of the Reformation. Stokesley, Lee, Gardiner, and other prelates and priests, feeling themselves guilty towards Rome, which they had sacrificed to their personal ambition, desired to expiate their faults by sacrificing the reformers. Seeing at their feet a fatal gulf, dug between them and the Roman pontiff by their faithlessness, they desired to fill it up with corpses. The persecution continued.

There was at that time a pious evangelist in the dungeons of the bishop of London. He was fastened upright to the wall, with chains round his neck, waist, and legs. Usually the most guilty prisoners were permitted to sit down, and even to lie on the floor; but for this man there was no rest. It was Richard Bayfield, accused of bringing from the continent a number of New Testaments translated by Tyndale.[1] When one of his gaolers told him of Bilney's martyrdom, he exclaimed: "And I too, and hundreds of men with me, will die for the faith he has confessed." He was brought shortly afterwards before the episcopal court. "With what intent," asked Bishop Stokesley, "did you bring into the country the errors

[1] See Volume I, pp. 267–8, 460–1.

of Luther, Œcolampadius the great heretic, and others of that damnable sect?"—"To make the Gospel known," answered Bayfield, "and to glorify God before the people." Accordingly, the bishop, having condemned and then degraded him, summoned the lord mayor and sheriffs of London, "by the bowels of Jesus Christ" (he had the presumption to say), to do to Bayfield "according to the *laudable custom* of the famous realm of England." "O ye priests," said the gospeller, as if inspired by the Spirit of God, "is it not enough that your lives are wicked, but you must prevent the life according to the gospel from spreading among the people?" The bishop took up his crosier and struck Bayfield so violently on the chest that he fell backwards and fainted. He revived by degrees, and said, on regaining his consciousness: "I thank God that I am delivered from the wicked church of Antichrist, and am going to be a member of the true Church which reigns triumphant in heaven." He mounted the pile; the flames, touching him only on one side, consumed his left arm. With his right hand Bayfield separated it from his body, and the arm fell. After enduring the flames for three quarters of an hour, he ceased to pray, because he had ceased to live.

John Tewkesbury,[1] one of the most respected merchants in London, whom the bishops had put twice to the rack already, and whose limbs they had broken, felt his courage revived by the martyrdom of his friend. CHRIST ALONE, he said habitually: these two words were all his theology. He was arrested, taken to the house of Sir Thomas More at Chelsea, shut up in the porter's lodge, his hands, feet, and head being held in the stocks; but they could not obtain from him the recantation they desired. The officers took him into the chancellor's garden, and bound him so tightly to the *tree of truth*, as the renowned scholar called it, that the blood started out of his eyes; after which they scourged him. Tewkesbury remained firm.

On the 16th of December the bishop of London went to Chelsea and held a court at the house of Sir Thomas More. "Thou art a heretic," said Stokesley, " a backslider; thou hast incurred the great excommunication. We shall deliver thee

[1] See Volume I, pp. 392–3.

up to the secular power." He was burnt alive at Smithfield on the 20th of December, 1531.

Such were at this period the cruel *utopias* of the bishops and of the witty Sir Thomas More. Other evangelical Christians were thrown into prison. In vain did one of them exclaim: "The more they persecute this sect, the more will it increase." That opinion did not check the persecution. "It is impossible," says Foxe (doubtless with some exaggeration), "to name all who were persecuted before the time of Queen Anne Boleyn. As well try to count the grains of sand on the seashore!"

Thus did the real Reformation show by the blood of its martyrs that it had nothing to do with the policy, the tyranny, the intrigues, and the divorce of Henry VIII. If these men of God had not been burnt by that prince, it might possibly have been imagined that he was the author of the transformation of England; but the blood of the reformers cried to heaven that he was its executioner.

CHAPTER THIRTEEN

The King Despoils the Pope and Clergy

(March to May 1532)

HENRY VIII having permitted the bishops to execute their task of persecution, proceeded to carry out his own, that of making the papacy disgorge. Unhappily for the clergy, the king could not attack the pope and leave them unscathed. The duel between Henry and Clement was about to become more violent, and in the space of three months (March, April, and May, 1532) the Romish Church, stripped of important prerogatives, would learn that, after so many ages of wealth and honour, the hour of its humiliation in England had come at last.

Henry was determined, above all things, not to permit his cause to be tried at Rome. What would be thought if he yielded? "Could the pope," wrote Henry to his envoys, "constrain kings to leave the charge God had entrusted to them, in order to humble themselves before him? That would be to tread under foot the glory of our person and the privileges of our kingdom. If the pope persists, take your leave of the pontiff and return to us immediately."—"The pope," added Norfolk, "would do well to reflect if he intend the continuance of good obedience of England to the see apostolic."

Catherine on her part did not remain inactive: she wrote a pathetic letter to the pope, informing him that her husband had banished her from the palace. Clement, in the depths of his perplexity, behaved, however, very properly: he called upon the king (25th January) to take back the queen, and to dismiss Anne Boleyn from court. Henry spiritedly rejected the pontiff's demand. "Never was prince treated by a pope as your Holiness has treated me," he said; "not painted reason, but the truth alone, must be our guide." The king prepared to begin the emancipation of England.

Thomas Cromwell is the representative of the political reform achieved by that prince. He was one of those powerful natures which God creates to work important things. His prompt and sure judgment taught him what it would be possible to do under a Tudor king, and his intrepid energy put him in a position to accomplish it. He had an instinctive horror of superstitions and abuses, tracked them to their remotest corner, and threw them down with a vigorous arm. Every obstacle was shattered under the wheels of his car. He even defended the evangelicals against their persecutors, without committing himself, however, and encouraged the reading of Holy Scripture; but the royal supremacy, of which he was the staunch advocate, if not (as some claim) the originator, was his idol.

The events of 1532, involving as they did the royal supremacy, the impact upon the political and ecclesiastical scene of the new secretary Cromwell, the vigorous work of the Commons, and the position and authority of Convocation in a world of change, were of primary importance for both Church and State. In the outcome the constitutional independence of the Church in England was terminated.

The struggles of the Parliamentary session of 1532 commenced with a petition of the Commons against Church courts originally presented in 1529. At that time the matter had been allowed to fall into the background, but under Cromwell's energetic direction it was now revived and focussed on one special issue—the freedom of the Church to legislate for itself. This freedom was no longer acceptable to the king. By the secretary's skilful strategy the Commons were moved to present to Henry their "Supplications against the Ordinaries," a document stressing their orthodoxy, reciting their complaints against the Church courts, and urging the desirability of taking from the Church its powers of independent legislation. This was precisely what Henry desired. He presented the Supplication to Convocation and required it to produce its observations. To Gardiner, now Bishop of Winchester, fell the distasteful task of drawing up the reply. Its principal feature was a compromise proposal that while Convocation should continue to legislate for the Church, the laws it made should not become operative without royal sanction. This proved unacceptable to the king, and Cromwell and he craftily suggested that the Commons would doubtless like to adopt the same attitude as the crown. Their willingness to do so led the king to press his demands, and in a short time an overawed Convocation accepted them in their completeness.

Henry's final argument proved more potent than all others. Cromwell drew his master's attention to the oaths which the bishops took at their consecration, both to the king and to the pope. Henry first read the oath to the pope. "I swear," said the bishop, "to defend the papacy of Rome, the regality of St. Peter, against all men. If I know of any plot against the pope, I will resist it with all my might, and will give him warning. Heretics, schismatics, and rebels to our holy father I shall resist and persecute with all my power." On the other hand, the bishops took an oath to the king at the same time, wherein they renounced every clause or grant which, coming from the pope, might be in any way detrimental to his Majesty. In one breath they must obey the pope and disobey him.

Such contradictions could not last: the king wanted the English to be not with Rome but with England. Accordingly he sent for the Speaker of the Commons, and said to him: "On examining the matter closely, I find that the bishops, instead of being wholly my subjects, are only so by halves. They swear an oath to the pope quite contrary to that they swear to the crown; so that they are the pope's subjects rather than mine. I refer the matter to your care." Parliament was prorogued three days later on account of the plague; but the king did not allow the matter to rest.

The prelates felt that all their defences against the throne had been completely broken down. They knew well that it was their union with powerful pontiffs, always ready to defend them against kings, which had given them so much strength in the middle ages, and that now they must yield. They therefore lowered their flag before the authority which they had themselves set up. Convocation did, indeed, make a last effort. It represented that "the authority of bishops proceeds immediately from God, and from no power of any secular prince, as *your Highness hath shown in your own book*

most excellently written against Martin Luther." But the king was
firm, and made the prelates yield at last. As for Gardiner, he
lost the king's favour and any hopes he had of succeeding to
the see of Canterbury when the aged Warham died were
shattered.

The 15th May was fateful for the church. On that day
Convocation made its surrender in a document known as the
Submission of the Clergy. As in 1531 the clergy had, with
reservations, acknowledged Henry as their supreme head, so
now they accepted him, without reservations, as their supreme
legislator. The days of papal power in England were numbered.
Thus a great revolution was accomplished: the spiritual power
was taken away from the arrogant priests who had so long
usurped the rights of the members of the Church. It was only
justice: but it ought to have been placed in better hands
than those of Henry VIII.

The 16th May witnessed another notable event. To the
last the English priests had hoped in Sir Thomas More. That
disciple of Erasmus had acted like his master. After assailing
the Romish superstitions with biting jests, he had turned
round, and seeing the Reformation attack them with weapons
still more powerful, he had fought against the evangelicals
with fire and scourge. For two years he had filled the office of
lord-chancellor with unequalled activity and integrity. Convocation having offered him four thousand pounds sterling
"for the pains he had taken in God's quarrel," he answered:
"I will receive no recompense save from God alone;" and
when the priests urged him to accept the money, he said:
"I would sooner throw it into the Thames." He did not
persecute from any mercenary motives; but the more he
advanced, the more bigoted and fanatical he became. Every
Sunday he put on a surplice and sang mass at Chelsea. The
duke of Norfolk surprised him one day in this equipment.
"What do I see?" he exclaimed. "My lord-chancellor acting
the parish clerk . . . you dishonour your office and your king."
—"Not so," answered Sir Thomas seriously, "for I am
honouring his Master and ours."

The great question of the bishop's oath warned him that
he could not serve both the king and the pope. His mind
was soon made up. In the afternoon of the 16th of May he

went to Whitehall gardens, where the king awaited him, and in the presence of the duke of Norfolk resigned the seals. On his return home, he cheerfully told his wife and daughters of his resignation, but they were much disturbed by it. As for Sir Thomas, delighted at being freed from his charge, he indulged more than ever in his flagellations, without renouncing his witty sayings—Erasmus and Loyola combined in one.

Henry gave the seals to Sir Thomas Audley, a man well disposed towards the Gospel: this was preparing the emancipation of England. Yet the Reformation was still exposed to great danger.

Henry struck another blow against the papacy in 1532. It was being prepared while the struggle between the crown and the clergy was causing deep and bitter searchings of heart. Annates were the payments made by the bishops to the pope when they entered into possession of their sees. A Bill was introduced into Parliament—it became the famous First Act of Annates—which proposed to abolish these payments. Lest the pope should retaliate by refusing consecration to bishops-elect, the Bill further proposed arrangements for their consecration at the hands of their fellow-bishops, apart from his authority. Actually the Bill was intended as a weapon to cause the pope to yield to Henry's wishes, for one of the clauses suspended its operation until the king was pleased to issue confirmatory letters patent. The Bill therefore had the nature of a Damocles' sword suspended over the tiara-crowned head of the pope.

Clearly the work of reformation was gathering momentum. Henry VIII wished to abolish popery and set catholicism in its place—maintain the doctrine of Rome, but substitute the authority of the king for that of the pontiff. He was wrong in keeping the catholic doctrine; he was wrong in establishing the jurisdiction of the prince in the Church. Evangelical Christians had to contend against these two evils in England, and to establish the supreme and exclusive sovereignty of the Word of God. Can we blame them if they have not entirely succeeded? To attain their object they willingly have poured out their blood.

CHAPTER FOURTEEN

Liberty of Inquiry and Preaching
(1532)

THERE are writers who seriously ascribe the Reformation in England to the divorce of Henry VIII, and thus silently pass over the Word of God and the labours of the evangelical men who really founded English protestant Christianity, some of whom loved not their lives unto the death. As well forget that light proceeds from the sun. But for the faith of such men as Bilney, Latimer, and Tyndale, the Church of England, with its king, ministers of state, parliament, bishops, cathedrals, liturgy, hierarchy, and ceremonies, would have been a gallant bark, well supplied with masts, sails, and rigging, and manned by able sailors, but acted on by no breath from heaven. The Church would have stood still. It is in the humble members of the kingdom of God that its real strength lies. "Those whom the Lord has exalted to high estate," says Calvin, "most often fall back little by little, or are ruined at one blow." England, with its wealth and grandeur, needed a counterpoise: the living faith of the poor in spirit. If a people attain a high degree of material prosperity; if they conquer by their energy the powers of nature; if they compel industry to lavish its stores on them; if they cover the seas with their ships, the more distant countries with their colonies and marts, and fill their warehouses and their dwellings with the produce of the whole earth, then great dangers encompass them. Material things threaten to extinguish the sacred fire in their bosoms; and unless the Holy Ghost raises up a salutary opposition against such snares, that people, instead of acting a moralizing and civilizing part, may turn out nothing better than a huge noisy machine, fitted only to satisfy vulgar appetites. For a nation to do justice to a high and glorious calling, it must have within itself the life of faith, holiness of conscience, and the hope of incorruptible riches. At this time there were men in England in whose hearts God had kindled a holy flame, and who were to become the most important instruments of its moral transformation.

About the end of 1531, a young minister, John Nicholson, surnamed Lambert, was on board one of the ships that traded between London and Antwerp. He was chaplain to the merchants in the English House at the latter place, well versed in the writings of Luther and other reformers, intimate with Tyndale, and had preached the Gospel with power. Being accused of heresy by a certain Barlow, he was seized, put in irons, and sent to London. Alone in the ship, he retraced in his memory the principal events of his life—how he had studied in the university of Cambridge and had been converted by Bilney's ministry; how, mingling with the crowd round St. Paul's Cross, he had heard the bishop of Rochester preach against the New Testament; and how, terrified by the impiety of the priests, and burning with desire to gain the knowledge of God, he had crossed the sea to the Netherlands. When he reached England, he was taken to Lambeth, where he underwent a preliminary examination. He was then taken to Otford, near Sevenoaks, Kent, where Archbishop Warham had a fine palace, and was brought before the archbishop, and called upon to reply to forty-five different articles.

Lambert, during his residence on the Continent, had become thoroughly imbued with the principles of the Reformation. He believed that it was only by entire freedom of inquiry that men could be convinced of the truth. But he had not wandered without a compass over the vast ocean of human opinions: he had taken the Bible in his hand, believing firmly that every doctrine found therein is true, and everything that contradicts it is false. On the one hand he saw the papal system which opposes religious freedom, freedom of the press, and even freedom of reading; on the other hand protestantism, which declares that every man ought to be free to examine Scripture and submit to its teachings.

The archbishop, attended by his officers, having taken his seat in the palace chapel, Lambert was brought in, and the examination began.

"Have you read Luther's books?" asked the prelate.

"Yes," replied Lambert, "and I thank God that ever I did so, for by them hath God shown me, and a vast multitude of others also, such light as the darkness cannot abide." Then testifying to the freedom of inquiry, he added: "Luther desires above all things that his writings and the writings of all his adversaries might be translated into all languages, to the intent that all people might see and know what is said on each side, whereby they might better judge what is the truth. And this is done not only by hundreds and thousands, but by whole cities and countries, both high and low. But (he continued) in England our prelates are so drowned in voluptuous living that they have no leisure to study God's Scripture; they abhor it, no less than they abhor death, giving no other reason than the tyrannical saying of Sardanapalus: *Sic volo, sic jubeo: sit pro ratione voluntas*, So I will, so do I command, and let my will for reason stand. Moreover they curse as black as pitch men who keep and read the books written by Luther."

Lambert, wishing to make these matters intelligible to the people, said: "When you desire to buy cloth, you will not be satisfied with seeing one merchant's wares, but go from the first to the second, from the second to the third, to find who has the best cloth. Will you be more remiss about your soul's health? . . . When you go a journey, not knowing perfectly the way, you will inquire of one man after another; so ought we likewise to seek about entering the kingdom of heaven. Chrysostom himself in his commentary on Matthew, teaches you this. . . . Read the works not only of Luther, but also of all others, be they ever so ill or good. No good law forbids it, but only constitutions pharisaical."

Warham, who was as much opposed then to the liberty of the press as the popes are now, could see nothing but a boundless chaos in this freedom of inquiry. "Images are sufficient," he said, "to keep Christ and His saints in our remembrance." But Lambert exclaimed: "What have we to do with senseless stones or wood carved by the hand of man? That Word which came from the breast of Christ Himself showeth us perfectly His blessed will."

Warham having questioned Lambert as to the number of

his followers, he answered: "A great multitude through all regions and realms of Christendom think in like wise as I have showed. I ween the multitude mounteth nigh unto the one half of Christendom." Lambert was taken back to prison; but More having resigned the seals, and Warham dying, this herald of liberty and truth saw his chains fall off. One day, however, he was to die by fire, and, forgetting all controversy, to exclaim in the midst of the flames: "None but Jesus Christ."

There was a minister of the Word in London who exasperated the friends of Rome more than all the rest; this man was Latimer. The court of Henry VIII, which was worldly, magnificent, fond of pleasures, intrigue, the elegances of dress, furniture, banquets, and refinement of language and manners, was not a favourable field for the Gospel. "It is very difficult," said a reformer, "that costly trappings, solemn banquets, the excesses of pride, a flood of pleasure and debauchery should not bring many evils in their train." Thus the priests and courtiers could not endure Latimer's sermons. If Lambert was for freedom of inquiry, the king's chaplain was for freedom of preaching: his zeal sometimes touched upon imprudence, and his biting wit, and extreme frankness did not spare his superiors. One day, some honest merchants, who hungered and thirsted for the Word of God, begged him to come and preach in one of the city churches. Thrice he refused, but yielded to their prayers at last. The death of Bilney and of the other martyrs had wounded him deeply. He knew that wild beasts, when they have once tasted blood, thirst for more, and feared that these murders, these butcheries, would only make his adversaries fiercer. He determined to lash the persecuting prelates with his sarcasms. Having entered the pulpit, he preached from these words in the epistle of the day: *Ye are not under the law, but under grace.* "What!" he exclaimed, "St. Paul teaches Christians that they are not under the law. . . . What does he mean? . . . No more law! St. Paul invites Christians to break the law. . . . Quick! inform against St. Paul, seize him and take him before my lord bishop of London! . . . The good apostle must be condemned to bear a faggot at St. Paul's Cross. What a goodly sight to see St. Paul with a faggot on his back, before my

lord of London, bishop of the same, sitting under the cross!
Nay, verily, I dare say, my lord should sooner have burned
him!"

This ironical language was to cost Latimer dear. To no
purpose had he spoken in one of those churches which, being
dependencies of a monastery, were not under episcopal
jurisdiction: everybody about him condemned him and
embittered his life. The courtiers talked of his sermons,
shrugged their shoulders, pointed their fingers at him when he
approached them, and turned their backs on him. The favour
of the king, who had perhaps smiled at that burst of pulpit
oratory, had some trouble to protect him. The court became
more intolerable to him every day, and Latimer, withdrawing
to his room, gave vent to many a heavy sigh. "What tortures
I endure!" he said; "in what a world I live! Hatred ever at
work; factions fighting one against the other; folly and
vanity leading the dance; dissimulation, irreligion, debauchery,
all the vices stalking abroad in open day. . . . It is too much.
If I were able to do something . . . but I have neither the
talent nor the industry required to fight against these
monsters. . . . I am weary of the court."

On the 14th January, 1531, Latimer was presented to the
living of West Kington, fourteen miles from Bristol.[1] Wishing
to uphold the liberty of the Christian Church, and seeing
that it existed no longer in London, he resolved to seek it
elsewhere. "I am leaving," he said to one of his friends:
"I shall go and live in my parish."—"What is that you say?"
exclaimed the other; "Cromwell, who is at the pinnacle of
honours, and has profound designs, intends to do great things
for you. . . . If you leave the court, you will be forgotten, and
your rivals will rise to your place."—"The only fortune I
desire," said Latimer, "is to be useful." He departed, turning
his back on the episcopal crosier to which his friend had
alluded.

Latimer began to preach with zeal in Wiltshire, and not
only in his own parish, but in the parishes around him. His

---

[1] [The parish of West Kington was in the diocese of Salisbury whose
bishop was none other than Cardinal Campeggio who had presided over
the legatine court which dealt with Henry's divorce suit. He had never
visited his diocese and Latimer was instituted by his Vicar General, Richard
Hiley.]

diligence was so great, his preaching so mighty, says Foxe, that his hearers must either believe the doctrine he preached or rise against it. "Whosoever entereth not into the fold by the door, which is Christ, be he priest, bishop, or pope, is a robber," said he. "In the Church there are more thieves than shepherds, and more goats than sheep." His hearers were astounded. One of them (Dr. William Sherwood) said to him: "What a sermon, or rather what a satire! If we believe you, all the hemp in England would not be enough to hang those thieves of bishops, priests, and curates. . . . It is all exaggeration, no doubt, but such exaggeration is rash, audacious, and impious." The priests looked about for some valiant champion of Rome, ready to fight with him the quarrel of the Church.

One day there rode into the village an old doctor of strange aspect; he wore no shirt, but was covered with a long gown that reached down to the horse's heels, "all bedirted like a slobber," says a chronicler. He took no care for the things of the body, in order that people should believe he was the more given up to the contemplation of the interests of the soul. He dismounted gravely from his horse, proclaimed his intention of fasting, and began a series of long prayers. This person, by name Hubbardin, the Don Quixote of Roman-catholicism, went wandering all over the kingdom, extolling the pope at the expense of kings and even of Jesus Christ, and declaiming against Luther, Zwingli, Tyndale, and Latimer.

On a feast-day Hubbardin put on a clerical gown rather cleaner than the one he generally wore, and went into the pulpit, where he undertook to prove that the new doctrine came from the devil—which he demonstrated by stories, fables, dreams, and amusing dialogues. He danced and hopped and leaped about, and gesticulated, as if he were a stage-player, and his sermon a sort of interlude. His hearers were surprised and diverted; Latimer was disgusted. "You lie," he said, "when you call the faith of Scripture a new doctrine, unless you mean to say that it makes new creatures of those who receive it."

Hubbardin being unable to shut the mouth of the eloquent chaplain with his mountebank tricks, the bishops and nobility of the neighbourhood resolved to denounce Latimer. A messenger handed him a writ, summoning him to appear personally before the bishop of London to answer touching certain excesses and crimes committed by him. Putting down the paper which contained this threatening message, Latimer began to reflect. His position was critical. He was at that time suffering from the stone, with pains in the head and bowels. It was in the dead of winter, and moreover he was alone at West Kington, with no friend to advise him. Being of a generous and daring temperament, he rushed hastily into the heat of the combat, but was easily dejected. "Jesu mercy! what a world is this," he exclaimed, "that I shall be put to so great labour and pains above my power for preaching of a poor simple sermon! But we must needs suffer, and so enter into the kingdom of Christ."

The terrible summons lay on the table. Latimer took it up and read it. He was no longer the brilliant court-chaplain who charmed fashionable congregations by his eloquence; he was a poor country minister, forsaken by all. He was sorrowful. "I am surprised," he said, "that my lord of London, who has so large a diocese in which he ought to preach the Word in season and out of season, should have leisure enough to come and trouble me in my little parish . . . wretched me, who am quite a stranger to him." He appealed to Richard Hiley, chancellor of the Salisbury diocese; but Bishop Stokesley did not intend to let him go, and being as able as he was violent, he prayed the archbishop, as primate of all England, to summon Latimer before his court, and to commission himself (the bishop of London) to examine him. The chaplain's friends were terrified, and entreated him to leave England; but he began his journey to London.

On the 29th of January, 1532, a court composed of bishops and doctors of the canon law assembled, under the presidency of Primate Warham, in St. Paul's Cathedral. Latimer having appeared, the bishop of London presented him a paper, and ordered him to sign it. The reformer took the paper and read it through. There were sixteen articles on belief in purgatory, the invocation of saints, the merit of pilgrimages, and lastly on the power of the keys which (said the document) belonged to the bishops of Rome, "even should their lives be wicked," and other such topics. Latimer returned the paper to Stokesley, saying: "I cannot sign it." Three times in one week he had to appear before his judges, and each time the same scene was repeated: both sides were inflexible. The priests then changed their tactics: they began to tease and embarrass Latimer with innumerable questions. As soon as one had finished, another began with sophistry and plausibility, and interminable subterfuges. Latimer tried to make his adversaries keep within the circle from which they were straying, but they would not hear him.

One day, as Latimer entered the hall, he noticed a change in the arrangement of the furniture. There was a chimney, in which there had been a fire before: on this day there was no fire, and the fireplace was invisible. Some tapestry hung down over it, and the table round which the judges sat was in the middle of the room. The accused was seated between the table and the chimney. "Master Latimer," said an aged bishop, whom he believed to be one of his friends, "pray speak a little louder: I am hard of hearing, as you know." Latimer, surprised at this remark, pricked up his ears, and fancied he heard in the fireplace the noise of a pen upon paper; in his own vivid words, "I heard a pen walking in the chimney, behind the cloth." "Ho ho!" thought he, "they have hidden some one behind there to take down my answers." He replied cautiously to captious questions, much to the embarrassment of the judges.

Latimer was disgusted, not only with the tricks of his enemies, but still more with their "troublesome unquietness": because by keeping him in London they obliged him to neglect his duties, and especially because they made it a crime to preach the truth. The archbishop, wishing to gain him over by marks of esteem and affection, invited him to come and see him; but Latimer declined, being unwilling at any price to renounce the freedom of the pulpit. The reformers of the sixteenth century did not contend that all doctrines should be preached from the same pulpit, but that evangelical truth should be freely preached everywhere. "I have desired and still desire," wrote Latimer to the archbishop, "that our people should learn the difference between the doctrines which God has taught and those which proceed only from ourselves. Go, said Jesus, and *teach all things*. . . . What things? . . . *all things whatsoever I have commanded you*, and not *whatsoever you think fit to preach*. Let us all then make an effort to preach with one voice the things of God. I have sought not my gain, but Christ's gain; not my glory, but God's glory. And so long as I have a breath of life remaining, I will continue to do so."

Thus spoke the bold preacher. It is by such unshakable fidelity that great revolutions are accomplished.

As Latimer was deaf to all their persuasion, there was nothing to be done but to threaten the stake. The charge was transferred to the Convocation of Canterbury, and on the 11th of March, 1532, he was summoned to appear before that body at Westminster. The fifteen articles were set before him.[1] "Master Latimer," said the archbishop, "the synod calls upon you to sign these articles."—"I refuse," he answered. All the bishops pressed him earnestly. "I refuse absolutely," he answered a second time. Warham, the friend of learning, could not make up his mind to condemn one of the finest geniuses of England. "Have pity on yourself," he said. "A third and last time we entreat you to sign these articles." Although Latimer knew that a negative would probably consign him to the stake, he still answered, "I refuse absolutely."

The patience of Convocation was now exhausted. "Heretic! obstinate heretic!" exclaimed the bishops. "We have heard

---

[1] [They included the following:
 1. that there is a purgatory to purge the souls of the dead,
 2. that the souls in purgatory are holpen by the masses, prayers, and alms of the living,
 3. that the saints in heaven pray for us as mediators,
 5. that the invocation of saints is profitable,
 6. that pilgrimages and oblationst o the relics and sepulchres of saints are meritorious,
 9. that fasting, prayer, and other good works merit favour at God's hands,
 11. that Lent and other fasts should be observed,
 14. that the crucifix and other images of saints should be kept in churches as memorials, and to the honour and worship of Jesus Christ and His saints,
 15. that it is laudable to deck those images and to burn candles before them.]

it from his own mouth. Let him be excommunicated." The sentence of excommunication was pronounced, and Latimer was taken to the Lollards' Tower.

Great was the agitation both in city and court. The creatures of the priests were already singing in the streets songs with a burden like this:

> Wherefore it were pity thou shouldst die for cold.

"Ah!" said Latimer in the Tower, "if they had asked me to confess that I have been too prompt to use sarcasm, I should have been ready to do so, for sin is a heavy load. O God! unto Thee I cry; wash me in the blood of Jesus Christ." He looked for death, knowing well that few left that tower except for the scaffold. "What is to be done?" said Warham and the bishops. Many of them would have handed the prisoner over to the magistrate to do what was customary, but the rule of the papacy was coming to an end in England, and Latimer was the king's chaplain. One dexterous prelate suggested a means of reconciling everything. "We must obtain something from him, be it ever so little, and then report everywhere that he has recanted."

Some priests went to see the prisoner: "Will you not yield anything?" they asked.—"I have been too violent," said Latimer, "and I humble myself accordingly."—"But will you not recognize the merit of works?"—"No!"—"Prayers to the saints?"—"No!"—"Purgatory?"—"No!"—"The power of the keys given to the pope?"—"No! I tell you."—A bright idea occurred to one of the priests. Luther taught that it was not only permitted, but praiseworthy, to have the crucifix and the images of the saints, provided that it was merely to remind us of them and not to invoke them. He had added that the Reformation ought not to abolish fast days, but to strive to make them realities. Latimer declared that he was of the same opinion.

The deputation hastened to carry this news to the bishops. The more fanatical of them could not make up their minds to be satisfied with so little. What! no purgatory, no virtue in the mass, no prayers to saints, no power of the keys, no meritorious works! It was a signal defeat; but the bishops

knew that the king would not suffer the condemnation of his
chaplain. Doubtless, Cromwell, too, worked hard to achieve
a compromise. Convocation decided, after a long discussion,
that if Master Latimer would sign the two articles, eleven
and fourteen, he should be absolved from the sentence of
excommunication. In fact, on the 10th of April the Church
withdrew the condemnation it had already pronounced.[1]

[1] [The original documents that bear on these matters are incomplete,
and in at least one instance "tantalizingly mutilated." According to the
records of Convocation (lost for this period, but reconstructed from a
variety of sources) Latimer, having first assented to the two articles,
shortly, of his own accord, assented to the remainder.

Even so, difficulties persisted. On the 15th April he was again examined
by Convocation, and, probably on the strongly-expressed advice of
Cromwell, he appealed from Convocation to the king. It seems likely that
the king received Latimer in audience, and gave him the counsel which
proved too strong for his wearied conscience to resist. He must submit
himself unreservedly to his fellow-clergy. Their doctrine must be his
doctrine, their practices his practices. Latimer yielded to the royal
mandate. At great cost to his comfort, though it was comfort he sought,
he obtained his freedom. "This," says his biographer, "is the darkest
page in Latimer's history." It must have been with a vastly-troubled
breast that the would-be reformer hastened back to his remote rural
parish.]

CHAPTER FIFTEEN

Henry VIII Attacks Romanists and Protestants
(1532)

THE vital principle of the Reformation of Henry VIII
was its opposition both to Rome and the Gospel. He
did not hesitate, like many, between these two doctrines:
he punished alike, by exile or by fire, the disciples of the
Vatican and those of Holy Scripture.

Desiring to show that the resolution he had taken to
separate from Catherine was immutable, the king had lodged
Anne Boleyn in the palace at Greenwich, even when the
queen was still there, and had given her a reception room
and a royal state. The crowd of courtiers, abandoning the
setting star, turned towards that which was appearing above
the horizon. Henry respected Anne's person, and was eager
that all the world should know that if she was not actually
queen, she would be so one day. There was a want of delicacy
and principle in the king's conduct, at which the catholic
party were much irritated, and not without a cause.

The monks of St. Francis who officiated in the royal chapel
at Greenwich took every opportunity of asserting their
attachment to Catherine and to the pope. Anne vainly tried
to gain them over by her charms; if she succeeded with a
few, she failed with the greater number. Their superior, Father
Forest, Catherine's confessor, warmly defended the rights of
that unhappy princess. Preaching at St. Paul's Cross, he
delivered a sermon in which Henry was violently attacked,
although he was not named. Those who had heard it made a
great noise about it, and Forest was summoned to the court.
"What will be done to him?" people asked; but instead of
sending him to prison, as many expected, the king received
him well, spoke with him for half an hour, and "sent him a
great piece of beef from his own table."

On returning to his convent, Forest described with triumph

this flattering reception; but the king did not attain his
object. Among these monks there were men of independent,
perhaps of fanatical character, whom no favours could gain
over.

One of them, by name Peto, until then unknown, but
afterwards of great repute in the catholic world as cardinal
legate from the pope in England, thinking that Forest had
not said enough, determined to go further. Anne Boleyn's
elevation filled him with anger: he longed to speak out, and
as the king and all the court would be present in the chapel
on the 1st of May, he chose for his text the words of the
prophet Elijah to King Ahab: *The dogs shall lick thy blood.* He
drew a portrait of Ahab, described his malice and wickedness,
and although he did not name Henry VIII, certain passages
made the hearers feel uncomfortable. At the peroration,
turning towards the king, he said: "Now hear, O king, what
I have to say unto thee, as of old time Micaiah spoke to
Ahab. This new marriage is unlawful. There are other
preachers who, to become rich abbots or mighty bishops,
betray thy soul, thy honour, and thy posterity. Take heed
lest thou, being seduced like Ahab, find Ahab's punishment
. . . who had his blood licked up by the dogs."

The court was astounded; but the king, whose features
were unmoved during this apostrophe, waited until the end
of the service, left the chapel as if nothing had happened,
and allowed Peto to depart for Canterbury. But Henry could
not permit such invectives to pass unnoticed. A clergyman
named Kirwan was commissioned to preach in the same
chapel on the following Sunday. The congregation was still
more numerous than before, and more curious also. Some
monks of the order of Observants, friends of Peto, got into
the rood-loft, determined to defend him. The doctor began
his sermon. After establishing the lawfulness of Henry's
intended marriage, he came to the sermon of the preceding
Sunday and the insults of the preacher. "I speak to thee,
Peto," he exclaimed, "who makest thyself Micaiah; we
look for thee, but thou art not to be found, having fled for
fear and shame." There was a noise in the rood-loft, and one
of the Observants named Elstow rose and called out: "You
know that Father Peto is gone to Canterbury to a provincial

council, but I am here to answer you. And to this combat I
challenge thee, Kirwan, prophet of lies, who for thy own
vainglory art betraying thy king into endless perdition."

The chapel was instantly one scene of confusion: nothing
could be heard. Then the king rose: his princely stature, his
royal air, his majestic manners overawed the crowd. All were
silent, and the agitated congregation left the chapel respectfully. Peto and his friend were summoned before the council.
"You deserve to be sewn in a sack and thrown into the
Thames," said one. "We fear nothing," answered Elstow;
"the way to heaven is as short by water as by land."

Henry, having thus made war on the partisans of the pope,
turned to those of the Reformation. Like a child, he see-sawed
to and fro, first on one side, then on the other; but his sport
was a more terrible one, for every time he touched the ground
the blood spurted forth.

At that time there were many Christians in England to
whom the Roman worship brought no edification. Having
procured Tyndale's translation of the Word of God, they felt
that they possessed it not only for themselves but for others.
They sought one another's company, and met together to read
the Bible and receive spiritual graces from God. Several
Christian assemblies of this kind had been formed in London,
in garrets, in warehouses, schools and shops, and one of them
was held in a warehouse in Bow Lane. Among its frequenters
was the son of a Gloucestershire knight, James Bainham by
name, a man well read in the classics, and a distinguished
lawyer, respected by all for his piety and works of charity.
To give advice freely to widows and orphans, to see justice
done to the oppressed, to aid poor students, protect pious
persons, and visit the prisons were his daily occupations.
"He was an earnest reader of Scripture, and mightily addicted
to prayer." His marriage brought him under suspicion, for
his wife was the widow of Simon Fish whose book previously
mentioned had aroused a great storm of catholic opposition.
He was asked where his books were to be found but would
not divulge. When his wife denied that they were in his
house she was sent to the Fleet prison, and their goods were
confiscated. When he entered the meeting, every one could
see that his countenance expressed a calm joy; but for a

month past his Bow Lane friends noticed him to be agitated and cast down, and heard him sighing heavily. The cause was this. Some time before (in 1531), when he was engaged about his business in the Middle Temple, this "model of lawyers" had been arrested by order of More, who was still chancellor, and taken like a criminal to the house of the celebrated humanist at Chelsea. Sir Thomas, quite distressed at seeing a man so distinguished leave the Church of Rome, had employed all his eloquence to bring him back; but finding his efforts useless, he had ordered Bainham to be taken into his garden and tied to "the tree of truth." There the chancellor whipped him, or caused him to be whipped: we adopt the latter version, which is more probable. Bainham having refused to give the names of the gentlemen of the Temple tainted with heresy, he was taken to the Tower. "Put him on the rack," cried the learned chancellor, now become a fanatical persecutor. The order was obeyed in his presence. The arms and legs of the unfortunate protestant were fastened to the instrument and pulled in opposite directions: his limbs were dislocated, and he went lame out of the torture-chamber.[1]

Sir Thomas had broken his victim's limbs, but not his courage; and accordingly when Bainham was summoned before the bishop of London, he went to the palace rejoicing to have to confess his Master once more. "Do you believe in purgatory?" said Stokesley to him sternly. Bainham answered: "*The blood of Jesus Christ cleanseth us from all sin.*" "Do you believe that we ought to call upon the saints to pray for us?" He again answered: "*If any man sin, we have an advocate with the Father—Jesus Christ the righteous.*"

A man who answered only by texts from Scripture was embarrassing. More and Stokesley made the most alluring promises, and no means were spared to bend him. Before long they resorted to more serious representation: "The arms of the Church your mother are still open to you," they said; "but if you continue stubborn, they will close against you for ever. It is now or never!" For a whole month the bishop and the chancellor persevered in their entreaties; Bainham replied: "My faith is that of the holy Church." Hearing

[1] Foxe, *Acts*, iv, p. 698.

these words, Foxford, the bishop's secretary, took out a
paper. "Here is the abjuration," he said; "read it over."
Bainham began: "I voluntarily, as a true penitent returned
from my heresy, utterly abjure" . . . At these words he stopped,
and glancing over what followed, he continued: "No, these
articles are not heretical, and I cannot retract them." Other
springs were now set in motion to shake Bainham. The
prayers of his friends, the threats of his enemies, especially the
thought of his wife, whom he loved, and who would be left
alone in destitution, exposed to the anger of the world: these
things troubled his soul. He lost sight of the narrow path he
ought to follow, and five days later he read his abjuration
with a faint voice. But he had hardly got to the end before
he burst into tears, and said, struggling with his emotion:
"I reserve the doctrines." He consented to remain in the Roman
Church, still preserving his evangelical faith. But this was not
what the bishop and his officers meant. "Kiss that book,"
they said to him threateningly. Bainham, like one stunned,
kissed the book; that was the sign; the abjuration was looked
upon as completed. He was condemned to pay a fine of
twenty pounds sterling, and to do penance at St. Paul's
Cross. After that he was set at liberty, on the 17th of February.

Bainham returned to the midst of his brethren: they looked
sorrowfully at him, but did not reproach him with his fault.
That was quite unnecessary. The worm of remorse was
preying on him; he abhorred the fatal kiss by which he had
sealed his fall; his conscience was never quiet; he could neither
eat nor sleep, and trembled at the thought of death. At one
time he would hide his anguish and stifle it within his breast;
at another his grief would break forth, and he would try to
relieve his pain by groans of sorrow. The thought of appearing
before the tribunal of God made him faint. The restoration
of conscience to all its rights was the foremost work of the
Reformation. Luther, Calvin, and an endless number of
lesser reformers had reached the haven of safety through the
midst of such tempests. "A tragedy was being acted in all
protestant souls," says a writer who does not belong to the
Reformation—the eternal tragedy of conscience.

Bainham felt that the only means of recovering peace was
to accuse himself openly before God and man. Taking

Tyndale's New Testament in his hand, which was at once his joy and his strength, he went to St. Austin's church, sat down quietly in the midst of the congregation, and then at a certain moment stood up and said: "I have denied the truth." . . . He could not continue for his tears. On recovering, he said: "If I were not to return again to the doctrine I have abjured, this Word of Scripture would condemn me both body and soul at the day of judgment." And he lifted up the New Testament before all the congregation. "O my friends," he continued, "rather die than sin as I have done. The fires of hell have consumed me, and I would not feel them again for all the gold and glory of the world." He wrote in a similar strain to the bishop.

Then his enemies seized him again and shut him up in the bishop's coal-house, where, after putting him in the stocks, with his legs in irons, they left him for almost fourteen days. He was afterwards taken to the Tower, where he was scourged every day for a fortnight, and at last condemned as a relapsed heretic.

On the eve of the execution four distinguished men, one of whom was Latimer, were dining together in London. It was commonly reported that Bainham was to be put to death for saying that Thomas Becket was a traitor. "Is it worth a man's while to sacrifice his life for such a trifle?" said the four friends. "Let us go to Newgate and save him if possible." They were taken along several gloomy passages, and found themselves at last in the presence of a man sitting on a little straw, holding a book in one hand and a candle in the other. He was reading; it was Bainham. Latimer drew near him: "Take care," he said, "that no vainglory make you sacrifice your life for motives which are not worth the cost." "I am condemned," answered Bainham, "for trusting in Scripture and rejecting purgatory, masses, and meritorious works."— "I acknowledge that for such truths a man must be ready to die." Bainham was ready; and yet he burst into tears. "Why do you weep?" asked Latimer. "I have a wife," answered the prisoner, "the best that man ever had. A widow, destitute of everything and without a supporter, everybody will point at her and say, That is the heretic's wife." Latimer and his friends tried to console him, and then they departed from the gloomy dungeon.

2 +509

The next day (30th of April, 1532) Bainham was taken to the scaffold. Soldiers on horseback surrounded the pile: Master Pave, the city clerk, directed the execution. Bainham, after a prayer, rose up, embraced the stake, and was fastened to it with a chain. "Good people," he said to the persons who stood round him, "I die for having said it is lawful for every man and woman to have God's book. I die for having said that the true key of heaven is not that of the bishop of Rome, but the preaching of the Gospel. I die for having said that there is no other purgatory than the cross of Christ, with its consequent persecutions and afflictions."—"Thou liest, thou heretic," exclaimed Pave; "thou hast denied the blessed sacrament of the altar."—"I do not deny the sacrament of Christ's body," resumed Bainham, "but I do deny your transubstantiation and your idolatry to a piece of bread."— "Light the fire," shouted Pave. The executioners set fire to a train of gunpowder, and as the flame approached him, Bainham lifted up his eyes towards heaven, and said to the city clerk: "God forgive thee! and shew thee more mercy than thou showst to me! the Lord forgive Sir Thomas More . . . pray for me, all good people!" The arms and legs of the martyr were soon consumed, and thinking only how to glorify his Saviour, he exclaimed: "Behold! you look for miracles, you may see one here; for in this fire I feel no more pain than if I were on a bed of down, but it is to me as sweet as a bed of roses." The primitive Church hardly had a more glorious martyr.

Pave had Bainham's image continually before his eyes, and his last prayer rang day and night in his heart. In the garret of his house, far removed from noise, he had fitted up a kind of oratory, where he had placed a crucifix, before which he used to pray and shed bitter tears. He abhorred himself: half mad, he suffered indescribable sorrow, and struggled under great anguish. The dying Bainham had said to him: "May God show thee more mercy than thou hast shown to me!" But Pave could not believe in mercy: he saw no other remedy for his despair than death. About a year after Bainham's martyrdom, he sent his domestics and clerks on different errands, keeping only one servant-maid in the house. As soon as his wife had gone to church, he went out himself, bought a rope, and hiding it carefully under his gown, went up into the garret. He stopped before the crucifix, and began to groan and weep. The servant ran upstairs. "Take this rusty sword," he said, "clean it well, and do not disturb me." She had scarcely left the room when he fastened the rope to a beam and hanged himself.

The maid, hearing no sound, again grew alarmed, went up to the garret, and seeing her master hanging, was struck with terror. She ran crying to the church to fetch her mistress home; but it was too late: the wretched man could not be recalled to life.

If the deaths of the martyrs plunged the wicked into the depths of despair, it often gave life to earnest souls. The crowd which had surrounded the scaffold of these men of God dispersed in profound emotion. Some returned to their fields, others to their shops or workrooms; but the pale faces of the martyrs followed them, their words sounded in their souls, their virtues softened many hearts most averse to the Gospel. "Oh! that I were with Bainham!" exclaimed one. These people continued for some time to frequent the Romish churches, but ere long their consciences cried aloud to them: "It is Christ alone who saves us;" and they forsook the rites in which they could find no consolation. They courted solitude; they procured the writings of Wycliffe and of Tyndale, and especially the New Testament, which they read in secret, and if any one came near, hid them hastily under a bed, at the bottom of a chest, in the hollow of a tree, or even under stones, until the enemy had retired and they could take the books up again. Then they whispered about them to their neighbours, and often had the joy of meeting with men who thought as they did. A surprising change was taking place. While the priests were loudly chanting in the cathedrals the praises of the saints, of the Virgin, and of the *Corpus Domini,* the people were whispering together about the Saviour *meek and lowly in heart.* All over England was heard a still, small voice such as Elijah heard, and on hearing it wrapped his face in his mantle and stood silent and motionless, because the Lord was there. Great changes were about to take place.

It is not without a reason that we describe in some detail in this history the lives and deaths of these evangelical men.

We desire to show that the Church in England, as in all the world, is not a mere ecclesiastical hierarchy, in which prelates exercise dominion over the inheritance of the Lord; nor a confused assemblage of men, whose spirit imagines about religion all kinds of doctrines contrary to the revelation from heaven, and whose profession of faith comprehends all the opinions that are found in the nation from catholic scholasticism to pantheistic materialism. The Church of God, raised above the human systems of the superstitious and the incredulous alike, is the assembly of those who by a living faith are partakers of the righteousness of Christ, and of the new life of which the Holy Ghost is the creator—of those in whom selfishness is vanquished, and who give themselves up to the Saviour to achieve with their brethren the conquest of the world. Such is the true Church of God; very different, it will be seen, from all those invented by man.

CHAPTER SIXTEEN

The New Primate of All England

(February 1532 to March 1533)

A MAN who for more than thirty years had had an important voice in the management of the ecclesiastical affairs of the kingdom now disappeared from the scene to give place to the most influential of the reformers of England. Warham, archbishop of Canterbury, a learned canonist, a skilful politician, a dexterous courtier, and the friend of letters, had made it his special work to exalt the sacerdotal prerogative, and to that end had had recourse to the surest means, by fighting against the idleness, ignorance, and corruption of the priests. He had even hoped for a reform of the clergy, provided it emanated from episcopal authority. But when he saw another reformation accomplished in the name of God's Word, without priests and against the priests, he turned round and began to persecute the reformers and to strengthen the papal authority. Alarmed at the proceedings of the Commons, he sent for three notaries, on the 24th February, 1532, and protested in their presence against every act of parliament derogatory to the authority of the Roman pontiff.

On the 22nd August of the same year, just at the very height of the crisis, "the second pope," as he was sometimes called, was removed from his see by death, and the people anxiously wondered who would be appointed to his vacant place.

The choice was important, for the nomination might be the symbol of what the Church of England was to be. Would he be a prelate devoted to the pope, like Fisher; or a catholic favourable to the divorce, like Gardiner; or a moderate evangelical attached to the king, like Cranmer; or a decided reformer, like Latimer? At this moment, when a new era was beginning for Christendom, it was of consequence to know whom England would take for her guide; whether she would march at the head of civil and religious progress, like Germany; or bring up the rear, like Spain and Italy. The king did not favour either extreme, and hesitated between the two other candidates. All things considered, he had no confidence in such bishops as Longland of Lincoln, and Gardiner of Winchester, who might promise and not fulfil. He wanted somebody less political than the one, and less fanatical than the other—a man separated from the pope on principle, and not merely for convenience.

Cranmer, after passing a few months at Rome, had returned to England. Then departing again for Germany on a mission from the king, he had arrived at Nuremberg, probably in the autumn of 1531. He examined with interest that ancient city, its beautiful churches, its monumental fountains, its old and picturesque castle; but there was something that attracted him more than all these things. Being present at the celebration of the sacrament, he noticed that while the priest was muttering the gospel in Latin at the altar, the deacon went up into the pulpit and read it aloud in German. He saw that, although there was still some appearance of catholicism in Nuremberg, in reality the Gospel reigned there. One man's name often came up in the conversations he had with the principal persons in the city. They spoke to him of Andreas Osiander as of a man of great eloquence. Cranmer followed the crowd which poured into the church of St. Lawrence, and was struck with the minister's talents and piety. He sought his acquaintance, and the two doctors had many a conversation together, either in Cranmer's house or in Osiander's study; and the German divine, being gained over to the cause of Henry VIII, published shortly after a book on unlawful marriages.

Cranmer, who had an affectionate heart, loved to join the simple meals, the pious devotions, and the friendly conversations at Osiander's house; he was soon almost like a member of the family. But although his intimacy with the Nuremberg pastor grew stronger every day, he did not adopt all his opinions. When Osiander told him that he must substitute the authority of Holy Scripture for that of Rome, Cranmer gave his full assent; but the Englishman perceived that the German entertained views different from Luther's on the justification of the sinner. "What justifies us," said

Osiander, "is not the imputation of the merits of Christ by faith, but the inward communication of His righteousness." "On the contrary," said Cranmer, "Christ has paid the price of our redemption by the sacrifice of His body and the fulfilling of the law; and if we heartily believe in this work which He has perfected, we are justified. The justified man must be sanctified, and must work good works; but it is not the works that justify him." The conversation of the two friends turned also upon the Lord's Supper. Whatever may have been Cranmer's doctrine before, he soon came (like Calvin) to place the real presence of Christ not in the wafer which the priest holds between his fingers, but in the heart of the believer.[1]

In June 1532 protestant and Roman-catholic delegates arrived at Nuremberg to arrange the religious peace. The celibacy of the clergy immediately became one of the points discussed. It appeared to the chiefs of the papacy impossible to concede that article. "Rather abolish the mass entirely," exclaimed the archbishop of Mayence, "than permit the marriage of priests." "They must come to that at last," said Luther; "God is overthrowing the mighty from their seat." Cranmer was of his opinion: "It is better," he said, "for a minister to have his own wife, than to have other men's wives, like the priests." "What services may not a pious wife do for the pastor her husband," added Osiander, "among the poor, the women, and the children?"

Cranmer had lost his wife at Cambridge, and his heart yearned for affection. Osiander's family presented him a touching picture of domestic happiness. One of its members was a certain Margaret, a niece of Osiander's wife. Cranmer, charmed with her piety and candour, and hoping to find in her the virtuous woman who is a crown to her husband, asked her hand and married her, not heeding the unlawful command of those who "forbid to marry."

---

[1] ["Although Christ be not corporally in the bread and wine, yet Christ used not so many words in the mystery of his holy supper, without effectual signification: For he is effectually present, and effectually worketh not in the bread and wine, but in the godly receivers of them, to whom he giveth his own flesh spiritually to feed upon, and his own blood to quench their great inward thirst." (Cranmer, *On the Lord's Supper* Parker Society, pp. 34–5.)]

Still Cranmer did not forget his mission. The king of England was desirous of forming an alliance with the German protestants, and his agent made overtures to the electoral prince of Saxony. "First of all," answered the pious John Frederick, "the king must be in harmony with us as to the articles of faith." The alliance failed, but, at the same moment, affairs took an unexpected turn. The Emperor Charles V who was marching against Solyman the Magnificent, the greatest of all the Ottoman sultans, desired the help of the King of England, and Granvella, his minister, had some talk with Cranmer on the subject. The latter was procuring carriages, horses, boats, tents, and other things necessary for his journey, with the intention of rejoining the Emperor at Linz, when a courier suddenly brought him orders to return to London. It was very vexatious. Just as he was on the point of concluding an alliance with the nephew of Queen Catherine, in which the matter of the divorce would consequently be arranged, Henry's envoy had to give up everything. He wondered anxiously what could be the motive of this sudden and extraordinary recall: the letters of his friends explained it.

Warham was dead, and the king thought of Cranmer to succeed him as archbishop of Canterbury and primate of all England. The reformer was greatly moved. "Alas!" he exclaimed, "no man has ever desired a bishopric less than myself. If I accept it, I must resign the delights of study and the calm sweetness of an obscure condition." Knowing Henry's domineering character and his peculiar religious principles, Cranmer thought that with him the reformation of England was impossible. He saw himself exposed to disputes without end: there would be no more peace for the most peaceable of men. A brilliant career, an exalted position—he was terrified. "My conscience," he said, "rebels against this call. Wretch that I am! I see nothing but troubles, and conflicts, and insurmountable dangers in my path."

Upon mature reflection, Cranmer thought he might get out of his difficulty by gaining time, hoping that the king, who did not like delays, would doubtless give the see to another. He sent an answer that important affairs prevented his return to England. Solyman had retreated before the Emperor; the latter had determined to pass through Italy

to Spain, and had appointed a meeting with the pope at
Piacenza or Genoa. Henry's ambassador thought it his duty
to neutralize the fatal consequences of this interview; and
Charles having left Vienna on the 4th of October, Cranmer
followed him two days later. The exalted dignity that awaited
him oppressed him like the nightmare. On his road he found
neither inhabitants nor food, and hay was his only bed.
Sometimes he crossed battle-fields covered with the carcases
of Turks and Christians. A comet appeared in the east foreboding some tragic event. Many declared they had seen a
flaming sword in the heavens. "These strange signs," he
wrote to Henry, "announce some great mutation." Cranmer
and his colleagues could not gain the pope to their side.
Several months passed away, during which men's minds
became so excited, that the cardinals forgot all decorum.
"Alas!" says a catholic historian, "all the time this affair
continued, they went to the consistory as if they were going
to a play." Charles V prevailed at last.

A report having circulated in Italy that the king was
about to place Cranmer at the head of the English Church,
the imperial court treated him with unusual consideration.
Charles V, his ministers, and the foreign ambassadors said
openly that such a man richly deserved to hold a high place
in the favour and government of the king his master. In
November, the Emperor gave Cranmer his farewell audience;
and the latter returned to England not long after. But he
did so reluctantly enough, knowing what awaited him and
prolonging to seven weeks a journey which could easily have
been accomplished in three. Not wishing to act in opposition
to general usage and clerical opinion, he thought it more
prudent to leave his wife for a time with Osiander. He sent
for her somewhat later, but she was never presented at court.
It was not necessary, and it might only have embarrassed
the pious German lady.

As soon as Cranmer reached London, he waited upon the
king, being quite engrossed in thinking of what was about to
take place between his sovereign and himself. Henry went
straight to the point: he told him that he had nominated him
archbishop of Canterbury. Cranmer objected, but the king
would take no refusal. In vain did the divine urge his reasons:

the monarch was firm. It was no slight matter to contend
with Henry VIII. Cranmer was alarmed at the effect produced
by his resistance. "Your Highness," he said, "I most humbly
implore your Grace's pardon."

When he left the king, he hurried off to his friends, particularly to Cromwell. The burden which Henry was laying
upon him seemed more insupportable than ever. Knowing
how difficult it is to resist a prince of despotic character, he
foresaw conflicts and perhaps compromises, which would
embitter his life, and he could not make up his mind to
sacrifice his happiness to the imperious will of the monarch.
"Take care," said his friends, "it is as dangerous to refuse a
favour from so absolute a prince as to insult him." But
Cranmer's conscience was concerned in his refusal. "I feel
something within me," he said, "which rebels against the
supremacy of the pope, and all the superstitions to which I
should have to submit as primate of England. No, I will not be
a bishop!" He might sacrifice his repose and his happiness,
expose himself to painful struggles; but to recognize the pope
and submit to his jurisdiction was an insurmountable obstacle.
His friends shook their heads. "Your *nolo episcopari*," they said,
"will not hold against our master's *volo te episcopum esse*.[1] And
after all what is it? Permitting the king to place you at the summit of honours and power. . . . You refuse all that men desire."
"I would sooner forfeit my life," answered Cranmer, "than do
anything against my conscience to gratify my ambition."

Henry, vexed at all these delays, again summoned Cranmer
to the palace, and bade him speak without fear. "If I accept
this office," replied that sincere man, "I must receive it from
the hands of the pope, and this my conscience will not permit
me to do. . . . Neither the pope nor any other foreign prince
has authority in this realm." Such a reason as this had great
weight with Henry. He was silent for a little while, as if
reflecting, and then said to Cranmer: "Can you prove what
you have just said?" "Certainly I can," answered the doctor;
"Holy Scripture and the Fathers support the supreme authority
of kings in their kingdoms, and thus prove the claims of the
pope to be a miserable usurpation."

[1] "I am unwilling to be made a bishop." "I desire you to be a bishop."
(Fuller, *Church History*, Book V, p. 184.)

Such a statement bound Henry to take another step in his reforms. As he had not yet thought of establishing bishops and archbishops without the pope, he sent for some learned lawyers, and asked them how he could confer the episcopal dignity on Cranmer without wounding the conscience of the future primate. The lawyers proposed, that as Cranmer refused to submit to the Roman primacy, some one should be sent to Rome to do in his stead all that the law required. "Let another do it, if he likes," said Cranmer, "but *super animam suam*, at the risk of his soul. As for me, I declare I will not acknowledge the authority of the pope any further than it agrees with the Word of God; and that I reserve the right of speaking against him and of attacking his errors."

The lawyers found bad precedents to justify a bad measure. "Archbishop Warham," they said, "while preserving the advantages he derived from the state, protested against everything the state did prejudicial to Rome. If the deceased archbishop preserved the rights of the papacy, why should not the new one preserve those of the kingdom? . . . Besides (they added) the pope knows very well that when they make oath to him, every bishop does so *salvo ordine meo*, without prejudice to the rights of his order."

It having been conceded that in the act of consecration "the rights of the Word of God" should be reserved, Cranmer consented to become primate of England. Henry VIII, who was less advanced in practice than in theory, all the same demanded of Clement VII the bulls necessary for the inauguration of the new archbishop. The pontiff, only too happy still to have something to say to England, hastened to despatch them, addressing them directly to Cranmer himself. But the latter, who would accept nothing from the pope, sent them to the king, declaring that he would not receive his appointment from Rome.

By accepting the call that was addressed to him, Cranmer meant to break with the order of the Middle Ages, and re-establish, so far as was in his power, that of the Gospel. But he would not conceal his intentions: all must be done in the light of day. On the 30th of March, 1533, he summoned to the chapter-house of Westminster Watkins, the king's prothonotary,[1] with other dignitaries of the Church and State. On entering, he took up a paper, and read aloud and distinctly: "I, Thomas, archbishop of Canterbury, protest openly, publicly, and expressly, that I will not bind myself by oath to anything contrary to the law of God, the rights of the king of England, and the laws of the realm; and that I will not be bound in aught that concerns liberty of speech, the government of the Church of England, and the reformation of all things that may seem to be necessary to be reformed therein. If my representative with the pope has taken in my name an oath contrary to my duty, I declare that he has done so without my knowledge, and that the said oath shall be null. I desire this protest to be repeated at each period of the present ceremony." Then turning to the prothonotary: "I beg you to prepare as many copies as may be necessary of this my protest."

Cranmer left the chapter-house and entered the abbey, where the clergy and a numerous crowd awaited him. He was not satisfied with once declaring his independence of the papacy; he desired to do it several times. The greater the antiquity of the Romish power in Britain, the more he felt the necessity of proclaiming the supremacy of the divine Word. Having put on his sacerdotal robes, Cranmer stood at the top of the steps of the high altar, and said, turning towards the assembly: "I declare that I take the oath required of me only under the reserve contained in the protest I have made this day in the chapter-house." Then bending his knees before the altar, he read it a second time in presence of the bishops, priests, and people; after which the bishops of Lincoln, Exeter, and St. Asaph consecrated him to the episcopate.

The archbishop, standing before the altar, prepared to receive the pallium, but first he had a duty to fulfil: if he sacrificed his repose, he did not intend to sacrifice his convictions. For the third time he took up the protest, and again read it before the immense crowd that filled the cathedral. The accustomed order of the ceremony having been twice interrupted by an extraordinary declaration, all were at liberty to praise or blame the action of the prelate as they

[1] [A chief clerk in certain courts of law.]

pleased. Cranmer, having thus thrice published his reserves, read at last the oath which the archbishops of Canterbury were accustomed to make to St. Peter and to the holy apostolic Church of Rome, with the usual protest: *salvo meo ordine* (without prejudice to my order).

Cranmer's triple protest was an act of Christian decision. Some time afterwards he said: "I made that protest in good faith: I always loved simplicity and hated falseness." But it was wrong of him to use after it the formula ordinarily employed in consecrations. Doubtless it was nothing more than a form; a form that was imposed by the king, and Cranmer protested against all the bad it might contain: still "it is necessary to walk consistently in all things," as Calvin says; and we here meet with one of those weaknesses which sometimes appear in the life of the pious reformer of England. He ought at no price to have made oath to the pope; that oath was a stain which in some measure tinged the whole of his episcopate. Yet if we were to condemn him severely, we should be forgetting that striking truth—*in many things we offend all.* Cranmer was the first in the breach, and he has claims to the consideration of those who are comfortably established in a position gained by him with so much suffering. The energy with which he thrice proclaimed his independence deserves our admiration. Nevertheless all weakness is a fault, and when that fault is committed in high station it may lead to fatal consequences. The sanctity of the oath taken by churchmen was compromised by Cranmer's act, and we have seen in later times other divines secretly communing with Romish doctrines while appearing to reject popery. There have sometimes been disguised papists in the protestant Church of England.

After the ceremony the new archbishop returned to his palace at Lambeth. From that hour this patron of letters, a scholar himself, a truly pious man, a distinguished preacher, and of indefatigable industry, never ceased to labour for the good of the Church. He was able to introduce Christian faith into many hearts, and sometimes to defend it against the king's ill-humour. He constantly endeavoured to spread around him moderation, charity, truth, piety, and peace. When Cranmer became primate of all England, on the 30th

of March, 1533, in St. Stephen's, Westminster, the papal order
was interred, and it might be foreseen that the apostolic order
would be revived. England preserved episcopacy but she rejected that Roman superstition which makes bishops the sole
successors of the apostles and maintains (as at the Council of
Trent) that they are invested with an indelible character and
a spiritual power which no other minister possesses. "Most
assuredly," said Cranmer, "at the beginning of the religion of
Christ, bishops and presbyters (priests) were not two things,
but one only." He declared that a bishop was not necessary to
make a pastor; that not only presbyters possessed this right, but
"the people also by their election." "Before there were Christian
princes, it was the people," he said, "who generally elected the
bishops and priests." Cranmer was not the only man who professed these principles, which make of the episcopalian and the
presbyterian constitution two varieties, having many things
in common. The most venerable fathers of the Anglican
Church—Pilkington, Coverdale, Whitgift, Fulke, Tyndale,
Jewel, Bradford, Becon, and others—have acknowledged the
identity of bishops and presbyters. By the Reformation,
England belongs not to the papistical system of episcopacy,
but to the evangelical system. A public act which would
bring back that Church to her holy origin, would be a source
of great prosperity to her.

The great reformers of England did not separate from
Rome only, but also from the semi-catholicism that was
intended to be substituted for it. To them the spirit and the
life were in the ministry of the Word of God, and not in rites
and ceremonies. By their noble example they have called all
men of God to follow them.

CHAPTER SEVENTEEN

Catherine of Aragon Descends from the Throne and Anne Boleyn Ascends It

(November 1532 to July 1533)

CRANMER was on the archiepiscopal throne: if Anne Boleyn were now to take her seat on the royal throne by the side of Henry, it was the pope's opinion that everything would be lost. Clement recurred once more to his favourite suggestion of bigamy, already advised by him in 1528 and 1530. True, this suggestion could not be acceptable either to Henry or to Charles V, but that made it all the better in the eyes of the pontiff: he would then have the appearance of assenting to the king's plans without running the least risk of seeing them realized. "Rather than do what his Majesty asks," he said to one of the English envoys, "I would prefer granting him the necessary dispensation to have two wives: that would be a smaller scandal."

The tenacity with which the pope advised Henry again and again to commit the crime of bigamy has not prevented the most illustrious advocates of catholicism from exclaiming that "to have two wives at once is a mystery of iniquity, of which there is no example in Christendom." A singular assertion after a cardinal and then a pope had on several occasions advised what they call "a mystery of iniquity." Again, for the third time, the king refused a remedy that was worse than the disease.

The pope wished at any price to prevent Rome from losing England; and turning to the other side, he resolved to try to gain over Charles V and prevail upon him not to oppose the divorce. In order to succeed, Clement determined to undertake a journey to Bologna in the worst season of the year. He started on the 18th of November with six cardinals and a

certain number of attendants, and took twenty days to reach
that city by way of Perugia. Most of his officers had done
everything to dissuade him from this painful expedition, but
in vain. The rain fell in torrents; the rivers were swollen and
unfordable; the roads muddy and broken up; the mules sank
of fatigue one after another; the couriers who preceded him
solicited the pope to travel on foot; and at last his Holiness'
favourite mule broke its leg. It mattered not: he must oppose
the Reformation of England. But the discomforts of the
journey increased: the pope often arrived at inns where there
was no bed, and had to sleep among the straw. At last he
reached Bologna on the 7th of December, but in such a plight
that, notwithstanding his love for ceremonies, he entered the
city furtively.

Another disappointment awaited him. The cardinal of
Ancona died, the most influential member of the Sacred
College, and on whom Clement relied to gain over the
Emperor, who greatly respected him. But this did not cool
the pontiff's zeal: "I am thoroughly decided to please the
king in this great matter," he said to Henry's envoys, and
added: "To have universal concord between all the princes
of Christendom, I would give a joint of my hand." In fact
Clement set to work and went so far as to tell Charles that,
according to the theologians, the pope had no right to grant
a dispensation for a marriage between brother and sister;
but the Emperor was immovable. The pope then proposed
a truce of three or four years between Henry, Francis, and
Charles, during which he would convoke a general council,
to whom he would remit the whole affair. Francis informed
Henry that all this was nothing but a trick.

The king, convinced that the pope was trifling with him,
no longer hesitated to follow the course which the interests
of his people and his own happiness seemed to point out.
He determined that Anne Boleyn should be his wife and
queen of England also. It was now that the marriage took
place. Cranmer states in a letter written on the 17th of June,
1533, that he did not perform the ceremony, that he did not
hear of it until a fortnight after, and that it was celebrated
privately "much about Saint Paul's day last" (25th of
January, 1533).

Whatever may have been the exact date of the marriage,[1] it became the universal topic of conversation in the early months of 1533; people did not speak of it publicly, but in private, some attacking and others defending it. If the members of the Romish party circulated ridiculous stories and outrageous calumnies against Anne, the members of the national party replied that the purity of her life, her moderation, her chastity, her mildness, her discretion, her noble and exalted parentage, her pleasing manners, and (they added somewhat later) her fitness to give a successor to the crown of England, made her worthy of the royal favour. Men are apt to go too far in reproaches as well as in eulogies.

This important step on the part of Henry VIII was accompanied with an explosion of murmurs against Clement VII. "The pope," he said, "wanders from the path of the Redeemer, who was obedient in this world to princes. What! must a prince submit to the arrogance of a human being whom God has put under him? Must a king humble himself before that man above whom he stands by the will of God? No! that would be a perversion of the order God has established." This is what Henry represented to Francis through Lord Rochford; but the words did not touch the King of France, for the Emperor was just then making several concessions to him, and the evangelicals of Paris were annoying him. From that hour the cordial feeling between the two monarchs gradually decreased. England turned her eyes more and more towards the Gospel, and France towards Rome. Just at the time when Anne Boleyn was about to reign in the palaces of Whitehall and Windsor, Catherine de Medici was entering those of St. Germain and Fontainebleau. The contrast between the two nations became ever more distinct and striking: England was advancing towards liberty, and France towards the dragonnades.[2]

The divorce between Rome and Whitehall soon became manifest. A brief of Clement VII posted in February on the

---

[1] [Evidence for the exact date of the marriage is conflicting, but it is difficult to refuse credence to Cranmer's testimony. As Elizabeth, Anne's child, was born on the 7th September of the same year, it is clear that Henry had urgent reasons for speeding up all matters connected with the marriage.]

[2] [Persecutions of Huguenots under Louis XIV at the hands of dragoons.]

doors of all the churches in Flanders, in the states of the king's enemy, and as near to England as possible, attracted a great number of readers. "What shall we do?" said the pontiff to Henry. "Shall we neglect thy soul's safety? . . . We exhort thee, our son, under pain of excommunication, to restore Queen Catherine to the royal honours which are due to her, to cohabit with her, and to cease to associate publicly with Anne; and that within a month from the day on which this brief shall be presented to thee. Otherwise, when the said term shall have elapsed, we pronounce thee and the said Anne to be *ipso facto* excommunicate, and command all men to shun and avoid your presence." It would appear that this document, demanded by the imperialists, had been posted throughout Flanders without the pope's knowledge.

A copy was immediately forwarded to the king by his agents. He was surprised and agitated, but believed at last that it was forged by his enemies. How could he imagine that the pope, just at the very time he was showing the king especial marks of his affection, would (even conditionally) have anathematized and isolated him in the midst of his people? Henry sent a copy of the document to Benet, his agent at Rome, and desired him to ascertain carefully whether it did really proceed from the pope or not.

Benet presented the document to Clement as a paper forwarded to him by his friend in Flanders. The latter was "ashamed and in great perplexity," wrote the envoy. He then read it again more attentively, stopped at certain passages, and seemed as if he were choking. Having come to the end, he expressed his surprise, and pretended that the copy differed from the original. "There is one mistake in particular which almost chokes the pope every time it is mentioned," wrote Benet to Cromwell. This mistake was the inclusion of Queen Anne Boleyn in the censure, without giving her previous warning, which (they said) was contrary to all the commandments of God. Accordingly Dr. Benet received orders to bring up this mistake frequently in his audiences with the pope; and he did not fail to do so. At this moment, in which he was about to lose England, the pope was more uneasy at having committed an error of form with regard to Anne Boleyn, than with having struck the monarch of a powerful kingdom with an interdict. There is, besides, no doubt that he dictated the unhappy phrase himself.

Benet and his friends took advantage of the pope's vexation, and even increased it: they communicated the brief to the dignitaries of the Church in Clement's household, and the latter acknowledged that the document must be offensive to his Majesty of England, and that "the pope was much to blame." Benet transmitted the pontiff's *errata* to the king, but it was too late: the blow had taken effect. The indignant Henry was about to proceed ostentatiously to the very acts which Rome threatened with her thunders.

Whilst the pope was hesitating, England firmly pursued her emancipation. Parliament met on the 4th of February, and the boldest language was uttered. "The people of England, in accord with their king," said eloquent speakers, "have the right to decide supremely on all things both temporal and spiritual; and certainly the English possess intelligence enough for that. And yet, in spite of the prohibitions issued by so many of our princes, we see bulls arriving every moment from Rome to regulate wills, marriages, divorces, everything in short. We propose that henceforward these matters be decided solely before the national tribunals." The law passed. It was Cromwell's legislative masterpiece. Appeals, instead of being made to Rome, were to be made in the first instance to the bishop, then to the archbishop, and, if the king was interested in the cause, to the Upper Chamber of the ecclesiastical Convocation.

The king took immediate advantage of this law to inquire of Convocation whether the pope could authorize a man to marry his brother's widow. Out of sixty-six present, and one hundred and ninety-seven who voted by proxy, there were only nineteen in the Upper House who voted against the king. The opposition was stronger in the Lower House; but even this agreed with the other house in declaring that Pope Julius II had exceeded his authority in giving Henry a dispensation, and that the marriage was consequently null from the very first.

Nothing remained now but to proceed to the divorce. On the 11th of April, two days before Easter, Cranmer, as archbishop, wrote a letter to the king, in which he set forth, that desiring to fill the office of archbishop of Canterbury, "according to the laws of God and Holy Church, for the relief of the grievances and infirmities of the people, God's subjects and yours in spiritual causes," he prayed his Majesty's favour for that office. Cranmer did not decline the royal intervention, but he avoided confounding spiritual with temporal affairs.

Henry, who was doubtless waiting impatiently for this letter, was alarmed as he read the words, "according to the laws of God and Holy Church." God and the Church. . . . Well! but what of the king and the royal supremacy? The primate seemed to assert the right of acting *proprio motu*, and, while asking the king's favour, to be doing a simple act of courtesy. . . . Did the Church of England claim to take the pontiff's place and station, and leave the king aside? . . . That was not what Henry meant. Tired of the pretensions of the pope of Rome, would he suffer a pope on a small scale at his side? He intended to be master in his own kingdom—master of everything. The letter must be modified, and this Henry intimated to Cranmer.

That day, or the next after the one on which this letter had been written, there was a great festival at the court in honour of Anne Boleyn. "Queen Anne that evening went in state to her apartments openly as queen," says Hall. It was probably during this festival that the king, taking the prelate aside, desired him to suppress the unwelcome passage. The idea suggested by an eminent historian, that Cranmer sent both the letters together to Henry, that he might choose which he would prefer, seems to me inadmissible. Cranmer, as it would appear, submitted, waiting for better days. On returning to Lambeth, he recopied his letter, omitting the words which had been pointed out. Not content with asking the king's *favour*, he desired his *licence*, his authorization to proceed. (Actually, appropriate resolutions of Convocation had already virtually decided the issues, and Cranmer knew that he could take action with the Church supporting him.) He dated his second letter the same day, and sent it to his master, who was satisfied with it.

This alone did not satisfy Henry: in his reply to the archbishop, he marked still more strongly his intention not to have in England a primate independent of the crown: "Ye therefore duly recognizing that it becometh you not, being our subject, to enterprise any part of your said office *without our licence obtained so to do.* . . . In consideration of these things, albeit we being your king and sovereign, do recognize no superior upon earth but only God; yet because ye be under us, by God's calling and ours, the most principal minister of our spiritual jurisdiction, we will not refuse your humble request."

This language was clear. Henry VIII did not, however, claim the arbitrary authority to which the pope pretended: human and divine laws were to be the supreme rule in England, but he, the king, was to be their chief interpreter. Cranmer must understand that. "To these laws we, as a Christian king," wrote Henry, "have always heretofore submitted, and shall ever most obediently submit ourselves." The ecclesiastical system which Henry VIII established in England in 1533 was not a free Church in a free State, and there is no reason to be surprised at it.

Cranmer having received the royal licence, now prepared the measure for disposing of the problem which, for six years, had kept England and the continent in suspense. Taking the bishops of Lincoln and Winchester and some lawyers with him, he proceeded quietly, and without ostentation, to the priory of Dunstable, five miles from Ampthill in Bedfordshire, where Queen Catherine was staying. He wished to avoid the notoriety of a trial held in London.

The ecclesiastical court being duly formed, Henry and Catherine were summoned to appear before it on the 10th of May. The king was present by attorney: but the queen replied: "My cause is before the pope; I accept no other judge." A fresh summons was immediately made out for the 12th of May, and as the queen appeared neither in person nor by any of her servants, she was pronounced contumacious, and the trial went forward. The king was informed every night of each day's proceedings, and he was often in great anxiety. Some unexpected event, an appeal from Catherine, the sudden intervention of the pope or of the Emperor, might stop everything. His courtiers were on the watch for news. Anne said nothing, but her heart beat quick, and the ambitious Cromwell, whose fortunes depended on the success of the matter, was sometimes in great alarm. Cranmer rested on the declarations of Scripture, and showed much equity and uprightness during the trial. "I have willingly injured no human being," he said. But he knew the queen had numerous partisans; they would conjure her, perhaps, to appear before her judges; there would then be a great stir, and the voice of the people would be heard. The archbishop could hardly restrain his emotion as he thought of this. He must indeed expect an inflexible resistance on the part of the queen; but in the midst of all the agitation around her, she alone remained calm and resolute. Her hand had grasped the pope's robe, and nothing could make her let it go. "I am the king's lawful wife," she repeated; "I am queen of England. My daughter is the king's child: I place her in her father's hands."

On Wednesday the 23rd of May, the primate, attended by all the archiepiscopal court, proceeded to the church of St. Peter's priory at Dunstable, in order to deliver the final judgment of divorce. A few persons attracted by curiosity were present; but, although Dunstable was near Ampthill, all of Catherine's household kept themselves respectfully aloof from an act which was to deal their mistress such a grievous blow. The primate, after reciting the decisions of the several universities, provincial councils, and other premises, continued: "Therefore we, Thomas, archbishop, primate, and legate, having first called upon the name of Christ, and having God altogether before our eyes, do pronounce and declare that the marriage between our sovereign lord King Henry and the most serene Lady Catherine, widow of his brother, having been contracted contrary to the law of God, is null and void; and therefore we sentence that it is not lawful for the said most illustrious Prince Henry and the said most serene Lady Catherine to remain in the said pretended marriage." The announcement, drawn up very carefully by two notaries, was immediately sent to the king.

The divorce was pronounced, and Henry was free. Many persons gave way to feelings of alarm: they thought that all Europe would combine against England. "The pope will excommunicate the English," said some; "and then the Emperor will destroy them." But, on the other hand, the majority of the nation desired to have done with a subject which had been agitating their minds during the last seven years. England, getting out of a labyrinth from which she had never expected to find an issue, began to breathe again.

Catherine's marriage was declared to be null: it only remained now to recognize Anne Boleyn's. On the 28th of May, an archiepiscopal court held at Lambeth, in the primate's palace, officially declared that Henry and Anne had been lawfully wedded, and the king had now no thought but how to seal his union by the pomp of a coronation. It would certainly have been preferable had the new queen taken her seat quietly on the throne; but slanderous reports made it necessary for the king to present his wife to the people in all the splendour of royalty.

At three o'clock in the afternoon of Thursday before Whitsuntide, a magnificent procession started from Greenwich. Fifty barges, adorned with rich banners, conveyed the representatives of the different city companies, and the metropolis joyfully hailed a union that promised to inaugurate a future of light and faith: it was almost a religious festival. On the banner of the Fishmongers was the inscription, *All worship belongs to God alone;* on that of the Haberdashers, *My trust is in God only;* on that of the Grocers, *God gives grace;* and on that of the Goldsmiths, *To God alone be all the glory.* The city of London thus asserted, in the presence of the immense crowd, the principles of the Reformation. The lord mayor's barge immediately preceded the galley, all hung with cloth of gold, in which Anne was seated. Near it floated another gay barge, on which a little mountain was contrived, planted with red and white roses, in the midst of which sat a number of young maidens singing to the accompaniment of sweet music. A hundred richly ornamented barques, carrying the nobility of England, brought up the magnificent procession, and a countless number of boats and skiffs covered the river. The moment Anne set her foot on shore at the Tower, a thousand trumpets sounded notes of triumph, and all the guns of the fortress fired such a peal as had seldom been heard before.

Henry, who liked the sound of cannon, met Anne at the gate and kissed her, and the new queen entered in triumph that vast fortress from which, three years later, she was to issue, by order of the same prince, to mount, an innocent victim, the cruel scaffold. She smiled courteously on all around; and yet, seized with a sudden emotion, she sometimes trembled, as if, instead of the joyous flowers on which she trod with light and graceful foot, she saw a deep gulf yawning beneath her.

The king and queen passed the whole of the next day (Friday) at the Tower. On Saturday Anne left it for Westminster. The streets were gay with banners, and the houses were hung with velvet and cloth of gold. All the Orders of the State and Church, the ambassadors of France and Venice, and the officers of the court opened the procession. The queen was carried in a magnificent litter covered with white cloth shot with gold, her head, which she had modestly inclined, being encircled with a wreath of precious stones. The people who crowded the streets were full of enthusiasm, and seemed to triumph more than she did herself.

The next day, Whit-Sunday, she proceeded for the coronation to the ancient abbey of Westminster, where the bishops and the court had been summoned to meet her. She took her seat in a rich chair, whence she presently descended to the high altar and knelt down. After the prescribed prayers she rose, and the archbishop placed the crown of St. Edward upon her head. She then took the sacrament and retired; the Earl of Wiltshire, her father, trembling with emotion, took her right hand . . . he was at the pinnacle of happiness, and yet he was uneasy. Alas! a caprice of the man who had raised his daughter to the throne might be sufficient to hurl her from it! Anne herself, in the midst of all these pomps, greater than any ever seen before at the coronation of an English queen, could not entirely forget the princess whose place she had now taken. Might not she be rejected in her turn? . . . In such a thought there was enough to make her shudder.

Anne did not find in her marriage with Henry the happiness she had dreamt, and a cloud was often seen passing across those features once so radiant. The idol to which this young woman had sacrificed everything—the splendour of a throne—did not satisfy her longings for happiness: she looked within herself, and found once more,

as queen, that attraction towards the doctrine of the Gospel
which she had felt in the society of Margaret of Valois, and
which, amid her ambitious pursuits, had been almost
extinguished in her heart. She discovered that for those who
have everything, as well as for those who have nothing,
there is only one single good—God Himself. She did not
probably give herself up entirely to Him, for her best impressions were often fugitive; but there are occasional
indications that she took advantage of her power to assist
those who she knew were devoted to the Gospel. Foxe
intimates that the pardon granted to John Lambert, who
was still in prison, was in part the result of "the coming of
Queen Anne." That faithful confessor of Jesus Christ
settled in London, where he began to teach children Latin
and Greek, without however neglecting the defence of truth.

The king, who had informed Catherine through Lord
Mountjoy of the archiepiscopal sentence, officially communicated his divorce and marriage to the various crowned
heads of Europe, and particularly to the king of France, the
Emperor, and the pope. The pope on the 11th of July
annulled the sentence of the Archbishop of Canterbury,
declared the king's marriage with Anne Boleyn unlawful,
and threatened to excommunicate both, unless they separated
before the end of September. Henry angrily commanded
his theologians to demonstrate that the bull was a nullity,
recalled his ambassador, the Duke of Norfolk, and said that
the moment was come for all monarchs and all Christian
people to withdraw from under the yoke of the bishop of
Rome. "The pope and his cardinals," he wrote to Francis I,
"pretend to have princes, who are free persons, at their beck
and commandment. Sire, you and I and all the princes of
Christendom must unite for the preservation of our rights,
liberties, and privileges; we must alienate the greatest part of
Christendom from the see of Rome."

But Henry had scholastic prejudices which made him fall
into the strangest contradictions. While he was employing
his diplomacy to isolate the pope, he still prayed him to
declare the nullity of his marriage with Catherine. It is not
at the court of this prince that we must look for the real
Reformation: we must go in search of it elsewhere.

CHAPTER EIGHTEEN

Fryth in the Tower

(August 1532 to May 1533)

ONE of the leading scholars of England was about to seal the testimony of his faith with his blood. John Fryth had been one of the most brilliant stars of the university of Cambridge. "It would hardly be possible to find his equal in learning," said many. Accordingly Wolsey had invited him to his college at Oxford, and Henry VIII had desired to place him among the number of his theologians. But the mysteries of the Word of God had more attraction for Fryth than mere scholastic renown: the claims of conscience prevailed in him over those of the intellect, and neglecting his own glory, he sought only to be useful to mankind. A sincere, decided, and yet moderate Christian, preaching the Gospel with great purity and love, this man of thirty seemed destined to become one of the most influential reformers of England. Nothing could have prevented his playing the foremost part, if he had had Luther's enthusiastic energy or Calvin's indomitable will. There were less strong, but perhaps more amiable features in his character; he taught with gentleness those who were opposed to the truth, and while many, as Foxe says, "take the bellows in hand to blow the fire, but few there are that will seek to quench it," Fryth sought after peace. Controversies between protestants distressed him. "The opinions for which men go to war," he said, "do not deserve those great tragedies of which they make us spectators. Let there be no longer any question among us of Zwinglians or Lutherans, for neither Zwingli nor Luther died for us, and we must be one in Christ Jesus." This servant of Christ, meek and lowly of heart like his Master, never disputed even with papists, unless obliged to do so.

A true catholicism which embraced all Christians was

Fryth's distinctive feature as a reformer. He was not one of
those who imagine that a national Church ought to think
only of its own nation; but of those who believe that if a
Church is the depositary of the truth, she is so for all the
earth; and that a religion is not good, if it has no longing to
extend itself to all the races of mankind. There were some
strongly marked national elements in the English Reformation—the activity of the king and the parliament, but there
was also a universal element—a lively faith in the Saviour
of the world. No one in the sixteenth century represented
this truly catholic element better than Fryth. "I understand
the Church of God in a wide sense," he said. "It contains
all those whom we regard as members of Christ. It is a net
thrown into the sea." This principle, sown at that time as a
seed in the English Reformation, was one day to cover the
world with missionaries.

Fryth, having declined the brilliant offers the king had
made to him through Cromwell and Vaughan, joined Tyndale
in translating and publishing the Holy Scriptures in English.
While labouring thus for England, an irresistible desire came
over him to circulate the Gospel there in person. He therefore
quitted the Low Countries, returned to London, and directed
his course to Reading, where the prior had been his friend.
Exile had not used him well, and he entered that town
miserably clothed, and more like a beggar than one whom
Henry VIII had desired to place near himself. This was in
August 1532.

His writings had preceded him. Having received, when in
the Netherlands, three works composed in defence of purgatory
by three distinguished men—Rastell, Sir Thomas More's
brother-in-law, More himself, and Fisher, bishop of Rochester
—Fryth had replied to them: "A purgatory! there is not *one*
only, there are *two*. The first is the *Word of God*, the second
is the *cross of Christ:* I do not mean the cross of wood, but
the cross of tribulation. But the lives of the papists are so
wicked that they have invented a third."

Sir Thomas, exasperated by Fryth's reply, said with that
humorous tone he often affected, "I propose to answer the
good young father Fryth, whose wisdom is such that three
old men like my brother Rastell, the bishop of Rochester,

Henry VIII with his father, Henry VII, in the background. Holbein's drawing for the
mural in the Tudor Palace of Whitehall. "Reginald Pole, in the book which he addressed
to him, observed that in matters touching the pope, we must not regard either his character
or his life, but only his authority, and that the lapses of a pope in morals detract nothing
from his infallibility in faith. Henry understood this distinction very clearly, and showed
himself a pope in every way." See page 319.

Catherine of Aragon, first wife of Henry VIII and mother of Queen Mary Tudor.

o:Moor Lᵈ Chancelour.

Sir Thomas More, drawing by Holbein. Though he had been Chancellor of England, More was executed in 1535 for his refusal to recognize the Royal supremacy in the Church. "This eminent man protested against the aberrations of a cruel prince, who usurped the title given by the Bible to Jesus Christ alone." A firm Catholic, More recognized more clearly than some of his Protestant contemporaries the implications of this issue, and at his trial before Cranmer in 1534, when the Primate counselled obedience to the Prince, More saw that if the Archbishop's argument was right "it would be an easy way out of every perplexity".

Hampton Court. The old palace, part of which still stands facing the river, was erected by Wolsey at the height of his power. To bolster his favour at Court he presented it to Henry VIII in 1526, but four years later, facing death and a charge of high treason, the Cardinal made his pathetic lament: "If I had served God as diligently as I have served the king, he would not have given me over in my grey hairs!"

Anne Boleyn, who, "when every passion was at work to paralyse the power of right", was executed on May 19th, 1536. On the night preceding that event, Alesius, the Scottish Reformer, was awakened by a terrible dream in which he saw the Queen's severed head; hastening across the river to Lambeth he found Cranmer walking in the gardens at four o'clock in the morning in an agony of grief. "Do not you know what is to happen today?" exclaimed the Primate; "she who has been the Queen of England upon earth will today become a queen in Heaven."

Thomas Cromwell, Earl of Essex. Painting by Holbein. Rising from obscurity to the summit of power, he was responsible for many ecclesiastical and political reforms and played an important role in the English Reformation. Falling from favour, however, he was sent to the block in 1540.

Thomas Cranmer, Archbishop of Canterbury. Painting by G. Flicke. As Jasper Ridley, in his recent biography of Cranmer (Clarendon Press, 1962), points out, Merle d'Aubigné was one of the first nineteenth-century historians to vindicate Cranmer's character. Ridley's work is an important additional source of information on the man whose part in the Reformation has repeatedly occasioned controversy.

and myself are mere babies when confronted with father Fryth alone." The exile having returned to England, More had now the opportunity of avenging himself more effectually than by his jokes.

At Reading, Fryth's strange air and his look as of a foreigner arriving from a distant country attracted attention, and he was taken up for a vagabond. "Who are you?" asked the magistrate. Fryth, suspecting that he was in the hands of enemies of the Gospel, refused to give his name, which increased the suspicion, and he was set in the stocks. As they gave him but little to eat, with the intent of forcing him to tell his name, his hunger soon became insupportable. Knowing the name of the master of the grammar-school, he asked to speak with him. Leonard Coxe had scarcely entered the prison, when the pretended vagabond all in rags addressed him in correct Latin, and began to deplore his miserable captivity. Never had words more noble been uttered in a dungeon so vile. The school-master, astonished at so much eloquence, compassionately drew near the unhappy man and inquired how it came to pass that such a learned scholar was in such profound wretchedness. Presently he sat down, and the two men began to talk in Greek about the universities and languages. Coxe could not make it out: it was no longer simple pity that he felt, but love, which turned to admiration when he heard the prisoner recite with the purest accent those noble lines of the *Iliad* which were so applicable to his own case:—

> Sing, O Muse,
> The vengeance deep and deadly, whence to Greece
> Unnumbered ills arose; which many a soul
> Of mighty warriors to the viewless shades
> Untimely sent.

Filled with respect, Coxe hurried off to the mayor, complained bitterly of the wrong done to so remarkable a man, and obtained his liberation. Homer saved the life of a reformer.

Fryth departed for London and hastened to join the worshippers who were accustomed to meet in Bow Lane. He conversed with them and exclaimed: "Oh! what consolation to see such a great number of believers walking in the way of the Lord!" These Christians asked him to expound the

E(II)

Scriptures to them, and, delighted with his exhortations, they exclaimed in their turn: "If the rule of St. Paul were followed, this man would certainly make a better bishop than many of those who wear the mitre." Instead of the crosier he was to bear the cross.

One of those who listened was in great doubt relative to the doctrine of the Lord's Supper; and one day, after Fryth had been setting Christ before them as the food of the Christian soul through faith, this person followed him and said: "Our prelates think differently: they believe that the bread transformed by consecration becomes the flesh, blood, and bones of Christ; that even the wicked eat this flesh with their teeth, and that we must adore the host. . . . What you have just said refutes their errors, but I fear that I cannot remember it. Pray commit it to writing." Fryth, who did not like discussions, was alarmed at the request, and answered: "I do not care to touch that terrible tragedy;" for so he called the dispute about the supper. The man having repeated his request, and promised that he would not communicate the paper to anybody, Fryth wrote an explanation of the doctrine of the Sacrament and gave it to this London Christian, saying: "We must eat and drink the body and blood of Christ, not with the teeth, but with the hearing and through faith." The brother took the treatise, and, hurrying home with it, read it carefully.

In a short time every one at the Bow Lane meeting spoke about this writing. One man, a false brother, named William Holt, listened attentively to what was said, and thought he had found an opportunity of destroying Fryth. Assuming a hypocritical look, he spoke in a pious strain to the individual who had the manuscript, as if he had desired to enlighten his faith, and finally asked him for it. Having obtained it, he hastened to make a copy, which he carried to Sir Thomas More, who was still chancellor.

Fryth soon perceived that he had tried in vain to remain unknown: he called with so much power those who thirsted for righteousness to come to Christ for the waters of life, that friends and enemies were struck with his eloquence. Observing that his name began to be talked of in various places, he quitted the capital and travelled unnoticed through several counties, where he found some little Christian congregations whom he tried to strengthen in the faith.

Tyndale, who remained on the continent, having heard of Fryth's labours, began to feel great anxiety about him. He knew but too well the cruel disposition of the bishops and of More. "I will make the serpent come out of his dark den," Sir Thomas had said, speaking of Tyndale, "as Hercules forced Cerberus, the watch-dog of hell, to come out to the light of day. . . . I will not leave Tyndale the darkest corner in which to hide his head."[1] In Tyndale's eyes Fryth was the great hope of the Church in England; he trembled lest the redoubtable Hercules should seize him. "Dearly beloved brother Jacob," he wrote, calling him Jacob to mislead his enemies, "be cold, sober, wise, and circumspect, and keep you low by the ground, avoiding high questions that pass the common capacity. But expound the law truly, and open the veil of Moses to condemn all flesh and prove all men sinners. Then set abroach the mercy of our Lord Jesus, and let the wounded consciences drink of him. . . . All doctrine that casteth a mist on these two to shadow and hide them, resist with all your power. . . . Beloved in my heart, there liveth not one in whom I have so great hope and trust, and in whom my heart rejoiceth, not so much for your learning and what other gifts else you may have, as because you walk in those things that the conscience may feel, and not in the imagination of the brain. Cleave fast to the rock of the help of God; and if aught be required of you contrary to the glory of God and His Christ, then stand fast and commit yourself to God. He is our God and His is the glory. I hope our redemption is nigh."

Tyndale's fears were but too well founded. Sir Thomas More held Fryth's new treatise in his hand: he read it and gave way by turns to anger and sarcasm. "Whetting his wits, calling his spirits together, and sharpening his pen," to use the words of the chronicler, he answered Fryth, and described his doctrine under the image of a cancer. This did not satisfy him. Although he had returned the seals to the king in May, he continued to hold office until the end of the

[1] *Confutation of Tyndale's Answer*, by Sir Thomas More, lord-chancellor of England (1532).

year. He ordered search to be made for Fryth, and set all his
bloodhounds on the track. If the reformer was discovered he
was lost: when Sir Thomas More had once caught his man,
nothing could save him—nothing but a merry jest, perhaps.
For instance, one day when he was examining a gospeller
named Silver: "You know," he said with a smile, "that
silver must be tried in the fire." "Yes," retorted the accused
instantly, "but not quicksilver." More, delighted with the
repartee, set the poor wretch at liberty. But Fryth was no
jester: he could not hope, therefore, to find favour with the
ex-chancellor of England.

Sir Thomas hunted the reformer by sea and by land,
promising a great reward to any one who should deliver
him up. There was no county where More did not look for
him, no sheriff or justice of the peace to whom he did not
apply, no harbour where he did not post some officer to
catch him. But the answer from every quarter was: "He is
not here." Indeed, Fryth, having been informed of the great
exertions of his enemy, was fleeing from place to place, often
changing his dress, and finding a safe retreat nowhere. Determining to leave England and return to Tyndale, he went to
Milton Shone in Essex with the intention of embarking. A
ship was ready to sail, and quitting his hiding-place he went
down to the shore with all precaution. But he had been
betrayed. More's agents, who were on the watch, seized him
as he was stepping on board, and carried him to the Tower.
This occurred in October 1532.

Sir Thomas More was uneasy and soured. He beheld a
new power lifting its head in England and all Christendom,
and he felt that in despite of his wit and his influence he was
unable to check it. That man so amiable, that writer of a
style so pure and elegant, did not so much dread the anger
of the king; what exasperated him was to see the Scriptures
circulating more widely every day, and a continually increasing number of his fellow-citizens converted to the evangelical
faith. These new men, who seemed to have more piety than
himself—he an old follower of the old papacy!—irritated him
sorely. He claimed to have alone—he and his friends—the
privilege of being Christians. The zeal of the partisans of the
Reformation, the sacrifice they made of their repose, their

money, and their lives confounded him. "These diabolical people," he said, "print their books at great expense, notwithstanding the great danger; not looking for any gain, they give them away to everybody, and even scatter them abroad by night. They fear no labour, no journey, no expense, no pain, no danger, no blows, no injury. They take a malicious pleasure in seeking the destruction of others, and these disciples of the devil think only how they may cast the souls of the simple into hell-fire." In such a strain as this did the elegant utopist give vent to his anger—the man who had dreamt all his life of the plan of an imaginary world for the perfect happiness of every one. At last he had caught one of the chief of these disciples of Satan, and hoped to put him to death by fire.

The news soon spread through London that Fryth was in the Tower, and several priests and bishops immediately went thither to try to bring him back to the pope. Their great argument was that More had confuted his treatise on the Lord's Supper. Fryth asked to see the confutation, but it was refused him. One day the Bishop of Winchester, having called upon the prisoner, showed it to Fryth, and, holding it up, asserted that the book quite shut his mouth: Fryth put out his hand, but the bishop hastily withdrew the volume. More himself was ashamed of the apology, and did all he could to prevent its circulation. Fryth could only obtain a written copy, but he resolved to answer it immediately. There was no one with whom he could confer, not a book he could consult, and the chains with which he was loaded scarcely allowed him to sit and write. But reading in his dungeon by the light of a small candle the insults of More, and finding himself charged with having collected all the poison that could be found in the writings of Wycliffe, Luther, Œcolampadius, Tyndale, and Zwingli, this humble servant of God exclaimed: "No! Luther and his doctrine are not the mark I aim at, but the Scriptures of God." "He shall pay for his heresy with the best blood in his body," said his enemies; and the pious disciple replied: "As the sheep bound by the hand of the butcher with timid look beseeches that his blood may soon be shed, even so do I pray my judges that my blood may be shed *to-morrow*, if by my death the king's eyes should be opened."

Before he died, Fryth desired to save, if it were God's will, one of his adversaries. There was one of them who had no obstinacy, no malice: it was John Rastell, More's brother-in-law. Being unable to speak to him or to any of the enemies of the Reformation, he formed the design of writing in prison a treatise which should be called the *Bulwark*. But strict orders had recently arrived that he should have neither pen, ink, nor paper. However, some evangelical Christians of London, who succeeded in getting access to him, secretly furnished him with the means of writing, and Fryth began. He wrote . . . but at every moment he listened for fear the lieutenant of the Tower or the warders should come upon him suddenly and find the pen in his hand. Often a bright thought would occur to him, but some sudden alarm drove it out of his mind, and he could not recall it. He took courage, however: he had been accused of asserting that good works were of no service: he proceeded to explain with much eloquence all their utility, and every time he repeated: "Is that nothing? is that still nothing? Truly, Rastell," he added, "if you only regard that as useful which justifies us, the sun is not useful, because it justifieth not."

As he was finishing these words he heard the keys rattling at the door, and, being alarmed, immediately threw paper, ink, and pen into a hiding-place. However, he was able to complete the treatise and send it to Rastell. More's brother-in-law read it; his heart was touched, his understanding enlightened, his prejudices cleared away; and from that hour this choice spirit was gained over to the Gospel of Christ. God had given him new eyes and new ears. A pure joy filled the prisoner's heart. "Rastell now looks upon his natural reason as foolishness," he said. "Rastell, become a child, drinks the wisdom that cometh from on high."

The conversion of Sir Thomas More's brother-in-law made a great sensation, and the visits to Fryth's cell became every day more numerous. Although separated from his wife and from Tyndale, whom he had been forced to leave in the Low Countries, he had never had so many friends, brothers, mothers, and fathers; he wept for very joy. He took his pen and paper from their hiding-place, and, always indefatigable, began to write first the *Looking-glass of Self-knowledge*, and

next a *Letter to the Faithful Followers of the Gospel of Christ.*
"Imitators of the Lord," he said to them, "mark yourselves
with the sign of the cross, not as the superstitious crowd does,
in order to worship it, but as a testimony that you are ready
to bear that cross as soon as God shall please to send it. Fear
not when you have it, for you will also have a hundred fathers
instead of one, a hundred mothers instead of one, a hundred
mansions already in this life (for I have made the trial), and
after this life, joy everlasting."

At the beginning of 1533, Anne Boleyn having been
married to the King of England, Fryth saw his chains fall
off: he was allowed to have all he asked for, and even permitted to leave the Tower at night on parole. He took
advantage of this liberty to visit the friends of the Gospel,
and consult with them about what was to be done. One
evening in particular, after leaving the Tower, Fryth went
to Petit's house, anxious to embrace once more that great
friend of the Reformation, that firm member of parliament,
who had been thrown into prison as we have seen, and at
last set free. Petit, weakened by his long confinement, was
near his end; the persecution agitated and pained him, and
it would appear that his emotion sometimes ended in
delirium. As he was groaning over the captivity of the young
and noble reformer, Fryth appeared. Petit was confused, his
mind wandered. Is it Fryth or his ghost? He was like the
believers, when Rhoda came to tell them that Peter was at
the gate waiting to see them. But gradually recovering himself,
Petit said: "You here! how have you escaped the vigilance of
the warders?" "God Himself," answered Fryth, "gave me this
liberty by touching their hearts." The two friends then
conversed about the true Reformation of England, which in
their eyes had nothing to do with the diplomatic proceedings
of the king. In their opinion it was not a matter of loading the
external Church with new frippery, but "to increase that
elect, sanctified, and invisible congregation, elect before the
foundation of the world." Fryth did not conceal from Petit
the conviction he felt that he would be called upon to die for
the Gospel. The night was spent in such Christian conversation,
and the day began to dawn before the prisoner hastened to
return to the Tower.

The evangelist's friends did not think as he did. Anne Boleyn's accession seemed as if it ought to open the doors of Fryth's prison, and in imagination they saw him at liberty, and labouring either on the continent or at home at that real reformation which is accomplished by the Scriptures of God.

But it was not to be so. Most of the evangelical men raised up by God in England during the reign of Henry VIII found —not the influence which they should have exercised, but— death. Yet their blood has weighed in the divine balance; it has sanctified the Reformation of England, and been a spiritual seed for future ages. If the Church in England has witnessed the development of a powerful evangelical life in its bosom, it must not forget the cause, but understand, with Tertullian, that *the blood of the martyrs is the seed of the Church.*

CHAPTER NINETEEN

A Reformer Chooses rather to Lose his Life than Save it

(May to July 1533)

THE enemy was on the watch: the second period of Fryth's captivity, that which was to terminate in martyrdom, was beginning. Henry's bishops, who, while casting off the pope to please the king, had remained devoted to scholastic doctrines, feared lest the reformer should escape them: they therefore undertook to solicit Henry to put him to death. Fryth had on his side the queen, Cromwell, and Cranmer. This did not discourage them, and they represented to the king that although the man was shut up in the Tower of London, he did not cease to write and act in defence of heresy. It was the season of Lent, and Fryth's enemies came to an understanding with Dr. Curwin, the king's chaplain, who was to preach before the court. He had no sooner got into the pulpit than he began to declaim against those who denied the material presence of Christ in the host. Having struck his hearers with horror, he continued: "It is not surprising that this abominable heresy makes such great progress among us. A man now in the Tower of London has the audacity to defend it, and no one thinks of punishing him."

When the service was over, the brilliant congregation left the chapel, and each as he went out asked what was the man's name. "Fryth" was the reply, and loud were the exclamations on hearing it. The blow took effect, the scholastic prejudices of the king were revived, and he sent for Cromwell and Cranmer. "I am very much surprised," he said, "that John Fryth has been kept so long in the Tower without examination. I desire his trial to take place without delay; and if he does not retract, let him suffer the penalty he deserves." He then nominated six of the chief spiritual and

temporal peers of England to examine him: they were the
Archbishop of Canterbury, the bishops of London and
Winchester, the lord chancellor, the Duke of Suffolk, and the
Earl of Wiltshire. This demonstrated the importance which
Henry attached to the affair. Until now, all the martyrs had
fallen beneath the blows either of the bishops or of More;
but in this case it was the king himself who stretched out his
strong hand against the servant of God.

Henry's order plunged Cranmer into the cruellest anxiety.
On the one hand, Fryth was in his eyes a disciple of the
Gospel; but on the other, he attacked a doctrine which the
archbishop then held to be Christian; for, like Luther and
Osiander, he still believed in consubstantiation. "Alas!" he
wrote to Archdeacon Hawkins, "he professes the doctrine of
Œcolampadius." He resolved, however, to do everything in
his power to save Fryth.

The best friends of the young reformer saw that a pile was
being raised to consume the most faithful Christian in England.
"Dearly beloved," wrote Tyndale from Antwerp, "fear not
men that threat, nor trust men that speak fair. Your cause is
Christ's Gospel, a light that must be fed with the blood of
faith. The lamp must be trimmed daily, that the light go
not out." There was no lack of examples to confirm these
words. "Two have suffered in Antwerp unto the great glory
of the Gospel; four at Ryselles in Flanders. At Rouen in
France they persecute, and at Paris are five doctors taken for
the Gospel. See, you are not alone: follow the example of all
your other dear brethren, who choose to suffer in hope of a
better resurrection. Bear the image of Christ in your mortal
body, and keep your conscience pure and undefiled. . . .
Una salus victis, nullam sperare salutem: the only safety of the
conquered is to hope for no safety. If you may write, tell us how
it goes with you." In this letter from a martyr to a martyr
there was one sentence honourable to a Christian woman:
"Your wife is well content with the will of God, and would
not for her sake have the glory of God hindered."

If friends were thinking of Fryth on the banks of the
Scheldt, they were equally anxious about him on the banks
of the Thames. Worthy citizens of London asked what was
the use of England's quitting the pope to cling to Christ, if

she burnt the servants of Christ? The little Church had recourse to prayer. Archbishop Cranmer wished to save Fryth:
he loved the man and admired his piety. If the accused
appeared before the commission appointed by the king, he
was lost: some means must be devised without delay to rescue
him from an inevitable death. The archbishop declared that,
before proceeding to trial, he wished to have a conference
with the prisoner, and to endeavour to convince him, which
was very natural. But at the same time the primate appeared
to fear that if the conference took place in London the people
would disturb the public peace, as in the time of Wycliffe.
He settled therefore that it should be held at Croydon, where
he had a palace. The primate's fear seems rather strange. A
riot on account of Fryth, at a time when king, commons, and
people were in harmony, appeared hardly probable. Cranmer
had another motive.

Among the persons composing his household was a gentleman of benevolent character, and with a leaning towards the
Gospel, who was distressed at the cruelty of the bishops, and
looked upon it as a lawful and Christian act to rob them, if
possible, of their victims. Giving him one of the porters of
Lambeth Palace as a companion, Cranmer committed Fryth
to his care to bring him to Croydon. They were to take the
prisoner a journey of four or five hours on foot through fields
and woods, without any constables or soldiers. A strange walk
and a strange escort!

Lord Fitzwilliam, first Earl of Southampton and governor
of the Tower, at the time lay sick in his house at Westminster,
suffering such severe pain as to force loud groans from him.
On the 10th of June, at the desire of my lord of Canterbury,
the archbishop's gentleman, and the Lambeth porter, Gallois,
surnamed Perlebeane, were introduced into the nobleman's
bedchamber, where they found him lying upon his bed in
extreme agony. Fitzwilliam, a man of the world, was greatly
enraged against the evangelicals, who were the cause, in his
opinion, of all the difficulties of England. The gentleman
respectfully presented to him the primate's letter and the
king's ring. "What do you want?" he asked sharply, without
opening the letter. "His Grace desires your lordship to deliver
Master Fryth to us." The impatient Southampton flew into

a passion at the name, and cursed Fryth and all the heretics. He thought it strange that a gentleman and a porter should have to convey a prisoner of such importance to the episcopal court: were there no soldiers in the Tower? Had Fitzwilliam any suspicion, or did he regret to see the reformer leave the walls within which he had been kept so long? We cannot tell: but he must obey, for they brought him the king's signet. Accordingly, taking his own ring hastily from his finger: "Fryth," he said, "Fryth. . . . Here, show this to the lieutenant of the Tower, and take away your heretic quickly. I am but too happy to get rid of him."

A few hours later Fryth, the gentleman, and Perlebeane entered a boat moored near the Tower, and were rowed speedily to the archbishop's palace at Lambeth. At first the three persons preserved a strict silence, only interrupted from time to time by the deep sighs of the gentleman. Being charged to begin by trying to induce Fryth to make some compromise, he broke the silence at last. "Master Fryth," he said, "if you are not prudent you are lost. What a pity! you that are so learned in Latin and Greek and in the Holy Scriptures, the ancient doctors, and all kinds of knowledge, you will perish, and all your admirable gifts will perish with you, with little profit to the world, and less comfort to your wife and children, your kinsfolk and friends." . . . The gentleman was silent a minute, and then began again: "Your position is dangerous, Master Fryth, but not desperate: you have many friends who will do all they can in your favour. On your part do something for them, make some concession, and you will be safe. Your opinion on the merely spiritual presence of the body and blood of the Saviour is premature: it is too soon for us in England; wait until a better time comes!"

Fryth did not say a word: no sound was heard but the plash of the water and the noise of the oars. The gentleman thought he had shaken the young doctor, and after a moment's silence he resumed: "My lord Cromwell and my lord of Canterbury feel great affection for you; they know that if you are young in years you are old in knowledge, and may become a most profitable citizen of this realm. . . . If you will be somewhat advised by their counsel, they will never permit you to be harmed; but if you stand stiff to your opinion, it is not possible to save your life, for as you have good friends so have you mortal enemies."

The gentleman stopped and looked at the prisoner. It was by such language that Bilney had been seduced; but Fryth kept himself in the presence of God, ready to lose his life that he might save it. He thanked the gentleman for his kindness, and said that his conscience would not permit him to recede, out of respect to man, from the true doctrine of the Lord's Supper. "If I am questioned on that point, I must answer according to my conscience, though I should lose twenty lives if I had so many. I can support it by a great number of passages from the Holy Scriptures and the ancient doctors, and if I am fairly tried I shall have nothing to fear."— "Indeed!" quoth the gentleman, "if you be fairly tried, you would be safe, but that is what I very much doubt. Our master Christ was not fairly tried, nor would He be, as I think, if He were now present again in the world. How then should you be, when your opinions are so little understood and are so odious?"—"I know," answered Fryth, "that the doctrine which I hold is very hard meat to be digested just now; but listen to me." As he spoke, he took the gentleman by the hand: "If you live twenty years more, you will see this whole realm of my opinion concerning this sacrament of the altar—all, except a certain class of men. My death, you say, would be sorrowful to my friends, but it will be only for a short time. But, all things considered, my death will be better unto me and all mine than life in continual bondage. God knoweth what He hath to do with His poor servant, whose cause I now defend. He will help me, and no man shall prevail on me to step backwards."

The boat reached Lambeth. The travellers landed, entered the archbishop's palace, and, after taking some refreshment, started on foot for Croydon, ten miles south of London.

The three travellers proceeded over the hills and through the plains of Surrey: here and there flocks of sheep were grazing in the scanty pastures, and to the east stretched vast woods. The gentleman walked mournfully by the side of Fryth. It was useless to ask him again to retract, but another idea engrossed Cranmer's officer: that of letting Fryth escape. The country was then thinly inhabited: the woods which covered it on the east and the chalky hills might serve as a hiding-place for the fugitive. The difficulty was to persuade Perlebeane. The gentleman slackened his pace, called to the porter, and they walked by themselves behind the prisoner. When they were so far off that he could not hear their conversation, the gentleman said: "You have heard this man, I am sure, and noted his talk since he came from the Tower." — "I never heard so constant a man," Perlebeane answered, "nor so eloquent a person."—"You have heard nothing," resumed the gentleman, "in respect both of his knowledge and his eloquence. If you could hear him at the university or in the pulpit, you would admire him still more. England has never had such a one of his age with so much learning. And yet our bishops treat him as if he were a very dolt or an idiot. . . . They abhor him as the devil himself, and want to get rid of him by any means."—"Surely," said the porter, "if there were nothing else in him but the consideration of his person both comely and amiable, his disposition so gentle, meek, and humble, it were pity he should be cast away."—"Cast away," interrupted the gentleman, "he will certainly be cast away if we once bring him to Croydon." And lowering his voice, he continued: "Surely before God I speak it, if thou, Perlebeane, wert of my mind, we should never bring him thither." —"What do you mean?" asked the astonished porter. Then, after a moment's silence, he added: "I know that you have a great deal more responsibility in this matter than I have; and therefore if you can honestly save this man I will yield to your proposal with all my heart." The gentleman breathed again.

Cranmer had desired that all possible efforts should be made to change Fryth's sentiments; and these failing, he wished to save him in another way. It was his desire that the reformer should go on foot to Croydon, that he should be accompanied by two only of his servants, selected from those best disposed towards the new doctrine. The primate's gentleman would never have dared take upon himself, except by his master's desire, the responsibility of conniving at the escape of a prisoner who was to be tried by the first personages of the realm, appointed by the king himself. Happy at having gained the porter to his enterprise, he began to discuss with him the ways and means. He knew the country well, and his plan was arranged.

"You see yonder hill before us," he said to Perlebeane; "it is Brixton Causeway, two miles from London. There are great woods on both sides. When we come to the top we will permit Fryth to escape into the woods on the left hand, whence he may easily get into Kent, where he was born, and where he has many friends. We will linger an hour or two on the road, after his flight, to give him time to reach a place of safety, and when night approaches we will go to Streatham, which is a mile and a half off, and make an outcry in the town that our prisoner has escaped into the woods on the right hand towards Wandsworth, that we followed him for more than a mile, and at length lost him because we were not many enough. At the same time we will take with us as many people as we can, to search for him in that direction; if necessary, we will be all night about it; and before we can send the news to Croydon of what has happened, Fryth will be in safety, and the bishops will be disappointed."

The gentleman, we see, was not very scrupulous about the means of rescuing a victim from the Roman priests. Perlebeane thought as he did. "Your plan pleases me," he answered; "now go and tell the prisoner, for we are already at the foot of the hill."

The delighted gentleman hurried forward: "Master Fryth," he said, "let us talk together a little. I cannot hide from you that the task I have undertaken, to bring you to Croydon, as a sheep to the slaughter, grieves me exceedingly, and there is no danger I would not brave to deliver you out of the lion's mouth. Yonder good fellow and I have devised a plan whereby you may escape: listen to me." The gentleman having described his plan, Fryth smiled amiably and said: "This then is the result of your long consultation together. You have wasted your time. If you were both to leave me here and go to Croydon, declaring to the bishops you had lost me, I should follow after as fast as I could, and bring them news that I had found and brought Fryth again."

The gentleman had not expected such an answer. A prisoner refuse his liberty! . . . "You are mad," he said: "do you think your reasoning will convert the bishops? At Milton

Shone you tried to escape beyond the sea, and now you refuse to save yourself!"—"The two cases are different," answered Fryth; "then I was at liberty, and according to the advice of St. Paul I would fain have enjoyed my liberty for the continuance of my studies. But now the higher power, as it were by Almighty God's permission, has seized me, and my conscience binds me to defend the doctrine for which I am persecuted, if I would not incur our Lord's condemnation. If I should now run away, I should run from my God; if I should fly, I should fly from the testimony I am bound to bear to his Holy Word, and I should deserve a thousand hells. I most heartily thank you both for your good will towards me, but I beseech you to bring me where I was appointed to be brought, for else I will go thither all alone."

Those who desired to save Fryth had not counted upon so much integrity. Such were, however, the martyrs of protestantism. The archbishop's two servants continued their journey along with their strange prisoner. Fryth had a calm eye and cheerful look, and the rest of the journey was accomplished in pious and agreeable conversation. When they reached Croydon, he was delivered to the officers of the episcopal court, and passed the night in the porter's lodge.

The next morning he appeared before the bishops and peers appointed to examine him. Cranmer and Lord Chancellor Audley desired his acquittal, but some of the other judges were men without pity.

The examination began:

"Do you believe," they said, "that the sacrament of the altar is or is not the real body of Christ?" Fryth answered simply and firmly: "I believe that the bread is the body of Christ in that it is *broken*, and thus teaches us that the body of Christ was to be broken and delivered unto death to redeem us from our iniquities. I believe the bread is the body of Christ in that it is *distributed*, and thus teaches us that the body of Christ and the fruits of His passion are distributed unto all faithful people. I believe that the bread is the body of Christ so far as it is *received*, and thus it teaches us that even as the outward man receiveth the sacrament with his teeth and mouth, so doth the inward man truly receive through faith the body of Christ and the fruits of his passion."

The judges were not satisfied: they wanted a formal and complete retraction. "Do you not think," asked one of them, "that the natural body of Christ, his flesh, blood, and bones, are contained under the sacrament and are there present without any figure of speech?"—"No," he answered; "I do not think so;" adding with much humility and charity: "notwithstanding I would not have that any should count my saying to be an article of faith. For even as I say, that you ought not to make any necessary article of the faith of your part; so I say again, that we make no necessary article of the faith of our part, but leave it indifferent for all men to judge therein, as God shall open their hearts, and no side to condemn or despise the other, but to nourish in all things brotherly love, and to bear one another's infirmities."

The commissioners then undertook to convince Fryth of the truth of transubstantiation; but he quoted Scripture, St. Augustine and Chrysostom, and eloquently defended the doctrine of the spiritual eating. The court rose. Cranmer had been moved, although he was still under the influence of Luther's teaching. "The man spoke admirably," he said to Dr. Heath as they went out, "and yet in my opinion he is wrong." Not many years later he devoted one of the most important of his writings to an explanation of the doctrine now professed by the young reformer; it may be that Fryth's words had begun to shake him.

Full of love for him, Cranmer desired to save him. Four times during the course of the examination he sent for Fryth and conversed with him privately, always asserting the Lutheran opinion. Fryth offered to maintain his doctrine in a public discussion against anyone who was willing to attack it, but nobody accepted his challenge. Cranmer, distressed at seeing all his efforts useless, found there was nothing more for him to do; the cause was transferred to the ordinary, the Bishop of London, and on the 17th of June the prisoner was once more committed to the Tower. The bishop selected as his assessors for the trial, Longland, bishop of Lincoln, and Gardiner, bishop of Winchester: there were no severer judges to be found on the episcopal bench. At Cambridge Fryth had been the most distinguished pupil of the clever and ambitious Gardiner; but this, instead of exciting the compassion of that hard man, did but increase his anger, "Fryth and his friends," he said, "are villains, blasphemers, and limbs of the devil."

On the 20th of June Fryth was taken to St. Paul's before the three bishops, and though of a humble disposition and almost timid character, he answered boldly. A clerk took down all his replies, and Fryth, snatching up the pen, wrote: "I Fryth think thus. Thus have I spoken, written, defended, affirmed, and published in my writings." The bishops having asked him if he would retract his errors, Fryth replied: "Let justice have its course and the sentence be pronounced." Stokesley did not keep him waiting long. "Not willing that thou, Fryth, who art wicked," he said, "shouldest become more wicked, and infect the Lord's flock with thy heresies, we declare thee excommunicate and cast out from the Church, and leave thee unto the secular powers, most earnestly requiring them in the truth of our Lord Jesus Christ that thy execution and punishment be not too extreme, *nor yet the gentleness too much mitigated.*"

Fryth was taken to Newgate and shut up in a dark cell, where he was bound with chains on the hands and feet as heavy as he could bear, and round his neck was a collar of iron, which fastened him to a post, so that he could neither stand upright nor sit down. Truly the "gentleness" was not "too much mitigated." His charity never failed him. "I am going to die," he said, "but I condemn neither those who follow Luther nor those who follow Œcolampadius, since both reject transubstantiation." A tailor's apprentice, twenty-four years of age, Andrew Hewet by name, was placed in his cell. Fryth asked him for what crime he was sent to prison. "The bishops," he replied, "asked me what I thought of the sacrament, and I answered, 'I think as Fryth does.' Then one of them smiled, and the Bishop of London said: 'Why Fryth is a heretic, and already condemned to be burnt, and if you do not retract your opinion you shall be burnt with him.' 'Very well,' I answered, 'I am content.' So they sent me here to be burnt along with you."

On the 4th of July they were both taken to Smithfield: the executioners fastened them to the post, back to back; the torch was applied, the flame rose in the air, and Fryth, stretching out his hands, embraced it as if it were a dear friend whom he would welcome. The spectators were touched, and showed marks of lively sympathy. "Of a truth," said an evangelical Christian in after days, "he was one of those prophets whom God, having pity on this realm of England, raised up to call us to repentance." His enemies were there. Dr. Cooke, a fanatic priest, observing some persons praying, called out: "Do not pray for such folks, any more than you would for a dog." At this moment a sweet light shone on Fryth's face, and he was heard beseeching the Lord to pardon his enemies. Hewet died first, and Fryth thanked God that the sufferings of his young brother were over. Committing his soul into the Lord's hands, he expired. "Truly," exclaimed many, "great are the victories Christ gains in His saints."

So many souls were enlightened by Fryth's writings, that this reformer contributed powerfully to the reformation in England. "One day, an Englishman," says Thomas Becon, prebendary of Canterbury and chaplain to Archbishop Cranmer, "having taken leave of his mother and friends, travelled into Derbyshire, and from thence to the Peak, a marvellous barren country," and where there was then "neither learning nor yet no spark of godliness." Coming into a little village named Alsop in the Dale, he chanced upon a certain gentleman also named Alsop, lord of that village, a man not only ancient in years, but also ripe in the knowledge of Christ's doctrine. After they had taken "a sufficient repast," the gentleman showed his guest certain books which he called his *jewels* and *principal treasures:* these were the New Testament and some books of Fryth's. In these godly treatises this ancient gentleman occupied himself among his rocks and mountains both diligently and virtuously. "He did not only love the Gospel," adds Cranmer's chaplain, "he *lived it also*."[1]

Fryth's writings were not destined to be read always with the same avidity: the truth they contain is, however, good for all times. The books of the apostles and of the reformers which that gentleman of Alsop read in the sixteenth century are better calculated to bring joy and peace to the soul than the light works read with such avidity in the modern world.

[1] Becon, *The Jewel of Joy* (Parker Society), p. 420.

CHAPTER TWENTY

The Isolation of England

(1533)

WHEN Fryth was consigned to the flames, Anne
Boleyn had been seated a month on the throne
of England. The salvoes of artillery which had
saluted the new queen had re-echoed all over Europe. There
could be no more doubt: the Earl of Wiltshire's daughter,
radiant with grace and beauty, wore the Tudor crown;
every one, especially the imperial family, must bear the
consequences of the act. One day Sir John Hacket, English
envoy at Brussels, arrived at court just as Mary of Hungary,
regent of the Low Countries, was about to mount her horse.
"Have you any news from England?" she asked him in
French.—"None," he replied. Mary gave him a look of
surprise, and added: "Then I have, and not over good,
methinks." She then told him of the king's marriage, and
Hacket rejoined with an unembarrassed air: "Madam, I
know not if it has taken place, but everybody who considers
it coolly and without family prejudice will agree that it is a
lawful and a conscientious marriage." Mary, who was niece
of the unhappy Catherine, replied: "Mr. Ambassador, God
knows I wish all may go well; but I do not know how the
Emperor and the king my brother will take it, for it touches
them as well as me."—"I think I may be certain," returned
Sir John, "that they will take it in good part."—"That I do
not know, Mr. Ambassador," said the regent, who doubted
it much; and then, mounting her horse, she rode out for the
chase.

Charles V was exasperated: he immediately pressed the
pope to intervene, and on the 12th of May Clement cited
the king to appear at Rome. The pontiff was greatly embarrassed: having a particular liking for Benet, Henry's
agent, he took him aside, and said to him privately: "It is

146

an affair of such importance that there has been none like it for many years. I fear to kindle a fire that neither pope nor Emperor will be able to quench." And then he added unaffectedly: "Besides, I cannot pronounce the king's excommunication before the Emperor has an army ready to constrain him." Henry being told of this *aside* made answer: "Having the justice of our cause for us, with the entire consent of our nobility, commons, and subjects, we do not care for what the pope may do." Accordingly, he appealed from the pope to a general council.

The pope was now more embarrassed than ever: "I cannot stand still and do nothing," he said. On the 12th of July he revoked all the English proceedings and excommunicated the king, but suspended the effects of his sentence until the end of September. "I hope," said Henry contemptuously, "that before then the pope will understand his folly."

He reckoned on Francis I to help him to understand it; but that prince was about to receive the pope's niece into his family. The King of England, who had already against him the Netherlands, the Empire, Rome, and Spain, saw France also slipping from him. He was isolated in Europe, and that became a serious matter. Agitated and indignant, he came to an extraordinary resolution, namely, to turn to the disciples and friends of that very Luther whom he had formerly so disdainfully treated.

Stephen Vaughan and Christopher Mann were despatched, the former to Saxony, the other to Bavaria. Vaughan reached Weimar on the 1st of September, where he had to wait five days for the Elector of Saxony, who was away hunting. On the 5th of September he had an audience of the prince, and spoke to him first in French and then in Latin. Seeing that the elector, who spoke neither French, English, nor Latin, answered him only with nods, he begged the chancellor to be his interpreter. A written answer was sent to Vaughan at seven in the evening: the Elector of Saxony turned his back on the powerful King of England. He was unworthy, he said, to have at his court ambassadors from his royal Majesty; and besides, the Emperor, who was his only master, might be displeased. Vaughan's annoyance was extreme. "Strange rudeness!" he exclaimed. "A more uncourteous refusal has never been made to such a gracious proposition. And to my greater misfortune, it is the first mission of this kind with which I have ever been entrusted." He left Weimar, determined not to deliver his credentials either to the Landgrave of Hesse or to the Duke of Lauenberg, whom he was instructed to visit: he did not wish to run the chance of receiving fresh affronts.

A strange lot was that of the King of England! the pope excommunicating him, and the heretics desiring to have nothing to do with him! No more allies, no more friends! Be it so: if the nation and the monarch are agreed, what is there to fear? Besides, at the very moment this affront was offered him, his joy was at its height: the hope of soon possessing that heir, for whom he had longed so many years, quite transported him. He ordered an official letter to be prepared announcing the birth of a prince, "to the great joy of the king," it ran, "and of all his loving subjects." Only the date of the letter was left blank.

On the 7th of September, two days after the Elector's refusal, Anne, then residing in the palace at Greenwich, gave birth to a fine well-formed child, reminding the gossips of the features of both parents; but alas! it was a girl. Henry, agitated by two strong affections, love for Anne and desire for a son, had been kept in great anxiety during the time of labour. When he was told that the child was a girl, the love he bore for the mother prevailed, and though disappointed in his fondest wishes, he received the babe with joy. But the famous letter announcing the birth of a prince . . . what must be done with it now? Henry ordered the queen's secretary to add an *s* to the word *prince*, and despatched the circular without making any change in the expression of his satisfaction. The christening was celebrated with great pomp; two hundred torches were carried before the princess, a fit emblem of the light which her reign would shed abroad. The child was named Elizabeth, and Henry declared her his successor in case he should have no male offspring. In London the excitement was great: *Te Deums*, bells, and music filled the air. The adepts of judicial astrology declared that the stars announced a glorious future. A bright star was indeed rising over England; and the English people, throwing off the yoke of Rome, were about to start on a career of freedom, morality, and greatness. Elizabeth was not destined to shine by the amiability which distinguished her mother, and the restrictions she placed upon liberty tend rather to remind us of her father. Yet while on the continent kings were trampling under foot the independence of their subjects, the English people, under Anne Boleyn's daughter, were to develop themselves, to flourish in letters and in arts, to extend navigation and commerce, to reform abuses, to exercise their liberties, to watch energetically over the public good, and to set up the torch of the Gospel of Christ.

The King of France, very adverse to England's becoming independent of Rome, at last prevailed upon Henry to send two English agents (Gardiner and Bryan) to Marseilles. "You will keep your eyes open," said Henry VIII to them, "and lend an attentive ear, but you will keep your mouths shut." The English envoys, being invited to a conference with Pope Clement and Francis I, and solicited by those great personages to speak, declared that they had no powers. "Why then were you sent?" exclaimed the king, unable to conceal his vexation. The ambassadors only answered with a smile. Francis, who meant to uphold the authority of the pope in France, was unwilling that England should be free. Accordingly he took the ambassadors aside, and prayed them to enter immediately on business with the pontiff. "We are not here for his Holiness," dryly answered Gardiner, "or to negotiate anything with him, but only to do what the King of England commands us." The tricks of the papacy had ruined it in the minds of the English people. Francis I, displeased at Gardiner's silence and irritated by his stiffness, intimated to the King of England that he would be pleased to see "better instruments" sent. Henry did send another instrument to Marseilles, but he took care to choose one sharper still.

Edmund Bonner, late chaplain to Wolsey, and future bishop of London, was a clever, active man, but ambitious, coarse and rude, wanting in delicacy and consideration towards those with whom he had to deal, violent, and, as he showed himself later to the protestants, a cruel persecutor. For some time he had got into Cromwell's good graces, and as the wind

was against popery, Bonner was against the pope. Henry
gave him his appeal to a general council, and charged him to
present it to Clement VII: it was the "bill of divorcement"
between the pope and England. Bonner, proud of being the
bearer of so important a message, arrived at Marseilles,
firmly resolved to give Henry a proof of his zeal. If Luther
had burnt the pope's bull at Wittenberg, Bonner would do
as much; but while Luther had acted as a free man, Bonner
was only a slave, pushing to fanaticism his submission to the
orders of his despotic master.

Gardiner was astounded when he heard of Bonner's arrival.
What a humiliation for him! He hung his head, "making a
plaicemouth with his lip" (says Foxe), and then lifted up his
eyes and hands, as if cursing the day and hour when Bonner
appeared. Never were two men more discordant to one
another. Gardiner could not believe the news. A scheme
contrived without him! A bishop to see one of his inferiors
charged with a mission more important than his own!
Bonner having paid him a visit, Gardiner affected great
coldness, and brought forward every reason calculated to
dissuade him from executing his commission.—"But I have
a letter from the king," answered Bonner, "sealed with his
seal, and dated from Windsor: here it is." And he took from
his satchel the letter in which Henry VIII intimated that he
had appealed from the sentence of the pope recently
delivered against him. "Good," answered Gardiner, and
taking the letter he read: "Our good pleasure is that if you
deem it *good* and *serviceable* (Gardiner dwelt upon those two
words) you will give the pope notice of the said appeal,
according to the forms required by law; if not, you will
acquaint us with your opinion in that respect."—"That is
clear," said Gardiner; "you should advise the king to abstain,
for that notice just now will be neither good nor serviceable."—
"And I say that it is both," rejoined Bonner.

One circumstance brought the two Englishmen into
harmony, at least for a time. Catherine de Medici, the pope's
niece, had been married to the son of Francis I, and Clement
made four French prelates cardinals. But not one Englishman, not even Gardiner! That changed the question: there
could be no more doubt. Francis is sacrificing Henry to the

pope, and the pope insults England. Gardiner himself desired Bonner to give the pontiff notice of the appeal, and the English envoy, fearing refusal if he asked for an audience of Clement, determined to overleap the usual formalities, and take the place by assault.

On the 7th of November, Bonner, accompanied by Penniston, a gentleman who had brought him the king's last orders, went early to the pontifical palace, preparing to let fall from the folds of his mantle war between England and the papacy. As he was not expected, the pontifical officers stopped him at the door; but the Englishman forced his way in, and entered a hall through which the pope must pass on his way to the consistory.

Ere long the pontiff appeared, wearing his stole, and walking between the cardinals of Lorraine and Medicis, his train following behind. His eyes, which were of remarkable quickness, immediately fell upon the distant Bonner, and as he advanced he did not take them off the stranger, as if astonished and uneasy at seeing him. At length he stopped in the middle of the hall, and Bonner, approaching the datary, said to him: "Be pleased to inform his Holiness that I desire to speak to him." The officer refusing, the intrepid Bonner made as if he would go towards the pope. Clement, wishing to know the meaning of these indiscreet proceedings, bade the cardinals stand aside, took off the stole, and going to a window recess, called Bonner to him. The latter, without any formality, informed the pope that the King of England appealed from his decision to a general council, and that he (Bonner), his Majesty's envoy, was prepared to hand him the authentic documents of the said appeal, taking them (as he spoke) from his portfolio. Clement, who expected nothing like this, was greatly surprised: "it was a terrible breakfast for him," says a contemporary document. Not knowing what to answer, he shrugged his shoulders, "after the Italian fashion;" and at last, recovering himself a little, he told Bonner that he was going to the consistory, and desired him to return in the afternoon. Then beckoning the cardinals, he left the hall.

Henry's envoy was punctual to the appointment, but had to wait for an hour and a half, his Holiness being engaged in giving audience. At length he and Penniston were conducted to the pope's chamber. Clement fixed his eyes on the latter, and Bonner having introduced him, the pope remarked with a mistrustful air: "It is well, but I also must have some members of my council;" and he ordered Simonetta, Capisuchi, and the datary to be sent for. While awaiting their arrival, Clement leant at the window, and appeared absorbed in thought. At last, unable to contain himself any longer, he exclaimed: "I am greatly surprised that his Majesty should behave as he does towards me." The intrepid Bonner replied: "His Majesty is not less surprised that your Holiness, who has received so many services from him, repays him with ingratitude." Clement started, but restrained himself on seeing the datary enter, and ordered that officer to read the appeal which Bonner had just delivered to him.

The datary began: "Considering that we have endured from the pope many wrongs and injuries (*gravaminibus et injuriis*)." . . . Clasping his hands and nodding dissent, Clement exclaimed ironically: "*O questo è molto vero!*" meaning to say that it was false, remarks Bonner. The datary continued: "Considering that his most holy Lordship strikes us with his spiritual sword, and wishes to separate us from the unity of the Church; we, desiring to protect with a lawful shield the kingdom which God has given us, appeal by these presents, for ourselves and for all our subjects, to a holy universal council."

At these words, the pope burst into a transport of passion, and the datary stopped. Clement's gestures and broken words uttered with vehemence, showed the horror he entertained of a council. . . . A council would set itself above the pope, a council might perhaps say that the Germans and the King of England were right.

The pope gave way to convulsive movements, folding and unfolding his handkerchief, which was always a sign of great anger in him. At last, as if to hide his passion, he said: "Continue, I am listening." When the datary had ended, the pope said coldly to his officers: "It is well written!"

Then turning to Bonner, he asked: "Have you anything more to say to me?" Bonner was not in the humour to show the least consideration. A man of the north, he took a pleasure

in displaying his roughness and inflexibility in the elegant,
crafty, and corrupt society of Rome. He boldly repeated the
protest, and delivered the king's "provocation" to the pope,
who broke out into fresh lamentations. "Ha!" he exclaimed
vehemently, "his Majesty affects much respect for the Church,
but does not show the least to me." . . . Just at this moment,
one of his officers announced the King of France. Francis
could not have arrived at a more seasonable moment.
Clement rose and went to the door to meet him. The king
respectfully took off his hat, and holding it in his hand made
a low bow, after which he enquired what his Holiness was
doing. "These English gentlemen," said the pontiff, "are
here to notify me of certain provocations and appeals . . .
and for other matters," he added, displaying much ill-
humour. Francis sat down near the table at which the pope
was seated; and turning their backs to Henry's envoy, who
had retired into an adjoining room, they began a conversation in a low tone, which Bonner, notwithstanding all
his efforts, could not hear.

That conversation possibly decided the separation between
England and France. The king showed that he was offended
at a course of proceeding which he characterized as unbecoming; and Clement learnt, to his immense satisfaction,
that the English had not spoken to Francis about the council.
"If you will leave me and the Emperor free to act against
England," he said to the king, "I will ensure you possession
of the duchy of Milan." Bonner, who had not lost sight of the
two speakers, remarked that at this moment the king and
the pope "laughed merrily together," and appeared to be
the best friends in the world.

The king having withdrawn, Bonner again approached
the pope, and the datary finished the reading. The Englishman
had not been softened by the mysterious conversation and
laughter of Clement and Francis: he was as rough and abrupt
as the Frenchman had been smooth and amiable. It was
long since the papacy had suffered such insults openly, and
even the German Reformation had not put it to such torture.
The Cardinal de Medici, chief of the malcontents, who had
come in, listened to Bonner, with head bent down and eyes
fixed upon the floor: he was humiliated and indignant. "This

is a matter of great importance," said Clement; "I will consult the consistory and let you know my answer."

In the afternoon of Monday, 10th of November, Bonner returned to the palace to learn the pope's pleasure: but there was a grand reception that day. The lords and ladies of the court of Francis I were presented to Clement, who did nothing for two hours but bless chaplets, bless the spectators, and put out his foot for the nobles and dames to kiss.

At last Bonner was introduced: *"Domine doctor, quid vultis?* (Sir doctor, what do you want?)" said the pope. "I desire the answer which your Holiness promised me." Clement, who had had time to recover himself, replied: "A constitution of Pope Pius, my predecessor, condemns all appeals to a general council. I therefore reject his Majesty's appeal as unlawful." The pope had pronounced these words with calmness and dignity, but an incident occurred to put him out of temper. Bonner, hurt at the little respect paid to his sovereign, bluntly informed the pope that the archbishop of Canterbury—that Cranmer—desired also to appeal to a council. This was going too far: Clement, restraining himself no longer, rose, and approaching Henry's envoy, said to him: "If you do not leave the room instantly, I will have you thrown into a caldron of molten lead."—"Truly," remarked Bonner, "if the pope is a shepherd, he is, as the king my master says, a violent and cruel shepherd." And not caring to take a leaden bath, he departed for Lyons. Such is the story told by the historian Burnet.

Clement was delighted not only at the departure, but still more at the conduct of Bonner: the insolence of the English envoy helped him wonderfully; and accordingly he made a great noise about it, complaining to everybody, and particularly to Francis. "I am wearied, vexed, disgusted with all this," said that prince to his courtiers. "What I do with great difficulty in a week for my good brother (Henry VIII), his own ministers undo in an hour." Clement endeavoured in secret interviews to increase this discontent, and he succeeded. The mysterious understanding was apparent to everyone, and Vannes, the English agent, who never lost sight either of the pope or the king, informed Cromwell of the close union of their minds.

When Henry VIII learnt that the King of France was slipping from him, he was both irritated and alarmed. Abandoned by that prince, he saw the pope launching an interdict against his kingdom, the Emperor invading England, and the people in insurrection. He had no repose by night or day: his anger against the pope continued to increase. Wishing to prevent at least the revolts which the partisans of the papacy might excite among his subjects, he dictated a strange proclamation to his secretary: "Let no Englishman forget the most noble and loving prince of this realm," he said, "who is most wrongfully judged by the great idol and most cruel enemy to Christ's religion, which calleth himself Pope. Princes have two ways to attain right—the general council and the sword. Now the king, having appealed from the unlawful sentence of the Bishop of Rome to a general council lawfully congregated, the said usurper hath rejected the appeal, and is thus outlawed. By holy Scripture, there is no more jurisdiction granted to the Bishop of Rome than to any other bishop. Henceforth honour him not as an idol, who is but a man usurping God's power and authority; and a man neither in life, learning, nor conversation like Christ's minister or disciple."

Henry having given vent to his irritation, bethought himself, and judged it more prudent not to publish the proclamation. But to the subjects of Henry it was becoming increasingly clear that between the English throne and the papacy there was a great gulf fixed, and there seemed good reason to think that it would yet grow wider and deeper.

CHAPTER TWENTY-ONE

Parliament Abolishes Papal Usurpations in England

(January to March 1534)

WHILE the papacy was intriguing with France and the Empire, England was energetically working at the utter abolition of the Roman authority. "One loud cry must be raised in England against the papacy," said Cromwell to the council. "It is time that the question was laid before the people. Bishops, parsons, curates, priors, abbots, and preachers of the religious orders should all declare from their pulpits that the Bishop of Rome, styled the Pope, is subordinate, like the rest of the bishops, to a general council, and that he has no more rights in this kingdom than any other foreign bishop."

It was necessary to pursue the same course abroad. Henry resolved to send ambassadors to Poland, Hungary, Saxony, Bavaria, Pomerania, Prussia, Hesse, and other German states, to inform them that he was touched with the zeal they had shown in defence of the Word of God and the extirpation of ancient errors, and to acquaint all men that he was himself "utterly determined to reduce the pope's power to the just and lawful bounds of his mediocrity."

He did not stop here. Keenly desiring to withdraw France from under the influence of Rome, he instructed his ambassadors to tell Francis I in his name and in the name of the people: "We shall shortly be able to give unto the pope such a buffet as he never had before." This was quite in Henry's style. "Things are going at such a rate here," wrote the Duke of Norfolk to Montmorency, "that the pope will soon lose the obedience of England; and other nations, perceiving the great fruits, advantage, and profit that will result from it, will also separate from Rome."

All this was serious: there was some chance that Norfolk's prophecy would be fulfilled. The pontiff could think of nothing else, and began to believe that the idea of a council was not so unreasonable after all, since the place and time of meeting and mode of proceeding would lead to endless discussions; and if the meeting ever took place, he would thus be relieved of a responsibility which became more oppressive to him every day. He therefore bade Henry VIII be informed that he agreed to call a general council. But events had not stood still: the position was not the same. "It is no longer necessary," the king answered coldly. In his opinion, the Church of England was sufficient of herself, and could do without the Church of Rome.

The King of France, in the interests of the pope, immediately resumed his part of mediator. Du Bellay, his ambassador at Rome, made indefatigable efforts to inspire the consistory with an opinion favourable to Henry VIII. According to that diplomatist, the King of England was ready to re-establish friendly relations with Clement VII, and it was parliament alone that desired to break with the papacy for ever: it was the people who wished for reform, it was the king who opposed it. "Make your choice," he exclaimed with eloquence. "All that the king desires is peace with Rome; all that the commonalty demands is war. With whom will you go—with your enemies or with your friend?" Du Bellay's assertions, though strange, were based upon a truth that cannot be denied. It was the best of the people who wanted protestantism in England, and not the king.

The court of Rome felt that the last hour had come, and determined to despatch to London the papers necessary to reconcile Henry. It was believed on the continent that the King of England was going to gain his cause at last, and people ascribed it to the ascendancy of French policy at Rome since the marriage of Catherine de Medici with Henry of Orleans. But the more the French triumphed, the more indignant became the Imperialists. To no purpose did the pope say to them: "You do not understand the state of affairs: the thing is done. . . . The King of England is married to Anne Boleyn. If I annulled the marriage, who would undertake to execute my sentence?"—"Who?" exclaimed the ambassadors of Charles V, "who? . . . The Emperor." The weak pontiff knew not which way to turn: he had but one hope left—if Henry VIII were to re-establish Roman catholicism in his kingdom, a fact so important would silence Charles V.

This fact was not to be feared: a movement had begun in the minds of the people of England which it was no longer possible to stop. While many pious souls received the Word of God in their hearts, the king and the most enlightened part of the nation were agreed to put an end to the intolerable usurpations of the Roman pontiff. "We have looked in the Holy Scriptures for the rights of the papacy," said the members of the Commons house of parliament, "but instead of finding therein the institution of popes, we have found that of kings—and, according to God's commandments, the priests ought to be subject to them as much as the laity."—"We have reflected upon the wants of the realm," said the royal council, "and have come to the conclusion that the nation ought to form one body; that one body can have but one head, and that head must be the king." The parliament which met in January 1534 was to give the death-blow to the supremacy of the pope.

This blow came strictly neither from Henry nor from Cranmer, but from Thomas Cromwell. Without possessing Cranmer's lively faith, Cromwell desired that the preachers should open the Word of God and preach it "with pure sincereness" before the people, and he afterwards procured for every Englishman the right to read it. Being pre-eminently a statesman of sure judgment and energetic action, he was in advance of his generation; and it was his fate, like those generals who march boldly at the head of the army, to procure victory to the cause for which he fought; but, persecuted by the traitors concealed among his soldiers, to be sacrificed by the prince he had served, and to meet a tragical death before the hour of his triumph.

The Commons, wishing to put an end to the persecutions practised by the clergy against the evangelical Christians, summoned—it was a thing unprecedented—the Lord-bishop of London to appear at their bar to answer the complaint made against him by Thomas Philips, one of the disciples of the Reformation. The latter had been lying in prison three years under a charge of heresy. The parliament, unwilling

that a bishop should be able at his own fancy to transform
one of his Majesty's subjects into a heretic, brought in a bill
for the repression of doctrines condemned by the Church.
They declared that, the authority of the Bishop of Rome
being opposed to Holy Scripture and the laws of the realm,
the words and acts that were contrary to the decisions of the
pontiff could not be regarded as heresies. Then turning to the
particular case which had given rise to the grievance, parliament declared Philips innocent and discharged him from
prison.

After having thus upheld the cause of religious liberty, the
Commons proceeded to the definitive abolition of the privileges
which the bishops of Rome had successively usurped to the
great detriment of both Church and people. They restored to
England the rights of which Rome had despoiled her. They
prohibited all appeals to the pope, of what kind soever they
might be, and substituted for them an appeal to the king in
chancery. They voted that the election of bishops did not
concern the court of Rome, but belonged to the chief ecclesiastical body in the diocese, to the chapter . . . at least in
appearance; for it really appertained to the crown, the king
designating the person whom the chapter was to elect. This
strange constitution was abolished under Edward VI, when
the nomination of the bishops was conferred purely and simply
on the king. If this was not better, it was at least more sincere;
but the singular *congé d'élire* was restored under Elizabeth.

At the same time new and loud complaints of the Romish
exactions were heard in parliament. "For centuries the
Roman bishops have been deceiving us," said the eloquent
speakers, "making us believe that they have the power of
dispensing with everything, even with God's commandments.
We send to Rome the treasures of England, and Rome sends
us back in return . . . a piece of paper. The monster which
has fattened on the substance of our people bears a hundred
different names. They call it relicfs, dues, pensions, provisions,
procurations, delegation, rescript, appeal, abolition, re-
habilitation, relaxation of canonical penalties, licences, Peter's
pence, and many other names besides. And after having thus
caught our money by all sorts of tricks, the Romans laugh at
us in their sleeves." Parliament forbade all Englishmen, even

F(II)

the king himself, to apply to Rome for any dispensation or delegation whatsoever, and ordered them, in case of need, to have recourse to the Archbishop of Canterbury. Then, immediately putting these principles into practice, they declared the king's marriage with Catherine to be null, for "no man has power to dispense with God's laws," and ratified the marriage between Henry and Anne, proclaiming their children heirs to the crown. At the same time, wishing England to become entirely English, they deprived two Italians, Campeggio and Ghinucci, of the sees of Salisbury and Worcester, which they held.

It was during the month of March, 1534—an important date for England—that the main branches of the tree of popery were thus lopped off one after another. The trunk indeed remained, although stripped; but yet a few months, and that too was to strew the earth with its fall. Still the Commons showed a certain degree of consideration. When Clement had threatened the king with excommunication, he had given him three months' grace; England, desiring to return his politeness, informed the pope that he might receive some compensation. At the same time she made an important declaration: "We do not separate from the Christian Church," said the Commons, "but merely from the usurped authority of the Pope of Rome; and we preserve the catholic faith, as *it is set forth in the Holy Scriptures.*" All these reforms were effected with great unanimity, at least in appearance. The bishops, even the most scholastic, such as Stokesley of London, Tunstall of Durham, Gardiner of Winchester, and Rowland Lee of Coventry, declared the Roman papacy to be of human invention, and that the pope was, in regard to them, only a *bishop*, a *brother*, as his predecessors had been to the bishops of antiquity. Every Sunday during the session of parliament a prelate preached at St. Paul's Cross "that the pope was not the head of the Church," and all the people said AMEN.

Meanwhile Du Bellay, the French ambassador at Rome, was waiting for the act by which the King of England was to bind himself once more to the pope—an act which Francis I still gave him reason to expect. Every morning he fancied it would arrive, and every evening his expectations were disappointed. He called upon the English envoys, and afterwards at the Roman chancery, to hear if there was any news; but everywhere the answer was the same—nothing.

The term fixed by Clement VII having elapsed, he summoned the consistory for Monday the 23rd of March. Du Bellay attended it, still hoping to prevent anything being done that might separate England from the papacy. The cardinals represented to him, that as the submission of Henry VIII had not arrived, nothing remained but for the pope to fulminate the sentence. "Do you not know," exclaimed Du Bellay in alarm, "that the courier charged with that prince's despatches has seas to cross, and the winds may be contrary? The king of England waited your decision for six years, and cannot you wait six days?" "Delay is quite useless," said a cardinal of the imperial faction; "we know what is taking place in England. Instead of thinking of reparation, the king is widening the schism every day. He goes so far as to permit the representation of dramas at his court, in which the holy conclave, and some of your most illustrious selves in particular, are held up to ridicule." The last blow, although a heavy one, was unnecessary. The priests could no longer contain their vexation; the rebellious prince must be punished. Nineteen out of twenty-two cardinals voted against Henry VIII; the remaining three only asked for further enquiry. Clement could not conceal his surprise and annoyance. To no purpose did he demand another meeting, in conformity with the custom which requires two, and even three, consultations: overwhelmed by an imposing and unexpected majority, he gave way.

Simonetta then handed him the sentence, which the unhappy pope took and read with the voice of a criminal rather than of a judge. "Having invoked the name of Christ, and sitting on the throne of justice, we decree that the marriage between Catherine of Aragon and Henry king of England was and is valid and canonical; that the said king Henry is bound to cohabit with the said queen; to pay her royal honours; and that he must be constrained to discharge these duties." After pronouncing these words, the pontiff, alarmed at the bold act he had just performed, turned to the envoys of Charles V and said to them: "I have done my duty; it is now for the Emperor to do his, and to carry the sentence into

execution." "The Emperor will not hold back," answered
the ambassadors; but the thing was not so easily done as said.

Thus the great affair was ended; the king of England was
condemned. It was dark when the pope quitted the consistory;
the news so long expected spread immediately through the
city; the Emperor's partisans, transported with joy, lit bonfires
in all the open places, and cannons fired repeated salvoes.
Bands of Ghibelines paraded the streets, shouting, *Imperio e
Espagna* (the Empire and Spain). The whole city was in
commotion. The pope's disquietude was still further increased
by these demonstrations. "He is tormented," wrote Du Bellay
to his master. Clement spent the whole night in conversation
with his theologians. "What must be done? England is lost
to us. How can I avert the king's anger?" Clement VII
never recovered from this blow: the thought that under his
pontificate Rome lost England made him shudder. The
slightest mention of it renewed his anguish, and sorrow soon
brought him to the tomb.

Yet he did not know all. The evil with which Rome was
threatened was greater than he had imagined. If in this
matter there had been nothing more than the decision of a
prince discontented with the court of Rome, a contrary
decision of one of his successors might again place England
under the dominion of the pontiffs; and these would be sure
to spare no pains to recover the good graces of the English
kings. But in despite of Henry VIII, a pure doctrine, similar
to that of the apostolic times, was spreading over the different
parts of the nation; a doctrine which was not only to wrest
England from the pope, but to establish in that island a true
Christianity—a vast evangelical propaganda which should
ultimately plant the standard of God's Word even at the ends
of the world. The empire of Christendom was thus to be taken
from a church led astray by pride, and which bade mankind
unite with it that they might be saved; and to be given to
those who taught that, according to the divine declarations,
none could be saved except by uniting with Jesus Christ.

BOOK TWO

England Breaks with Rome

CHAPTER ONE

A Conspiracy against the Reformation

(March and April 1534)

THE parliament of 1534 had greatly advanced the cause of the Reformation. The voices of the most enlightened men of England had been heard in it with still greater power than in 1529; and accordingly an historian,[1] referring to the meeting of 1534, speaks of it as "that great session." These enlightened men, however, formed but a small minority, and among them were many who, from a want of independence, never voted on the side of liberty but when the king authorized them. The epoch was a critical one for the nation. It might as easily fall back to the pope as advance towards the Gospel. Hesitating between the Middle Ages and modern times, it had to choose either life or death. Would it make a vigorous effort and reach those bracing heights, like travellers scaling the rugged sides of the Alps? England appeared too weak for so daring a flight. The mass of the people seemed chained by time-worn prejudices to the errors and practices of Rome. The king no doubt had political views which raised him above his age; but, a slave to his passions, and the docile disciple of the old ways, he detested a real Reformation and real liberty. The clergy were superstitious, selfish, and excitable; and the advisers of the crown knew no other rule than the will of their master. By none of these powers, therefore, could a transformation be accomplished. The safety of England came from that sovereign hand, that mysterious power, which was already stirring the western world. The nation began to feel its energetic impulse. A strange breeze seemed to be filling the sails and driving the bark of the state towards the harbour, notwithstanding the numerous shoals that lay around it.

The thought which at that time mainly engrossed the minds of the most intelligent men of England—men like Cranmer,

[1] Bishop Burnet.

165

Cromwell, and their friends—was the necessity of throwing off the papal authority. They believed that it was necessary to root out the foreign and unwholesome weed, which had spread over the soil of Britain, and tear it up so thoroughly that it could never grow again. Parliament had declared that all the powers exercised by the bishop of Rome in England must cease and be transferred to the crown; and that no one, not even the king, should apply to Rome for any dispensation whatsoever. A prelate had preached every Sunday at St. Paul's Cross that the pope was not the head of the Church. On the other hand, the pontiff, who was reckoning on Henry's promised explanations and satisfactory propositions, seeing that the messenger whom he expected from London did not arrive, had solemnly condemned that prince on the 23rd March, 1534. But immediately startled at his own boldness, Clement asked himself with agony how he could repair this wrong and appease the king. He saw it was impossible, and in the bitterness of his heart exclaimed: "Alas! England is lost to us!"

Two days after the famous consistory in which Henry's condemnation had been pronounced, an English courier entered Rome, still in a state of agitation and trouble, and went straight to the papal palace. "What is his business?" people said; "and what can give him such boldness?" The Englishman was bringing to the ministers of the Vatican the long-expected act by which the King of England declared himself prepared to enter into an arrangement with the pope, provided the cardinals of the imperial faction were excluded. The messenger at the same time announced that Sir Edward Carne and William Revett, two envoys from Henry VIII, would soon arrive to conclude the business. Cardinal Farnese, who erelong succeeded Clement under the title of Paul III, and the more moderate prelates of the sacred college waited upon the pope at once, and begged him to summon the consistory without delay. It was just what Clement desired; but the imperialists, more furious than ever, insisted on the confirmation of the sentence condemning Henry, and spared no means to ensure success. Monks went about repeating certain stories which their English brethren sent them, and which they furthermore exaggerated. They asserted that the

English people were about to rise in a body against the king and throw themselves at the feet of the holy father. The pope ratified the sentence, and the consistory, taking one more step, urged the Emperor to carry it out.

It has been said that a delay of two days was the cause of the Reformation of England. That is a mistake. The Reformation came from the Holy Scriptures, from God, from His mighty grace, and not from princes, their passions, or delays. Even had the pontifical court at last conceded to Henry the divorce he asked for, that prince would probably not have renounced the rights he had acquired, and which made him sole and true monarch of England. Had he done so, it is doubtful whether he was strong enough to check the Reformation. The people were in motion, Christian truth had reappeared among them: neither pontifical agitations nor concessions could stop the rapid current that was carrying them to the pure and living waters of the Gospel.

However, Sir Edward Carne and William Revett, Henry's envoys, arrived in Italy full of hope, and pledged themselves (as they wrote to the king) to reconcile England and the papacy "in conformity to his Highness' purpose." Having learnt on reaching Bologna that Du Bellay, the bishop of Paris, who was instructed to support them, was in that city, they hurried to him to learn the exact state of affairs. The bishop was one of those enlightened catholics who believed that the extreme papal party was exposing the papacy to great danger, and who would have prevented schism in the Church by giving some satisfaction to Germany and England. Hence the envoys from Henry VIII found the prelate dejected and embarrassed. "All is over," he told them. "The pope has pronounced sentence against his Majesty." Carne and Revett were thunderstruck; the burden was too heavy for them. "All our hopes have vanished in a moment," they said. Du Bellay assured them that he had spared no pains likely to prevent so precipitate and imprudent an act on the part of a pope. "But the imperialists," he said, "moved heaven and earth, and constrained Clement VII to deliver a sentence in opposition to his own convictions." The ambassador of Francis I added that there was still one gleam of hope. "Raincé, secretary to the French embassy at Rome, with an oath, wished himself at perdition," said Du Bellay rather coarsely, "if our holy father does not patch up all that has been damaged." The Englishmen desired to go to the pope forthwith, in order to prevent the execution of the sentence. "Do nothing of the kind," said the French bishop. "Do not go to Rome on any pretext whatsoever."

Perhaps Du Bellay wanted first to know what his master thought of the matter. Carne, undecided what to do, despatched a messenger to Henry VIII to ask for orders; and then, ten days later, wishing to do something, he appealed from the bishop of Rome ill-informed to the bishop of Rome better-informed.

When the King of England received his ambassador's message, he could hardly restrain his anger. At the very moment when he had made a concession which appeared to him the height of condescension, Rome treated him with contempt and sacrificed him to Charles V. Even the nation was aroused. The pope, it was said, commissions a foreign prince to execute his decrees; soldiers, newly raised in Germany, and brimful of insults and threats, are preparing to land in England. National pride arrayed the people on the king's side. Henry no longer hesitated; his offended honour demanded reparation: a complete rupture alone could satisfy it. Many writers supported him. "The pope," said Dr. Sampson, dean of the Chapel Royal, "has no more power in England than the Archbishop of Canterbury in Rome. It was only by tacit consent that the pope crept into the kingdom, but we intend to drive him out now by express consent." The two houses of parliament were almost unanimously of that opinion. The privy council proposed to call upon the lord mayor to see that anti-Romish doctrines were taught in every house in London. Lastly, the people showed their opposition after their fashion, indulging in games and masquerades, in which a cardinal at one time, the pope at another, were represented. To call a man a "papist" or "a priest of the pope" was one of the greatest insults. Even the clergy declared against Rome. On the 31st March the lower house of convocation discussed whether the Roman pontiff had in England, according to Scripture, a higher jurisdiction than any other foreign bishop. Thirty-three voted in the negative, only four in the affirmative. The king immediately forwarded the same question to all the ecclesiastical corporations of the kingdom. The friends of the Gospel were filled with joy. The pope had made a great mistake when, imitating the style of ancient Rome, he had hurled the bolts of the Vatican, as Jupiter had in days of old launched the thunders of the Capitol. A great revolution seemed to be working itself out unopposed in this island, so long the slave of the Roman pontiffs. There was just at this time nothing to be feared from without: Charles V was overwhelmed with business; the King of Scotland was on better terms with his uncle of England, and Francis I was preparing for a friendly interview with Henry VIII. And yet the danger had never been greater; but the mine was discovered in March 1534, before the match could be applied to it.

A dangerous political and clerical conspiracy had been for some time silently organizing in the monasteries. It was possible, no doubt, to find here and there in the cloisters monks who were learned, pious, and loyal; but the greater number were ignorant and fanatical, and terribly alarmed at the dangers which threatened their order. Their arrogance, grossness, and loose manners irritated the most enlightened part of the nation; their wealth, endowments, and luxury aroused the envy of the nobility. A religious and social transformation was taking place at this memorable epoch, and the monks foresaw that they would be the first victims of the revolution. Accordingly they were resolved to fight to the uttermost for their altars and homes. But who was to take the first step in the perilous enterprise—who to give the signal?

As in the days of the Maid of Orleans, it was a young woman who grasped the trumpet and sounded the charge. But if the first was a heroine, the other was an ecstatic—nay, a fanatic.

There lived in the village of Aldington in Kent a young woman of singular appearance. Although of an age which is usually distinguished by a fresh and clear complexion, her face was sallow and her eyes haggard. All of a sudden she would be seized with a trembling of the whole body; she lost the use of her limbs and of her understanding, uttered strange and incoherent phrases, and fell at last stiff and lifeless to the ground. She was, moreover, exemplary in her conduct. The people declared her state to be miraculous, and Richard Masters, the rector of the parish, a cunning and grasping priest, noticing these epileptic attacks, resolved to take advantage of them to acquire money and reputation. He suggested to the poor sufferer that the extraordinary words she uttered proceeded from the inspiration of Heaven, and declared that she would be guilty if she kept secret this wonderful work of God. An official of Canterbury, Dr. Edward Bocking, joined the priest with the intention of turning the girl's disease to the profit of the Romish party. They represented to Elizabeth Barton—such was the name of the Kentish maiden—that the cause of religion was exposed to great danger in England; that it was intended to turn out the monks and priests; but that God, whose hand defends His Church by the humblest instruments, had raised her up in these inauspicious days to uphold that holy ark, which king, ministers, and parliament desired to throw down. Such language pleased the girl: on the faith of the priests, she regarded her attacks as divine transports; a feeling of pride came over her; she accepted the part assigned her. On a sudden her imagination kindled; she announced that she had held communications with saints and angels, even with Satan himself. Was this sheer imposture or enthusiasm? There was, perhaps, a little of both; but, in her eyes, the end justified the means. When speaking, she affected strange turns, unintelligible figures, poetical language, and clothed her visions in rude rhymes, which made the educated smile, but helped to circulate her oracles among the people. Erelong she set herself unscrupulously above the truth, and, inspired by a feverish energy, did not fear to excite the people to bloodshed.

There was somewhere out in the fields, in one part of the parish, a wretched old chapel that had been long deserted, and where a coarse image of the Virgin still remained. Masters determined to make it the scene of a lucrative pilgrimage. He suggested the notion to Elizabeth Barton, and erelong she gave out that the Virgin would cure her of her disorder in that holy consecrated edifice. She was carried thither with a certain pomp, and placed devoutly before the image. Then a crisis came upon her. Her tongue hung out of her mouth, her eyes seemed starting from their sockets, and a hoarse sepulchral voice was heard speaking of the terrors of hell; and then, by a singular transformation, a sweet and insinuating voice described the joys of paradise.[1] At last the ecstasy ended, Elizabeth came to herself, declared that she was perfectly cured, and announced that God had ordered her to become a nun and to take Dr. Bocking as her confessor. The prophecy of the Kentish maiden touching her own disease being thus verified, her reputation increased.

Elizabeth Barton's accomplices imagined that the new prophetess required a wider stage than the fields of Aldington, and hoped that, once established in the ecclesiastical metropolis of England, she would see her followers increase throughout the kingdom. Immediately after her cure, the ventriloquist entered the convent of St. Sepulchre at Canterbury, to which Dr. Bocking belonged. Once in this primatial city, her oracles and her miracles were multiplied. Sometimes in the middle of the night, the door of her cell opened miraculously: it was a call from God, inviting her to the chapel to converse with Him. Sometimes a letter in golden characters was brought to her by an angel from heaven. The monks kept a record of these wonders, these oracles; and, selecting some of them, Masters laid the miraculous collection, this bible of the fanatics, before Archbishop Warham. The prelate, who appeared to believe in the nun's inspiration, presented the document to the king, who handed it to Sir Thomas More, and ordered the words of the Kentish maiden to be carefully taken down and communicated to him. In this Henry VIII showed probably more curiosity and distrust than credulity.

Elizabeth and her advisers were deceived, and thought they might enter into a new phase, in which they hoped to reap the reward of their imposture. The Aldington girl passed from a purely religious to a political mission. This is what her advisers were aiming at. All, and especially Dr. Bocking, who contemplated restoring the authority of the papacy—even were it necessary to their end to take the king's life—began to denounce in her presence Henry's tolerance of heresy and the new marriage he desired to contract. Elizabeth eagerly joined

---

[1] "A voice speaking within her belly."—Cranmer, *Letters and Remains* (Parker Society), p. 273.

this factious opposition. "If Henry marries Anne Boleyn," she told Bishop Fisher, "in seven months' time there will be no king in England." The circle of her influence at once grew wider. The Romish party united with her. Abell, Queen Catherine's agent, entered into the conspiracy; twice Elizabeth Barton appeared before the pope's legates; Fisher supported her, and Sir Thomas More, one of the most cultivated men of his day, though at first little impressed in her favour, admitted afterwards the truth of some of her foolish and guilty revelations.

One thing was yet wanting, and that was very essential in the eyes of the supporters of the movement: Elizabeth must appear before Henry VIII as Elijah appeared before Ahab: they expected great results from such an interview. At length they obtained permission, and the Kentish maiden prepared herself for it by exercises which over-excited her. When brought into the presence of the prince, she was at first silent and motionless, but in a moment her eyes brightened and seemed to flash fire; her mouth was drawn aside and stretched, while from her trembling lips there fell a string of incoherent phrases. "Satan is tormenting me for the sins of my people," she exclaimed, "but our blessed Lady shall deliver me by her mighty hand. . . . O times! O manners! . . . Abominable heresies, impious innovations! . . . King of England, beware that you touch not the power of the holy Father. . . . Root out the new doctrines. . . . Burn all over your kingdom the New Testament in the vulgar tongue. Henry, forsake Anne Boleyn and take back your wife Catherine. . . . If you neglect these things, you shall not be king longer than a month, and in God's eyes you will not be so even for an hour. You shall die the death of a villain, and Mary, the daughter of Catherine, shall wear your crown."

This noisy scene produced no effect on the king. Henry, though prompt to punish, would not reply to Elizabeth's nonsense, and was content to shrug his shoulders. But the fanatical young woman was not discouraged: if the king could not be converted, the people must be roused. She repeated her threats in the convents, castles, and villages of Kent, the theatre of her frequent excursions. She varied them according to circumstances. The king must fall: but at one time she announced it would be by the hands of his subjects; at another, of the priests; and at a third, by the judgment of God. One point alone was unchanged in her utterances: Henry Tudor must perish. Erelong, like a prophetess lifted above the ordinary ministers of God, she reprimanded even the sovereign pontiff himself. She thought him too timid, and, taking him to task, declared that if he did not bring Henry's plans to naught, "the great stroke of God which then hung over his head" would inevitably fall upon him.[1]

This boldness added to the number of her partisans. Monks, nuns, and priests, knights, gentlemen, and scholars, were carried away by her. Young folks especially and men of no culture eagerly embraced this mad cause. There were also men of distinction who did not fear to become her defenders. Bishop Fisher was gained over: he believed himself certain of the young woman's piety. Being a man of melancholy temperament and mystic tendency, a lover of the marvellous, he thought that the soul of Elizabeth might well have a supernatural intercourse with the Infinite Being. He said in the House of Lords: "How could I anticipate deceit in a nun, to whose holiness so many priests bore witness?" The Roman catholics triumphed. A prophetess had risen up in England, like Deborah in Israel.

One eminent and large-hearted catholic, Sir Thomas More, had however some doubts; and the monks who were Elizabeth's advisers set every engine at work to win him over. During the Christmas of 1532, Father Risby, a Franciscan of Canterbury, arrived at Chelsea to pass the night there. After supper, he said: "What a holy woman this nun of Kent is! It is wonderful to see all that God is doing through her."—"I thank God for it," answered More coldly.—"By her mediation she saved the cardinal's soul," added the monk. The conversation went no farther. Some time later a fresh attempt was made: Father Rich, a Franciscan of Richmond, came and told More the story of the letter written in letters of gold and brought by an angel. "Well, father," said the chancellor, "I believe the nun of Kent to be a virtuous woman, and that God is working great things by her; but stories like that you have told me are not part of our *Credo*, and before repeating them, one

[1] Cranmer, *Letters and Remains* (Parker Society), p. 273.

should be very sure about them." However, as the clergy generally countenanced Elizabeth, More could not bear the idea of forming a sect apart, and went to see the prophetess at Sion monastery. She told him a silly story of the devil turned into a bird. More was satisfied to give her a double ducat and commend himself to her prayers. The chancellor, like other noble intellects among the catholics, was prepared to admit certain superstitions; but he would have had the nun keep in her religious sphere; he feared to see her touch upon politics. "Do not speak of the affairs of princes," he said to her. "The relations which the late Duke of Buckingham had with a holy monk were in great part the cause of his death." More had been Chancellor of England, and perhaps feared the duke's fate.

Elizabeth Barton did not profit by this lesson. She again declared that, according to the revelations from God, no one should deprive the Princess Mary of the rights she derived through her birth, and predicted her early accession. Father Goold immediately carried the news to Catherine. The nun and her advisers, who chided the pope only through their zeal for the papacy, had communications with the nuncio; they thought it necessary for him to join the conspiracy. They agreed upon the course to be adopted: at a given time, monks were to mingle with the people and excite a seditious movement. Elizabeth and her accomplices called together such as were to be the instruments of their criminal design. "God has chosen you," said the nun to them, "to restore the power of the Roman pontiff in England." The monks prepared for this meritorious work by devout practices: they wore sackcloth next to their skin; they fastened iron chains round their bodies, fasted, watched, and made long prayers. They were seriously intent on disturbing the social order and banishing the Word of God.

The violent Henry VIII—easy-tempered for once in his life—persisted in his indifference. The seven months named by the prophetess had gone by, and the dagger with which she had threatened him had not touched him. He was in good health, had the approbation of parliament, saw the nation prosper under his government, and possessed the wife he had so passionately desired. Everything appeared to succeed with him, which disconcerted the fanatics. To encourage them Elizabeth said: "Do not be deceived. Henry is no longer really king, and his subjects are already released from every obligation towards him. But he is like King John, who, though rejected by God, seemed still to be a king in the eyes of the world."

The conspirators intrigued more than ever: not content with Catherine's alliance, they opened a communication with Margaret Plantagenet, Countess of Salisbury, niece of Edward IV, and with her children, the representatives of the party of the White Rose. Hitherto this lady had refrained from politics; but, her son Reginald Pole having united with the pope and quarrelled with Henry VIII, they prevailed upon her to carry over to the Princess Mary, whose household she directed, the forces of the party of which she was the head.

The conspirators believed themselves sure of victory; but at the very moment when they imagined themselves on the point of restoring the papacy in England, their whole scheme suddenly fell to the ground. The country was in danger: the state must interfere. Cranmer and Cromwell were the first to discover the approaching storm. Canterbury, the primate's archiepiscopal city, was the centre of the criminal practices of the Kentish woman. One day the prioress of St. Sepulchre received the following note from Cranmer: "Come to my palace next Friday; bring your nun with you. Do not fail." The two women duly came; Elizabeth's head was so turned that she saw in everything that happened the opportunity of a new triumph. This time she was deceived. The prelate questioned her; she obstinately maintained the truth of her revelations, but did not convince the archbishop, who had her taken to Cromwell, by whom she was sent to the Tower with five other nuns of her party. At first Elizabeth proudly stuck to her character of prophetess; but imprisonment, the searching questions of the judges, and the grief she felt on seeing her falsehoods discovered, made her give way at last. The unhappy creature, a blind tool of the priests, was not entirely wanting in proper feeling. She began to understand her offence and to repent of it: she confessed everything. "I never had a vision in all my life," she declared; "whatever I said was of my own imagination; I invented it to please the

people about me and to attract the homage of the world."
The disorder which had weakened her head had much to do
with her aberrations. Masters, Bocking, Goold, Deering, and
others more guilty than she appeared before the Star Chamber.
Elizabeth's confession rendered their denials impossible, and
they acknowledged having attempted to get up an insurrection
with a view of re-establishing the papacy. They were condemned to make a public disavowal of their impostures, and
the following Sunday at St. Paul's was appointed for that
purpose. The bishop of Bangor preached; the nun and her
accomplices, who were exposed on a platform in front of him,
confessed their crimes before the people, and were then led
back to the Tower.

Personages far more illustrious than these were involved.
Besides an epileptic woman and a few monks, the names of
Fisher and of More were in the indictment. Cromwell urged
both the bishop and the statesman to petition the king for
pardon, assuring them they would obtain it. "Good Master
Cromwell," exclaimed Sir Thomas More, who was much
excited and ashamed of his credulity, "my poor heart is
pierced at the idea that his Majesty should think me guilty.
I confess that I did believe the nun to be inspired; but I put
away far from me every thought of treason. For the future,
neither monk nor nun shall have power to make me faithless
to my God and my king." Cranmer, Cromwell, and the
chancellor prevailed on Henry VIII to strike More's name out
of the bill. The illustrious scholar escaped the capital punishment with which he was threatened. His daughter, Margaret
Roper, came in a transport of joy to tell him the news: "In
faith, Meg," said More with a smile, "*quod differtur non aufertur*,"
(what is postponed is not dropped).

The case of the bishop of Rochester was more serious: he
had been in close communication with all those knaves, and
the honest but proud and superstitious churchman would not
acknowledge any fault. Cromwell, who desired to save the old
man, conjured him to give up all idea of defending himself;
but Fisher obstinately wrote to the House of Lords that he
had seen no deception in the nun. The name of the king's old
tutor was left, therefore, in the bill of attainder, but he was
charged with misprision, i.e. failure of duty in respect to the

crime of another, and not with treason. In the outcome he was condemned to the loss of his goods and to imprisonment at the king's pleasure, penalties from which he escaped by the payment to the king of a fine of £300.

The bill was introduced into the House of Lords on the 21st February, and received the royal assent on the 21st March. The prisoners charged with treason were brought together in the Star Chamber to hear their sentence. Their friends had still some hope; but the Bull which the pope had issued against Henry VIII on the 23rd March, endangering the order of succession, made indulgence difficult. The king and his ministers felt it their duty to anticipate, by a severe example, the rebellion which the partisans of the pontiff were fomenting in the kingdom. Sentence of death was pronounced upon all the criminals.

During this time the unfortunate Elizabeth Barton saw all the evils she had caused rise up before her eyes: she was grieved and agitated, she was angry with herself and trembled at the idea of the temporal and eternal penalties she had deserved. Death was about to end this drama of fanaticism. On the 20th April the false prophetess was carried to Tyburn with her accomplices, in the midst of a great crowd of people. On reaching the scaffold, she said: "I am the cause not only of my own death, which I have richly deserved, but of the death of all those who are going to suffer with me. Alas! I was a poor wretch without learning, but the praises of the priests about me turned my brain, and I thought I might say anything that came into my head. Now I cry to God and implore the king's pardon." These were her last words. She fell—she and her accomplices—under the stroke of the law.

These were the means to which fervent disciples of Rome had recourse to combat the Reformation in England. Such weapons recoil against those who employ them. The blindest partisans of the Church of the popes continued to look upon this woman as a prophetess, and her name was in great favour during the reign of Mary. But the most enlightened Roman catholics are now careful not to defend the imposture.[1] The

---

[1] Lingard, the Roman-catholic historian, acknowledges the deception, as do almost all other historians.

fanatical episode was not without its use: it made the people understand what these pretended visions and false miracles were, through which the religious orders had acquired so much influence; and so far contributed to the suppression of the monasteries within whose walls such a miserable deception had been concocted.

CHAPTER TWO

The Church Becomes a Department of State

(Christmas 1533 to June 1534)

THE maid of Kent having been executed, her partisans rallied round another woman, who represented the Romish system in its highest features, as Elizabeth Barton had represented it in its more vulgar phase. After the nun came the queen.

Catherine had always claimed the honours due to the Queen of England, and her attendants yielded them to her. "We made oath to her as queen," they said, "and the king cannot discharge our consciences." Whenever Lord Mountjoy, royal commissioner to the daughter of Ferdinand and Isabella, called her *"princess,"* she raised her head haughtily and said to him: "You shall answer for this before God." "Ah!" exclaimed Mountjoy, fretted by the vexations of his office, "I would a thousand times rather serve the king in the most dangerous cause!" Mary having also received an injunction to drop her title of princess, made answer: "I shall believe no such order, unless I see his Majesty's signature." The most notable partisans of Roman catholicism, and even the ambassador of Charles V, paid the queen frequent visits. Henry became uneasy, and shortly before Christmas 1533 he took measures to remove her from her friends. Catherine opposed everything. Suffolk wrote to the king: "I have never seen such an obstinate woman." But there was a man quite as obstinate, and that was Henry.

His most cherished desires had not been satisfied: he had no son. Should he chance to die, he would leave two daughters, Mary and Elizabeth; the former supported by the partisans of the old times, the latter by those of the new. Civil war would probably decide to whom the crown should belong. It was necessary to prevent such a misfortune. The Lords and Commons, therefore, petitioned the king, no doubt at his instigation, that his marriage with Lady Catherine should be declared null, and her child illegitimate; that his marriage with Queen Anne should be recognized as valid, and the children issuing from it alone entitled to succeed. All classes of people immediately took the statutory oath; even the monks bowed their heads. They said: "Bound to render to our king Henry VIII, and to him alone after Jesus Christ, fidelity and worship, we promise inviolable obedience to our said lord as well as to our most serene Queen Anne, his wife, and to their children; and we profess perpetual respect for the holy and chaste marriage which they have legitimately contracted."[1] This forced testimony, borne to Anne by the monastic orders, is one of the numerous monuments of the despotism of Henry VIII and of the moral weakness of the monks.

But in this oath of allegiance the king had meditated a more important object—to banish the papacy from England. The monks bound themselves not only to recognize the prescribed order of succession, but further to substitute the primacy of the king for that of the pope. "We affirm," they said, "that King Henry is the head of the Anglican Church, that the Roman bishop, falsely styled pope and sovereign pontiff, has no more authority than any other bishop; and we promise to preach Christ simply and openly according to the rule of Scripture and of the orthodox and catholic doctors." A sign, a word from the State was sufficient to make the papal army pass from the camp of Rome to the camp of the king.

The "famous question," that of the Romish jurisdiction, was also put before the two universities. On the 2nd May, 1534, Cambridge declared that "all its doctors, having carefully examined the Holy Scriptures, had not discovered the primacy of the pope in them." The clergy of the province of York, led by the archbishop, Edward Lee, a churchman full of talent, activity, and vanity, stoutly resisted at first; but eventually the prelate wrote to the king on the 2nd June that "according to the unanimous opinion of his clergy, the pope in conformity with the Holy Scriptures had no more authority in England than any other foreign ecclesiastic." Henry, not content with the proclamations of his council and the declarations of parlia-

[1] Rymer, *Acta*, p. 192.

ment, required for his separation from Rome the suffrage of the Church; and the Church, probably more from weakness than conviction, gave it. However, without reckoning the members of the clergy who, like the primate, wanted no pope, there were many bishops who, at heart, were not sorry to be liberated from the perpetual encroachments of the Roman court.

A rumour from the continent suddenly alarmed the king among all his easy triumphs; a more formidable enemy than monks and bishops was rising against him. It was reported that the Emperor was not only recruiting soldiers in Flanders, but was preparing considerable numbers from Bohemia, Germany, Italy, and Spain for the invasion of England. Francis I could not permit this kingdom, so close to his own, to be occupied by the armies of Charles V, his constant enemy; he determined therefore to have an interview with Henry, and to that intent sent over the Seigneur De la Guiche, his chamberlain and counsellor. Henry replied that it would be difficult to leave England just at a time when pope and Emperor spoke of invading him; the more so as he must leave his "most dearly beloved queen" (Anne Boleyn) and his young daughter, the Princess Elizabeth; as well as another daughter and her mother, the aunt of Charles V, whose partisans were conspiring against him. "Ask my good brother the king," said Henry to De la Guiche, "to collect a fleet of ships, galleys, and barks to prevent the Emperor's landing. And in case that prince should invade either France or England, let us agree that the one who is not called upon to defend his own kingdom shall march into Charles' territories." However, Henry consented to go as far as Calais.

There was another invasion which, in Henry's eyes, was much more to be dreaded. That king —a greater king perhaps than is ordinarily supposed—maintained that no prince, whether his name was Charles or Clement, had any business to meddle with his kingdom. The act of the 23rd March, by which the pope had condemned him, had terminated his long endurance: Clement VII had declared war against him and Henry VIII accepted it. A man, though he be ordinarily the slave of his passions, has sometimes impulses which belong to great characters. Henry determined to finish with the pope as the pope had finished with him. He will declare himself master in his own island; dauntlessly he will brave Rome and the imperial power ready to assail him. Erelong the fire which consumed him appeared to kindle his subjects. The political party, at the head of which were Suffolk and Gardiner, was ready to give up the papacy, even while maintaining the dogmas of catholicism. The evangelical party desired to go farther, and drive the catholic doctrines out of England. These two hostile sections united their forces against the common enemy.

At the head of the evangelicals, who were eventually to prevail under the son of Henry VIII, were two men of great intelligence, destined to be powerful instruments in the enfranchisement of England. Cranmer, the ecclesiastical leader of the party, gave way too easily to the royal pressure; but, being a moderate theologian, a conscientious Christian, a skilful administrator, and indefatigable worker, he carefully studied the Scriptures, the Fathers, and even the Schoolmen; he took note of their sayings and, strengthened by their opinions, continued the work of the Reformation with calmness and perseverance. Beside him stood Cromwell, the lay leader of protestant feeling. Gifted in certain respects with a generous character, he loved to benefit those who had helped him in adversity; but too attentive to his own interests, he profited by the Reformation to increase his riches and honours. Inferior to Cranmer in moral qualities, he had a surer and a wider glance than the primate; he saw clearly the end for which he must strive and the means necessary to be employed, and combined much activity with his talents. These leaders were strongly supported. A certain number of ministers and lay members of the Church desired an evangelical reform in England. Latimer, a popular orator, was the tribune commissioned to scatter through the nation the principles whose triumph Cranmer and Cromwell sought. He preached throughout the whole extent of the province of Canterbury; but if his bold language enlightened the well-disposed, it irritated the priests and monks. His great reputation led to his being invited to preach before the king and queen. Cranmer, fearing his incisive language and sarcastic tone, begged him to say nothing in the pulpit that would indicate any soreness about his late disgrace. "In your sermon let not any sparkle or suspicion of grudge appear to remain in you. If you feel authorized by the Word of God to attack any sin or superstition, let not the reproof be given without affection."[1] Latimer preached, and Anne Boleyn was so charmed by his evangelical simplicity, Christian eloquence, and apostolic zeal, that shortly she used her influence with the king to have the preacher elevated to the see of Worcester. Latimer takes his place by the side of Cranmer among the reformers of the English Church.

The evangelical and the political parties being thus agreed to support the prince, Henry determined to strike the decisive blow. On the 9th June, 1534, about three months after he had been condemned at Rome, he signed at Westminster the proclamation "for the abolishing of the usurped power of the pope." The king declared: "That having been acknowledged next after God, supreme head of the Church of England, he abolished the authority of the bishop of Rome throughout his realm, and commanded all bishops to preach and have preached, every Sunday and holy day, the true and sincere Word of the Lord; to teach that the jurisdiction of the Church belongs to him alone, and to blot out of all canons, liturgies, and other works the name of the bishop of Rome and his pompous titles, so that his name and memory be never more remembered in the kingdom of England, except to his contumely and reproach.[2] By so doing you will advance the honour of God Almighty, manifest the imperial majesty of your sovereign lord, and procure for the people unity, tranquillity, and prosperity."

Would these orders be executed? If there remained in any university, monastery, parish, or even in any wretched presbytery, a breviary in which the name of the *pope* was written; if on the altar of any poor country church a missal was found with these four letters unerased—it was a crime. If every weed be not plucked up, thought the king's counsellors, the garden will soon be entirely overrun. The obstinacy of the

[1] [Harleian MSS., 6148 (probably to be dated in the first week of January, 1534).]

[2] "And his name and memory to be never more remembered except to his contumely and reproach."—Wilkins, *Concilia*, p. 773.

clergy, their stratagems, their pious frauds were a mystery to nobody. Henry was persuaded, and his counsellors still more so, that the bishops would make no opposition; they resolved therefore to direct the sheriffs to see that the king's orders were strictly carried out. "We command you," said that prince, "under pain of our high indignation, to put aside all human respect, to place God's glory solely before you, and, at the risk of exposing yourselves to the greatest perils, to make and order diligent search to be made. Inform yourselves whether in every part of your county the bishop executes our commands without veil or dissimulation. And in case you should observe that he neglects some portion, or carries out our orders coldly, or presents this measure in a bad light, we command you strictly to inform us and our council with all haste.

"If you hesitate or falter in the commission we give you, rest assured that being a prince who loves justice, we will punish you with such severity that all our subjects will take care for the future not to disobey our commands."

Everybody could see that Henry was in earnest, and, immediately after this energetic proclamation, those who were backward hastened to make their submission. The dean and chapter of St. Paul's made their protest against the pope on the 20th June. On the 27th the University of Oxford, in an act where they described the king as "that most wise Solomon," declared unanimously that it was contrary to the Word of God to acknowledge any superiority whatsoever in the bishop of Rome. A great number of churches and monasteries set their seals to similar declarations.

Such was the first pastoral of the prince who claimed now to govern the Church. He seemed desirous of making it a mere department of the State. Henry allowed the bishops to remain, but he employed the functionaries of police and justice to overlook their episcopate; and that office was imposed upon them in such terms that they must necessarily look sharp after the transgressors. First and foremost the king wanted his own way in his family, in the State, and in the Church. The latter was to him as a ship which he had just captured: the captain was driven out, but for fear lest he should return, he threw overboard all who he thought might betray him. With haughty head and naked sword Henry VIII entered the new realm which he had conquered. He was far from resembling Him whom the prophets had announced: *Behold thy king cometh unto thee, meek and lowly.*

The power in the Church having been taken from the pope, to whom should it have been committed?

Scripture calls the totality of Christian people a holy nation, a royal priesthood;[1] words which show that, after God, the authority belongs to them. And, in fact, the first act of the Church, the election of an apostle in the place of Judas, was performed by the brethren assembled in one place.[2] When it became necessary to appoint deacons, the twelve apostles once more summoned "the multitude of the disciples."[3] And later still, the evangelists, the delegates of the flocks, were selected by the voice of the churches.[4]

It is a principle of reason, that authority, where a corporate body is concerned, resides in the totality of its members. This principle of reason is also that of the Word of God.

When the Church became more numerous it was called upon to delegate (at least partially) a power that it could no longer exercise wholly of itself. In the apostolic age the Christians, called to form this delegation, adopted the forms with which they were familiar. After the pattern of the council of elders, which existed in the Jewish synagogues, and of the assembly of decurions, which exercised municipal functions in the cities of the pagans, the Christian Church had in every town a council, composed of men of irreproachable life, vigilant, prudent, apt to teach,[5] but distinct from those who were called doctors, evangelists, or ministers of the Word.[6] Still the Christians never entertained the idea of giving themselves a universal chief, after the image of the emperor. Jesus Christ and His Word were amply sufficient. It was not until many centuries later that this anti-Christian institution appeared in history.

The authority, which in England had been taken away

[1] 1 Peter 2. 9.   [2] Acts 1. 15–26.
[3] Acts 6. 2.   [4] 2 Cor. 8. 19.
[5] 1 Timothy 3.; Titus 1.
[6] Ephesians 4. 11; 6. 21; Colossians 1. 7; 1 Timothy 4. 6.

from the pope, should return in accordance with scriptural principles to the members of the Church; and if, following the example of the primitive Christians, they had adopted the forms existing in their own country in the sixteenth century, they would have placed as directors of the Church—Christ remaining their sole king—one or two houses or assemblies, authorized to provide for the ecclesiastical administration, the maintenance of a pure faith, and the spiritual prosperity of that vast body. These assemblies would have been composed, as in the primitive times, of a majority of Christian laymen, with the addition of ministers; and both would have been elected by believers whose faith was in conformity with that of the Church.

But was there at that time in England a sufficient number of enlightened Christians to become members of these assemblies, and even to hold the elections which were to appoint them? It is doubtful. They were not to be found even in Germany. "I have nobody to put in them," said Luther; "but if the thing becomes feasible, I shall not be wanting in my duty."

This form of government not being possible in England then, according to the Reformer's expression, two other forms offered themselves. If the first were adopted, the authority would be remitted to the clergy; but that would have been to perpetuate the doctrines and rites of popery and to lead back infallibly to the domination of Rome. The most dangerous government for the Church is the government of priests: they commonly rob it of liberty, spontaneousness, evangelical faith, and life.

There remained no alternative then but to confide the supreme authority in the Church to the State; and this is what was generally done in the sixteenth century. But men of the greatest experience in these matters have agreed that the government of the religious society by the civil power can only be a temporary expedient, and have universally proclaimed the great principle "that the essence of all society is to be governed by itself" (Grotius). To deny this axiom would be utterly contrary not only to liberty, but, further still, contrary to justice.

We must not forget, when we speak of the relations between

Church and State, that there are three different systems:—
the government of the Church by the State; the union of the
Church, governing itself, with the State; and their complete
separation. There is no reason for pronouncing here upon the
relative value of the two last systems.

CHAPTER THREE

Tyndale and his Enemies

(1534 to August 1535)

TWO persons were at this time specially dreaded by the Roman party: one was at the summit of the grandeurs of the world, the other at the summit of the grandeurs of faith—the Queen and Tyndale. The hour of trial was approaching for both of them.

There existed another reformation than that of which the sheriffs were to be the agents; there were other reformers than Henry VIII. One man, desirous of reviving the Church of England, had made the translation of the Holy Scriptures the work of his life. Tyndale had been forced to leave his country; but he had left it only to prepare a seed which, borne on the wings of the wind, was to change the wildernesses of his native land into a fruitful garden.

The retired tutor from the vale of the Severn was living in 1534 as near as possible to England—at Antwerp, whence ships departed frequently for British harbours. The English merchants, of whom there were many in that city, welcomed him with fraternal cordiality. Among them was a friend of the Gospel, Thomas Poyntz, a member of the grocers' company and distantly related to Lady Walsh of Little Sodbury. This warm-hearted Christian had received Tyndale into his house, and the latter was unremittingly occupied in translating the Old Testament, when an English ship brought the news of the martyrdom of Fryth, his faithful colleague. Tyndale shed many tears, and could not make up his mind to continue his work alone. But the reflection that Fryth had glorified Jesus Christ in his prison aroused him: he felt it his duty to glorify God in his exile. The loss of his friend made his Saviour still more precious to him, and in Jesus he found comfort for his mind. "I have lost my brother," he said, "but in Christ, all Christians and even all the angels are father and mother, sister and brother, and God Himself takes care of me. O Christ, my Redeemer and my shield! Thy blood, Thy death, all that Thou art and all that Thou hast done—Thou Thyself art mine!"[1]

Tyndale, strengthened by faith, redoubled his zeal in his Master's service. While pursuing his study of the Scriptures with intense eagerness, he combined with learning the charity that maintains good works. The English merchants of Antwerp having made him an annual allowance, he consecrated it to the poor; but he was not content with mere giving. Besides Sunday he reserved two days in the week, which he called his "days of recreation." On Monday he visited the most out-of-the-way streets of Antwerp, hunting in garrets for the poor English refugees who had been driven from their country on account of the Gospel; he taught them to bear Christ's burden, and carefully tended their sick. On Saturday, he went about the city, seeking out the poor in "every hole and corner." Should he happen to meet some hardworking parents burdened with children, or some aged or infirm man, he hastened to share his substance with the poor creatures. "We ought to be for our neighbour," he said, "what Christ has been for us." This is what Tyndale called his "pastime." On Sunday morning he met with the merchants in a room prepared for evangelical worship, and read and explained the Scriptures with so much sweetness and unction and in such a practical spirit that the congregation (it was said) fancied they were listening to John the Evangelist. During the remainder of the week the laborious scholar gave himself entirely to his translation. He was not one of those who remain idle in the hope that grace may abound. "If we are justified by faith," he said, "it is in order that we may do Christian works."

There came good news from London to console him for the death of Fryth. In every direction people were asking for the New Testament; several Flemish printers began to reprint it, saying: "If Tyndale should print 2000 copies, and we as many, they would be few enough for all England." Four new editions of the sacred book issued from the Antwerp presses in 1534.

[1] Tyndale, *Treatises* (Parker Society), pp. 19, 110.

There was at that time living in the city a man little fitted to be Tyndale's associate. George Joye, a fellow of Cambridge, was one of those active but superficial persons, with little learning and less judgment, who are never afraid to launch out into works beyond their powers.[1] Joye, who had left England in 1527, noticing the consideration which Tyndale's labours brought to their author, and being also desirous of acquiring glory for himself, began, though he knew neither Hebrew nor Greek, to correct Tyndale's New Testament according to the Vulgate and his own imagination. One day when Tyndale had refused to adopt one of his extravagant corrections, Joye was touched to the quick: "I am not afraid to cope with him in this matter," he said, "for all his high learning in Hebrew, Greek, and Latin." Tyndale knew more than these. "He is master of seven languages," said Busche, Reuchlin's disciple: "Hebrew, Greek, Latin, Italian, Spanish, English, French, and so thoroughly that, whichever he is speaking, one might believe it to be his mother tongue."

In the month of August Joye's translation appeared at Antwerp: he had advertised it as "clearer and more faithful." Tyndale glanced over the leaves of the work that had been so praised by its author, and was vexed to find himself so unskilfully "corrected." He pointed out some of Joye's errors, and made this touching and solemn declaration: "Moreover, I take God, which alone seeth the heart, to record to my conscience, beseeching Him that my part be not in the blood of Christ, if I wrote of all that I have written, throughout all my books, aught of an evil purpose, of envy or malice to any man, or to stir up any false doctrine or opinion in the Church of Christ; or to be author of any sect; or to draw disciples after me. . . . Also, my part be not in Christ, if mine heart be not to follow and live according as I teach; and also, if mine heart weep not night and day for mine own sin, and other men's. . . . As concerning all I have translated, or otherwise written, I beseech all men to read it for that purpose I wrote it; even to bring them to the knowledge of the Scripture. And as far as the Scripture approveth it, so far to allow it; and if in any place the Word of God disallow it,

---

[1] [For a more sympathetic appraisal of Joye's work, see D. B. Knox, *The Doctrine of Faith* (James Clarke, 1961), especially pp. 55–63, 228–237.]

then to refuse it, as I do before our Saviour Christ and His congregation."[1]

While Joye was waging this petty war against Tyndale, every ship that came from London to Antwerp brought the cheering news that the great conflict seemed to be dying out in England, and that the king and those around him were drawing towards protestantism. A change had been worked in Anne's mind analogous to that which had been wrought in her position. She had been ambitious and worldly, but, from the moment she ascended the throne, her character had expanded; she had become queen, she wished to be the mother of her people, especially of those who trod in the paths of Holy Scripture. In the first transports of his affection, Henry had desired to share all the honours of sovereignty with her, and she had taken this high position more seriously than Henry had intended. When he saw her whom he had placed by his side imagine that she had any power, the selfish and jealous monarch knit his brows: this was the beginning of the storm that drove Anne Boleyn from the throne to the scaffold. She ventured to order Cromwell to indemnify the merchants who had suffered loss for having introduced the New Testament into England. "If a day passes," people said, "without her having an opportunity of doing a service to a friend of the Gospel, she is accustomed to say with Titus, 'I have lost a day.'" Harman, a merchant of Antwerp and a man of courage, who had helped Tyndale to publish the Gospel in English, had been kept seven months in prison by Wolsey and Hacket. Although set at liberty, he was still deprived of his privileges and compelled to suspend business. He came over to England, but instead of applying either to the lord chancellor or to Cromwell for the restoration of his rights, he went straight to the Queen. Anne, who was then at Greenwich Palace, was touched by his piety and sufferings, and, probably without taking counsel of the king, she dictated the following message to the chief minister, which we think worth quoting in full.

[1] [Quoted from the Second Preface to Tyndale's New Testament Revision of 1534, and dated August of that year. It appeared in print in the following November.]

G(II)

By the Queen

Anne the Queen. Trusty and right well-beloved, we greet you well. And whereas we be credibly informed that the bearer hereof, Richard Harman, merchant and citizen of Antwerp in Brabant, was in the time of the late lord cardinal put and expelled from his freedom and fellowship of and in the English house there, for nothing else, as he affirmeth like a good Christian man, but only for that, that he did, both with his goods and policy to his great hurt and hindrance in this world, help to the setting forth of the New Testament in English. We therefore desire and instantly pray you, that with all speed and favour convenient, you will cause this good and honest merchant, being my Lord's true, faithful, and loving subject, to be restored to his pristine freedom, liberty, and fellowship aforesaid. And the sooner at this our request: and at your good pleasure to hear him in such things as he hath to make further relation unto you in this behalf.

Given under our signet at my Lord's manor of Greenwich, the xiv day of May.

To our trusty and right well-beloved Thomas Cromwell, principal secretary to his Majesty, the king my lord.

This intervention of the queen in favour of a persecuted evangelical was much talked about. Some ascribed her conduct to the interests of her own cause, others to humanity: most of the friends of the Reformation regarded it as a proof that Anne was gained over to their convictions, and Tyndale manifested his gratitude to the queen by presenting her with a handsome copy of his New Testament.[1]

What gave such joy to Tyndale annoyed the king greatly. Such a private order as this coming from the queen singularly displeased a monarch whose will it was that no business should be discussed except in his council. There was also in this order, at least in Henry's eyes, a still greater evil. The evangelical reformation, which Henry had so stoutly combated and which he detested to the last, was making great progress in England. On the 4th of July, 1533, Fryth, the friend of Harman and Tyndale, was burnt at Smithfield, as being one of its followers; and ten months later, on the 14th of May, 1534, Harman, the friend of Tyndale and Fryth, had been declared "a good Christian" by the queen. Anne dared profess herself the friend of those whom the king hated. Did she design to make a revolution—to oppose the opinions of

---

[1] [It was printed on vellum with illuminations; the prefatory matter was omitted; and the fore-edges bore the words, "Anna, Regina Angliæ."]

her lord the king? That letter did not remain without effect: it was reported that the friends of the Word of God, taking advantage of these favourable dispositions, were printing at Antwerp six separate editions of the New Testament, and were introducing them into England.

It was not only the king who was irritated, the anger of the Romish party was greater still; but as they dared not strike the queen, they looked about for another victim. Neither Bishop Fisher, Sir Thomas More, nor Henry VIII appear to have had any part in this new crime. Gardiner, now bishop of Winchester, gave a force to the episcopal body of which it had long been deprived; and several prelates, "incensed and inflamed in their minds," says Foxe, called to remembrance that the best means of drying up the waters of a river is to cut off its springs. It was from Tyndale that all those writings proceeded—those Gospels which, in their opinion, were leading England astray. The moment seemed favourable for getting rid of him: he was actually in the territory of Charles V, that great enemy of the Reformation. Gardiner and his allies, the chief of whom was probably Stokesley, bishop of London, determined to send into the Low Countries two persons with instructions to keep an eye upon the reformer, to take him unawares, and have him put to death. For this purpose they selected a very clever monk of Stratford-le-Bow Abbey and a zealous young papist, who had the look of a gentleman, and who (they hoped) would soon gain Tyndale's heart by his amiability.

It was about the end of the year 1534, while the reformer was still living at Antwerp in the house of Thomas Poyntz, when one day, dining with another merchant, he observed among the guests a tall young man of good appearance whom he did not know. "He is a fellow-countryman," said the master of the house, "Mr. Harry Philips, a person of very agreeable manners." Tyndale drew near the stranger and was charmed with his conversation. After dinner, just as they were about to separate, he observed another person near Philips, whose countenance from being less open pleaded little in his favour. It was "Gabriel, his servant," he was told. Tyndale invited Philips to come and see him: the young layman accepted the invitation, and the candid reformer was so taken with him,

that he could not pass a day without him—inviting him at
one time to dinner, at another to supper. At length Philips
became so necessary to him that he prevailed upon him, with
Poyntz's consent, to come and live in the same house with
him. For some time they had lost sight of Gabriel, and on
Tyndale's asking what had become of him, he was informed
that he had gone to Louvain, the centre of Roman clericalism
in Belgium. When Tyndale and Philips were once lodged
beneath the same roof, their intimacy increased: Tyndale
kept no secrets from his fellow-countryman. The latter spent
hours in the library of the hellenist, who showed him his
books and manuscripts, and conversed with him about his
past and future labours, and the means that he possessed for
circulating the New Testament throughout England. The
translator of the Bible, all candour and simplicity, supposing
no evil, thinking nothing but good of his neighbour, un-
bosomed himself to him like a child.

Philips, less of a gentleman than he appeared, was the
son of a tax-collector in Dorsetshire and had disgraced
himself by robbing his father of money. In 1534, he was
living in London and seeking employment. The pretended
domestic, a disguised monk, was a crafty and vicious churchman, who had been brought from Stratford-le-Bow and given
to the so-called gentleman—apparently as a servant, but
really as his counsellor and master. Neither Wolsey, More,
nor Hacket had succeeded in getting hold of Tyndale; but
Gardiner and Stokesley, men of innate malice and indirect
measures, familiar with all holes and corners, all circumstances and persons, knew how to go to work without noise,
to watch their prey in silence, and fall upon it at the very
moment when they were least expected. Two things were
required in order to catch Tyndale: a bait to attract him,
and a bird of prey to seize him. Philips was the bait, and the
monk Gabriel Donne the bird of prey.[1] The noble-hearted
Poyntz, a man of greater experience than the reformer, had
been for some time watching with inquisitive eye the new

---

[1] [J. F. Mozley in his *William Tyndale* (pub. in 1937) considers it possible
that although Gabriel Donne was made use of by Philips, he may have been
ignorant of his sinister designs against the reformer. The evidence is not
entirely conclusive.]

guest introduced into his house. It was of no use for Philips to try to be agreeable, there was something in him which displeased the worthy merchant. "Master Tyndale," he said one day to the reformer, "when did you make that person's acquaintance?"—"Oh! he is a very worthy fellow," replied Tyndale, "well-educated and a thorough gentleman." Poyntz said no more.

Meanwhile the monk had returned from Louvain, where he had gone to consult with some of the most fanatical papal leaders. If he and his companion could gain Mr. Poyntz, it would be easy to lay hold of Tyndale. They thought it would be sufficient to show the merchant that they had money, imagining that every man was to be bought. One day Philips said to Poyntz: "I am a stranger here, and should feel much obliged if you would show me Antwerp." They went out together. Philips thought the moment had come to let Poyntz know that he was well supplied with gold, and even had some to give to others. "I want to make several purchases," he said, "and you would greatly oblige me by directing me. I want the best goods. I have plenty of money," he added. He then took a step farther, and sounded his man to try whether he would aid him in his designs. As Poyntz did not seem to understand him, Philips went no farther.

As stratagem did not succeed, it was necessary to resort to force. Philips by Gabriel's advice set out for Brussels in order to prepare the blow that was to strike Tyndale. The Emperor and his ministers had never been so irritated against England and the Reformation. The troops of Charles V were in readiness, and people expected to hear every moment that war had broken out between the Emperor and the king. On arriving at Brussels, the young Englishman appeared at court and waited on the government: he declared that he was a Roman catholic disgusted with the religious reforms in England and devoted to the cause of Catherine. He explained to the ministers of Charles V that they had in the Low Countries the man who was poisoning the kingdom; and that, if they put Tyndale to death, they would save the papacy in England. The Emperor's ministers, delighted to see Englishmen making common cause with them against Henry VIII, conceded to him all that he asked. Philips, sparing no expense to attain his end, returned to Antwerp, accompanied by the imperial prosecutor and other officers of the Emperor.

It was important to arrest Tyndale without having recourse to the city authorities, and even without their knowledge. Had not the Hanseatic judges the strange audacity to declare, in Harman's case, that they could not condemn a man without positive proof? The monk, who probably had not gone to Brussels, undertook to reconnoitre the ground. One day, when Poyntz was sitting at his door, Gabriel went up to him and said: "Is Master Tyndale at home? My master desires to call upon him." They entered into conversation. Everything seemed to favour the monk's designs: he learnt that in three or four days Poyntz would be going to Bergen-op-Zoom, where he would remain about six weeks. It was just what Gabriel wanted, for he dreaded the piercing eye of the English merchant.

Shortly after this, Philips arrived in Antwerp with the prosecutor and his officers. The former went immediately to Poyntz's house, where he found only the wife at home. "Does Master Tyndale dine at home to-day?" he said. "I have a great desire to dine with him. Have you anything good to give us?" "What we can get in the market," she replied laconically.

The new Judas hurried to meet the officers, and agreed with them upon the course to be adopted. When the dinner-hour drew near, he said: "Come along, I will deliver him to you." The imperial prosecutor and his followers, with Philips and the monk, proceeded towards Poyntz's house, carefully noting everything and taking the necessary measures not to attract observation. The entrance to the house was by a long narrow passage. Philips placed some of the agents a little way down the street; others, near the entrance of the alley. "I shall come out with Tyndale," he told the agents; "and the man I point out with my finger is the one you will seize." With these words Philips entered the house; it was about noon.

The creature was exceedingly fond of money; he had received a great deal from the priests in England for the payment of his mission; but he thought it would be only right to plunder his victim, before giving him up to death. Finding Tyndale, at home, he said to him after a few compliments: "I must tell you my misfortune. This morning I lost my purse

between here and Mechlin, and I am penniless. Could you
lend me some money?" Tyndale, simple and inexperienced
in the tricks of the world, went to fetch the required sum,
and lent him forty shillings. The delighted Philips put the
money carefully in his pocket, and then thought only of
betraying his kind-hearted friend. "Well, Master Tyndale,"
he said, "we are going to dine together." "No," replied
Tyndale, "I am going to dine out to-day; come along with
me, I will answer for it that you will be welcome." Philips
joyfully consented; promptitude of execution was one element
of success in his business. The two friends prepared to start.
The alley by which they had to go out was (as we have said)
so narrow that two persons could not walk abreast. Tyndale,
wishing to do the honours to Philips, desired him to go first.
"I will never consent," replied the latter, pretending to be
very polite. "I know the respect due to you—it is for you to
lead the way." Thus Tyndale, who was of moderate height,
went first, while Philips, who was very tall, came behind him.
He had placed two agents at the entrance, who were sitting
at each side of the alley. Hearing footsteps they looked up and
saw the innocent Tyndale approaching them without suspicion,
and over his shoulders the head of Philips. He was a lamb led
to slaughter by the man who was about to sell him. The officers
of justice, frequently so hard-hearted, experienced a feeling of
compassion at the sight. But the traitor, raising himself behind
the reformer, who was about to enter the street, placed his
forefinger over Tyndale's head, according to the signal which
had been agreed upon, and gave the men a significant look,
as if to say to them, "This is he!" The men at once laid hands
upon Tyndale, who, in his holy simplicity, did not at first
understand what they intended doing. He soon found out;
for they ordered him to move on, the officers following him,
and he was thus taken before the imperial prosecutor. The
latter who was at dinner invited Tyndale to sit down with
him. Then ordering his servants to watch him carefully, the
magistrate set off for Poyntz's house. He seized the papers,
books, and all that had belonged to the reformer; and returning home, placed him with the booty in a carriage, and
departed. The night came on, and after a drive of about
three hours they arrived in front of the strong castle of Vilvorde,

built in 1374 by duke Wenceslaus, situated two leagues north
of Brussels, on the banks of the Senne, surrounded on all sides
by water and flanked by seven towers. One of the three draw-
bridges was lowered, and Tyndale was delivered into the
hands of the governor, who put him into a safe place. The
reformer of England was not to leave Vilvorde as Luther left
the Wartburg.[1]

The object of his mission once attained, Philips, fearing the
indignation of the English merchants, escaped to Louvain.
Sitting in taverns or at the tables of monks, professors, and
prelates—sometimes even at the court of Brussels, he would
boast of his exploit, and desiring to win the favour of the
imperialists would call Henry VIII a tyrant and a robber of
the State.

Shortly Poyntz returned from Bergen-op-Zoom, and he and
his fellow merchants, deeply offended by the loss of their
friend and by the prosecutor's encroachment upon their rights
and privileges, addressed a letter to Mary of Hungary, at that
time Queen Regent of the Netherlands, urging her to agree
to the speedy release of Tyndale, but their protest proved
unavailing. Her officials objected strongly to the release of a
man who had, in their opinion, done such great harm to the
papal cause in England.

Tyndale, deprived of all hope, sought consolation in God.
"Oh! what a happy thing it is to suffer for righteousness'
sake," he said. "If I am afflicted on earth with Christ, I have
joy in the hope that I shall be glorified with Him in heaven.
Trials are a most wholesome medicine, and I will endure
them with patience. My enemies destine me for the stake, but
I am as innocent as a new-born child of the crimes of which
they accuse me. My God will not forsake me. O Christ, Thy
blood saves me, as if it had been mine own that was shed
upon the cross. God, as great as He is, is mine with all that
He hath." And again: "There is none other way into the
kingdom of life than through persecution and suffering of
pain and of very death, after the example of Christ."

Tyndale in his prison at Vilvorde was happier than Philips

---

[1] [The arrest occurred, as we now know from the Archives of Brussels,
on the 23rd or 24th May, 1535. In all, the reformer was a prisoner for a
hundred and thirty-five days.]

at court. If we carefully study the history of the reformers, we recognize at once that they were not simply masters of a pure doctrine, but also men of lofty soul, Christians of great morality and exalted spirituality. We cannot say as much of their adversaries: what a contrast here between the traitor and his victim! The calumnies and insults of the enemies of protestantism will deceive nobody. If it is sufficient to read the Bible with a sincere heart in order to believe it, it is sufficient also to know the lives of the reformers in order to honour them.

CHAPTER FOUR

Henry VIII as King-Pontiff
(1534 and 1535)

WHILE the Roman papacy was triumphing in the Low Countries, a lay papacy was being established in England. Henry VIII gave his orders like a sovereign bishop, *summus episcopus*, and the majority of the priests obeyed him. They believed that such an extraordinary state of things would be but of short duration, and thought that it was not worth the trouble of dying in battle against what would perish of itself. They muttered with their lips what the king ordered them, and waited for the coming deliverance.

Every preacher was bound to preach once at least against the usurpations of the papacy; to explain on that occasion the engagements made by the pope with the king of England, the duplicity shown by Clement, and the obligation by which the monarch was bound to thwart so much falsehood and trickery. The ministers of the Church were ordered to proclaim the Word of Christ purely, but to say nothing about the adoration of saints, the marriage of priests, justification by works and other doctrines rejected by the reformers, which the king intended to preserve. The secular clergy generally obeyed.

There were however numerous exceptions, particularly in the north of England, and the execution of Henry's orders gave rise to scenes more or less riotous. Due credit must be given to those who ventured to resist a formidable power in obedience to conscientious principles. There were here and there a few signs of opposition. On the 24th of August, 1534, Father Ricot, when preaching at Sion Monastery, called the king, according to his orders, "the head of the Church"; but added immediately after, that he who had given the order was alone responsible before God, and that he "ought to take steps for the discharge of his conscience." The other monks went farther still: as soon as they heard Henry's new title proclaimed, there was a movement among them. Father Lache, who, far from resembling his name (meaning "lax"), was inflexible even to impudence, got up; eight other monks rose with him and left the chapel "contrary to the rule of their religion" and to the great scandal of all the audience. These nine, boldly quitting the church one after another, were the living protest of the monks of England. They wanted to maintain the dominion of the pope in the Church, and in the State also. The king-pope would have none of these freaks of independence. Dr. Bedyll, a fellow of New College, Oxford, who had received Cromwell's order to inspect this monastery, proposed to send the nine monks to prison, "to the terrible example of their adherents."

The priests, finding that they must act with prudence, avoided a repetition of such outbreaks and began secretly to school their penitents in the confessional, bidding them employ mental reservations, in order to conciliate everything. They set the example themselves: "I have abjured the pope *in the outward man*, but not *in the inward man*," said one of them to some of his parishioners. The confessor at Sion Monastery had proclaimed the king's new title and even preached upon it; yet when one of his penitents showed much uneasiness because he had heard Latimer say that the pope himself could not pardon sin: "Do not be afraid," said the confessor; "the pope is assuredly the head of the Church. True, king and parliament have turned him out of office here in England; but that will not last long. The world will change again, you will see, and that too before long."—"But we have made oath to the king as head of the Church," said some persons to a priest. "What matters!" replied he. "An oath that is not very strictly made may be broken the same way."

These mental reservations, however, made many ecclesiastics and laymen too feel uneasy. They longed for deliverance: they were on the look-out; they turned their eyes successively towards Ireland, which had risen for the pope, and towards the Low Countries, whence they hoped an imperial fleet would sail for the subjugation of England. Men grew excited. In the monasteries there were fanatical and visionary monks who, maddened by the abuses of power under which they suffered, and fired by persecution, dreamt of nothing but reaction and vengeance, and expressed their cruel wishes in daring language. One of them named Maitland, belonging to the Dominican order in London, exclaimed presumptuously, as if he were a prophet: "Soon I shall behold a scaffold erected. . . . On that scaffold will pass in turn the heads of all those who profess the new doctrine, and Cranmer will be one of them. . . . The king will die a violent and shameful death, and the queen will be burnt." Being addicted to the black art, Maitland pretended to read the future by the help of Satanic beings. All were not so bold: there were the timid and fearful. Several monks of Sion House, despairing of the papacy, were making preparations to escape and hide themselves in some wilderness or foreign cloister. "If we succeed," they said, "we shall be heard of no more, and nobody will know where we are." This being told to Bedyll, Cromwell's agent, he was content to say: "Let them go; the loss will not be great." Roman-catholicism was, however, to find more honourable champions.

Two men, a bishop and a layman, celebrated throughout Christendom, John Fisher and Sir Thomas More, were about to present an opposition to the king which probably he had not expected. Since More had fathomed the king's intentions, and resigned the office of chancellor, he often passed whole nights without sleep, shuddering at the future which threatened him, and watering his bed with tears. He feared that he was not firm enough to brave death. "O God!" he exclaimed during his agitated vigils, "come and help me. I am so weak I could not endure a fillip" (*i.e.* even a trifling blow). His children wept, his wife stormed against her husband's enemies, and he himself employed a singular mode of preparing his family for the fate that awaited him. One day, when they were all at table, a serjeant entered the room and summoned him to appear before the king's commissioners. "Be of good cheer," said More; "the time is not yet come. I paid this man in order to prepare you for the calamity that hangs over you." It was not long delayed.

Shortly after the condemnation of Elizabeth Barton the nun, Sir Thomas More, Fisher, and many other influential men were summoned to the archbishop's palace to take the oath prescribed in the Act of Succession. More confessed, received the sacrament, and, forbidding his wife and children to accompany him, as was their custom, to the boat which was to carry him to Lambeth, he proceeded in great emotion towards the place where his future would be decided. His startled family watched him depart. The ex-chancellor, taking his seat in the boat along with his son-in-law William Roper, endeavoured to restrain his tears and struggled but without success against his sorrow. At length his face became more serene, and, turning to Roper, he whispered in his ear, "I thank our Lord, my son; the field is won." On his arrival at Lambeth Palace, where Bishop Fisher (of Rochester) and a great number of ecclesiastics were assembled, More, who was the only layman, was introduced first. The chancellor read the form to him: it stated in the preamble that the troubles of England, the oceans of blood that had been shed in it, and many other afflictions, originated in the usurped power of the popes; that the king was the head of the Anglican Church, and that the bishop of Rome possessed no authority out of his own diocese. "I cannot subscribe that form," said More, "without exposing my soul to everlasting damnation. I am ready to give my adhesion to the Act of Succession which is a political act—but without the preamble." "You are the first man who has refused," said the chancellor. "Think upon it." A great number of bishops, doctors, and priests who were successively introduced took the required oath. But More remained firm, and so did Bishop Fisher.[1]

Cranmer, who earnestly desired to save these two con-scientious men, asked Cromwell to accept the oath they proposed, and the latter consulted the king upon it. "They must give way," exclaimed Henry, "or I will make an example of them that shall frighten others." As the king was inexorable, they were attainted by act of parliament for refusing to take the required oath, and sent to the Tower.

The family of Sir Thomas More was plunged in affliction. His daughter Margaret, having obtained permission to see him, hurried to the Tower, penetrated to his cell, and, incapable of speaking, fell weeping into his arms. "Daughter," said More, restraining himself with an effort, "let us kneel down." He

[1] 17th April, 1534. Cranmer, *Letters and Remains* (Parker Society), p. 286.

repeated the seven penitential Psalms, and then, rising up, said: "Dear Meg, those who have put me here think they have done me a high displeasure, but God treats me as He treats His best friends." Margaret, who thought of nothing but to save her father, exclaimed: "Take the oath! death is hanging over your head." "Nothing will happen to me but what pleases God," replied Sir Thomas More. His daughter left the Tower, overwhelmed with grief. His wife, who also went to see him, chancellor Audley, the dukes of Norfolk and Suffolk, Cromwell, and other of the king's counsellors were not more successful than Margaret. Bishop Fisher met similar solicitations with a similar refusal.

As the king's government did not wish to hurry on the trial of these illustrious men, they turned from the chiefs to the followers. The Carthusians of London were in great odour of sanctity; they never spoke except at certain times, ate no meat, and affirmed that God had visited them in visions and miracles. Their house was not free from disorders, but many of the monks took their vocation seriously. When the royal commissioners visited them to tender the oath of succession, Prior Haughton, a man of small stature but agreeable appearance and noble carriage, appeared before them. The commissioners required him to acknowledge Henry's second marriage to be lawful; Haughton at first sought a loophole, and answered that the king might be divorced and married without him or his monks having anything to say to it. "It is the king's command," answered the commissioners, "that you and your brethren acknowledge by oath the lawfulness of his union. Call the monks together." The Carthusians appeared, and all refused to take the oath. The prior and proctor were consequently sent to the Tower. The Bishop of London used all his influence to make them change their opinions, and succeeded in persuading them that they might take the oath, by making several reservations. They therefore returned to the Charter-House and prevailed upon their brethren to do as they had done.

Immediately all was confusion in the monastery. Several monks in deep distress could not tell which course to follow: others, more decided, exclaimed that they would not yield at any price. "They are minded to offer themselves in sacrifice to the great idol of Rome," wrote Bedyll to Cromwell. At last, when the soldiers appeared to take the rebels to the Tower, the terrified monks lost heart, and took the oath to the new marriage of Henry VIII "so far as it was lawful." The bitter cup was removed, but not for long.

Whilst England was separating from Rome, Clement VII was dying of vexation. The hatred felt by the Romans towards him was only equalled by the joy they experienced at the election of his successor. Alexander Farnese, the choice of the French party, was a man of the world, desirous of putting down the protestants, recovering England, reforming the Church, and above all enriching his own family. When Da Casale, Henry's envoy, presented his homage: "There is nothing in the world," said Paul III to him, "that I have more at heart than to satisfy your master." It was too late.

Clement's behaviour had produced an evil influence on the character of the Tudor king. The services rendered by this prince to the papacy had been overlooked, his long patience had not been rewarded: he fancied himself despised and deceived. His pride was irritated, his temper grew fiercer, his violence, for some time restrained, broke out, and, unable to reach the pope, he revenged himself on the papacy. Until now, he had scarcely been worse than most of the sovereigns of Christendom: from this moment, when he proclaimed himself head of the Church, he became harsh, and cared for nothing but gratifying his evil inclinations, his despotic humours, his bloodthirsty cruelty. As a *prince*, he had at times shown a few amiable qualities; as a *pope*, he was nothing but a tyrant.

Henry VIII, observing the agitation his pretensions caused in England, and wishing to strengthen his new authority, had caused several bills concerning the Church to be brought into the parliament, which met on the 3rd of November, 1534, and continued in session until the 18th of December. The ministers who had drafted them, far from being protestants, were zealous partisans of scholastic orthodoxy. They included the cunning Gardiner, a furious Catholic; the duke of Norfolk, who assisted in the king's movements against Rome only to prevent him from falling into the arms of the reformers; and the politic Cromwell, who, despite his zeal against the pope, declared at his death, possibly giving a particular meaning to the words, that he died in the catholic faith.[1]

The first act passed by parliament was the ratification of the king's new title, already officially recognized by the clergy. Henry's ministers knew how to make the law strict and rigorous. "It is enacted," so ran the act, "that our lord the king be acknowledged sole and supreme head on earth of the Church of England; that he shall possess not only the honours, jurisdictions, and profits attached to that dignity, but also full authority to put down all heresies and enormities, whatever be the customs and the laws that may be opposed to it."[2] Parliament also enacted that "whoever should do anything tending to deprive the king or his heirs of any of their titles, or should call him heretic, schismatic, usurper, &c., should be guilty of high treason."[3]

Thus Henry VIII united the two swords in his hand, and virtually became a pope in his own dominions. Whether a pope claims to be king, or a king claims to be pope, it comes to nearly the same thing. At the time when the Reformation was emancipating the long-enslaved Church, a new master was given it, and what a master! The consciences of Christians revolted against this order of things. One day—it was some time later—Cranmer was asked: "Who is the supreme head of the Church of England?"—"Christ," was the reply, "as He is of the universal Church."—"But did you not recognize the king as supreme head of the Church?"—"We recognized him as head of *all the people of England*," answered Cranmer, "of *churchmen* as well as of *laymen*."[4]—"What! not of the Church?" "No! *Supreme head of the Church* never had any other meaning than what I tell you." This is explicit. If the title given to Henry only signified that he was king of the clergy as well as of the laity, and that the former were under the jurisdiction of the royal courts as well as the latter, in all matters of common law, there can be nothing fairer. But how was it that Cranmer did not find as much courage in Henry's

---

[1] "I die in the catholic faith, not doubting in any article of my faith."— Foxe, *Acts*, v. p. 402.

[2] Act of Supremacy: 26 Henry VIII, c. 1.

[3] *Ibid.* c. 13.

[4] "Of all the people of England, as well ecclesiastical as temporal."— Cranmer, *Letters and Remains* (Parker Society), p. 224.

lifetime to speak according to his conscience, as when examined in 1555 by Brokes, the papal sub-delegate? An interpretative document drawn up by the government at almost the same time as the act of parliament, corroborates however the explanation made by Cranmer; it said: "The title of supreme head of the Church gives the king no new authority: it does not signify that he can assume any spiritual power." This document declares that the words *reform abuses and heresies* indicate the authority which the king possesses to suppress the powers which the bishop of Rome or other bishops have usurped in his realm. "We heartily detest," said William Fulke, Master of Pembroke Hall, Cambridge, "the notion that the king can do what he likes in matters of religion."[1] Even Elizabeth refused the title of head of the Church.[2] Probably these are facts which are not generally known.

[1] Fulke's *Defence* (Parker Society), p. 489.
[2] Jewel's *Works*, (Parker Society), iv. p. 1144.

CHAPTER FIVE

Henry Destroys his Opponents

(1534–1535)

IN England it was reserved for Catholics as well as for evangelicals to give the world, amid great misery, remarkable examples of Christian virtues. Latimer and others preached the truth courageously; martyrs like Bilney, Tewkesbury, and Fryth had laid down their lives for the Gospel. Now in the other party, laymen, monks, and priests, with unquestionably a less enlightened piety, were about to furnish proofs of their sincerity. There were Roman martyrs also. Two armies were in presence; many fell on both sides; but there was a sensible difference between this spiritual war and the wars of nations. Those who bit the dust did not fall under the weapons of a hostile army: there was a third power, the king-pope, who took his station between the two lines, and dealt his blows now to the right, now to the left. Leaders of the pontifical army were to be smitten in the struggle in which so many evangelicals had already fallen.

Sir Thomas More, while in prison, strove to banish afflicting thoughts by writing a history of Christ's passion. One day when he came to these words of the Gospel: *Then came they and laid hands on Jesus, and took him*, the door opened, and Sir William Kingston, the constable of the Tower, accompanied by Sir Richard Rich, the solicitor-general, appeared. "Sir Thomas," said Rich, "if an act of parliament ordered all Englishmen to acknowledge me as their king, would you acknowledge me?"—"Yes, sir."—"And if an act of parliament ordered all Englishmen to recognize me as pope?"—"Parliament has no authority to do it," answered More. Sir Thomas held that an act of parliament was sufficient to dethrone a king of England: it is to a great-grandson of More that we are indebted for this opinion, which a grand-nephew of Cromwell put into practice a hundred years later. Was Henry

VIII exasperated because More disposed so freely of his crown? It is possible, but be that as it may, the harshness of his imprisonment was increased. Suffering preceded martyrdom. The illustrious scholar was forced to pick up little scraps of paper on which to write a few scattered thoughts with a coal. This was not the worst. "I have neither shirt nor sute," he wrote to the chief secretary of state, "nor yet other clothes that are necessary for me to wear, but that be ragged and rent too shamefully. Notwithstanding, I might easily suffer that if that would keep my body warm. And now in my age my stomach may not away but with a few kind of meats; which, if I want, I decay forthwith, and fall into crases and diseases of my body, and cannot keep myself in health. . . . I beseech you be a good master unto me in my necessity, and let me have such things as are necessary for me in mine age. Restore me to my liberty out of this cold and painful imprisonment. Let me have some priest to hear my confession against this holy time, and some books to say my devotions more effectually. The Lord send you a merry Christmas.

"At the Tower, 23rd December."

It is a relief to hope that this scandalous neglect proceeded from heedlessness and not from cruelty. His requests were granted.

While these sad scenes were enacted in the Tower, there was great confusion in all England, where the most opposite parties were in commotion. When the traditional yoke was broken, every man raised up his own banner. The friends of More and Fisher wished to restore the papacy of the Roman bishop; Henry VIII, Cromwell, and the court thought how to establish the supremacy of the king; Cranmer and a few men of the same stamp endeavoured to steer between these quicksands, and aspired to introduce the reign of Holy Scripture under the banner of royalty. This contest between forces so different, complicated too by the passions of the sovereign, was a terrible drama destined to wind up not in a single catastrophe, but in many. Illustrious victims, taken indiscriminately from all parties, were to fall beneath the oft-repeated blows and be buried in one common grave.

The prudent Cranmer lived in painful anxiety. Surrounded

by enemies who watched every step, he feared to destroy the
cause of truth by undertaking reforms as extensive as those on
the Continent. The natural timidity of his character, the
compromises he thought it his duty to make with regard to
the hierarchy, his fear of Henry VIII, his moderation, gentleness, and plasticity of character and in some respects of
principle, prevented his applying to the work with the decision
of a Luther, a Calvin, or a Knox. Tyndale, if he had possessed
the influence that was his due, would have accomplished a
reform similar to that of those great leaders. To have had
him for a reformer would, in Wycliffe's native land, have
been the source of great prosperity; but such a thing was
impossible: his country gave him—not a professor's chair but
exile. Cranmer moved forward slowly: he modified an
evangelical movement by a clerical concession. When he
had taken a step forward, he stopped suddenly, and apparently
drew back; not from cowardice, but because his extreme
prudence so urged him. The boldness of a Farel or a Knox
is in our opinion far more noble; and yet this extreme
moderation saved Cranmer and English protestantism with
him. Near a throne like that of Henry's, it was only a man
of extreme caution who could have retained his position in
the see of Canterbury. Cranmer knew that if he came into
collision with the Tudor's sceptre, he would find it a sword.
God gives to every people and to every epoch the man
necessary to it. Cranmer was this man for England, at the
time of her separation from the papacy. Notwithstanding his
compromises, he never abandoned the great principles of the
Reformation; notwithstanding his concessions, he took advantage of every opportunity to encourage those who shared his
faith to march towards a better future. The primate of
England held a torch in his hand which had not the brilliancy
of that borne by Luther and Calvin, but the tempest that
blew upon it for fifteen or twenty years could not extinguish
it. Sometimes he was seized with terror: as he heard the lion
roar, he bent his head, kept in the background, and concealed the truth in his bosom; but again he rose and again
held out to the Church the light he had saved from the fury
of the tyrant. He was a reed and not an oak—a reed that bent
too easily, but through this very weakness he was able to do

what an oak with all its strength would never have accomplished. The truth triumphed.

At this time Cranmer thought himself in a position to take a step—the most important step of all: he undertook to give the Bible to the laity. When the convocation of clergy and parliament had assembled, he made a proposition that the Holy Scriptures should be translated into English by certain honourable and learned men, and be circulated among the people. To present Holy Scripture as the supreme rule instead of the pope was the bold act that decided the evangelical reformation. Stokesley, Gardiner, and the other bishops of the catholic party cried out against such a monstrous design: "The teaching of the Church is sufficient," they said; "we must prohibit Tyndale's Testament and the heretical books which come to us from beyond the sea." The archbishop saw that he could only carry his point by giving up something: he consented to a compromise. Convocation resolved on the 19th of December, 1534, to lay Cranmer's proposal before the king, but with the addition that the Scriptures translated into the vulgar tongue should only be circulated among the king's subjects in proportion to their knowledge, and that all who possessed suspected books should be bound to give them up to the royal commissioners: others might have called this resolution a defeat, Cranmer looked upon it as a victory. The Scriptures would no longer be admitted stealthily into the kingdom, like contraband goods: they would appear in broad daylight with the royal sanction. This was something.

Henry granted the petition of Convocation, but hastened to profit by it. His great fixed idea was to destroy the Roman papacy in England, not because of its errors, but because he felt that it robbed princes of the affection and often of the obedience of their subjects. "If I grant my bishops what they ask for," he said, "in my turn I ask them to make oath never to permit any jurisdiction to be restored to the Roman bishop in my kingdom; never to call him *pope*, universal *bishop*, or most holy lord, but only bishop of Rome, colleague and brother, according to the ancient custom of the oldest bishops." All the prelates were eager to obey the king; but the archbishop of York, secretly devoted to the Roman Church, added, to acquit his conscience, "that he took the oath in order to preserve the unity of the faith and of the Catholic Church."

Cranmer was filled with joy by the victory he had won. "If we possess the Holy Scriptures," he said, "we have at hand a remedy for every disease. Beset as we are with tribulations and temptations, where can we find arms to overcome them? In Scripture. It is the balm that will heal our wounds, and will be a more precious jewel in our houses than either gold or silver." He therefore turned his mind at once to the realization of the plan he had so much at heart. Taking for groundwork an existing translation (doubtless that by Tyndale) he divided the New Testament into ten portions, had each transcribed separately, and transmitted them to the most learned of the bishops, praying that they might be returned to him with their remarks. He even thought it his duty not to omit such decided catholics as Stokesley and Gardiner.

The day appointed for the return and examination of these various portions having arrived (June 1535) Cranmer set to work, and found that the *Acts of the Apostles* were wanting: they had fallen to the lot of the bishop of London. When the primate's secretary went to ask for the manuscript, Stokesley replied in a very bad humour: "I do not understand my lord of Canterbury. By giving the people the Holy Scriptures, he will plunge them into heresy. I certainly will not give an hour to such a task. Here, take the book back to my lord." When the secretary delivered his message, Thomas Lawney, one of Cranmer's friends, said with a smile: "My lord of London will not take the trouble to examine the Scriptures, persuaded that there is nothing for him in the Testament of Jesus Christ." Many of the portions returned by the other bishops were pitiable. The Archbishop saw that he must find colleagues better disposed.

Cranmer had soon to discharge another function. As popery and rebellion were openly preached in the dioceses of Winchester and London, the metropolitan announced his intention to visit them. The two bishops cried out vehemently, and Gardiner hurried to the king: "Your Grace," he said, "here is a new pope!" All who had anything to fear began to reproach the primate with aspiring to honours and dominion. "God forgive me," he said with simplicity, "if there is any title in the world I care for more than *the paring of an apple*.[1] Neither paper, parchment, lead, nor wax, but the very Christian conversation of the people, are the letters and seals of our office." The king supported Cranmer, knowing that certain of the clergy preached submission to the pope. The visitation took place. Even in London priests were found who had taken the oath prescribed by Henry VIII, and who yet "made a god of the Roman pontiff, setting his power and his laws above those of our Lord." "I command you," said the king, "to lay hold of all who circulate those pernicious doctrines."

Francis I watched these severities from afar. He feared they would render an alliance between France and England impossible. He therefore sent Bryon, high-admiral of France, to London, to reconcile the king with the pope, to strengthen the bonds that united the two countries, and at the same time, he prevailed upon Paul III to withdraw the decree of Clement VII against Henry VIII. But success did not crown his efforts: the king of England had no great confidence in the sincerity of the pope or of the French king. He was well pleased to be no longer confronted by a foreign authority in his own dominions, and thought that his people would never give up the Reformation. Instead of being reconciled with the Roman pontiff, he found it more convenient to imitate the pope, and to break out against those subjects who refused to recognize him, the king, as head of the Church.

He first attacked the Carthusians, the most respectable of the religious orders in England, and whom he considered as the most dangerous. Where there was the most goodness, there was also the most strength; and that strength gave umbrage to the despotic Tudor king.

Monastic life, abominable in its abuses, was, even in principle, contrary to the Gospel. But we must confess that there was a certain harmony between the wants of society in the Middle Ages and monastic establishments. Many and various motives drove into the cloisters the men that filled them; and if some were condemnable, there were others whose value deserves to be appreciated. It was these earnest

[1] Cranmer, *Letters and Remains* (Parker Society), p. 305.

monks who, even while defending the royalty of the pope, rejected most energetically the papacy of the king: this was enough to draw down upon them the royal vengeance. One day a messenger from the court brought to the Charter-House of London an order to reject the Roman authority. The monks, summoned by their prior, remained silent when they heard the message, and their features alone betrayed the trouble of their minds. "My heart is full of sorrow," said Prior Haughton. "What are we to do? If we resist the king, our house will be shut up, and you young men will be cast into the midst of the world, so that after commencing here in the spirit you will end there in the flesh. But, on the other hand, how can we obey? Alas! I am helpless to save those whom God has entrusted to my care!" At these words the Carthusians "fell all a-weeping"; and then, taking courage from the presence of danger, they said: "We will perish together in our integrity; and heaven and earth shall cry out against the injustice that oppresses us."—"Would to God it might be so," exclaimed the Superior; "but this is what they will do. They will put me to death—me and the oldest of us— and they will turn the younger ones into the world, which will teach them its wicked works. I am ready to give up my life to save you; but if one death does not satisfy the king, then let us all die!"—"Yes, we will all die," answered the brethren. —"And now let us make preparation by a general confession," said the prior, "so that the Lord may find us ready."

Next morning the chapel-doors opened and all the monks marched in. Their serious looks, their pale countenances, their fixed eyes seemed to betoken men who were awaiting their last moments. The prior went into the pulpit and read the sixtieth Psalm: "*O God, thou hast cast us off.*" On coming to the end, he said: "My brethren, we must die in charity. Let us pardon one another." At these words Haughton came down from the pulpit, and knelt in succession before every brother, saying: "O my brother, I beg your forgiveness of all my offences!" The other monks, each in his turn, made this last confession.

Two days afterwards they celebrated the mass of the Holy Ghost. Immediately after the elevation, the monks fancied they heard "a small hissing wind." Their hearts were

filled with a tender affection: they believed that the Holy
Ghost was descending upon them, and the prior, touched
by this surprising grace, burst into tears. Enthusiasm mingled
extraordinary fantasies with their pious emotions.

The king had evidently not much to fear in this quarter.
His crown was threatened by more formidable enemies. In
various parts, especially in Lincolnshire and Yorkshire, there
were daring partisans of the papacy to be found who endeavoured to stir up the people to revolt; and thousands of
Englishmen in the North were ready to help them by force of
arms. At the same time Ireland wished to transport her
soldiers across St. George's Channel and hurl the king from
his throne. The decision with which Fisher, Sir Thomas More,
and the Carthusians resisted Henry had not immediate
insurrection for its object, but it encouraged the multitude to
revolt. The government, thinking, therefore, that it was time
to strike, sent the Carthusians an absolute order to acknowledge
the royal supremacy.

At this time there was in reality no liberty on one side or
the other. Rome, by not granting it, was consistent with
herself; but not so the protestantism that denies it. The
Reformation, acknowledging no other sovereign Lord and
Teacher than God, must of necessity leave the conscience to
the Supreme Master, man having nothing to do with it. But
the Roman Church, acknowledging a man as its head, and
honouring the pope as the representative of God on earth,
claims authority over the soul. Men may say in vain that
they are in harmony with God and His Word: that is not the
question. The great business is to be in accord with the pope.
That old man, throned in the Vatican on the traditions of the
Church and the bulls of his predecessors, is their judge: they
are bound to follow exactly his line, without wavering either
to the right or the left. If they reject an article, a jot of a
papal constitution, they must be cast away. Such a system,
the enemy of every liberty, even of the most legitimate, rose
in the sixteenth century like a high wall to separate Rome
and the new generation. It threatened to destroy in the future
that power which had triumphed in the past.

After the festival of Easter 1535, the heads of two other
Carthusian houses—Robert Laurence, prior of Belleval, and

Augustine Webster, prior of Axholm—arrived in London in obedience to an order they had received, and, in company with Prior Haughton, waited upon Cromwell. As they refused to acknowledge the royal supremacy, they were sent to the Tower. A week later, they consented to take the oath, adding: "So far as God's law permits."—"No restrictions," answered Cromwell. On the 29th of April they were placed on their trial, when they said: "We will never believe anything contrary to the law of God and the teaching of our holy mother Church." At first the jury expressed some interest in their behalf; but Haughton uselessly embittered his position. "You can only produce in favour of your opinion," he said, "the parliament of one single kingdom; for mine, I can produce all Christendom." The jury found the three prisoners guilty of high-treason. Thence the government proceeded to more eminent victims.

Fisher and More, confined in the same prison, were now treated with more consideration. It was said, however, that these illustrious captives were endeavouring, even in the Tower, to excite the people to revolt. The king and Cromwell could hardly have believed it, but they imagined that if these two leading men gave way, their example would carry the recalcitrants with them: they were therefore exposed to a new examination. But they proved as obstinate as their adversaries, and perhaps more skilful. "I have no more to do with the titles to be given to popes and princes," said Sir Thomas; "my thoughts are with God alone."

The court hoped to intimidate these eminent personages by the execution of the three priors, which took place on the 4th May, 1535. Margaret hurried to her father's side. Before long the procession passed under his window, and the affectionate young woman used every means to draw Sir Thomas away from the sight; but he would not avert his eyes. When all was over, he turned to his daughter: "Meg," he said, "you saw those saintly fathers; they went as cheerfully to death as if they were bridegrooms going to be married."

The prisoners walked calmly along: they wore their clerical robes, the ceremony of degradation not having been performed, no doubt to show that a papal consecration could not protect offenders. Haughton, prior of the London Charter-House, mounted the ladder first. "I pray all who hear me," he said, "to bear witness for me in the terrible day of judgment, that it is not out of obstinate malice or rebellion that I disobey the king, but only for the fear of God." The rope was now placed round his neck. "Holy Jesus!" he exclaimed, "have mercy on me," and he gave up the ghost. The other priors then stepped forward. "God has manifested great grace to us," they said, "by calling us to die in defence of the catholic faith. No, the king is not head of the Church in England." A few minutes later and these monks, dressed in the robes of their order, were swinging in the air. This was one of the crimes committed when the unlawful tiara of the pontiffs was placed unlawfully on the head of a king of England. Other Carthusians were put to death somewhat later.

Meanwhile Henry VIII desired to preserve a balance between papists and heretics. The Roman tribunals struck one side only, but this strange prince gloried in striking both sides at once. An opportunity of doing so occurred. Some anabaptists from the Low Countries were convicted on the 25th of May: two of them were taken to Smithfield and twelve others sent to different cities, where they suffered the punishment by fire. All of them went to death with cheerful hearts.

The turn of the illustrious captives was at hand.

CHAPTER SIX

Two Notable Executions

(May to September 1535)

Not long after the death of the Carthusians, Cromwell paid More a visit. Henry VIII loved his former chancellor, and desired to save his life. "I am your friend," said Cromwell, "and the king is a good and gracious lord towards you." He then once again invited More to accept the act of parliament which proclaimed the king's supremacy; and the same steps were taken with Fisher. Both refused what was asked. From that moment the execution of the sentence could not be long delayed. More felt this, and, as soon as the Secretary of State had left him, he took a piece of coal and wrote some verses upon the wall, expressive of the peace of his soul.

Henry and his minister seemed however to hesitate. It had not troubled them much to punish a few papists and obscure anabaptists; but to put to death an ex-chancellor of the realm and an old tutor of the king—both personages so illustrious and so esteemed throughout Christendom—was another thing. Several weeks passed away. It was an act of the pope that hastened the death of these two men. On the 20th of May, Paul III created a certain number of cardinals: John Du Bellay, Contarini, Caracciolo, and lastly, Fisher, bishop of Rochester. The news of this creation burst upon Rome and London like a clap of thunder. Da Casale, Henry's agent at the papal court, exclaimed that it was offering his master the greatest affront possible: the matter was the talk of the whole city. "Your Holiness has never committed a more serious mistake than this," said De Casale to the pope. Paul tried to justify himself. As England desired to become reconciled with the Vatican, he said, it seemed to him that he could not do better than nominate an English cardinal. When Fisher heard the news, he said piously: "If the cardinal's hat were at my feet, I would not stoop to pick it up." But Henry did not take the matter so calmly: he considered the pope's proceedings as an insolent challenge. Confer the highest honours on a man convicted of treason—is it not encouraging subjects to revolt? Henry seemed to have thought that it would be unnecessary to take away the life of an old man whose end could not be far off; but the pope exasperated him. Since they place Fisher among the cardinals in Rome, in England he shall be counted among the dead. Pope Paul may, as long as he likes, send him the hat; but when the hat arrives, there shall be no head on which to place it.

On the 14th of June, 1535, Thomas Bedyll and other officers of justice proceeded to the Tower. The Bishop would give no answer to the demand that he should recognize the king as head of the Church. Sir Thomas More, when questioned in his turn, replied: "My only study is to meditate on Christ's passion." "Do you acknowledge the king as supreme head of the Church?" asked Bedyll. "The royal supremacy is established by law."—"That law is a two-edged sword," returned the ex-chancellor. "If I accept it, it kills my soul; if I reject it, it kills my body."

Three days later the bishop was condemned to be beheaded. When the order for his execution arrived, the prisoner was asleep: they respected his slumber. At five o'clock the next morning, 22nd of June, 1535, Kingston, entering his cell, aroused him and told him that it was the king's good pleasure he should be executed that morning. "I most humbly thank his Majesty," said the old man, "that he is pleased to relieve me from all the affairs of this world. Grant me only an hour or two more, for I slept very badly last night." Then turning towards the wall, he fell asleep again. Between seven and eight o'clock he called his servant, took off the hair-shirt which he wore next his skin to mortify the flesh, and gave it to the man. "Let no one see it," he said. "And now bring me my best clothes."—"My lord," said the astonished servant, "does not your lordship know that in two hours you will take them off never to put them on again?"—"Exactly so," answered Fisher; "this is my wedding-day, and I ought to dress as if for a holiday."

At nine o'clock the lieutenant appeared. The old man—he

was about seventy-six years old—took up his New Testament, made the sign of the cross, and left the cell. He was tall, being six feet high, but his body was bent with age, and his weakness so great that he could hardly get down the stairs. He was placed in an arm-chair. When the porters stopped near the gate of the Tower to know if the sheriffs were ready, Fisher stood up, and, leaning against the wall, opened his Testament, and, lifting his eyes to heaven, said: "O Lord! I open it for the last time. Grant that I may find some word of comfort to the end that I may glorify Thee in my last hour." The first words he saw were these: *And this is life eternal, that they might know thee the only true God, and Jesus Christ whom thou hast sent.*[1] Fisher closed the book and said: "That will do. Here is learning enough to last me to my life's end."

The funeral procession was set in motion. Clouds hid the face of the sun; the day was gloomy; the streets through which they passed seemed dull and in harmony with men's hearts. A large body of armed men surrounded the pious old man, who kept repeating in a low tone the words of his Testament: *Hæc est autem vita æterna, ut cognoscant te solum verum Deum et quem misisti Jesum Christum* (John 17. 3). They reached Smithfield. "We will help you to ascend," said his bearers at the foot of the scaffold. "No, Sirs," he replied, and then added in a cheerful tone: "Come, feet! do your duty, you have not far to go." Just as he mounted the scaffold, the sun burst out and shone upon his face: *They looked unto him and were lightened,* he cried, *and their faces were not ashamed.* It was ten o'clock. The noble bearing and piety of the aged bishop inspired all around him with respect. The executioner knelt before him and begged his forgiveness. "With all my heart," he made answer. Having laid aside his robe and furred gown, he turned to the people, and said with gravity and joy: "Christians, I give my life for my faith in the holy catholic Church of Christ. I do not fear death. Assist me, however, with your prayers, so that when the axe falls I may remain firm. God save the king and the kingdom!" The brightness of his face at this moment struck the spectators. He fell on his knees and said: "Eternal God, my hope is in Thy deliverance." The executioner approached and bound his eyes. The bishop raised his hands,

[1] John 17. 3. The Testament was in Latin.

uttered a cry towards heaven, and laid his head on the block. The doomsman seized his heavy axe, and cut off the head at one blow. It was exposed for a time by Henry's orders on London Bridge and then thrown into the river; but soldiers carried the body to Barking church-yard, where they dug a lowly grave for it with their halberds. Later, it was removed to St. Peter's *ad vincula* in the Tower, where it lies beside that of Sir Thomas More. Doubts have been thrown upon the details of this death; we believe them to be authentic, and it is a pleasure by reporting them to place a crown on the tomb of a Roman-catholic bishop whose end was that of a pious man.

It was now the turn of Sir Thomas More. On the 1st of July, 1535, he was summoned before a special commission and a packed jury. The former Chancellor of England quitted his prison in a frieze cloak, which had grown foul in the dungeon, and proceeded on foot through the most frequented streets of London on his road to Westminster. His thin pale face; his white hair, the effect not of time but of sorrow and imprisonment; the staff on which he leant, for he walked with difficulty, made a deep impression on the people. When he arrived at the bar of the tribunal, and looked around him, though weakened by suffering, with a countenance full of mildness, all the spectators were moved. The indictment was long and involved: he was accused of high-treason. Sir Thomas, endeavouring to keep on his feet, said: "My Lords, the charges brought against me are so numerous, that I fear, considering my great weakness, I shall be unable to remember them all." He stopped: his body trembled and he was near falling. A chair was brought him, and after taking his seat, he continued: "I have never uttered a single word in opposition to the statute which proclaims the king head of the Church." "If we cannot produce your words," said the king's attorney, "we can produce your silence."—"No one can be condemned for his silence," nobly answered More. "*Qui tacet consentire videtur* (Silence gives consent) according to the lawyers."

Nothing could save him: the jury returned a verdict of guilty. "Now that all is over," said the prisoner, "I will speak. Yes, the oath of supremacy is illegal. The Great Charter laid down that *the Church of England is free*, so that its rights and liberties might be equally preserved."—"The Church must be *free*," said the lawyers; "it is not therefore the slave of the pope."—"Yes, *free*," retorted More; "it is not therefore the slave of the king." The chancellor then pronounced sentence, condemning him to be hanged and quartered. Henry spared his illustrious subject and old friend from this degrading treatment, and instead ordered that he should be beheaded. "God save all my friends from his Majesty's favour," said Sir Thomas, "and spare my children from similar indulgences. . . . I hope, my lords," said the ex-chancellor, turning meekly towards his judges, "that though you have condemned me on earth, we may all meet hereafter in heaven."

Sir William Kingston approached; armed guards surrounded the condemned man, and the sad procession moved forward. One of the Tower wardens marched in front, bearing an axe with the edge turned towards More; it was a token to the people of the prisoner's fate. As soon as he crossed the threshold of the court, his son, who was waiting for him, fell at his feet distracted and in tears: "Your blessing, father," he exclaimed, "your blessing!" More raised him up, kissed him tenderly, and blessed him. His daughter Margaret was not there: she had fainted immediately on hearing of her father's condemnation. He was taken back to prison in a boat, perhaps to withdraw this innocent and illustrious man, treated like a criminal, from the eyes of the citizens of London. When they got near the Tower, the governor, who had until then kept his emotion under, turned to More and bade him farewell, the tears running down his cheeks. "My dear Kingston," said the noble prisoner, "do not weep; we shall meet again in heaven."—"Yes!" said the lieutenant of the Tower, adding: "you are consoling me, when I ought to console you." An immense crowd covered the wharf at which the boat was to land. Among this crowd, so eager for the mournful spectacle, was a young woman, trembling with emotion and silently waiting for the procession: it was Margaret. At length she heard the steps of the approaching guards, and saw her father appear. She could not move, her strength failed her; she fell on her knees just where she had stood. Her father, who recognized her at a distance, giving way to the keenest emotions, lifted up his hands and blessed her. This was not

enough for Margaret. The blessing had caused a strong
emotion in her, and had restored life to her soul. Regardless
of her sex, her age, and the surrounding crowd, that feeble
woman, to whom at this supreme moment filial piety gave the
strength of many men, says a contemporary, rushed towards
her father, and bursting through the officers and halberdiers
by whom he was surrounded, fell on his neck and embraced
him, exclaiming: "Father, father!" She could say no more;
grief stopped her voice: she could only weep, and her tears
fell on her father's bosom. The soldiers halted in emotion;
Sir Thomas, the prey at once of the tenderest love and
inexpressible grief, felt as if a sword had pierced his heart.
Recovering himself, however, he blessed his child, and said
to her in a voice whose emotion he strove to conceal: "Daughter,
I am innocent; but remember that however hard the blow with
which I am struck, it comes from God. Submit thy will to the
good pleasure of the Lord."

The captain of the escort, wishing to put an end to a scene
that might agitate the people, bade two soldiers take Margaret
away; but she clung to her father with arms that were like
bars of iron, and it was with difficulty that she could be
removed. She had been hardly set on the ground a few steps
off, when she sprang up again, and thrusting those who had
separated her from him she so loved, she broke through the
crowd once more, fell upon his neck, and kissed him several
times with a convulsive effort. In her, filial love had all the
vehemence of passion. More, whom the sentence of death
had not been able to move, lost all energy, and the tears
poured down his cheeks. The crowd watched this touching
scene with deep excitement and "they were very few in all
the troop who could refrain from weeping; no, not the guards
themselves." Even the soldiers wept, and refused to tear the
daughter again from her father's arms. Two or three, however,
of the less agitated stepped forward and carried Margaret
away. The women of her household, who had accompanied
her, immediately surrounded her and bore her away from a
sight of such inexpressible sadness. The prisoner entered the
Tower.

Sir Thomas spent six more days and nights in prison. We
hear certainly of his pious words, but the petty practices of

H(II)

an ascetic seemed to engross him. His macerations were increased: he walked up and down his cell, wearing only a winding-sheet, as if he were already a corpse waiting to be buried. He often scourged himself for a long time together, and with extraordinary violence. Yet at the same time he indulged in Christian meditations. "I am afflicted," he wrote to one of his friends, "shut up in a dungeon; but God in His mercy will soon deliver me from this world of tribulation. Walls will no longer separate us, and we shall have holy conversations together, which no gaoler will interrupt." On the 5th of July, desiring to bid his daughter a last farewell, More took a piece of charcoal (he had nothing else) and wrote to her: "To-morrow is St. Thomas's day, and my saint's day; accordingly, I desire extremely that it may be the day of my departure. My child, I never loved you so dearly as when last you kissed me. I like when daughterly love has no leisure to look unto worldly courtesy. . . . Farewell my dearly beloved daughter; pray for me. I pray for you all, to the end that we may meet in heaven."

Thus one of the closest and holiest affections, that of a father for his daughter, and of a daughter for her father, softened the last moments of this distinguished man. Sir Thomas sent Margaret his hair-shirt and scourge, which he desired to conceal from the eyes of the indifferent. What an inheritance!

That night he slept quietly, and the next morning early (6th of July, 1535) a fortnight after the death of Bishop Fisher, Sir Thomas Pope, one of his familiar friends, came to inform him that he must hold himself in readiness. "I thank the king," said More, "for shutting me up in this prison, whereby he has put me in a condition to make suitable preparation for death. The only favour I beg of him is, that my daughter may be present at my burial." Pope left the cell in tears. Then the prisoner put on a fine silk robe which his wealthy friend Bonvisi, the merchant of Lucca, had given him. "Leave that dress here," said Kingston, "for the man to whom it falls by custom is only a gaoler."—"I cannot look upon that man as a gaoler," answered More, "who opens the gates of heaven for me."

At nine o'clock the procession quitted the Tower. More

was calm, his face pale, his beard long and curly; he carried a crucifix in his hand, and his eyes were often turned towards heaven. A numerous and sympathetic crowd watched him pass along—a man one time so honoured, privy councillor, speaker of the House of Commons, president of the House of Lords—whom armed men were now leading to the scaffold. Just as he was passing in front of a house of mean appearance, a poor woman standing at the door, went up to him and offered him a cup of wine to strengthen him: "Thank you," he said gently, "thank you, Christ drank vinegar only." On arriving at the place of execution: "Give me your hand to help me up," he said to Kingston, adding: "As for my coming down, you may let me shift for myself." He mounted the scaffold. Sir Thomas Pope, at the king's request, had begged him to make no speech, fearing the effect this illustrious man might produce upon the people. More desired however to say a few words, but the sheriff stopped him. "I die," he was content to say, "in the faith of the catholic Church, and a faithful servant of God and the king." He then knelt down and repeated the fifty-first Psalm:[1] *Have mercy upon me, O God, according to thy loving-kindness: according unto the multitude of thy tender mercies blot out my transgressions.* When he rose up, the executioner begged his forgiveness: "Why do you talk of forgiveness?" replied More; "you are doing me the greatest kindness I ever received from man." He desired the man not to be afraid to do his office, and remarked that his neck was very short. With his own hands he fastened a bandage over his eyes, and then laid his head on the block. The executioner, holding the axe, was preparing to strike, when More stopped him, and, putting his beard carefully on one side, said: "This at least has not committed treason." Such words, almost jesting, no doubt startle us at such a moment; but strong men have often been observed to manifest the calmness of their souls in such a manner. More probably feared that his long beard would embarrass the executioner, and deaden the blow. At length that head fell through which so many noble thoughts had passed; that keen clear eye was closed; those eloquent lips were the lips of a corpse. The head was exposed on London Bridge, and Margaret discharged the

[1] The fiftieth of the Vulgate: *Miserere mei, Deus.*

painful duty her father had bequeathed her, by piously burying his body.[1]

Thus, at the cost of his life, this eminent man protested against the aberrations of a cruel prince, who usurped the title given by the Bible to Jesus Christ alone. The many evangelical martyrs who had been sacrificed in different countries and who were yet to be sacrificed, showed in general, to a greater extent than Fisher and More, an ardent love for the Saviour, a lively hope of eternal life; but none showed greater calmness than they. These two good men wanted discernment as to what constitutes the pure Gospel; their piety bound them too much, as we have said, to monastic practices; they had (and More especially) in the days of their power persecuted the disciples of the Lord, and though they rejected the usurpations of the king, had acted as fanatical defenders of those of the pope. But at a time when there were so many cringing bishops and servile nobles—when almost everyone bent the head timidly before the mad popery of Henry VIII, these two firmly held up theirs. More and Fisher were companions in misfortune with Bilney and Fryth: the same royal hand struck them all. Our sympathies are for the victims, our aversion for the executioner.

The death of these two celebrated men caused an immense sensation. In England, the people and even the nobility were struck with astonishment. Could it be true, men asked, that Thomas More, whom Henry had known since he was nine years old, with whom he used to hold friendly conversations by night on the terrace of his country-house, at whose table he used to love to sit down familiarly, whom he had chosen, although a layman and a knight only, to succeed the powerful Wolsey:—could it be true that by the king's orders he had perished by the axe? Could it be true that Fisher had met with the same fate—that venerable old man of almost fourscore years, who had been his preceptor, the trusty friend of his grandmother, and to whose teaching he owed the progress he had made in learning? Men began to see that resistance to a Tudor meant the scaffold. Every one trembled, and even those who had not known the two victims could not restrain their tears.

---

[1] [When Margaret died, by her wish her father's head, which she had herself preserved, was buried with her, in her arms.]

The horror which these executions caused among the enlightened men of the continent was displayed with more liberty and energy. "I am dead," exclaimed Erasmus, "since More is dead; for, as Pythagoras says, we had but one soul between us."—"O England! O dearly beloved country," said Reginald Pole; "he was not only Margaret's father, but thine also!"—"This year is fatal to our order," said Melanchthon the reformer;[1] "I hear that More has been killed and others also. You know how such things wring my heart."—"We banish such criminals," said Francis I sharply to the English ambassador, "but we do not put them to death."—"If I had two such lights in my kingdom," said Charles V, "I would sooner give two of my strongest cities than suffer them to be extinguished." At Rome in particular the anger was extreme. They were still flattering themselves that Henry VIII would return to his old sympathies; but now there was no more hope! The king had put to death a prince of the Church, and as he had sworn, the cardinal's hat could find no head to wear it. A consistory was immediately summoned: the French Cardinal de Tournon's touching letter was read, and all who heard it were moved even to tears. The embarrassed and speechless agents of England knew not what to do; and as they reported, there was everything to be feared.

Perhaps nobody was so much confounded as the pontiff himself. Paul III was circumspect, prudent, deliberative, and temporizing; but when he thought the moment arrived, when he believed further manœuvring was not required, he no longer hesitated, but struck forcibly. It is known that he had two young relations whom, in his blind tenderness, he had created cardinals, notwithstanding their youth and the Emperor's representations. "Alas!" he exclaimed, "I feel as mortally injured as if my two nephews had been killed before my eyes." His most devoted partisans, and above all a cardinal of his creation put to death! There was a violent movement in his heart; he worked himself into a fury; he desired to strike the prince whose cruel deeds had wounded him so deeply. His anger burst out in a thunder-clap. On the 30th of August he sanctioned a bull worthy of Gregory VII, which the more zealous partisans of the papacy would like to remove from the

---

[1] The "order" means that of men of letters.

papal records.[1] "Let King Henry repent of his crimes," said
the pontiff; "we give him ninety days and his accomplices sixty
to appear at Rome. In case of default, we strike him with the
sword of anathema, of malediction, and of eternal damnation;
we take away his kingdom from him: we declare that his body
shall be deprived of ecclesiastical burial; we launch an interdict
against his States; we release his subjects from their oath of
fidelity; we call upon all dukes, marquises and earls to expel
him and his accomplices from England; we unbind all Christian
princes from their oaths towards him, command them to march
against him and constrain him to return to the obedience due
to the Holy Apostolic See, giving them all his goods for their
reward, and he and his to be their slaves."

Anger had the same effect upon the pontiff as inebriety; he
had lost the use of his reason, and allowed himself to be
carried away to threats and excesses of which he would have
been ashamed, had he been sober. Accordingly the drunkenness was hardly over before the unfortunate Paul hastened to
hide his bull, and carefully laid aside his thunderbolts in the
arsenal, free to bring them out later.

Henry VIII, more calm than the pope, having heard of
his discontent, feared to push him to extremities; and Cromwell,
a month after the date of the bull, instructed Da Casale to
justify the king to the Vatican. "Fisher and More," he was to
say, "had on all points of the internal policy of England come
to conclusions diametrically opposed to the quiet and prosperity
of the kingdom. They had held secret conversations with certain
men notorious for their audacity, and had poured into the
hearts of these wretches the poison which they had first prepared in their own. Could we permit their crime, spreading
wider and wider, to give a death-blow to the State? Fisher
and More alone opposed laws which had been accepted by
the general consent of the people, and were necessary to the
prosperity of the kingdom. Our *mildest* of sovereigns could not
longer tolerate an offence so atrocious."[2]

Even these excuses accuse and condemn Henry. Neither
More nor Fisher had entered into a plot against the State;
their resistance had been purely religious; they were free to

[1] Lingard's *History*, iii. ch. iv.
[2] *State Papers*, vii. pp. 634–5.

act according to their consciences. It might have been necessary to take some prudential measures in an age as yet little fitted for liberty; but nothing could excuse the scaffold, erected by the king's orders, for men who were regarded with universal respect.

CHAPTER SEVEN

The Dissolution of the Smaller Monasteries
(September 1535 to 1536)

THE death of the late tutor and friend of the prince was to be followed by a measure less cruel but far more general. The pope who treated kings so rudely should not be surprised if kings treated the monks severely. Henry knew—had indeed been a close witness of their lazy and often irregular lives. One day, when he was hunting in the forest of Windsor, he lost his way, perhaps intentionally, and about the dinner hour knocked at the gate of Reading Abbey. As he represented himself to be one of his Majesty's guards, the abbot said: "You will dine with me"; and the king sat down to a table covered with abundant and delicate dishes. After examining everything carefully: "I will stick to this sir-loin," said he, pointing to a piece of beef of which he ate heartily.[1] The abbot looked on with admiration. "I would give a hundred pounds," he exclaimed, "to eat with as much appetite as you; but alas! my weak and squeazie (qualmish) stomach can hardly digest the wing of a chicken."—"I know how to bring back your appetite," thought the king. A few days later some soldiers appeared at the abbey, took away the abbot, and shut him up in the Tower, where he was put upon bread and water. "What have I done," he kept asking, "to incur his Majesty's displeasure to such a degree?" After a few weeks, Henry went to the state prison, and, concealing himself in an ante-room whence he could see the abbot, ordered a sirloin of beef to be set before him. The famished monk in his turn fell upon the joint, and (according to tradition) ate it all. The king now showed himself: "Sir abbot," he said, "I have

---

[1] "A Sir Loyne of beaf, so knighted by this king Henry."—Fuller, p. 299. [Other traditions attribute the "Sir Loyne" joke to James I and Charles II.]

cured you of your qualms; now pay me my wages. It is a hundred pounds, you know." The abbot paid and returned to Reading; but Henry never after forgot the monks' kitchen.

The state of the monasteries was an occasion of scandal: all religious life had largely died out in most of those establishments. The monks lived, generally, in idleness, gluttony, and licentiousness, and what should have been houses of saints had become in many cases mere sties of lazy gormandizers and impure sensualists. "The only law they recognize," said Luther, speaking of these cloisters, "is that of the seven deadly sins." History encounters here a twofold danger: one is that of keeping back what is essential, the scandalous facts that justified the suppression of monasteries; the other is that of saying things that cannot be named. We must strive to steer between these two quicksands.

All classes of society had become disgusted with the monasteries: the common people would say to the monks: "We labour painfully, while you lead easy and comfortable lives." The nobility regarded them with looks of envy and irony which threatened their wealth. The lawyers considered them as parasitical plants which drew away from others the nutriment they required. These things made the religious orders cry out with alarm: "If we no longer have the pope to protect us, it is all over with us and our monasteries." And they set to work to prevent Henry from separating from the pope: they circulated anonymous stories, seditious songs, trivial lampoons, frightful prophecies and biting satires against the king, Anne Boleyn, and the friends of the Reformation. They held mysterious interviews with the discontented, and took advantage of the confessional to alarm the weak-minded. "The supremacy of the pope," they said, "is a fundamental article of the faith; none who reject it can be saved." People began to fear a general revolt.

When Luther was informed that Henry VIII had abolished the authority of the pope in his kingdom, but had suffered the religious orders to remain, he smiled at the blunder: "The king of England," he said, "weakens the body of the papacy but at the same time strengthens the soul." That could not endure for long.

Cromwell had now attained high honours and was to

mount higher still. He thought with Luther that the pope and the monks could not exist or fall one without the other. After the abolition of the rule of the Roman pontiff, it became necessary to abolish the monasteries. It was he who had prevailed on the king to take the place of head of the Church; and now he wished him to be so really. "Sire," he said to Henry, "cleanse the Lord's field from all the weeds that stifle the good corn, and scatter everywhere the seeds of virtue. In 1525, 1528, 1531 and 1534 the popes themselves lent you their help in the suppression of monasteries; now you no longer require their aid. Do not hesitate, Sire: the most fanatical enemies of your supreme authority are to be found in the religious houses. There is buried the wealth necessary to the prosperity of the nation. The revenues of the religious orders are far greater than those of all the nobility of England. The cloister schools have fallen into decay, and the wants of the age require better ones. To suppress the pope and to keep the monks is like deposing the general and delivering the fortresses of the country up to his army. Sire, imitate the example of the protestants and suppress the monasteries."

Such language alarmed the friends of the papacy, who stoutly opposed a scheme which they believed to be sacrilegious. "These foundations were consecrated to Almighty God," they told the king; "respect therefore those retreats where pious souls live in contemplation." "Contemplation!" said Sir Henry Colt, smiling; "to-morrow, Sire, I undertake to produce proofs of the kind of contemplation in which these monks indulge." Whereupon, says an historian, Colt, knowing that a certain number of the monks of Waltham Abbey had a fondness for the conversation of ladies, and used to pass the night with the nuns of Chesham Convent, went to a narrow path through which the monks would have to pass on their return, and stretched across it one of the stout nets used in stag-hunting. Towards daybreak, as the monks, lantern in hand, were making their way through the wood, they suddenly heard a loud noise behind them—it was caused by men whom Colt had stationed for the purpose—and instantly blowing out their lights they were hurrying away, when they fell into the toils prepared for them.[1] The next morning, he presented

[1] Fuller, *Church History* (1655), p. 317.

them to the king, who laughed heartily at their piteous looks. "I have often seen better game," he said, "but never fatter. Certainly," he added, "I can make a better use of the money which the monks waste in their debaucheries. The coast of England requires to be fortified, my fleet and army to be increased, and harbours to be built for the commerce which is extending every day. All that is well worth the trouble of suppressing houses of impurity."

The protectors of the religious orders were not discouraged, and maintained that it was not necessary to shut all the monasteries, because of a few guilty houses.

Dr. Layton, a former officer of Wolsey, proposed a middle course: "Let the king order a general visitation of monasteries," he said, "and in this way he will learn whether he ought to secularize them or not. Perhaps the mere fear of this inspection will incline the monks to yield to his Majesty's desires." Henry charged Cromwell with the execution of this measure, and for that purpose he at once used him as his vicar-general, conferring on him all the ecclesiastical authority which belonged to the king. "You will visit all the churches," he said, "even the metropolitan, whether the see be vacant or not; all the monasteries both of men and women; and you will correct and punish whoever may be found guilty." Henry gave to his vicar precedence over all the peers, and decided that the layman should preside over the assembly of the clergy instead of the primate; overlook the administration not only of the bishops but also of the archbishops; confirm or annul the election of prelates, deprive or suspend them, and assemble synods. This was at the beginning of September 1535. The influence of the laity thus re-entered the Church, but not through the proper door. They came forward in the name of the king and his proclamations, whilst they ought to have appeared in the name of Christ and of His Word. The king informed the primate, and through him all the bishops and archdeacons, that as the general visitation was about to commence, they should no longer exercise their jurisdiction. The astonished prelates made representations, but they were unavailing: they and their sees were to be inspected by laymen.

The monks began to tremble. Faith in the religious houses no longer existed—not even in the houses themselves. Confidence in monastic practices, relics, and pilgrimages had grown weaker; the timbers of the monasteries were worm-eaten, their walls were just ready to fall, and the edifice of the Middle Ages, tottering on its foundations, was unable to withstand the hearty blows dealt against it. When an antiquary explores some ancient sepulchre, he often comes upon a skeleton, apparently well preserved, but crumbling into dust at the slightest touch of the finger; in like manner the puissant hand of the sixteenth century had only to touch most of these monastic institutions to reduce them to powder. The real dissolver of the religious orders was neither Henry VIII nor Cromwell: it was the devouring worm which, for years and centuries, they had carried in their bosom.

The vicar-general appointed his commissioners and then assembled them as a commander-in-chief calls his generals together. In the front rank was Dr. Richard Layton, his old comrade in Wolsey's household, a skilful man who knew the ground well and did not forget his own interests. After him came Dr. John London, Warden of New College, a man of unparalleled activity, but without character and a weather-cock, turning to every wind. With him was Sir Richard Cromwell, nephew of the vicar-general, an upright man, though desirous of making his way through his uncle's influence. He was the ancestor of another Cromwell, far more celebrated than Henry VIII's vice-gerent. Other two were Dr. Thomas Legh and Dr. John ap Rice, the most daring of the colleagues of the king's ministers; besides other individuals of well-known ability. The vice-gerent handed to them the instructions for their guidance, the questions they were to put to the monks, and the injunctions they were to impose on the abbots and priors; after which they separated on their mission.

The Universities, which sadly needed a reform, were not overlooked by Henry and his representative. Since the time when Garret, the priest of a London parish, circulated the New Testament at Oxford, the sacred volume had been banished from that city, as well as the *Beggars' Supplication* and other evangelical writings. Slumber had followed the awakening. The members of the university, especially certain ecclesiastics who, forsaking their parishes, had come and settled at Oxford, "to enjoy the delights of Capua," passed their lives in idleness and sensuality. The royal Commissioners aroused them from this torpor. They dethroned Duns Scotus, "the subtle doctor," who had reigned there for three hundred years, and the leaves of his books were scattered to the winds. Scholasticism fell; new lectures were established; philosophical teaching, the natural sciences, Latin, Greek, and divinity were extended and developed. The students were forbidden to haunt taverns, and the priests who had come to Oxford to enjoy life were sent back to their parishes.

The visitation of the monasteries began with those of Canterbury, the primatial church of England. In October 1535, shortly after Michaelmas, Dr. Layton, the Visitor, entered the cathedral, and Archbishop Cranmer went up into the pulpit. He had seen Rome: he had an intimate conviction that that city exerted a mischievous influence over all Christendom; he desired, as primate, to take advantage of this important opportunity to break publicly with her. "No," he said, "the bishop of Rome is not God's vicar. In vain you will tell me that the See of Rome is called *Sancta Sedes*, and its bishop entitled *Sanctissimus Papa:* the pope's holiness is but a holiness in name.[1] Vain-glory, worldly pomp, unchaste living and vices innumerable prevail in Rome. I have seen it with my own eyes. The pope claims by his ceremonies to forgive men their sins: it is a serious error. One work only blots them out, namely, the death of our Lord Jesus Christ. So long as the See of Rome endures, there will be no remedy for the evils which overwhelm us. These many years I have daily prayed unto God that I might see the power of Rome destroyed."[2] Language so frank necessarily displeased the adherents of the pope, and accordingly, when Cranmer alluded to his energetic daily prayer, the Superior of the Dominicans, trembling with excitement, exclaimed: "What a want of charity!"

He was not the only person struck with indignation and fear. As soon as the sermon was over, the Dominicans assembled to prevent the archbishop from carrying out his intentions. "We must support the papacy," they said, "but do it prudently." The prior was selected, as being the most eloquent of

---

[1] Cranmer's *Letters and Remains* (Parker Society), p. 326.
[2] *Ibid.*, p. 327.

the brothers, to reply to Cranmer. Going into the pulpit, he said: "The Church of Christ has never erred. The laws which it makes are equal in authority to the laws of God Himself. I do not know a single bishop of Rome who can be reproached with vice." Evidently the prior, however eloquent he might be, was not learned in the history of the Church.

The visitation of the Canterbury monasteries began. The immorality of most of these houses was manifested by scandalous scenes, and gave rise to questions which we are forced to suppress. The abominable vices that prevailed in them are mentioned by St. Paul in his description of the pagan corruptions (Rom. 1). The Commissioners having taken their seats in one of the halls of the Augustine monastery, all the monks came before them, some embarrassed, others bold, but most of them careless. Strange questions were then put to men who declared themselves consecrated to a devout and contemplative life: "Are there any among you," asked the Commissioners, "who, disguising themselves, leave the convent and go vagabondizing about? Do you observe the vow of chastity, and has anyone been convicted of incontinence? Do women enter the monastery, or live in it habitually?" We omit the questions that followed. The result was scandalous: eight of the brothers were convicted of abominable vices. The black sheep having been set apart for punishment, Layton called the other monks together, and said to them: "True religion does not consist in shaving the head, silence, fasting, and other observances; but in uprightness of soul, purity of life, sincere faith in Christ, brotherly love, and the worship of God in spirit and in truth. Do not rest content with ceremonies, but rise to sublimer things, and be converted from all these outward practices to inward and deep considerations."

One visitation still more distressing followed this. The Carthusian monastery at Canterbury, four monks of which had died piously, contained several rotten members. Some of them used to put on lay dresses, and leave the convent during the night. There was one house for monks and another for nuns, and the blacksmith of the monastery confessed that a monk had asked him to file away a bar of the window which separated the two cloisters. It was the duty of the monks to confess the nuns; but by one of those refinements of corruption which mark the lowest degree of vice, the sin and absolution often followed close upon each other. Some nuns begged the Visitors not to permit certain monks to enter their house again.

The visitation being continued through Kent, the Visitors came on the 22nd of October to Langdon Abbey, near Dover. William Dyck, abbot of the monastery of the Holy Virgin, possessed a very bad reputation. Layton, who was determined to surprise him, ordered his attendants to surround the abbey in such a manner that no one could leave it. He then went to the abbot's house, which looked upon the fields, and was full of doors and windows by which anyone could escape. Layton began to knock loudly, but no one answered. Observing an axe, he took it up, dashed in the door with it, and entered. He found a woman with the monk, and the visitors discovered in a chest the men's clothes which she put on when she wished to pass for one of the younger brethren. She escaped, but one of Cromwell's servants caught her and took her before the mayor at Dover, where she was placed in the cage. As for the holy father abbot, says Layton, he was put in prison. A few of the monks signed an act by which they declared that their house being threatened with utter ruin, temporal and spiritual, the king alone could find a remedy, and they consequently surrendered it to his Majesty.

The abbot of Fountains had ruined his abbey by publicly keeping six women. One night he took away the golden crosses and jewels belonging to the monastery, and sold them to a jeweller for a small sum. At Mayden-Bradley, Layton found another father prior, one Richard, who had five women, six sons, and a daughter pensioned on the property of the monastery: his sons, tall, stout young men, lived with him and waited on him. Seeing that the Roman Church prohibited the clergy from obeying the commandment of Scripture, which says: *A bishop must be the husband of one wife,* these wretched men took five or six. The impositions of the monks to extort money injured them in public opinion far more than their debauchery. Layton found in St. Anthony's house at Bristol a tunic of our Lord, a petticoat of the Virgin, a part of the Last Supper, and a fragment of the stone upon which Jesus was born at Bethlehem. All these brought in money.

Every religious and moral sentiment is disgusted at hearing of the disorders and frauds of the monks, and yet the truth of history requires that they should be made known. Here is one of the means—of the blasphemous means—they employed to deceive the people. At Hales in Gloucestershire, the monks pretended that they had some of Christ's blood preserved in a bottle. The man whose deadly sins God had not yet pardoned could not see it, they said; while the absolved sinner saw it instantaneously. Thousands of penitents crowded thither from all parts. If a rich man confessed to the priest and laid his gift on the altar, he was conducted into the mysterious chapel, where the precious vessel stood in a magnificent case. The penitent knelt down and looked, but saw nothing. "Your sin is not yet forgiven," said the priest. Then came another confession, another offering, another introduction into the sanctuary; but the unfortunate man opened his eyes in vain, he could see nothing until his contribution satisfied the monks. The Commissioners, having sent for the vessel, found it to be "a crystall very thick on one side and very transparent on the other." "You see, my lords," said a candid monk, "when a rich penitent appears, we turn the vessel on the thick side; that, you know, opens his heart and his purse." The transparent side did not appear until he had placed a large donation on the altar.

No discovery produced a greater sensation in England than that of the practices employed at Boxley in Kent. It possessed a famous crucifix, the image on which, carved in wood, gave an affirmative nod with the head if the offering was accepted, winked the eyes, and bent the body. If the offering was too small, the indignant figure turned away its head and made a sign of disapproval. One of the Commissioners took down the crucifix from the wall, and discovered the pipes which carried the wires that the priestly conjuror was wont to pull. Having put the machine in motion, he said: "You see what little account the monks have made of us and our forefathers." The monks trembled with shame and alarm, while the spectators, says the record, roared with laughter, like Ajax. The king sent for the machine, and had it worked in the presence of the court. The figure rolled its eyes, opened its mouth, turned up its nose, let its head fall, and bent its back.

"Upon my word," said the king, "I do not know whether I ought not to weep rather than laugh, on seeing how the poor people of England have been fooled for so many centuries."

These vile tricks were the least of the sins of the monks. In several monasteries the Visitors found implements for coining base money. In others they discovered traces of the horrible cruelties practised by the monks of one faction against those of another. Descending into the gloomy dungeons, they perceived, by the help of their torches, the bones of a great number of wretched people, some of whom had died of hunger and others had been crucified. But debauchery was the most frequent offence. Those pretended priests of a God who has said: *Be ye holy, for I the Lord am holy*, covered themselves with the hypocritical mantle of their priesthood, and indulged in infamous impurities. They discovered one monk, who, turning auricular confession to an abominable purpose, had carried adultery into two or three hundred families. The list was exhibited, and some of the Commissioners, to their great astonishment, says a contemporary writer, found the names of their own wives upon it.

There were sometimes riots, sieges, and battles. The royal Commissioners arrived at Norton Abbey in Cheshire, the abbots of which were notorious for having carried on a scandalous traffic with the monastic plate. On the last day of their visit, the abbot sent out his monks to muster his supporters, and collected a band of two or three hundred men, who surrounded the monastery to prevent the Commissioners from carrying anything away. The latter took refuge in a tower, which they barricaded. It was two hours past midnight: the abbot had ordered an ox to be killed to feed his rabble, seated round the fires in front of the monastery, and even in the courtyard. On a sudden Sir Piers Dulton, a justice of the peace, arrived, and fell with his posse upon the monks and their defenders. The besiegers were struck with terror, and ran off as fast as they could, hiding themselves among the fish-ponds and in the out-houses. The abbot and three canons, the instigators of the riot, were imprisoned in Halton Castle.

Be it said that the king's Commissioners met with houses of another character. When George Gifford was visiting the monasteries of Lincolnshire, he came to a lonely district,

abounding in water but very poor, where the abbey of
Woolstrop was situated. The inhabitants of the neighbourhood,
notwithstanding their destitution, praised the charity of the
recluses. Entering the house, Gifford found an honest prior
and some pious monks, who copied books, made their own
clothes, and practised the arts of embroidering, carving,
painting, and engraving. The Visitor petitioned the king for
the preservation of this monastery.

The Commissioners had particular instructions for the
women's convents. "Is your house perfectly closed?" they
asked the abbess and the nuns. "Can a man get into it? Are
you in the habit of writing love-letters?" At Lichfield the
nuns declared that there was no disorder in the convent; but
one good old woman told everything, and when Layton reproached the prioress for her falsehood, she replied: "Our
religion compels us to it. At our admission we swore never to
reveal the secret sins that were committed among us." There
were some houses in which nearly all the nuns trampled
under foot the most sacred duties of their sex, and were
without mercy for the unhappy fruits of their disorders.

Such were frequently in those times the monastic orders of
the West. The eloquent apologists who eulogize their virtues
without distinction, and the exaggerating critics who pronounce the same sentence of condemnation against all are
both mistaken. We have rendered homage to the monks who
were upright; we may blame those who were guilty. The
scandals, let us say, did not proceed from the founders of
these orders. Sentiments, opposed beyond a doubt to the
principles of the Gospel, although they were well-intentioned,
had presided over the formation of the monasteries. The
hermits Paul, Anthony, and others of the third and fourth
centuries gave themselves up to an anti-evangelical asceticism,
but still they struggled courageously against temptation.
However, one must be very ignorant not to see that corruption
must eventually issue from monastic institutions. *Every plant
which my heavenly Father hath not planted shall be rooted up*, is the
language of the Gospel.

We do not exaggerate. The monasteries were sometimes an
asylum in which men and women, whose hearts had been
wrecked in the tempests of life, sought a repose which the

world did not offer. They were mistaken; they ought to have lived with God, but in the midst of society. And yet there is a pleasure in believing that behind those walls, which hid so much corruption, there were some elect souls who loved God. Such were found at Catesby, at Godstow, near Oxford, and in other places. The Visitors asked for the preservation of these houses.

If the visitation of the religious houses was a bitter draught to many of the inmates, it was a cup of joy to the greater number. Many monks and nuns had been put into them during their infancy, and were detained in them against their will. No one ought to be forced, according to Cromwell's principles. When the visitation took place, the Visitors announced to every monk under twenty-four years of age, and to every nun under twenty-one, that they might go free. Almost all to whom the doors were thus opened hastened to profit by it. A secular dress was given them, with some money, and they departed with pleasure. But great was the sorrow among many whose age exceeded the limit. Falling on their knees, they entreated the Commissioners to obtain a similar favour for them. "The life we lead here," they said, "is contrary to our conscience."

The Commissioners returned to London, and made their report to the Council. They were distressed and disgusted. "We have discovered," they said, "not seven, but more than seven hundred thousand deadly sins. . . . These abominable monks are the *ravening wolves* whose coming Christ has announced, and who under sheep's clothing devour the flock. Here are the confessions of the monks and nuns, subscribed with their own hands. This book may well be called *The Book of God's Judgment*. The monasteries are so full of iniquity that they ought to fall down under such a weight. If there be here and there any innocent cloister, they are so few in number that they cannot save the others. Our hearts melt and all our limbs tremble at the thought of the abominations we have witnessed. O Lord! what wilt Thou answer to the five cities which Thou didst consume by fire, when they remind Thee of the iniquities of those monks, with whom Thou hast so long borne? The eloquence of Ptolemy, the memory of Pliny, and the pen of St. Augustine would not be able to give us the detestable history of these abominations."

The Council began to deliberate, and many of the members called for the secularization of a part of the monasteries. The partisans of the religious orders took up their defence, and acknowledged that there was room for reform. "But," they added, "will you deprive of all asylum the pious souls who desire to quit the world, and lead a devout life to the glory of their Maker?" They tried even to invalidate in some points the testimony of the Visitors; but the latter declared that, far from having recorded lightly those scandalous facts, they had excluded many.

Men of influence supported the Commissioners' conclusions; a few members of the Council were inclined to indulgence; even Cromwell seemed disposed to attempt the reform of whatever was susceptible of improvement; but many believed that all amendment was impossible. "We must, above all things, diminish the wealth of the clergy," said Dr. Cox; "for so long as they do not imitate the poverty of Christ, the people will not follow their teaching. I have no doubt," he added, with a touch of irony, "that the bishops, priests, and monks will readily free themselves from the heavy burden of wealth of every kind, which renders the fulfilment of their spiritual duties impossible." Other reasons were alleged. "The income of the monasteries," said one of the privy-councillors, "amounts to 500,000 ducats, while that of all the nobility of England is only 380,000. This disproportion is intolerable, and must be put an end to. For the welfare of his subjects and of the Church, the King should increase the number of bishoprics, parishes, and hospitals. He must augment the forces of the State, and prepare to resist the Emperor, whose fleets and armies threaten us. Shall we ask the people for taxes, who have already so much trouble to get a living, while the monks continue to consume their wealth in laziness and debauchery? It would be monstrous injustice. The treasures which the religious houses derive from the nation ought no longer to be useless to the nation."[1]

---

[1] [In *English Monasteries on the Eve of the Dissolution* (Oxford Studies, 1919), A. Savine estimates the gross income of the religious houses to have been about £163,000. The ordinary annual income of the government was slightly more than £100,000.]

In February 1536, this serious matter was laid before Parliament. It was Thomas Cromwell whose heavy hand struck these receptacles of impurity, and whom men called "the hammer of the monks," who proposed this great reform. He laid on the table of the Commons that famous *Black Book*, in which were inscribed the misdeeds of the religious orders, and desired that it should be read to the House. The book is no longer in existence: it was destroyed in the reign of Queen Mary by those who had an interest in its suppression.[1] But it was then opened before the Parliament of England. There had never before been such a reading in any assembly. The facts were clearly recorded—the most detestable enormities were not veiled: the horrible confessions of the monks, signed with their own hands, were exhibited to the members of the Commons. The recital produced an extraordinary effect. Men had had no idea of such abominable scandals. The House was horror-stricken, and "Down with them—down with them!" was shouted on every side.

The debate commenced. Personally, the members were generally interested in the preservation of the monasteries: most of them had some connection with one cloister or another; priors and other heads had relations and friends in Parliament. Nevertheless the condemnation was general, and men spoke of those monkish sanctuaries as, in former times, men had spoken of the priests of Jezebel—"Let us pull down their houses, and overturn their altars." There were, however, some objections. Twenty-eight abbots, heads of the great monasteries, were entitled to sit as barons in the Upper House: these were respected. Besides, the great monasteries were less disorderly than the small ones. Cromwell restricted himself for the moment to the suppression of 372 cloisters, in each of which the annual income was less than £200.[2] The abbots, flattered by the exception made in their favour, were silent, and even the bishops hardly cared to defend institutions which had

---

[1] [It was alleged by the Protestant historians of Elizabeth's reign that the *Black Book* was destroyed by Bishop Bonner. The Romanists affirmed that it was destroyed by the reforming party, who wished to destroy the evidence on which they acted.]

[2] [G. Baskerville in his *English Monks and the Suppression of the Monasteries* (1937) calculates that immediate suppression came to only about 220 houses, the remainder gaining a brief respite.]

long been withdrawn from their authority. "These monasteries," said Cromwell, "being the dishonour of religion, and all the attempts, repeated through more than two centuries, having shown that their reformation is impossible, the King, as supreme head of the Church under God, proposes to the Lords and Commons, and these agree, that the possessions of the said houses shall cease to be wasted for the maintenance of sin, and shall be converted to better uses."

There was immediately a great commotion throughout England. Some rejoiced, while others wept: superstition became active, and weak minds believed everything that was told them. "The Virgin," they were assured, "had appeared to certain monks, and ordered them to serve her as they had hitherto done." "What! no more religious houses," exclaimed others, through their tears. "On the contrary," said Latimer; "look at that man and woman living together piously, tranquilly, in the fear of God, keeping His Word and active in the duties of their calling: they form *a religious house*, one that is truly acceptable to God. Pure religion consists not in wearing a hood, but in visiting the fatherless and the widows, and keeping ourselves unspotted from the world. What has hitherto been called a religious life was an unreligious life; yea, rather an hypocrisy." "And yet," said the devout, "the monks had more holiness than those who live in the world." To this Latimer replied: "When St. Anthony lived in the desert on bread and water, and thought himself the most holy of men, he asked God who should be his companion in heaven, if it were possible for him to have one. 'Go to Alexandria,' said the Lord; 'in such a street and house you will find him.' Anthony left the desert, sought the house, and found a poor cobbler in his shop mending old shoes. The saint took up his abode with him, that he might learn by what mortifications the cobbler had made himself worthy of such great celestial honour. Every morning the poor man knelt down in prayer with his wife, and then went to work. When the dinner-hour arrived, he sat down at a table on which were bread and cheese; he gave thanks, ate his meal with joy, brought up his children in the fear of God, and faithfully discharged all his duties. At this sight, St. Anthony looked inwards, became contrite of heart, and put away his pride.

Such is the new sort of *religious houses*," added Latimer, "that we desire to have now."[1]

And yet, strange to say, Latimer, now bishop of Worcester, was almost the only person among the Evangelicals who raised his voice in favour of the religious bodies. He feared that if the property of the monasteries passed into the greedy hands of Henry's courtiers, the tenants, accustomed to the mild treatment of the abbots, would be oppressed by the lay landlords, desirous of realising the fruits of their estate unto the very last drop. Hence he was anxious that a few monasteries should be preserved as houses of study, prayer, hospitality, charity, and preaching. Cranmer, who had more discernment and a more practical spirit, had no hope of the monks. "Satan," he said, "lives in the monasteries; he is satisfied and at his ease, like a gentleman in his inn, and the monks and nuns are his very humble servants."[2] The primate, however, took little if any part in this great measure. His episcopal jurisdiction was suspended while the business was in hand, and he could do no other than acquiesce in the work of the Vicar-General.

The Bill for the suppression of the monasteries was introduced into the House of Commons on the 11th of March, 1536. The confiscated wealth of the monasteries was taken by the Crown. The possessions hitherto employed by a few to gratify their carnal appetites seemed destined to contribute to the prosperity of the whole nation.

Unhappily, the shameless cupidity of the monks was replaced by a cupidity of a different nature. Petitions poured in to Cromwell from every quarter. The saying of Scripture was fulfilled, *Wheresoever the carcase is, there will the eagles be gathered together*. Thomas Cobham, brother of Lord Cobham, represented that the Grey Friars' house at Canterbury was in a convenient position for him; that it was the city where he was born, and where all his friends lived. He consequently asked that it should be given him, and Cranmer, whose niece he had married, supported the prayer. "My good Lord," said Lord-Chancellor Audley, "my only salary is that of the chancellorship; give me a few good houses; I will give you my friendship during my life, and twenty pounds sterling

---

[1] Latimer's *Sermons* (Parker Society), pp. 391–3.
[2] Cranmer's *Letters and Remains* (Parker Society), p. 64.

for your trouble." "My specially dear Lord," said Sir Thomas
Eliot, "I have been the king's ambassador at Rome; my
services deserve some recompense. Pray his Majesty to grant
me some of the suppressed monastic lands. I will give your
lordship the income of the first year."

History has to record evils of another nature. Some of the
finest libraries in England were destroyed, and works of great
value sold for a trifle. Friends of learning on the continent
bought many of them, and carried away whole shiploads.
One man changed his religion for the sake of a piece of
abbey land. Some persons had imagined that the suppression
of the monasteries would lead to the abolition of taxes and
subsidies; but it was not so, and the nation found itself burdened
with a new need to make provision for the poor, in addition
to the ordinary taxes. There were, however, more worthy
cases than those of the king and his courtiers. "Most dread,
mighty, and noble prince," wrote the lord-mayor of London
to the king, "give orders that the three city hospitals shall
henceforward subserve not the pleasures of those canons,
priests, and monks, whose dirty and disgusting bodies en-
cumber our streets; but be used for the comfort of the sick
and blind, the aged and crippled."

The Act of Parliament suppressing the poorer religious
houses was immediately carried out. The earl of Sussex,
Sir John St. Clair, Anthony Fitzherbert, Richard Cromwell,
and several other Commissioners, travelled through England
and made known to the religious communities the statutory
dissolution. The voice of truth was heard from a small number
of monasteries. "Assuredly," said the Lincolnshire Franciscans,
"the perfection of Christian life does not consist in wearing a
grey frock, in disguising ourselves in strange fashion, in bending
the body and nodding the head, and in wearing a girdle full
of knots. The true Christian life has been divinely manifested
to us in Christ; and for that reason we submit with one consent
to the king's orders." The monks of the house of St. Andrew
at Northampton acknowledged to the Commissioners that they
had taken the habit of the order to live in comfortable idleness
and not by virtuous labour, and had indulged in continual
drunkenness, and in carnal and voluptuous appetites. "We
have covered the gospel of Christ with shame," they said.

"Now, seeing the gulf of everlasting fire gaping to swallow us up and impelled by the stings of our conscience, we humble ourselves with lowly repentance, and pray for pardon, giving up ourselves and our monastery to our sovereign king and lord."

But they did not all use the same language. There was a ceaseless movement in the cloisters; bursts of sorrow and fear, of anger and despair. What! No more monasteries! no more religious pomps! no more gossip! no more refectory! Those halls, wherein their predecessors had paced for centuries; those chapels in which they had worshipped kneeling on the pavement were to be converted to vulgar uses. A few monasteries endeavoured to bribe Cromwell: "If you save our house," said the abbot of Peterborough, "I will reward the king and you well." But Cromwell had conceived a great national measure, and wished to carry it out. Neither the eloquence of the monks, their prayers, their promises, nor their money could move him.

Some of the abbots set themselves in open revolt against the king, but were forced to submit at last. The old halls, the long galleries, the narrow cells of the religious houses became emptier from day to day. The monks received a pension in proportion to their age. Those who desired to continue in the religious life were sent to the large monasteries. Many were dismissed with a few shillings for their journey and a new gown. "As for you," said the Commissioners to the young monks under twenty-five, "you must earn a living by the work of your hands." The same rule was applied to the nuns.

There was great suffering at this period. The inhabitants of the cloisters were strangers in the world: England was to them an unknown land. Monks and nuns might be seen wandering from door to door, seeking an asylum for the night. Many, who were young then, grew old in beggary. Their sin had been great, and so was their chastisement. Some of the monks fell into a gloomy melancholy, even into frightful despair: the remembrance of their faults pursued them; God's judgment terrified them; the sight of their miseries infuriated them. "I am like Esau," said one of them, "I shall be eternally damned." And he strangled himself with his collar. Another stabbed himself with a penknife. Some compassionate people having deprived him of the power of injuring himself, he exclaimed with rage, "If I cannot die in this manner, I shall easily find another"; and taking a piece of paper, he wrote on it: "The king oppresses his people like a tyrant." This he placed in one of the church books, where it was found by a parishioner, who in great alarm called out to the persons around him. The monk, full of hope that he would be brought to trial, drew near and said, "It was I who did it: here I am; let them put me to death."

Erelong those gloomy clouds, which seemed to announce a day of storms, appeared to break. There were tempests afterwards, but, speaking generally, England found in this energetic act one of the sources of her greatness, instead of the misfortunes with which she was threatened. At the moment when greedy eyes began to covet the revenues of Cambridge and Oxford, a recollection of the pleasant days of his youth was awakened in Henry's mind. "I will not permit the wolves around me," he said, "to fall upon the universities." Indeed, the wealth of a few monasteries was employed in the foundation of new schools, and particularly of Trinity College, Cambridge; and these institutions helped to spread throughout England the lights of the Renaissance and of the Reformation. An eloquent voice was heard from those antique halls, saying: "O most invincible prince, great is the work that you have begun. Christ had laid the foundation; the apostles raised the building. But alas! barren weeds had overrun it; the papal tyranny had bowed all heads beneath its yoke. Now, you have rejected the pope; you have banished the race of monks. What more can we ask for? We pray that those houses of cenobites, where an ignorant swarm of drones was wont to buzz, should behold in their academic halls a generous youth, eager to be taught, and learned men to teach them. Let the light which has been restored to us spread its rays far and wide and kindle other torches, so that the darkness may be put to flight by the dawn of a new day."

It was not learning alone that gained by the suppression of the monasteries. Monastic wealth, hitherto useless, helped to strengthen England's defences and to build up her navy. At the same time, by the Reformation the moral force of the nation gained even more than the material force. The abolition of the papacy restored to the people that national unity which Rome had taken away; and England, freed from subjection to a foreign power, could oppose her enemies with a sword of might and a front of iron.

Political economy, rural economy, all that concerns the collection and distribution of wealth then took a start that nothing has been able to check. The estates, taken from the easy-going monks, produced riches. The king and the nobility, desirous of deriving the greatest gain possible from the domains that had fallen to them, endeavoured to improve agriculture. Many men, until that time useless, electrified by the movement of minds, sought the means of existence. The Reformation, from which the nation expected only purity of doctrine, helped to increase the general prosperity, industry, commerce, and navigation. The poor remembered that God had commanded man to eat his bread, not in the shade of the monasteries, but *in the sweat of his brow*. To this epoch we must ascribe the origin of those mercantile enterprises, of those long and distant voyages which were to be one day the strength of Great Britain. Henry VIII was truly the father of Elizabeth.

Moral, social, and political development was no less a gainer by the order that was established. At the first moment, no doubt, England presented the appearance of a vast chaos: but from that chaos there sprang a new world. Forces which had hitherto been buried in obscure cells were employed for the good of society. The men who had been dwelling carelessly within or without the cloister walls, and had expended all their activity in listlessly giving or listlessly receiving alms, were violently shaken by the blows from the *Malleus mona-chorum* (the hammer of the monks): they aroused themselves, and made exertions which turned to the public good. Their children, and especially their grandchildren, became useful citizens. The third estate appeared. The population of the cloisters was transformed into an active and intelligent middle class. The very wealth acquired, it is true greedily, by the nobility, secured them an independence, which enabled them to oppose a salutary counterpoise to the pretensions of the crown. The Upper House, where the ecclesiastical element had predominated, became essentially a lay house by the absence of the abbots and priors. A new life animated antique institutions that had remained almost useless. It was not, in truth, until later that England, having become decidedly evangelical and constitutional, emerged in greatness from the ruins of feudalism and popery; but an important step was taken under Henry VIII. That great transformation extended its influence even beyond the shores of Britain. The blow aimed at the system of the Middle Ages re-echoed throughout Europe, and everywhere shook the artificial scaffolding. Spain and Italy alone remained almost motionless in the midst of their ancient darkness.

The suppression of the monasteries, begun in 1535, was brought to a conclusion in 1539 by a second Act of Parliament.

A voice was heard from these ruined houses exclaiming: "Praise and thanksgiving to God! *For other foundation can no man lay than Jesus Christ.* Whoever believes that Jesus Christ is the *pacifier* who turneth away from our heads the strokes of God's wrath, lays the true foundation; and on that firm base he shall raise a better building than that which had the monks for its pillars!" This prophecy of Sir William Overbury did not fail of accomplishment.

CHAPTER EIGHT

Henry Negotiates with German Lutherans

(1534 to 1535)

Henry viii having thrown down the *chief pillar of the papacy* in England—the monks—felt the necessity of strengthening the work he had begun by alliances with the continental protestants. He did not turn to the Swiss or the French Reformers: their small political importance, as well as the decided character of their Reform, alienated him from them. "What inconsiderate men they are," said Calvin, "who exalt the king of England. To ascribe sovereign authority to the prince in everything, to call him supreme head of the Church under Christ, is blasphemy."[1]

Henry hoped more from Germany than from Switzerland. As early as 1534 three senators of Lubeck had presented to him the Lutheran Confession of Augsburg of 1530, and proposed an alliance against the Roman pontiff.[2] Anne Boleyn pressed the king to unite with the protestants, and in the spring of 1535 Henry's chaplain, Dr. Anthony Barnes, was sent to Wittenberg, where he endeavoured to induce the Reformers to claim his master's protection. Melanchthon, who was more inclined than Luther to have recourse to princes, did not

---

[1] [The words of Calvin which precede this quotation from his Commentary on Amos 7. 13 (Calvin Translation Society: *Minor Prophets*, Vol. II, p. 349) are worth quoting as further illustrative of the strong feelings which the reformer entertained on this subject: " 'Prophesy not again any more at Bethel, for it is the king's sanctuary and it is his court.' Amaziah wished here to prove by the king's authority that the received worship at Bethel was legitimate. How so? 'The king has established it; it is not then lawful for anyone to say a word to the contrary; the king could do this by his own right; for his majesty is sacred.' We see the object in view. And how many are there at this day under the Papacy who accumulate on kings all the authority and power they can, in order that no dispute may be made about religion; but power is to be vested in one king to determine according to his own will whatever he pleases, and this is to remain fixed without any dispute."]

[2] Rymer, *Fœdera*, VI. II. p. 214.

reject the advances of Henry VIII. "Sire," he wrote in
March 1535, "this is now the golden age for Britain. In times
of old, when the armies of the Goths had stifled letters in
Europe, your island restored them to the universe. I entreat
you in the name of Jesus Christ to plead for us before kings."
The illustrious doctor dedicated to this prince the new edition
of his *Common-Places*, and commissioned Alexander Alesius, a
Scot, to present it with the hope that he should see England
become the salvation of many nations, and even of the whole
Church of Christ. Alesius, who had taken refuge in Saxony,
was happy to return to that island from which the fanaticism
of the Scottish clergy had compelled him to flee. He was
presented to the uncle of his king, and Henry, delighted with
the Scot, said to him: "I name you my scholar," and directed
Cranmer to send Melanchthon two hundred florins. They
were accompanied by a letter for the illustrious professor, in
which the king signed himself: *Your friend Henry*.

But it was not long before the hopes of a union between
Germany and England seemed to vanish. Scarcely had
Melanchthon vaunted in his dedication to Henry VIII the
moderation of the king—a moderation worthy (he had said)
of a wise prince—when he heard of the execution of Fisher and
More. He shrank back with terror. "More," he exclaimed,
"has been put to death, and others with him." The cruelties
of the king tortured the gentle Philip. The idea that a man of
letters like More should fall by the hands of the executioner
scandalized him. He began to fear for his own life. "I am
myself," he said, "in great peril."

Henry did not suspect the horror which his crime would
excite on the continent, and had just read with delight a
passage of Melanchthon in which the latter compared him
to Ptolemy Philadelphus! He therefore said to Barnes: "Go
and bring him back with you." Barnes returned to Wittenberg
in September and delivered his message. But the doctor of
Germany had never received so alarming an invitation before.
He imagined it to be a treacherous scheme. "The mere thought
of the journey," he said, "overwhelms me with distress."
Barnes tried to encourage him. "The king will give you a
magnificent escort," he said, "and even hostages, if you desire
it." Melanchthon, who had More's bleeding head continually

before him, was immovable. Luther also regarded Barnes with an unfavourable eye, and called him *the dark Englishman.*

The envoy was more fortunate with the Elector of Saxony. John Frederick, hearing that the king of England was desirous of forming an alliance with the princes of Germany, replied that he would communicate this important demand to them. He then entertained Barnes at a sumptuous breakfast, made him handsome presents, and wrote to Henry VIII that the desire manifested by him to reform religious doctrine augmented his love for him, "for," he added, "it belongs to kings to propagate Christ's gospel far and wide."

Luther also, but from other motives than those of the elector, did not look so closely as Melanchthon; the suppression of the monasteries prepossessed him in favour of his ancient adversary. The penalties with which the Carthusians and others had been visited did not alarm him. Vergerio, the papal legate, who was at Wittenberg at the beginning of November, invited Luther to breakfast with him. "I know," he said, "that King Henry kills cardinals and bishops, but . . ." and biting his lips, he made a significant movement with his hand, as if he wished to cut off the king's head. When relating this anecdote to Melanchthon, who was then at Jena, Luther added: "Would to God that we possessed several kings of England to put to death those bishops, cardinals, legates, and popes who are nothing but robbers, traitors, and devils!" Luther was less tender than he is represented when contrasted with Calvin. Those hasty words expressed really the thoughts of all parties. The spiritual leaven of the gospel had to work for a century or more upon the hard material of which the heart of man is made, before the errors of Romish teachings, a thousand years old, were banished. No doubt there was an immediate mitigation produced by the Reformation; but if anyone had told the men of the sixteenth century that it was wrong to put men to death for acts of impiety, they would have been as astonished, and perhaps more so, than our judges, if they were abused because, in conformity with the law, they visited murder with capital punishment. It is strange, however, that it required so many centuries to understand those glorious words of our Saviour: *The Son of man is not come to destroy men's lives, but to save them* (Luke 9. 56).

The condition which the German protestants placed on their union with Henry VIII rendered the alliance difficult. "We only ask one thing," said the Reformers to Barnes, "that the doctrine which is in *conformity with Scripture* be restored to the *whole world;*" but Henry still observed the catholic doctrine. He was told, however, that the Lutherans and Francis I, thanks to Melanchthon's mediation, were probably coming to an agreement, and that a general council would be summoned. What treatment could he expect from such an assembly, he who had so grievously offended the papacy! Desirous of preventing a council at any price, the King determined in September, 1535, to send a more important embassy to the Lutherans, in order to persuade them to renounce the idea of coming to terms with the pope, and rather to form an alliance with England.

Consequently Edward Fox, bishop of Hereford, a proud and insolent courtier, and Nicholas Heath, archdeacon of Stafford, an amiable and enlightened man, with some others, started for Germany and joined Barnes, who had preceded them. On the 24th of December they were admitted into the presence of the Elector of Saxony, the Landgrave of Hesse, and other protestant deputies and princes: "The king our master," they said, "has abolished the power of the Roman bishop throughout his dominions, and rejected his pretended pardons and his old wives' stories. Accordingly the pope, in a transport of fury, has summoned all the kings of the earth to take arms against him. But neither pope nor papists alarm our prince. He offers you his person, his wealth, and his sceptre to combat the Roman power. Let us unite against it, and the Spirit of God will bind our confederation together." The princes replied to this eloquent harangue, "that if the king engaged to propagate the pure doctrine of the faith as it had been confessed at the diet of Augsburg; if he engaged, like them, never to concede to the Roman bishop any jurisdiction in his States, they would name him Defender and Protector of their confederation." They added that they would send a deputation, including one man of excellent learning (meaning Melanchthon), to confer with the king upon the changes to be made in the Church. The Englishmen could not conceal their joy, but the theologian had lost all confidence in Henry VIII. "The death of More distresses me: I will have nothing to do with the business." On the 25th December, 1535, the German princes at Schmalkald presented Fox with detailed propositions for a league with England. Henry VIII consulted Bishop Gardiner, at that time his ambassador in France, and then declined the terms, Gardiner having advised that the outcome of a league would be the establishment of protestantism in England.

Meanwhile, at home, Henry's relations with the most decided partisans of the papacy were far from improving. His daughter Mary, whose temper was melancholy and irritable, observed no bounds as regards her father's friends or acts, and refused to submit to his orders. "I bid her renounce the title of princess," said Henry in a passion.—"If I consented not to be regarded as such," she answered, "I should go against my conscience and incur God's displeasure." Henry, no friend of half-measures, talked of putting his daughter to death, and thus frightening the rebels. That wretched prince had a remarkable tendency for killing those who were nearest to him. We may see a father correct his child with a stripe; but with this man, a blow from his hand was fatal. There was already some talk of sending the princess to the Tower, when the evangelical Cranmer ventured to intercede in behalf of the catholic Mary. He reminded Henry that he was her father, and that if he took away her life, he would incur universal reprobation. The king gave way to these representations, predicting to the archbishop that this intervention would some day cost him dear. In fact, when Mary became queen she put to death the man who had saved her life. Henry was content to order his daughter to be separated from her mother. On the other hand, the terrified Catherine endeavoured to mollify the princess. "Obey the king in all things," she wrote from Buckden,[1] where she was living, "except in those which would destroy your soul. Speak little; trouble yourself about nothing, play on the spinet or lute." This unhappy woman, who had found so much bitterness in the conjugal estate, added: "Above all, do not desire a husband, nor even think of it, I beg you in the name of Christ's passion. Your loving mother, CATHERINE THE QUEEN."

[1] [Four miles from Huntingdon: formerly known as Bugden, where was a palace belonging to the bishop of Lincoln.]

But the mother was not less decided than the daughter in maintaining her rights, and would not renounce her title of queen, notwithstanding Henry's orders. A commission composed of the Duke of Suffolk, Lord Sussex, and others arrived at Buckden to try to induce her to do so, and all the household of the princess was called together. The intrepid daughter of Ferdinand and Isabella said with a firm voice: "I am the queen, the king's true wife." Being informed that it was intended to remove her to Somersham and separate her from some of her best friends, she answered: "I will not go unless you bind me with ropes." And to prevent this she took to her bed and refused to dress, saying she was ill. The king sent two catholic prelates, the archbishop of York and the bishop of Durham, hoping to soften her. "Madam," said the archbishop, "your marriage being invalid. . . ."—"It is a lawful marriage," she exclaimed with passionate vehemence. "Until death I shall be his Majesty's wife."—"Members of your own council," continued the archbishop, "acknowledge that your marriage with Prince Arthur was actually consummated."—"It is all false!" she exclaimed in a loud tone.—"The divorce was consequently pronounced. . . ."—"By whom?" she asked. —"By my lord of Canterbury."—"And who is he?" returned the queen. "A shadow! The pope has declared in my favour, and he is Christ's vicar."—"The king will treat you like a dear sister," said bishop Tunstall."—"Nothing in the world," answered Catherine, "neither the loss of my possessions nor the prospect of death, will make me give up my rights."

In October, 1535, Catherine was still at Buckden. That noble but fanatical woman increased her austerity, indulged in the harshest practices of an ascetic life, prayed frequently bare-kneed on the floor, while at the same time a deadly sorrow was undermining her health. At last consumption declared itself; and as it was judged that her condition required a change of air, she was removed to Kimbolton-castle, some eight miles to the west. She longed for the society of her daughter, which would no doubt have alleviated her sufferings; but she asked in vain with tears to see her. Mary also entreated the king to let her visit her mother: he was inflexible.

Henry's harshness towards the aunt of Charles V excited the wrath of that monarch to the highest degree. He was then returning victorious from his expedition against the corsair Barbarossa, whom he had driven out of Tunis, and determined to delay no longer in carrying out the mission he had received from the pope. To that end it was necessary to obtain, if not the co-operation, at least the neutrality of Francis I. That was not easy. The king of France had always courted the alliance of England: he had signed a treaty with Henry against the Emperor and against the pope, and had just sought an alliance with the Lutheran princes. But the Emperor knew that the acquisition of Italy, or at least of Lombardy, was the favourite idea of Francis I. Charles was equally desirous of it, but he was so impatient to re-establish Catherine of Aragon on the throne, and bring England again under the dominion of the pope, that he determined to sacrifice Italy, if only in appearance. Sforza, duke of Milan, having just died without children, the Emperor offered Francis I the duchy of Milan for his second son, the duke of Orleans, if he would not oppose his designs against England. The king of France eagerly accepted the proposal, and wishing to give a proof of his zeal, he even proposed that the pope should summon all the princes of Christendom to force the king of England to submit to the See of Rome. The love he had for Milan went so far as to make him propose a crusade against his natural ally, Henry VIII.

The matter was becoming serious: rarely had a greater danger threatened England, when an important event suddenly removed it. At the very time when Charles V, aided by Francis I, desired to rouse Europe in order to replace his aunt on the throne, she died. About the end of December, 1535, Catherine became seriously ill, and felt that God was bringing her great sorrows to an end. The king, wishing to keep up appearances, sent to enquire after her. The queen, firm to the last in her principles, sent for her lawyers and dictated her will to them. "I am ready," she said, "to yield up my soul unto God. . . . I supplicate that five hundred masses be said for my soul; and that some personage go in pilgrimage for me to Our Lady of Walsingham. I bequeath my gowns to the convent, and the furs of the same I give to my daughter." Then Catherine thought of the king: to her he was always her husband, and despite his injustice, she would not address him but with respect. Feeling that the end was not far off, she dictated the following letter, at once so simple and so noble:—

"My most dear Lord, King, and Husband,

"The hour of my death now approaching, I cannot choose but, out of the love I bear you, advise you of your soul's health. You have cast me into many calamities and yourself into many troubles; but I forgive you all, and pray God to do likewise. I commend unto you Mary our daughter, beseeching you to be a good father to her. Lastly, I make this vow, that mine eyes desire you above all things."

The queen, therefore, sought to bid farewell to him who had wrought her so much evil. Henry was moved, and even shed tears, but did not comply with the queen's wish: his conscience reproached him with his faults. On the 7th January Catherine received the last sacraments, and at two o'clock she expired.

Anne felt at the bottom of her heart the rights of this princess. She had yielded to her imagination, and to the absolute will of the king; her marriage had given her some moments of happiness, but her soul was often troubled. She thought to herself that the proud Spanish woman was the one to whom Henry had given his faith; and doubted whether the crown did not belong to the daughter of Isabella. Catherine's death removed her anxieties. "Now," she said, "now I am indeed a queen." The tears of the people accompanied to the tomb that unhappy and (to say truth) superstitious woman; but she was an affectionate mother, a high-spirited wife, and a queen of indomitable pride.

This decease was destined to effect great changes in Europe. The Emperor, who was forming a holy alliance to restore his aunt to the throne, and who, to succeed, had gone so far as to sacrifice the northern part of Italy, having nothing more to do with Catherine, sheathed his sword and kept Milan. Francis I, vexed at seeing the prey slip from him which he had so eagerly coveted, and fancied already in his hands, went into a furious passion, and prepared for a war to the death. The Emperor and the king of France, instead of marching together against Henry, began each of them to court him, desiring to have him for an ally in the fierce struggle that was about to begin.

At the same time Catherine's death facilitated, as we have said, the alliance of the king with the protestants of Germany, who had maintained the validity of his marriage with the princess of Aragon. One of their chief grievances against Henry VIII had thus disappeared. Both sides now thought they could take a step forward and strive to come to an understanding theologically. The points on which they differed were important. "The king of England," they said at Wittenberg, "wishes to be pope in the place of the pope, and maintains most of the errors of the old popery, such as monasteries,[1] indulgences, the mass, prayers for the dead, and other Romish fables."

The discussion began at Wittenberg. The champions in the theological tournament were Bishop Fox and Archdeacon Heath on one side; Melanchthon and Luther on the other. Heath, one of the young doctors whom Queen Anne had maintained at Cambridge University, charmed Melanchthon exceedingly. "He excels in urbanity and sound doctrine," said the latter. Fox, on the other hand, who was the king's man, showed, in Philip's opinion, no taste either for philosophy or for agreeable and graceful conversation. The doctrine of the mass was the principal point of the discussion. They could not come to an understanding. Luther, who thought it would be only a three days' matter, seeing the time slip away, said to the Elector: "I have done more in four weeks than these Englishmen in twelve years. If they continue reforming in that style, England will never be *inside* or *out*." This definition of the English Reformation amused the Germans. They did not discuss, they disputed: it became a regular quarrel. "I am disgusted with these debates," said Luther to vice-chancellor Burkhard, "they make me sick." Even the gentle Melanchthon exclaimed: "All the world seems to me to be burning with hatred and anger."

Accordingly the theological discussions were broken off, and the ambassadors of Henry VIII were admitted on the 12th of March into the presence of the Elector. "England is tranquil now," said the bishop of Hereford; "the death of a

---

[1] The *great* monasteries were not yet suppressed.

woman has for ever terminated all wrangling. At this moment
the creed of Jesus Christ alone is the concern of his Majesty.
The king therefore prays you to make an alliance between
you and him possible, by modifying a few points of your
Confession." Whereupon the vice-chancellor of Saxony
addressed Luther: "What can we concede to the king of
England?"—"Nothing," answered the reformer. "If we had
been willing to concede anything, we might just as well have
come to terms with the pope." After this very positive declaration, Luther softened down a little. He knew well, as Calvin
has said, "that some men are weaker than others, and if we
do not treat them very mildly, they lose their courage and
turn away from religion; and that Christians who are more
advanced in doctrine are bound to comfort the infirmities of the
ignorant." The Saxon reformer, retracing his steps a little,
wrote to the vice-chancellor: "It is true that England cannot
embrace the whole truth all at once." He thought it possible
in certain cases to adopt other expressions, and tolerate some
diversity of usages. "But," he said, always firm in the faith,
"the great doctrines can neither be given up nor modified.
Whether to make an alliance or not with the king is for my
most gracious lord to decide: it is a secular matter. Only it
is dangerous to unite outwardly, when the hearts are not in
harmony." The protestant States, assembled on the 24th of
April, 1536, at Frankfort on the Main, required Henry VIII
to receive *the faith confessed at Augsburg*, and in that case
expressed themselves ready to acknowledge him as protector
of the evangelical alliance. The Elector, who was much displeased with certain English ceremonies, added: "Let your
Majesty thoroughly reform the *pontifical idolomania* in England."
It was agreed that Melanchthon, Sturm, Bucer, and Dracon
should go to London to complete this great work of union.
England and evangelical Germany were about to join hands.

This proposed alliance of the king with the Lutherans
deeply chafed the catholics of the kingdom, already so seriously
offended by the suppression of the monasteries and the
punishment of the two men to whom Henry (they said) was
most indebted. While the Roman party was filled with anger,
the political party was surprised by the bold step the prince
had taken. But the blow which had struck two great victims

had taught them that they must submit to the will of the monarch or perish. The scaffolds of Fisher and More had read them a great lesson of docility, and moulded all those around Henry to that servile spirit which leaves in the palace of a king nothing but a master and slaves.

They were about to see an illustrious instance in the trial of Anne Boleyn.

CHAPTER NINE

The Accusation of the Queen

(1535 to May 1536)

IF feeble minds did not shrink from bending beneath the
royal despotism, men of fanatical mould cherished vengeance in their hearts. Great wounds had been inflicted on
the papacy, and they burnt to strike some signal blow against
the cause of Reform. That also, they said, must have its
victim. For all these monasteries sacrificed, one person must
be immolated: one only, but taken from the most illustrious
station. The king having, on the one side, struck his tutor
and his friend, must now, to maintain the balance, strike
his wife on the other. A tragedy was about to begin which
would terminate in a frightful catastrophe. Anne Boleyn had
not been brought up, as some have said, "in the worst school
in Europe," but in one of the best—in the household of the
pious Margaret of Angoulême, who was the enlightened
protectress not only of the learned, but of all friends of the
Gospel. Anne certainly seems to have had strong leanings
towards the Reformation and the Reformers. And accordingly
she was in the eyes of the papal partisans the principal cause
of the change that had been wrought in the king's mind, and
by him throughout the kingdom. The Reformation, as we
have seen, began in England about 1517 with the reading
of the Holy Scriptures in the universities; but the most
accredited Roman doctors have preferred to assign it another
origin, and, speaking of Cranmer's connexion with Anne
Boleyn, thirteen years later, have said, "Such is the beginning
of the Reformation in England."[1] In this assertion there is an
error both of chronology and history.

Since her coronation, the queen had been in almost daily
communication with the archbishop of Canterbury, and
habitually—even her enemies affirmed it—the interests of the

[1] Bossuet, *Histoire des Variations*, liv. vii. art. 8.

evangelical cause were treated of. At one time Anne prayed
Cranmer to come to the assistance of the persecuted protestants. At another, full of the necessity of sending reapers
into the harvest, she interested herself about such young
persons as were poor, but whose pure morals and clear intellect
seemed to qualify them for the practice of virtue and the
study of letters;[1] these she assisted with great generosity.
The queen did not encourage these students heedlessly: she
required testimonials certifying as to the purity of their morals
and the capacity of their intellect. If she was satisfied, she
placed them at Oxford or Cambridge, and required them to
spread around them, even while studying, the New Testament
and the writings of the reformers. Many of the queen's
pensioners did great service to the Church and State in after
years. With these queenly qualities Anne combined more
domestic ones. Cranmer saw her, like good Queen Claude,
gathering round her a number of young ladies distinguished
by their birth and their virtues, and working with them at
tapestry of admirable perfection for the palace of Hampton
Court, or at garments for the indigent. She established in
certain poor parishes warehouses, filled with such things as the
needy wanted. "Her eye of charity, her hand of bounty,"
says a biographer, "passed through the whole land." "She
is said in three quarters of a year," adds Lord Herbert of
Cherbury, the celebrated seventeenth-century philosopher and
historian, "to have bestowed fourteen or fifteen thousand
pounds in this way," that is, in alms. And this distinguished
writer, ambassador of England at the court of Louis XIII,
and known in France by the exertions he made in behalf of
the protestants, adds: "She had besides established a stock
for poor artificers in the realm." Such were the works of
Queen Anne. Cranmer, who had great discernment of men
and things, being touched by the regard which the queen
had for those who professed the Gospel, and seeing all that
she did for the Reformation and the consolation of the
wretched, declared that next to the king, Anne was of all
creatures living "the one to whom he was most bound."

Cranmer was not the only person among the evangelicals

[1] Letter of Sir John Cheke, 1535. Parker's *Correspondence* (Parker Society),
pp. 2–3.

with whom Anne Boleyn maintained relations. From the first day she had seen Latimer, the Christian simplicity and apostolic manners of the reformer had touched her. When she heard him preach, she was delighted. The enthusiasm for that bold Christian preacher was universal. "It is as impossible," said his hearers, "for us to receive into our minds all the treasures of eloquence and knowledge which fall from his lips, as it would be for a little river to contain the waters of the ocean in its bed." From the period (1535) when Latimer preached the Lent Sermons before the king, he was one of the most regular instruments of the queen's active charity.

A still more decided reformer had a high esteem for Anne Boleyn: this was Tyndale. No one, in his opinion, had declared with so much decision as the queen in favour of the New Testament and its circulation in English: and mention has already been made of the specially bound copy of his translation of the New Testament which he sent to England for the queen's acceptance in 1534.[1] This remarkable volume, now preserved in the library of the British Museum, is a monument of the veneration of the prisoner of Vilvorde for Anne Boleyn. A manuscript manual of devotion for the use of this princess has also been preserved: she used to present copies of it to her maids of honour. We see in it the value she attached to the Holy Scriptures: "Give us, O Father of mercies," we read, "the greatest of all gifts Thou hast ever conferred on man—the knowledge of Thy holy will, and the glad tidings of our salvation. Roman tyranny has long hidden it from us under Latin letters; but now it is promulgated, published, and freely circulated."

Anne, having in 1535 lost Dr. Betts, one of her chaplains, looked out for a man devoted to the Gospel to take his place, for she loved to be surrounded by the most pious persons in England. She cast her eyes upon Matthew Parker, a native of Norwich, Fellow of Corpus Christi College, Cambridge, and a man who for two years had been preaching the truth with fervour. Parker loved retirement and obscurity; accordingly, when he received shortly after Palm Sunday two letters summoning him to court "because the queen wished to see him," he was amazed and confounded. At first he wanted to

---

[1] Tyndale, *Doctrinal Treatises*, p. lxiv.

refuse so brilliant a call; but Latimer wrote to him: "Show yourself to the world; hide yourself no longer; work good while it is day, the night comes when no man can work. We know what you can do; let not your will be less than your power." Parker went to London, and in a short time his knowledge, piety, and prudence gained the entire esteem of the queen. That modest, intelligent, active man was just the person Anne wanted, and she took pleasure thenceforward in bestowing on him marks of her consideration. Parker was from this time one of those employed by Anne to distribute her benevolence. He had hardly arrived at court, when he presented to the queen one William Bill, a very young and very poor man, but by no means wanting in talent. Anne, rich in discernment, placed him in the number of students whom she was preparing for the ministry: he afterwards became dean of Westminster. Parker, who began his career with Anne, was to finish it with Elizabeth. When he was deprived of all his offices by Queen Mary in 1554, he exclaimed: "Now that I am stripped of everything, I live in God's presence, and am full of joy in my conscience. In this charming leisure I find greater pleasures than those supplied by the busy and perilous life I led at the court." Forced to hide himself, often to flee by night, to escape the pursuit of his persecutors, the peace which he enjoyed was never troubled. He looked upon trials as the privilege of the child of God. All of a sudden a strange and unexpected calamity befell him. The daughter of Anne Boleyn, having ascended the throne, desired to have her mother's chaplain for archbishop of Canterbury and primate of all England. "I kneel before your Majesty," he said to Queen Elizabeth, "and pray you not to burden me with an office which requires a man of much more talent, knowledge, virtue, and experience than I possess." A second letter from Nicholas Bacon, lord keeper of the great seal, repeated the summons. Then the unhappy Parker exclaimed in the depth of his sorrow: "Alas! alas! Lord God! for what times hast Thou preserved me! I am come into deep waters, where the floods overflow me. O Lord, I am oppressed: undertake for me. O Lord! strengthen me by Thy mighty Spirit!" Parker was at the head of the Church of England for sixteen years, and dignified the elevated seat on which he had been constrained to sit. Such were the men whom Anne Boleyn gathered round her.

We should be mistaken, however, if we represented the young queen as a bigot, living like Catherine in the practices of a rigid austerity. It appears even doubtful whether she knew by experience that inner, spiritual, and living Christianity which was found in Latimer, Tyndale, Cranmer, and Parker. She was a virtuous wife, a good protestant, attached to the Bible, opposed to the pope, fond of good works, esteeming men of God more than courtiers; but she had not renounced the world and its pomps. A woman of the world, upright, religious, loving to do good, a class of which there is always a large number, she was unacquainted with the pious aspirations of a soul that lives in communion with God. Her position as queen and wife of Henry VIII may have hindered her from advancing in the path of a Christian life. She thought it possible to love God without renouncing the enjoyments of the age, and looked upon worldly things as an innocent recreation. Desiring to keep her husband's heart, she endeavoured to please him by cheerful conversation, by organizing pleasure parties of which she was the life, and by receiving all his courtiers gracefully. Placed on slippery ground and watched by prejudiced eyes, she may occasionally have let fall some imprudent expression. Her sprightliness and gaiety, her amiable freedom were in strong contrast with the graver and stiffer formalities of the English ladies. Latimer, who saw her closely, sometimes admonished her respectfully, when he was alone with her, and the grateful Anne would exclaim unaffectedly: "You do me so much good! Pray never pass over a single fault."

It is not from the writings of the pamphleteers that we must learn to know Anne Boleyn. Towards the end of the sixteenth century, opposite parties, in their extreme excitement, have painted her at one time in colours too dark, at another in colours too flattering. We must in this matter especially listen to men whose testimony is sanctioned by universal respect. There are not many princesses in history who have enjoyed, like Anne, the esteem of the most elevated minds—of Cranmer and Latimer, of Tyndale and Parker, and other Christians less illustrious, perhaps, but not less respectable. In the eyes

of the papal partisans, however, she had committed an unpardonable crime: *she had separated England from the papacy:*
and accordingly their savage hatred has known no bounds,
and they have never ceased to blacken her memory with
their vile calumnies. Of all the misdeeds that history can
commit, the greatest consists in representing the innocent as
if they were guilty. Many writers have forged and still forge
base imputations against the reformers Luther, Calvin, and
others. Anne Boleyn has had her full share of slander in this
huge conspiracy of falsehood.[1]

The grandeur with which Anne was surrounded had opened
her heart to the tenderest sympathies. To be the joy of her
husband and the delight of her relations, to protect the friends
of the Gospel and to be loved by England—these were for
some time the dreams of her young imagination. But ere long
the crown of St. Edward pressed heavily on her brow. The
members of her own family became her enemies. Her uncle,
the proud duke of Norfolk, the chief along with Gardiner of
the papal party, was animated by a secret hatred against the
young woman who was the support of the evangelical party.
Her father, the earl of Wiltshire, imagining he saw that the
king was not flattered at being his son-in-law, had quitted
London, regretting a union which his ambition had so much
desired. Lady Rochford, wife of Anne's brother, a woman of
despicable character, whose former perfidies the queen had
pardoned, and whom she had attached to the court, repaid
this generous magnanimity by secretly plotting the ruin of a
sister-in-law whose elevation had filled her with jealousy. At
length, one of those who ate her bread and received favours
from her was about to shew her ingratitude to the unfortunate
queen.

Among her ladies of honour was Jane Seymour, who united
all the attractions of youth and beauty, and whose disposition

[1] This sort of conspiracy extends from the publication of the work
entitled, *De origine ac progressu schismatis Anglicani,* 1585, by Sanders—"a
book," says Bayle, "in which there is much passion and very little accuracy"
—down to the *Histoire de Henri VIII,* by Audin, a worthy successor of
Sanders, and whose work is in high favour in all papal coteries. This
miserable manufacture of outrageous fictions began even before Sanders,
and is not yet ended. [The most easily accessible life of Anne Boleyn for
the general reader is that to be found in Agnes Strickland's *Lives of the
Queens of England,* vol. ii.]

held a certain mean between the severe gravity of Queen
Catherine and the fascinating sprightliness of Queen Anne.
Constancy in affection was not a feature of Henry's character;
his heart was easily inflamed; his eye rested on the youthful
Jane, and no sooner had he become sensible of her graces
than the charms of Anne Boleyn, which had formerly captivated
him, became unendurable. The genial gaiety of the queen
fatigued him; the accomplishments which are ordinarily the
means of pleasing gave him umbrage; the zeal she manifested
for Protestantism alienated him. Anne's enemies, especially
the duke of Norfolk and Lady Rochford, observed this, and
resolved to take advantage of it to ruin the woman who
overshadowed them.

One circumstance, innocent enough of itself, favoured the
designs of the queen's enemies. Anne, who had been brought
up in France, among a people distinguished for their in-
exhaustible stores of gaiety, easy conversation, witty and
ingenious sallies, ironical phrases, and amiable hearts, had
brought something of all this to London. Frank and pre-
possessing, she loved society; and her ordinary manners
seemed too easy among a nation which, with deep affections,
possesses much gravity and external coldness. Anne had
found a certain freedom of speech in the court of France—it
does not appear that she imitated it; but in a moment of gaiety
she might have let slip some keen railleries, some imprudent
words, and thus furnished her enemies with weapons. She had
some difficulty in conforming with the strict etiquette of the
court of England, and had not been trained to the circum-
spection so necessary with a husband like Henry VIII.

Anne was not understood. Her gaiety did not degenerate
into frivolity: she did not possess that love of pleasure which,
carried to excess, engenders corruption of manners; we have
named the truly pious men whom she loved to gather round
her. But it was quite enough for some persons that Anne was
agreeable, like the ladies of St. Germains and Fontainebleau,
to suspect her of being a flirt, like many of them. Moreover,
she had married above her station. Having lived at court
as the equal of the young nobles belonging to it, she was not
always able, after she ascended the throne, to keep herself
on the footing of a queen. From that time her enemies inter-

preted unfavourably the innocent amiability with which she received them. The mistrustful Henry VIII began to indulge in suspicions, and Lady Rochford endeavoured to feed that prince's jealousy by crafty and perfidious insinuations.

Anne soon noticed the king's inclination for Jane Seymour: a thousand trifles, apparently indifferent, had struck her. She often watched the maid of honour; her pride was offended, and jealousy tortured her heart night and day. She endeavoured to win back the king's love; but Henry, who perceived her suspicions, grew more angry with her every hour. The queen was not far from her confinement; and it was at the very moment when she hoped to give Henry the heir he had longed for during so many years, that the king withdrew from her his conjugal affection. Her heart was wrung, and, foreseeing a mournful future, she wondered whether a blow similar to that which had struck Catherine might not soon be aimed at her. Jane Seymour did not reject the king's advances. Historians of the most opposite parties relate that one day, towards the end of January 1536, the queen, unexpectedly entering a room in the palace, found the king paying his court to the young maid of honour in too marked a manner. They may possibly exaggerate, but there is no doubt that Henry gave cause for very serious complaints on the part of his wife. It was as if a sword had pierced the heart of the unfortunate Anne Boleyn: she could not bear up against so cruel a blow, and prematurely gave birth to a dead son. God had at length granted Henry that long-desired heir, but the grief of the mother had cost the child's life. What an affliction for her! For some time her recovery was despaired of. When the king entered her room, she burst into tears. That selfish prince, soured at the thought that she had borne him a dead son, cruelly upbraided her misfortune, instead of consoling her. It was too much: the grief-stricken mother could not restrain herself. "You have no one to blame but yourself," she exclaimed. Henry, still more angry, answered her harshly and left the apartment. These details are preserved by a well-informed writer of the time of Elizabeth. To present Henry under so unfavourable a light, if it were untrue, could hardly have been an agreeable mode of paying court, as some have insinuated, to a queen who took more after her father than her mother.

Anne now foresaw the misfortunes awaiting her: she recovered indeed after this storm, and exerted herself by taking part once more in social gatherings and fêtes; but she was melancholy and uneasy, like a foundering ship, which reappears on the waves of the sea after the storm, and still keeps afloat for a time, only to be swallowed up at last. All her attempts to regain her husband's affections were useless, and frightful dreams disturbed her during the slumbers of the night. This agony lasted three months.

The wind had changed: everybody noticed it, and it was, to certain heartless courtiers, like the signal given to an impatient pack of hounds. They set themselves to hunt down the prey, which they felt they could rend without danger. The extreme catholics regained their courage. They had feared that, owing to Anne's intervention, the cause of Rome was lost in England, and their alarm was not unreasonable. Cranmer, realizing that he possessed the goodwill of the queen, never ceased pushing forward the Reformation. When some one spoke in the House of Lords about a General Council in Italy, he exclaimed: "It is the Word of God alone that we must listen to in religious controversies." At the same time, in concert with Anne, he circulated all over England a new Prayer-book, *the Primer*, intended to counter the dangerous books of the priests.[1] The people used it. A pious and spiritual reader of that book exclaimed one day, after meditating upon it: "O bountiful Jesu! O sweet Saviour! despise not him whom Thou hast ransomed at the price of such a treasure— with Thy blood! I look with confidence to the throne of mercy." Religion was becoming personal with Anne Boleyn.

The queen and the archbishop had not stopped there: they had attempted, so far as Henry would permit, to place true shepherds over the flocks, instead of merchants who traded with their wool. The bishopric of Worcester, which had been taken from Jerome de Ghinucci, was given (as we have seen) to Latimer; so that the valley of the Severn, which four Italian bishops had plundered for fifty years, possessed at last a pastor who "planted there the plenteousness of all spiritual

[1] "Pestilent and infectious books."—*Preface to the Primer.*

blessings in Jesus Christ."[1] Shaxton, one of Anne's chaplains, who at this time professed a great attachment to Holy Scripture, had been appointed bishop of Salisbury, in place of the famous Cardinal Campeggio. Hilderly, formerly a Dominican prior— who had at one time defended the immaculate conception of the Virgin, but had afterwards acknowledged and worshipped Jesus Christ as the only Mediator—had been nominated to the see of Rochester, in place of the unfortunate Bishop Fisher. Finally, George Brown, ex-provincial of the Augustines in England—an upright man, a friend of the poor, and who, caught by the truth, had exclaimed from the pulpit, "Go to Christ and not to the saints!"—had been elected archbishop of Dublin, and thus became the first evangelical prelate of Ireland, a difficult post, which he occupied at the peril of his life.[2] Other prelates, like Fox, bishop of Hereford, although not true Protestants, proved themselves to be anti-Papists.

The members of the papal party saw the influence of the queen in all these nominations. Who resisted the proposal that the English Church should be represented at the General Council? Who endeavoured to make the king advance in the direction of the Reformation? Who threw England into the arms of the princes of Germany?—The queen, none but the queen. She felt unhappy, it was said, when she saw a day pass without having obtained some favour for the Reformation. Men knew that the pope was ready to forgive everything, and even to unite with Henry against Charles V, if the king would submit to the conditions laid down in the bull—that is to say, if he would put away Anne Boleyn.

The condition required by the pontiff was not an impossible one, for Henry liked to change his wives: he had six. Marriage was not to him a oneness of life. At the end of 1535, Anne had been his wife for three years; it was a long time for him, and he began to turn his eyes upon others. Jane Seymour's youth eclipsed the queen's. Unfortunate Boleyn! Sorrow had gradually diminished her freshness. Jane had natural allies, who might help her to ascend the throne. Her two brothers, Edward and Thomas—the elder more moderate, the younger

---

[1] Latimer's *Sermons* (Parker Society), p. 82.
[2] "It was to the hazard of his life."—Strype's *Memorials of Thomas Cranmer*, p. 38.

more arrogant—each possessing great ambition and remarkable capacity, thought that a Seymour was as worthy as a Boleyn to wear the English crown. The first blow did not however proceed from them, but from a member of the queen's family—from her sister-in-law. There is no room for indifference between near relations: they love or, if they do not love, they hate. Lady Rochford, so closely allied to the queen, felt continually piqued at her. Jealousy had engendered a deep dislike in her heart, and this dislike was destined to lead her on to contrive the death of the detested object. Rendered desperate by the happiness and especially by the greatness of Anne Boleyn, it became her ruling passion to destroy them. One obstacle, however, rose up before her. Lord Rochford, her husband and Anne's brother, would not enter into her perfidious schemes. That depraved woman, who afterwards suffered capital punishment for conniving at crime, determined to ruin her sister-in-law and her husband together. It was arranged that three of the courtiers should give Henry the first hints. "Thus began," says an author of that day, "a comedy which was changed into a sorrowful tragedy."[1] Nothing was omitted that tended to the success of one of the most infamous court intrigues recorded in history.

Anne became cognizant almost at the same time of her sister-in-law's hatred of her and of her husband's love for Jane Seymour. From that moment she foreboded an early death, and her most anxious thoughts were for her daughter. She wondered what would become of the child, and, desirous of having her brought up in the knowledge of the Gospel, she sent for the pious, simple-minded Parker, told him of her apprehensions and her wishes, and commended Elizabeth to him with all a mother's love. Anne's words sank so deep into his heart that he never forgot them; and twenty-three years later, when that child, who had become queen, raised him to the primacy, he declared to Lord Burghley that if he were not under such great obligations to her mother, he would never have consented to serve the daughter in such an elevated station. After consigning the youthful Elizabeth to the care

---

[1] *Histoire de Anne Boleyn, royne d'Angleterre*, p. 181.—This History, written in French verse of the sixteenth century, is from the pen of Crespin, lord of Milherve, who was in London at the time of which he speaks.

of a man of God, the unhappy queen was more at ease.

Meantime the plot was forming in silence, and two or three circumstances, such as occur in the most innocent life, were the pretext for Anne's destruction. One day, when she was with the king at Winchester, she sent for one of the court-musicians, named Mark Smeaton, "to play on the virginals." This was the first count in the indictment.

Norris, a gentleman of the king's chamber, was engaged to Margaret, one of Anne's maids of honour, and consequently was often in the queen's apartments. Slanderous tongues affirmed that he went more for the sake of his sovereign than for his betrothed. The queen hearing of it, and desiring to stop the scandal, determined to bind Norris to marry Margaret. "Why do you not go on with your marriage?" she asked him. "I desire to wait a little longer," answered the gentleman. Anne, with the intent of making him understand that there were serious reasons for not putting it off any longer, added: "It is said at court that you are waiting for a dead man's shoes, and that if any misfortune befell the king, you would look to have me for your wife." "God forbid!" exclaimed Norris, in alarm; "if I had such an idea, it would be my destruction." "Mind what you are about," resumed the queen, with severity. Norris, in great emotion, went immediately to Anne Boleyn's almoner. "The queen is a virtuous woman," he said; "I am willing to affirm it upon oath." This was the second count in the indictment.

Sir Francis Weston, a bold frivolous man, was (although married) very attentive to a young lady of the court, a relative of the queen. "Sir Francis," said Anne, who was distressed at his behaviour, "you love Mistress Skelton, and neglect your wife." "Madam," answered the audacious courtier, "there is one person in your house whom I love better than both." "And who is that?" said the queen. "Yourself," answered Weston. Offended by such insolence, Anne ordered him, with scorn and displeasure, to leave her presence. This was the third count of the indictment.

Lord Rochford, a man of noble and chivalrous character, indignant at the calumnies which were beginning to circulate against his sister, endeavoured to avert the storm. One day, when she kept her bed, he entered her room to speak to her;

and, the maids of honour being present, he leant towards the queen, to say something on this matter which was not fit for the ears of strangers to the family. The infamous Lady Rochford made use of this innocent circumstance to accuse her husband and sister-in-law of an abominable crime.

Such are the four charges that were to cost Anne Boleyn her life. Futile observations, malicious remarks to which persons are exposed in the world, and especially at court, reached the ears of the king, and inspired him with jealousy, reproaches, angry words, and coldness. There was no more happiness for Anne.

There was enough in these stories to induce Henry VIII to reject his second wife, and take a third. This prince—and it was the case generally with the Tudors—had a temper at once decided and changeable, a heart susceptible and distrustful, an energetic character, and passions eager to be satisfied at any price. Very mistrustful, he did not easily get the better of his suspicions, and when any person had vexed him, he was not appeased until he had got rid of him. Common-sense generally appreciates at their true worth such stories as those we have reported; but the characters now on the stage were more rancorous than those usually to be found in the world. "A tempest," says Lord Herbert of Cherbury on this subject, "though it scarce stir low and shallow waters, when it meets a sea, both vexeth it, and makes it toss all that comes thereon."

Henry, happy to have found the pretext which his new passion made him long for, investigated nothing; he appeared to believe everything he was told. He swore to prove Anne's guilt to others by the greatness of his revenge. Of his six wives, he got rid of two by divorce, and two by the scaffold; only two escaped his criminal humour. This time he was unwilling to proceed by divorce; the tediousness of Catherine's affair had wearied him. He preferred a more expeditious mode—the axe.

On the 25th of April the king appointed a commission to enquire into Anne's conduct, and placed on it the duke of Norfolk, a maternal uncle but (as we have said) an implacable enemy of the unfortunate queen; the duke of Suffolk, who, as Henry's brother-in-law, served him in his least desires; the earl of Oxford, a skilful courtier; William Paulet, comptroller of the royal household, whose motto was, "To be a willow and not an oak"; Audley, the most honest of all, but still his master's humble servant; Lord Delawarr, and several other lords and gentlemen, to the number of twenty-six. It has been said, by Burnet and others, that the king named Anne's father, the earl of Wiltshire, one of the judges. It would, no doubt, have been the most striking trait of cruelty, of which Henry gave so many proofs; but we must in justice declare that the wretched prince did not perpetrate such a monstrosity. Burnet, after the most searching investigations, retracted his error.[1] On Thursday, the 27th of April, the king, understanding the necessity of a Parliament to repeal the laws made in favour of Anne and her children, issued writs for its assembling. He was resolved to hurry on the business—equally impatient to hear no more of his wife, and to possess her who was the object of his desires.

Anne, who was ignorant of what was going on, had gradually recovered a little serenity, but it was not so with those around her. The court was agitated and uneasy. The names of the commissioners were canvassed, and people wondered where the terrible blows of the king would fall. Would the storm burst on Sir Thomas Wyatt, who wrote verses in Anne's honour? or on Lord Northumberland, whom the queen had loved before Henry cast his eyes upon her? The king did not intend to go so high.

The indecision did not last long. At two o'clock on the 27th of April—the very day when the writs for the new Parliament were issued—William Brereton, one of the gentlemen of the king's household pointed out by the queen's enemies, was arrested and taken to the Tower. Two days later, on the 29th of April, Anne was crossing the presence-chamber, where a miserable creature happened to be present at that moment. It was Mark Smeaton, the court-musician—a vain, cowardly, corrupt man, who had felt hurt because, since the day when he had played before the queen at Winchester, that princess had never even looked at him. He was standing, in a dejected attitude, leaning against a window. It is possible that, having heard of the disgrace that threatened the queen, he hoped,

---

[1] Addenda to the Third Book of his History.—He acknowledges that this *mistake*, as he calls it, was an invention of Sanders.

by showing his sorrow, to obtain from her some mark of interest. Be that as it may, his unusual presence in that room, the posture he had assumed, the appearance of sorrow which he had put on, were evidently intended to attract her attention. The trick succeeded. Anne noticed him as she passed by. "Why are you sad?" she asked.—"It is no matter, madam." The queen fancied that Smeaton was grieved because she had never spoken to him. "You may not look to have me speak to you," she added, "as if you were a nobleman, because you are an inferior person." "No, madam," replied the musician, "I need no words; a look sufficeth me." He did not receive the look he asked for, and his wounded vanity urged him from that moment to ruin the princess, by whom he had the insolence to wish to be remarked. Smeaton's words were reported to the king, and next day (April 30) the musician was arrested, examined at Stepney, and sent to the Tower.

A magnificent festival was preparing at Greenwich, to celebrate the first day of May in the usual manner. This was the strange moment which Henry had chosen for unveiling his plans. In certain minds there appears to be a mysterious connexion between festivities and bloodshed; another prince (Nero) had shown it in old times, and some years later Charles IX was to celebrate the marriage of his sister Margaret by the massacres of St. Bartholomew. Henry VIII gave to two of the victims he was about to immolate the foremost places in the brilliant tournament he had prepared. Lord Rochford, the queen's brother, was the principal challenger, and Henry Norris was chief of the defenders. Sir Francis Weston was also to take part in these jousts. Henry showed himself very gracious to them, and hid with smiles their approaching destruction. The king having taken his place, and the queen, in a magnificent costume, being seated by his side, Rocheford and Norris passed before him, lowering their spears. The jousting began immediately after. The circumstances of the court gave a gloomy solemnity to the festival. The king, who was watching with fixed eyes the struggles of his courtiers, started up all of a sudden, with every appearance of anger, and hastily quitted the balcony. What had happened? The historian Sanders, notorious as being a most malicious and fabulous writer, mentions that the queen had dropped her handkerchief into the lists, and that Norris took it up and wiped his face with it. Lord Herbert, Burnet, and others affirm that there is nothing to corroborate the story, which, were it true, might be very innocent. However, the festivities were interrupted by the king's departure. The confusion was universal, and the alarmed queen withdrew, eager to know the cause of the strange procedure. Thus ended the rejoicings of the First of May.

Henry, who had gone back to the palace, hearing of the queen's return, refused to see her, ordered her to keep her room, mounted his horse, and, accompanied by six gentlemen, galloped back to London. Slackening his pace for a time, he took Norris aside, and, telling him the occasion of his anger, promised to pardon him if he would confess. Norris answered, with firmness and respect; "Sire, if you were to cut me open and take out my heart, I could only tell you what I know." On reaching Whitehall, Henry said to his ministers: "Tomorrow morning you will take Rochford, Norris, and Weston to the Tower; you will then proceed to Greenwich, arrest the queen, and put her in prison. Finally, you will write to Cranmer and bid him go immediately to Lambeth, and there await my orders." The victims were seized, and the high-priest summoned for the sacrifice.

The night was full of anguish to Anne Boleyn, and the next day, when she was surrounded by her ladies, their consternation increased her terror. It seemed to her impossible that a word from her would not convince her husband of her innocence. "I will positively see the king," she exclaimed. She ordered her barge to be prepared, but, just as she was about to set out, another barge arrived from London, bringing Cromwell, Audley, and the terrible Kingston, lieutenant of the Tower. That ominous presence was a death-warrant: on seeing him the queen screamed aloud.

They did not, however, remove her at once: the council, on which sat her most violent adversaries, assembled in the palace, and Anne was summoned to appear before it. The duke of Norfolk, the president, informed her coldly of what she was accused, and named her pretended accomplices. At these words, the queen, struck with astonishment and sorrow, fell on her knees and cried out: "O Lord, if I am guilty, may

I never be forgiven!" Then, recovering a little from her
emotion, she replied to the calumnious charges brought against
her, to which Norfolk answered carelessly and contemptuously,
as if he were still speaking to the little girl whom he had seen
born, "Tut, tut, tut," and shook his head disdainfully. "I
desire to see the king," said Anne. "Impossible," answered
the duke; "that is not included in our commission." "I have
been very cruelly treated," said Anne Boleyn, later, when
speaking of this horrible conversation with her uncle. "It is his
Majesty's good pleasure that we conduct you to the Tower,"
added Norfolk. "I am ready to obey," said the queen, and all
went in the same barge. When they reached the Tower, Anne
landed. The governor was there to receive her. Norfolk and
the other members of the council committed her into his
charge and departed. It was five in the afternoon.

  Then the gates of the fortress opened; and at this moment,
when she was crossing the threshold under the charge of
heinous crimes, Anne remembered how, three years before,
she had entered it in triumph for the ceremony of her
coronation, in the midst of the general acclamations of the
people. Struck by the fearful contrast, she fell on her knees,
"as a ball" and exclaimed, "O Lord, help me, as I am
guiltless of that whereof I am accused!" The governor raised
her up, and they entered. She expected to be put into close
confinement. "Mr. Kingston," she said, "do I go into a
dungeon?" "No, madam," answered the governor; "you will
be in your own lodging, where you lay at your coronation."
"It is too good for me," she exclaimed. She entered, however,
and on reaching those royal chambers, which occasioned such
different recollections, she knelt again and burst into tears.
The violence of her grief presently brought on convulsive
movements, and her tears were succeeded by hysterical
laughter. Gradually she came to herself, and tried to collect
her thoughts. Feeling the need of strengthening herself by the
evidences of the Lord's love, she said to Kingston, "Entreat his
Majesty to let me have the sacrament." Then, in the consciousness of innocence, she added, "Sir, I am as clear from the
company of man as I am of you. I am the king's true wedded
wife."

She was not absorbed in her own misfortunes: she was

moved by the sufferings of the others, and uneasy about her brother. "Can you tell me where Lord Rochford is?" she asked. Kingston replied that he had seen him at Whitehall. She was not tranquillized by this evasive answer. "Oh, where is my sweet brother?" she exclaimed. There was no reply. "Mr. Kingston," resumed Anne, after a few moments, "do you know why I am here?"—"No, madam." "I hear say that I am to be accused of criminal familiarities." (Norfolk had told her so in the barge.) "I can say no more than—Nay!" Suddenly tearing one of her garments, she exclaimed, as if distracted: "If they were to open my body, I should still say—No." After this her mind wandered. She thought of her step-mother, and the love she felt for the countess of Wiltshire made her feel more than anything else the bitterness of her situation: she imagined the proud lady was before her, and cried, with unutterable agony, "O my mother, my mother, thou wilt die for sorrow!" Then her gloomy thoughts were turned to other objects. She remembered that, while in the barge, the duke of Norfolk had named Norris and Smeaton as her accusers, which was partly false. The miserable musician was not grieved at being wrongfully accused of a crime likely to make him notorious, but Norris had stoutly rejected the idea that the queen could be guilty. "O Norris, hast thou accused me!" she ejaculated; "and thou too, Smeaton!" After a few moments' silence, Anne fixed her eyes on the governor. "Mr. Kingston," she asked, "shall I die without justice?" "Madam," answered the governor, "the meanest subject of the king has that." At these words the queen again laughed hysterically. "Justice—justice!" she exclaimed, with disdainful incredulity. She counted less upon justice than the humblest of her subjects. Gradually the tempest calmed down, and the silence of the night brought relief to her sorrow.

The same day (May 2) the news spread through London that the queen was arrested. Cranmer, who had received the royal intimation to go to his palace at Lambeth, and wait there until further orders, had arrived, and was thunderstruck on hearing what had happened. "What! the queen in prison! the queen an adulteress!" . . . A struggle took place in his bosom. He was indebted to the queen for much; he had always found her irreproachable—the refuge of the unhappy, the upholder of the truth. He had loved her like a daughter, respected her as his sovereign. That she was innocent, he had no doubt; but how to account for the behaviour of the king? The unhappy prelate was distracted by the most painful thoughts. This truly pious man showed excessive indulgence towards Henry VIII, and bent easily beneath his powerful hand; but his path was clearly traced—to maintain unhesitatingly the innocence of her whom he had always honoured. And yet he was to be an example of the fascination exerted by a despot over such characters—of the cowardice of which a good man may be guilty through human respect. Doubtless there are extenuating circumstances in his case. It was not only the queen's fate that made the prelate uneasy, but also the future of the Reformation. If love for Anne had helped to make Henry incline to the side of the Reformation, the hatred which he now felt against his unhappy wife might easily drive him in the other direction. Cranmer desired to prevent this at any price, and accordingly thought himself obliged to use extreme caution. But these circumstances are really no extenuation. No motive in the world can excuse a man from not frankly defending his friends when they are falsely accused—from not vindicating an innocent woman when she is declared to be guilty. Cranmer wrote to the king: "I cannot without your Majesty's command appear in your presence; but I can at least desire most humbly, as is my duty, that your great wisdom and God's help may remove the deep sorrow of your heart.

"I cannot deny that your Majesty has great cause to be overwhelmed with sorrow. In fact, whether the things of which men speak be true or not, your honour, Sire, according to the false appreciation of the world, has suffered; and I do not remember that Almighty God has ever before put your Majesty's firmness to so severe a test.

"Sire, I am in such a perplexity that I am clean amazed; for I never had a better opinion in woman than I had in her, which maketh me think that she cannot be culpable."[1]

This was tolerably bold, and accordingly Cranmer hastened

---

[1] Cranmer's *Letters and Remains* (Parker Society), letter clxxiv. to King Henry VIII, pp. 323–4.

to tone down his boldness. "And yet, Sire," he added, "would you have gone so far, if you had not been sure of her crime? . . . . Your Grace best knoweth that, next unto your Grace, I was most bound unto her of all creatures living. Wherefore I must humbly beseech your Grace to suffer me in that which both God's law, nature, and her kindness bindeth me unto, that I may (with your Grace's favour) wish and pray for her. And from what condition your Grace, of your only mere goodness, took her, and set the crown upon her head, I repute him not your Grace's faithful servant and subject, nor true to the realm, that would not desire the offence to be without mercy punished, to the example of all others. And as I loved her not a little, for the love I judged her to bear towards God and His Gospel; so, if she be proved guilty, there is not one that loveth God and His Gospel that will ever favour her . . . for then there never was creature in our time that so much slandered the Gospel.

"However," he added, appearing to recover his courage, "forget not that God has shown His goodness to your Grace in many ways, and has never offended you; whilst your Grace, I am sure, acknowledgeth that you have offended Him. Extend, therefore, to the Gospel the precious favour you have always shown it, and which proceedeth not from your love for the queen your wife, but from your zeal for the truth.

"From Lambeth, 3rd of May, 1536."

When Cranmer addressed these soothing words to the king, it was doubtless on the supposition (on which he gives no opinion) that Anne was guilty. But, even admitting this hypothesis, is it not carrying flattery of the terrible autocrat very far, to compare him with Job as the prelate does, for in another part of this letter he says: "By accepting all adversity, without despair and without murmuring, your Grace will give opportunity to God to multiply His blessings, as He did to His faithful servant Job, to whom, after his great calamity, and to reward his patience, He restored the double of what he had possessed." As regards the king, Cranmer had found for himself a false conscience, which led him into deceitful ways: his letter, although he still tries to defend Anne, cannot be justified.

He was about to despatch the letter, when he received a message from the lord-chancellor, desiring him to go to the Star-Chamber. The archbishop hastened across the Thames, and found at the appointed place not only Audley, but the Lords Oxford and Sussex, and the lord-chamberlain. These noblemen laid before him the charges brought against Anne Boleyn, adding that they could be proved, though they did not themselves produce any proof. On his return to Lambeth, Cranmer added a postscript to his letter, in which he expressed his extreme sorrow at the report that had just been made to him.

The morning of the same day (May 3) was a sad one in the Tower. By a refinement of cruelty, the king had ordered two of the queen's enemies—Lady Boleyn and Mistress Cosyns—to be always near her; to which end they slept in her room, while Kingston and his wife slept outside against her chamber-door. What could be the object of these strange precautions? We can only see one. Every word that fell from Anne, even in her convulsions or in her dreams, would be perfidiously caught up, and reported to the king's agents with malicious interpretations. Anne, pardoning the former conduct of these ladies, and wholly engrossed with her father's sorrow, thought she might ask for news about him from the persons who had been given her for companions; but the two women, who never spoke to her without rudeness, refused to give her any information. "The king knew what he was doing," said Anne to Kingston, "when he put these two women about me. I could have desired to have two ladies of my chamber, persons whom I love; but his Majesty has had the cruelty to give me those whom I could never endure."

The punishment continued. Lady Boleyn, hoping to detect some confusion in her niece's face, told her that her brother, Lord Rochford, was also in the Tower. Anne, who had somewhat recovered her strength, answered calmly, "I am glad to learn that he is so near me." "Madam," added Kingston, "Weston and Brereton are also under my charge." The queen remained calm.

She purposed, however, to vindicate herself, and her first thought turned towards two of the most pious men in England: "Oh, if God permitted me," she said, "to have my bishops (meaning Cranmer and Latimer), they would plead to the king for me." She then remained silent for a few minutes. A sweet reflection passed through her mind and consoled her. Since she had undertaken the defence of the persecuted evangelicals, gratitude would doubtless impel them to pray for her. "I think," she said, "that the greater part of England is praying for me."

Anne had asked for her almoner, and, as some hours had elapsed without his arrival, gloomy images once more arose to sadden her mind. "To be a queen," she said, "and to be treated so cruelly—treated as queen never was before!" Then, as if a ray of sunshine had scattered the clouds, she exclaimed: "No, I shall not die—no, I will not die! . . . The king has put me in prison only to prove me." The terrible struggle was too great for the young woman: distressed in her feelings beyond the bounds of endurance, she almost lost her senses. Then, attacked by a fresh hysterical paroxysm, the unfortunate lady burst into laughter. On coming to herself after a while, she cried: "I will have justice . . . justice . . . justice!" Kingston, who was present, bowed and said: "Assuredly, madam." "If any man accuses me," she continued, "I can only say—No. They can bring no witness against me." Then she had, all at once, an extraordinary attack: she fell down in delirium, and with eyes starting, as if she were looking into the future, and could foresee the chastisement with which God would punish the infamous wickedness of which she was the victim, she exclaimed: "If I am put to death, there will be great judgments upon England for seven years . . . And I . . . I shall be in heaven . . . for I have done many good deeds during my life."

CHAPTER TEN

The Execution of Anne Boleyn

(May 1536)

EVERYTHING was preparing for the unjust judgment which was to have so cruel a termination. Justice is bound to watch that the laws are observed, and to punish the guilty; but if law is to be just law, the judges must listen fairly to the accused, diligently discharge all the duties to which their office calls them, and not permit themselves to be influenced either by the presents or the solicitations, the threats or the favours, or the rank (even should it be royal) of the prosecutor. Their decisions should be inspired only by such motives as they can give an account of to the Supreme Judge; their sentences must be arrived at through attentive consideration and serious reflection. For them there are no other guides than impartiality, conscience, and law. But the queen was not to appear before such judges: those who were about to dispose of her life set themselves in opposition to these imperious conditions.

Henry's agents redoubled their exertions to obtain, either from the ladies of the court or from the accused men, some deposition against Anne; but it was in vain. Even the women whom her elevation had eclipsed could allege nothing against her. Henry Norris, William Brereton, and Sir Francis Weston were carefully interrogated, one after the other: the examiners tried to make them confess to adultery, but they stoutly denied it; whereupon the king's agents, who were determined to get at something, began a fresh enquiry, and cross-examined the prisoners. It is believed that the gentlemen of the court were exempted from torture, but that the rack was applied to Mark Smeaton, who was thus made to confess all they wanted. It is more probable that the vile musician, a man of weak head and extreme vanity, being offended that his sovereign had not condescended even to look at him, yielded to the vengeance of irritated self-esteem. The queen had not been willing to give him the honour of a look—he boasted of adultery. The three gentlemen persevered in their declaration touching the queen's innocence: Lord Rochford did the same. The disheartened prosecutor wrote to the Lord-Treasurer: "This is to inform you that no one, except Mark, will confess anything against her; wherefore I imagine, if there be no other evidence, the business will be injurious to the king's honour." The lawyers knew the value to be given to the musician's words. If the verdict was left to the equitable interpretation of the law—if the king did not bring his sovereign influence to bear upon the decisions of the judges, there could be no doubt as to the issue of the hateful trial.

But every passion was at work to paralyse the power of right. Vainly the queen's innocence shone forth on every side —the conspiracy formed against her grew stronger every day. To the wickedness of Lady Rochford, the jealousies of an intriguing *camarilla*, the hatred of the papal party, the un-bridled ambition aroused in certain families by the prospects of the despot's couch soon to be empty though stained with blood, and to the instability of weak men was added the strong will of Henry VIII, as determined to get rid of Anne by death as he had been to separate from Catherine by divorce. The queen understood that she must die; and, wishing to be prepared, she sought to wean herself from that life which had so many attractions for her. She felt that the pleasures she had so much enjoyed were vain; the knowledge that she had endeavoured to acquire, superficial; the virtue to which she had aspired, imperfect; and the active life she had desired, without decisive results. The vanity of all created things, once proclaimed by one who also had occupied a throne, struck her heart. Everything being taken from her, she renounced

Le vain espoir de ce muable monde.[1]

Anne, giving up everything, turned towards a better life, and sought to strengthen herself in God.[2]

Such were her affecting dispositions when the duke of

[1] "The vain hope of this changeable world."—*Histoire d'Anne de Boleyn* by Crespin, p. 140.
[2] *Ibid.*, p. 190.

Norfolk, accompanied by other noblemen, came in the king's name to set before her the charges brought against her, to summon her to speak the truth, and to assure her that, if she confessed her fault, the king might pardon her. Anne replied with the dignity of a queen still upon the throne, and with the calmness of a Christian at the gates of eternity. She threw back with noble indignation the vile accusations of which the royal commissioners were the channel.

"You call upon me to speak the truth," she said to Norfolk. "Well then, the king shall know it," and she dismissed the lords. It was beneath her to plead her cause before these malicious courtiers, but she would tell her husband the truth. Left alone, she sat down to write that celebrated letter, a noble monument of the elevation of her soul; a letter full of the tenderest complaints and the sharpest protests, in which her innocence shines forth, and which combines at once so much nature and eloquence that in the opinion of the most competent judges it deserves to be handed down to posterity.

It ran as follows:—

"Your Grace's displeasure and my imprisonment are things so strange unto me, that what to write, or what to excuse, I am altogether ignorant. Whereas you sent to me (willing me to confess a truth and so obtain your favour), by such a one whom you know to be my ancient professed enemy; I no sooner received this message by him,[1] than I rightly conceived your meaning; and if, as you say, confessing a truth indeed may procure my safety, I shall with all willingness and duty perform your command.

"But let not your Grace ever imagine that your poor wife will ever be brought to acknowledge a fault, where not so much as a thought thereof ever proceeded. And, to speak truth, never a prince had wife more loyal in all duty and in all true affection, than you have ever found in Anne Boleyn —with which name and place I could willingly have contented myself, if God and your Grace's pleasure had so pleased. Neither did I at any time so far forget myself in my exaltation or received queenship, but that I always looked for such alteration as I now find; for the ground of my prefer-

[1] [It is probable that Anne means the Duke of Suffolk.]

ment being on no surer foundation than your Grace's fancy, the least alteration was fit and sufficient (I knew) to draw that fancy to some other subject.

"You have chosen me from a low estate to be your queen and companion, far beyond my desert or desire. If then you found me worthy of such honour, good your Grace, let not any light fancy or bad counsel of my enemies withdraw your princely favour from me; neither let that stain—that un-worthy stain—of a disloyal heart towards your good Grace ever cast so foul a blot on me and on the infant princess, your daughter.

"Try me, good king, but let me have a lawful trial, and let not my sworn enemies sit as my accusers and as my judges; yea, let me receive an open trial, for my truth shall fear no open shames. Then shall you see either mine innocence cleared, your suspicions and conscience satisfied, the ignominy and slander of the world stopped—or my guilt openly declared; so that whatever God and you may determine of, your Grace may be freed from an open censure, and mine offence being so lawfully proved, your Grace may be at liberty, both before God and man, not only to execute worthy punishment on me, as an unfaithful wife, but to follow your affection already settled on that party, for whose sake I am now as I am; whose name I could, some good while since, have pointed unto, your Grace being not ignorant of my suspicion therein. But if you have already determined of me, and that not only my death but an infamous slander must bring you the joying of your desired happiness, then I desire of God that He will pardon your great sin herein, and likewise my enemies, the instruments thereof; and that He will not call you to a strict account for your unprincely and cruel usage of me at His general judgment-seat, where both you and myself must shortly appear; and in whose just judgment, I doubt not (whatsoever the world may think of me), mine innocency shall be openly known and sufficiently cleared.

"My last and only request shall be, that myself may only bear the burden of your Grace's displeasure, and that it may not touch the innocent souls of those poor gentlemen, who, as I understand, are likewise in strait imprisonment for my sake. If ever I have found favour in your sight—if ever the name of

K(II)

Anne Boleyn have been pleasing in your ears—then let me obtain this request; and so I will leave to trouble your Grace any further; with mine earnest prayer to the Trinity to have your Grace in His good keeping, and to direct you in all your actions.

"From my doleful prison in the Tower, the 6th of May.

"ANNE BOLEYN."

We see Anne thoroughly in this letter, one of the most touching that was ever written. Injured in her honour, she speaks without fear, as one on the threshold of eternity. If there were no other proofs of her innocence, this document alone would suffice to gain her cause in the eyes of an impartial and intelligent posterity.[1]

This noble letter aroused a tempest in the king's heart. The firm innocence stamped on it; the mention of Henry's tastes, and especially of his inclination for Jane Seymour; Anne's declaration that she had anticipated her husband's infidelity; the solemn appeal to the day of judgment; and the thought of the injury which such noble language would do to his reputation—all combined to fill that haughty prince with vexation, hatred, and wrath. The letter gives the real solution of the enigma. A guilty caprice had inclined Henry to Anne Boleyn; another caprice inclined him now to Jane Seymour. This explanation is so patent that no one need look for another.

Henry determined to inflict a great humiliation upon this daring woman. He would strip her of the name of wife, and pretend that she had only been his concubine. As his marriage with Catherine of Aragon had been declared null because of her union with his brother Arthur, Henry imagined that his marriage with Anne Boleyn might be annulled because of an attachment once entertained for her by Percy, afterwards duke of Northumberland. When that nobleman was summoned before Cromwell, he thought that he also was to be thrown into the Tower as the queen's lover; but the summons had reference

---

[1] A copy of this letter was found among the papers of Thomas Cromwell, at that time the king's chief minister. "It is universally known," says Sir Henry Ellis, "as one of the finest compositions in the English language." [The original must have been sent by Cromwell to the King. Although its authenticity has been called in question, it is undoubtedly genuine. It is impossible to regard it as "an Elizabethan forgery."]

to quite a different matter. "There was a pre-contract of marriage between you and Anne Boleyn?" asked the king's vicar-general. "None at all," he answered; and in order that his declaration might be recorded, he wrote it down and sent it to Cromwell. In it he said: "Referring to the oath I made in this matter before the archbishops of Canterbury and York, and before the Blessed Body of our Saviour, which I received in the presence of the duke of Norfolk and others of his Majesty's counsellors, I acknowledge to have eaten the Holy Sacrament to my condemnation, if there was any contract or promise of marriage between the queen and me. This 13th of May, in the twenty-eighth year of his majesty King Henry VIII." This declaration was clear, but the barbarous monarch did not relinquish his idea.

A special commission had been appointed, on the 24th of April, "to judge of certain offences committed at London, Hampton Court, and Greenwich." They desired to give to this trial the appearance at least of justice; and as the alleged offences were committed in the counties of Middlesex and Kent, the indictment was laid before the grand juries of both counties. On the 10th of May they found a true bill. The writers favourable to Henry VIII in this business—and they are few—have acknowledged that these "hideous charges" (to use the words of one of them) were but fables invented at pleasure, and which "overstepped all ordinary bounds of credulity." Various explanations have been given of the conduct of these juries; the most natural appears to be that they accommodated themselves, according to the servile manner of the times, to the king's despotic will, which was always to be feared, but more especially in matters that concerned his own person.

The acts that followed were as prompt as they were cruel. Two days later (on May 12) Norris, Weston, Brereton, and the musician were taken to Westminster, and brought before a commission composed of the dukes of Norfolk and Suffolk, Henry's two intimates, and other lords; it is even said that the earl of Wiltshire was present. The three gentlemen repelled the charge with unshakable firmness. "I would endure a thousand deaths," said Norris, "sooner than betray the innocent. I declare, upon my honour, that the queen is innocent, and am ready to support my testimony in arms against all the world." When this language of Henry VIII's favourite was reported to that prince, he cried out: "Hang him up, then—hang him up!"[1] The wretched musician alone confessed a crime which would give him a place in history. He did not reap the reward promised to his infamy. Perhaps it was imagined that his death would guarantee his silence, and that his punishment would corroborate his defamations. The three gentlemen were condemned to be beheaded, and the musician to be hanged.

Three days later (on May 15) the queen and her brother were taken before their peers in the great hall of the Tower, to which the Lord Mayor and a few aldermen and citizens alone were admitted. The duke of Norfolk had received orders to assemble a certain number of peers to form a court: they were twenty-six in all, and most of them enemies of Anne and of the Reformation. The earl of Wiltshire, Anne's father, was not of the number, as Sanders pretends. The duke of Norfolk, the personal enemy of the unfortunate queen, that uncle who hated her as much as he should have loved her, had been appointed to select the judges and to preside over the trial: a circumstance indicative of the spirit in which it was to be conducted. Norfolk took his seat, having the lord-chancellor on his right and the duke of Suffolk on his left, and in front of him sat as deputy earl-marshal the earl of Surrey, Norfolk's son, an upright man, but a proud and warm supporter of Romanism. The queen was announced: she was received in deep silence. Before her went the governor of the Tower, behind her came Lady Kingston and Lady Boleyn. Anne advanced with dignity, adorned with the ensigns of royalty, and, after gracefully saluting the court, took her seat in the chair accorded either to her weakness or her rank. She had no defender; but the modesty of her countenance, the dignity of her manner, the peace of her conscience, which found expression in the serenity of her look, touched even her enemies. She appeared before the tribunal of men, thinking only of the tribunal of God; and, relying

---

[1] Godwin's *Annals*, p. 139.—Queen Elizabeth raised his son to the peerage, and four of his grandsons were among the greatest of England's captains during the reign of Anne Boleyn's daughter.

upon her innocence, she did not fear those whom but yesterday she had ruled as a queen. One might have said from the calmness and nobility of her deportment, so assured and so majestic, that she was come, not to be tried as a criminal, but to receive the honours due to sovereigns. She was as firm, says a contemporary, as an oak that fears neither the hail nor the furious blasts of the wind.[1]

The court ordered the indictment to be read; it charged the queen with adultery, incest, and conspiracy against the king's person. Anne held up her hand and pleaded "not guilty," and then refuted and tore to tatters, calmly yet forcibly, the accusations brought against her. Having an "excellent quick wit," and being a ready speaker, she did not utter a word that did not strike home,[2] though full of moderation; but the tone of her voice, the calmness of her features, and the dignity of her countenance pleaded more eloquently than her words. It was impossible to look at her or to hear her, and not declare her innocent, says an eye-witness.[3] Accordingly there was a report in the Tower, and even in the city, that the queen had cleared herself by a most wise and noble speech and that she would be acquitted.

While Anne was speaking, the duke of Northumberland, who had once loved her and whom Henry had cruelly enrolled among the number of her judges, betrayed by his uneasy movements the agitation of his bosom. Unable to endure the frightful torment any longer, he rose, pretending indisposition, and hastily left the hall before the fatal verdict was pronounced.

The king waited impatiently for the moment when he could introduce Jane Seymour into Anne Boleyn's empty apartments. Unanimity of votes was not necessary among the "lords triers." In England, during the sixteenth century, there was pride in the people, but servility (with few exceptions) among the great. The axe that had severed the head

---

[1] *Histoire d'Anne Boleyn, royne d'Angleterre,* by Crespin, p. 200. The last lines of this narrative are dated 2nd of June, 1536, only seventeen days after the queen's trial and sentence. It would appear that the author, Crespin, lord of Milherve, was an eye-witness of the scene.

[2] "Having an excellent quick wit and being a ready speaker, she did so answer all objections."—*Harleian MSS.*

[3] *Histoire d'Anne Boleyn, royne d'Angleterre,* by Crespin, p. 201.

of the venerable bishop of Rochester and of the ex-chancellor More had taught a fearful lesson to all who might be disposed to resist the despotic desires of the prince. The court feared to confront the queen with the musician, the only witness against her, and declared her guilty without other formality. The incomprehensible facility with which the nobility were then accustomed to submit to the inflexible will of the monarch could leave no room for doubt as to the catastrophe by which this tragedy would be terminated.[1]

The duke of Norfolk, as lord high-steward, pronounced sentence: that the queen should be taken back to the Tower, and there on the green should be burnt or beheaded, *according to his Majesty's good pleasure*. The court, desirous of leaving a little space for Henry's compassion, left the mode of death to him: he might do the queen the favour of being only decapitated.

Anne heard this infamous doom with calmness. No change was observed in her features; the consciousness of innocence upheld her heart. Clasping her hands and raising her eyes to heaven, she cried out: "O Father, O Creator! Thou who art the way, the truth, and the life, knowest that I have not deserved this death!" Then, turning to her cruel uncle and the other lords, she said: "My lords, I do not say that my opinion ought to be preferred to your judgment; but if you have reasons to justify it, they must be other than those which have been produced in court, for I am wholly innocent of all the matters of which I have been accused, so that I cannot call upon God to pardon me. I have always been faithful to the king my lord; but perhaps I have not always shown to him such a perfect humility and reverence as his graciousness and courtesy deserved, and the honour he hath done me required. I confess that I have often had jealous fancies against him which I had not wisdom or strength enough to repress. But God knows that I have not otherwise trespassed against him. Do not think I say this in the hope of prolonging my life, for He who saveth from death has taught me how to die, and will strengthen my faith. Think not, however, that I am so bewildered in mind that I do not care to vindicate my innocence. I knew that it would avail me little to defend it

---

[1] The Catholic historian, Lingard, makes this remark. Vol. iii. ch. v.

at the last moment, if I had not maintained it all my life long, as much as ever queen did. Still the last words of my mouth shall justify my honour. As for my brother and the other gentlemen who are unjustly condemned, I would willingly die to save them; but as that is not the king's pleasure, I shall accompany them in death. And then afterwards I shall live in eternal peace and joy without end, where I will pray to God for the king—and for you, my lords."

The wisdom and eloquence of this speech, aided by the queen's beauty and the touching expression of her voice, moved even her enemies. But Norfolk, determined upon carrying out his hateful task, ordered her to lay aside her royal insignia. She did so, and commending herself to all their prayers, returned to her prison.

Lord Rochford's trial had preceded that of his sister the queen. He was calm and firm, and answered every question point by point, with much clearness and decision. But it was useless for him to affirm the queen's innocence—useless to declare that he had always respected her as a sister, as an "honoured lady": he was condemned to be beheaded and quartered.

The court broke up, and while the courtiers, who had just sealed with the blood of an innocent queen their servile submission to the most formidable of despots, were returning to their amusements and base flatteries, the Lord Mayor turned to a friend and said to him: "I can only observe one thing in this trial—the fixed resolution to get rid of the queen at any price." And that is the verdict of posterity.

The wretches who had entered into this iniquitous plot were eager to have it ended. On the 17th of May the gentlemen who were to be executed were brought together into a hall of the Tower. They embraced, commended each other to God, and prepared to depart. The constable of the Tower, fearing that they would speak upon the scaffold, reminded them that the honour due to the king would not permit them to doubt the justice of their sentence. When they reached the place of punishment, Lord Rochford, no longer able to keep silence, turned towards the spectators and said: "My friends, I am going to die, as such is his Majesty's pleasure. I do not complain of my death, for I have committed many sins

during my life, but *I have never injured the king*. May God grant
him a long and happy life!" Then, according to the chronicler,
he presented his head "to the sharp axe which severed it
at a blow." Norris, Weston, and Brereton were beheaded
after him.

The king, before putting his wife to death, desired to
perform an act not less cruel: he was determined to annul his
marriage with Anne, notwithstanding Northumberland's
denials. Did he wish to avoid the reproach of causing his wife
to perish by the hands of the executioner? or, in a fit of anger,
did he desire to strike the queen on all sides at once? We
cannot tell. Be that as it may, the king in his wrath did not
see that he was contradicting himself; that if there was no
marriage between him and Anne, there could be no adultery,
and that the sentence, based on this crime, was *ex facto* null.
Cranmer, the most unfortunate, but perhaps not the least
guilty of all the lords who lent themselves servilely to the
despotic wishes of the prince—Cranmer believed (as it
appears) that the position of the queen would thus become
better; that her life would be saved, if she could no longer be
regarded as having been Henry's wife. This excuses, although
only slightly, his great weakness. He told the unhappy lady that
he was commissioned to find the means of declaring null and
void the ties which united her to the king. Anne, stunned by
the sentence pronounced upon her, was also of opinion that
it was an expedient invented by some relics of Henry's regard,
to rescue her from the bitterness of death. Her heart opened
to hope, and imagining that she would only be sent into
banishment, she formed a plan of returning to the continent.
"I will go to Antwerp," she said at dinner, with an almost
happy look. She knew that she would meet with Protestants
in that city, who would receive her with joy. But vain hope!
In the very letter wherein the governor of the Tower reports
this ingenuous remark of the queen, he asks for the king's
orders as to the construction of the scaffold. Henry desired
personally to order the arrangement of those planks which he
was about to stain with innocent blood.

About nine o'clock in the forenoon of the 17th of May the
lord-chancellor, the duke of Suffolk, the earl of Essex
(Cromwell), the earl of Sussex, with several doctors and

archdeacons, entered the chapel of Lambeth. The archbishop having taken his seat, and the objections made against the marriage of Henry VIII and Anne Boleyn having been read, the proctors of the king and of the queen admitted them, and the primate declared the marriage to be null and void.

On the very day of Anne Boleyn's divorce, Da Casale, the English envoy at Rome, having heard of the queen's imprisonment, hurried to the pontifical palace to inform Paul III of the good news. "I have never ceased praying to heaven for this favour," said the pope with delight, "and I have always hoped for it. Now his Majesty may accomplish an admirable work for the good of Christendom. Let the king become reconciled with Rome, and he will obtain from the king of France all that he can wish for. Let us be friends. I will send him a nuncio for that purpose. When the news of Cardinal Fisher's death reached Rome," he continued, recollecting that terrible bull, "it is true I found myself driven to a measure somewhat severe . . . but I never intended to follow up my words by deeds." Thus, according to the pope and his adherents, the imprisonment of Anne Boleyn was to reconcile England and Rome. This fact points to one of the causes which made Norfolk and other catholics enter into the conspiracy against her.

On the same day also (17th of May), towards evening, the queen learnt that the sentence would assuredly be carried out. Although it was declared that she had never been the king's wife, the doom pronounced upon her for adultery must nevertheless be accomplished. This is what Henry VIII called administering justice.

Anne desired to take the Lord's Supper, and asked to be left alone. About two hours after midnight the chaplain arrived; but, before partaking of the holy rite, there was one thing she wished to do. One fault weighed heavily on her heart. She felt that she had sinned against queen Catherine by consenting to marry the king. Her conscience reproached her with having injured the princess Mary. It filled her with the deepest sorrow, and she was eager, before she died, to make reparation to the daughter of the woman whose place she had taken. Anne would have liked to see Mary, to fall a queen at her feet, and implore her pardon; but alas! she could not: she was only to leave the prison for the scaffold. Resolved, however, to confess her fault, she did so in a striking manner which showed all the sincerity of her repentance and her firm determination to humble herself before Catherine's daughter. She begged Lady Kingston, the wife of the constable of the Tower, who had little regard for her, to take her seat in the chair of state. When the latter objected, Anne compelled her, and kneeling before her, she said, all the while crying bitterly: "I charge you—as you would answer before God—to go in my name to the princess Mary, to fall down before her as I do now before you, and ask her forgiveness for all the wrongs I have done her. Until that is done," she added, "my conscience will have no rest." At the moment when she was about to appear before the throne of God, she wished to make reparation for a fault that weighed heavily upon her heart. "In fact," she said, "I wish to do what a Christian ought." This touching incident leads us to hope that if, during life, Anne was simply an honest Protestant, trusting too much to her own works, the trial had borne fruit and had made her a true Christian. But of this she was to give a still more striking proof.

As she rose from her knees, Anne felt more calm and prepared to receive the sacrament. Before taking it, she once more declared her innocence of the crime imputed to her. The governor was present, and he did not fail to inform Cromwell of this declaration, made as it were in the presence of God. Anne had found in Christ's death new strength to endure her own: she sighed after the moment that would put an end to her sorrows. Contrary to her expectation, she was told that the execution was put off until the afternoon. "Mr. Kingston," she said, "I hear that I am not to die this afternoon, and I am very sorry for it; for I thought by this time to be dead and past my pain."—"Madam," replied the governor, "you will feel no pain, the blow will be so sharp and swift."—"Yes," resumed Anne, "I have heard say that the headsman is very clever," and then she added: "and I have but a little neck," putting her hand about it and smiling. Kingston left the room.

Meanwhile the devout adherents of the Roman primacy were full of exultation, and allowed the hopes to appear which Anne's death raised in their bosoms. "Sire," they told the king, "the tapers placed round the tomb of queen Catherine suddenly burst into flame of their own accord." They concluded, from this prodigy, that Roman-catholicism was once more about to shed its light on England.

The hour appointed for Anne's death now drew near. Protesting her innocence to the last, she determined to send to Henry a final message. It was carried to him by a member of his privy-chamber. Thus she addressed him: "Commend me to his Majesty, and tell him that he has ever been constant in his career of advancing me. From a private gentlewoman he made me a marchioness, from a marchioness a queen; and now that he has no higher degree of honour left, he gives my innocence the crown of martyrdom."[1] The gentleman went and reported this noble farewell to his master. Even the gaoler bore testimony to the peace and joy which filled Anne Boleyn's heart at this solemn moment. "I have seen men and also women executed," wrote Kingston to Cromwell, "and they have been in great sorrow; but to my knowledge this lady has much joy and pleasure in death."

Everything was arranged so that the murder should be perpetrated without publicity and without disturbance. Kingston received orders to turn all strangers out of the Tower, and readily obeyed. About eleven in the forenoon of the 19th of May, the dukes of Suffolk and Richmond, the lord-chancellor, Cromwell, the lord mayor with the sheriffs and aldermen, entered the Tower, and took their stations on the green, where the instrument of punishment had been erected. The executioner, whom Henry had summoned from Calais, was there with his sword and his attendants. A cannon, mounted on the walls, was to announce both to king and people that all was over. A little before noon Anne appeared, dressed in a robe of black damask, and attended by four of her maids of honour. She walked up to the block on which she was to lay her head. Her step was firm, her looks calm; all indicated the most complete resignation. "Never had she looked so beautiful before," says a French contemporary, then in London. Her eyes expressed a meek submission; a pleasing

[1] "Purposing to make her by martyrdom a saint in heaven."—Strype, p. 437.

smile accompanied the look she turned on the spectators of this tragic scene. But just when the executioners had made the last preparations, her emotion was so keen that she nearly fainted. Gradually she recovered her strength, and her faith in the Saviour filled her with courage and hope.

It is important to know what, in this last and solemn moment, were her sentiments towards the king. She had desired that Mary should be asked to forgive her wrongs: it was her duty, if she died a Christian, also to pardon Henry's faults. She must obey her Saviour, who said: "*Love your enemies, bless them that curse you.*" She had pardoned everything; but it was her duty to declare it before she died, and if she was humble, she would do so without affectation. Addressing those who had been her subjects and were then standing round her, she said: "Good Christian people, I am not come here to justify myself; I leave my justification entirely to Christ, in whom I put my trust. I will accuse no man, nor speak anything of that whereof I am accused, as I know full well that aught that I could say in my defence doth not appertain unto you, and that I could draw no hope of life from the same. I come here only to die, according as I have been condemned. I commend my judges to the Lord's mercy. I pray God (and I beg you to do the same) to save the king and send him long to reign over you, for a gentler or more merciful prince there never was. To me he was ever a good, gentle, and sovereign lord. And thus I take my leave of the world and of you, and I heartily desire you all to pray for me. O Lord, have mercy upon me! To God I commit my soul!"

Such are the simple words in which Anne gave utterance to the feelings of peace with which her heart was filled towards her husband, at the moment when he was robbing her of life. Had she said that she forgave him, she would have called up the memory of the king's crime, and would thus have appeared to claim the merit of her generous pardon. She did nothing of the sort. During one part of their wedded life, Henry had been a "good lord" to her. She desired to recall the good only, and buried the evil in oblivion. She did so without any thought of self; for she knew that before the gracious words could reach the king's ears, the sword would have already fallen upon her, and it would be impossible for Henry to arrest the fatal blow.

This Christian discourse could not fail to make a deep impression on all who heard her. As they looked at the unfortunate queen, they felt the tenderest compassion and the sharpest pain. The firmer her heart became, the weaker grew the spectators of the tragedy. Ere long they were unable to check the tears which the sufferer had the strength to restrain. One of the ladies of the royal victim approached her to cover her eyes; but Anne refused, saying that she was not afraid of death, and gave her as a memorial of that hour a little manuscript prayer-book that she had brought with her.

The queen then removed her white collar and took off her hood, that the action of the sword might not be impeded; this head-dress formed a queue and hung down behind. Then falling on her knees, she remained a few moments silent and motionless, praying inwardly. On rising up, she approached the fatal block, and laid her head on it: "O Christ, into thy hands I commit my soul!" she exclaimed. The headsman, disturbed by the mild expression of her face, hesitated a few seconds, but his courage returned. Anne cried out again: "O Jesus, receive my soul!" At this instant the sword of the executioner flashed in the air and her head fell. A cry escaped from the lips of the spectators, "as if they had received the blow upon their own necks." This is honourable to Anne's enemies, so that we may well believe the evidence. But immediately another sound was heard: the gunner, placed as a signal-man on the wall, had watched the different phases of the scene, holding a lighted match in his hand; scarcely had the head fallen, when he fired the gun, and the report, which was heard at a distance, bore to Henry the news of the crime which gave him Jane Seymour. The ladies of queen Anne, though almost lifeless with terror, would not permit the noble remains of the mistress whom they had loved so much to be touched by rude hands; they gathered round the body, wrapped it in a white sheet, and carried it (almost fainting as they were) to an old elm chest, which had been brought out of the arsenal and had been used for storing arrows. This rough box was the last home assigned to her who had inhabited costly palaces: not so much as a coffin

had been provided for her. The ladies placed in it Anne's
head and body; "the eyes and lips were observed to move,"
says a document, as if her mouth was repeating the last words
it had uttered. She was immediately buried in the Tower
chapel.

Thus died Anne Boleyn. If the violent passions of a prince
and the meanness of his courtiers brought her to an untimely
death, hatred and credulity have killed her a second time.
But an infamous calumny, forged by dishonest individuals,
ought to be sternly rejected by all sensible men. Not in vain
did Anne, at the hour of death, place her cause in the hands
of God, and we willingly believe that all enlightened men,
without prejudice or partiality, among Roman-catholics as
among others, turn with disgust from the vile falsehoods of
malicious courtiers and the deceitful fables of the papist
Sanders and his followers.

On the morning of this day, Henry VIII had dressed
himself in white, as for a festival, and ordered a hunting-
party. There was a great stir round the palace: huntsmen
hurrying to and fro, dogs baying, horns sounding, nobles
arriving. The troop was formed and they all set off for Epping
Forest, where the sport began. At noon the hunters met to
repose themselves under an oak which still bears the name
of the *King's Oak*. Henry had taken his seat beneath it, surrounded by his suite and the dogs; he listened and seemed to
be agitated. Suddenly a cannon shot resounded through the
forest—it was the concerted signal—the queen's head had
fallen. "Ha, ha!" exclaimed the king, rising, "the deed is
done! uncouple the hounds and away." Horns and trumpets
were sounded, and dogs and horses were soon in pursuit.
The wretched prince, led away by his passions, forgot that
there is a God to whom he would have to render an account
not only of the execution in the Tower, but of the chase in the
forest; and by these cruel acts, which should have shocked
the hearts even of his courtiers, he branded himself with his
own hands as a great criminal. The king and his court returned
to the palace before night-fall.

At last Henry was free. He had desired Jane Seymour, and
everything had been invented—adultery, incest—to break the
bonds that united him to the queen. The proofs of Anne's

crimes failing, the ferocious acts of the king were to supply their place. Could those who witnessed the cruelty of the husband venture to doubt the guilt of the wife? Henry had become inhuman that he might not appear faithless. Now that the object was obtained, it only remained to profit by his crime. His impatience to gratify his passions made him flout all propriety. The mournful death of his queen; the Christian words that she had uttered, kissing as it were the cruel hand that struck her—nothing softened his heart. On the 19th May, the day of Anne's execution, Cranmer issued a special licence to enable the king to marry again. On the 20th, Henry and Jane Seymour were betrothed, and ten days later they were married privately at York Place. It would have been difficult to say in a more striking manner: "This is why Anne Boleyn is no more!" When we see side by side the bloodstained block on which Anne had received her death-blow, and the brilliant altar before which Henry and Jane were united, we can understand the story. The prince, at once voluptuous and cruel, liked to combine the most contrary objects in the same picture—crime and festivities, marriage and death, sensuality and hatred. He showed himself the most magnificent and most civilized monarch of Europe; but also the rival of those barbarous kings of savage hordes who take delight in cutting off the heads of those who have been their favourites and even the objects of their most passionate love. We must employ different standards in judging of the same person, when we regard him as a private and as a public individual. The Tudor prince, so guilty as a husband, father, and friend, did much good as a ruler for England. Louis XIV, as well as Henry VIII, had some of the characteristics of a great king; and his moral life was certainly not better than that of his prototype in England. He had as many, and even more mistresses than the predecessor of the Stuarts had wives; but the only advantage which the French monarch had over the English one is that he knew how to get rid of them without cutting off their heads.

The death of Anne Boleyn caused a great sensation in Europe, as that of Fisher and More had done before it. Her innocence, which Henry (it is said) acknowledged on his death-bed, was denied by some and maintained by others;

but all men of principle expressed a feeling of horror when they heard of her punishment. The Protestant princes and divines of Germany had not a doubt that this cruel act was the pledge of reconciliation offered to the pope by Henry VIII, and renounced the alliance they were on the point of concluding with England. "At last I am free from that journey," said Melanchthon, whom Anne Boleyn's death, added to that of Sir Thomas More, had rendered even less desirous of approaching the prince who had struck them. "The queen," he continued, "accused, rather than convicted, of adultery, has suffered the penalty of death, and that catastrophe has wrought great changes in our plans."

Somewhat later the Protestants ascribed Anne's death especially to the pope: "That blow came from Rome," they cried; "in Rome all these tricks and plots are contrived." In this I suspect there is a mistake. The plots of the Roman court against Elizabeth have caused it to be accused of similar designs against the mother of the great Protestant queen. The friends of that court in England were probably no strangers to the crime, but the great criminal was Henry.

CHAPTER ELEVEN

Catholicism versus Protestantism
(Summer 1536)

After queen Anne's death the two parties were agitated
in opposite directions. The friends of the Reformation
wished to show that the disgrace of that princess did
not carry with it the disgrace of the cause they had at heart,
and consequently believed that they ought to accelerate the
Reform movement. The friends of Rome and its doctrines
imagining, on their part, that the queen's death had put
their affairs in good train, thought they had but to redouble
their activity to gain a complete victory. The latter seemed
indeed to have some reasons for encouragement. If Catherine's
death four months earlier reconciled Henry VIII and the
Emperor just when the latter was threatening England with
invasion, the death of Anne Boleyn appeared as if it would
reconcile the king with Paul III, who was ready to issue his
terrible bull. Henry's wives played a great part in his private
history, but they had also a certain importance in his relations
with the powers of Europe, especially with the pope. The
court of Rome was very desirous of reviving the ancient
friendship which had united it to England. These desires
increased rapidly.

On the 20th of May, when the news of the queen's prosecution arrived in Rome, both pope and cardinals were transported
with joy. The frightful calumnies of which Anne was the
victim served the cause of the papacy too well not to be
accepted as truths, and all felt persuaded that, if she fell from
the throne, the acts done at London against the Italian
primacy would fall with her. When Henry's agent, Da Casale,
informed the pope that the queen had been sent to prison,
Paul exclaimed with delight: "I always thought, when I saw
Henry endowed with *so many virtues*, that heaven would not
forsake him. If he is willing to unite with me," he added, "I

303

shall have authority enough to enjoin the Emperor and the king of France to make peace with him; and the king of England, reconciled with the Church, will command the powers of Europe." At the same time Paul III confessed that he had made a mistake in raising Fisher to the cardinalate, and wound up this pontifical effusion in the kindest of terms. Da Casale, much delighted on his part, asked whether he was to repeat these matters to the king. "Tell him," answered the pope, "that his Majesty may, without hesitation, expect everything from me." Da Casale, therefore, made his report to London, and intimated that, if Henry made the least sign of reconciliation, the pope would immediately send him a nuncio. Thus Paul left not a stone unturned to win over the king of England. He extolled his virtues, promised him the foremost place in Europe, flattered his vanity as an author, and did not fear—he the infallible one—to acknowledge that he had made a mistake. Everybody at the court of Rome felt convinced that England was about to return to the bosom of the Church; Cardinal Campeggio even sent his brother to London to resume possession of the bishopric of Salisbury, of which he had been deprived in 1534. Up to the end of June, the pope and the cardinals became kinder and more respectful to the English, and entertained the most flattering expectations regarding the return of England.

Would these expectations be realized? Henry VIII was not one man, but two: his domestic passions and his public acts formed two departments entirely distinct. Guided as an individual by passion, he was, as a king, sometimes led by just views. He believed that neither pope nor foreign monarch had a right to exercise the smallest jurisdiction in England. He was therefore resolved—and this saved England—to maintain the rupture with Rome. One circumstance might have taught him that in all respects it was the best thing he could do.

Rome has two modes of bringing back princes under her yoke—flattery and abuse. The pope had adopted the first: a person, at that time without influence, Reginald Pole, an Englishman, and also a relative and *protégé* of Henry, undertook the second. In 1535 he was in the north of Italy. Burning with love for the papacy and hatred for the king, his benefactor, he wrote a defence of the unity of the Church, addressed to Henry VIII, and overflowing with violence. The wise and pious Contarini, to whom he showed it, begged him to soften a tone that might cause much harm. As Pole refused, Contarini entreated him at least to submit his manuscript to the pope; but the young Englishman, fearing that Paul would require him to suppress the untoward publication, declined to accede to his friend's request. His object was, not to convert the king, but to stir up the English against their lawful prince, and induce them to fall prostrate again before the Roman pontiff. The treatise, finished in the winter of 1535–36, before Anne's trial, reached London the first week in June. Tunstall, now bishop of Durham, and Pole's friend, read the book, which contained a few truths mixed up with great errors, and then communicated it to the king. Never did haughty monarch receive so rude a lesson.

"Shall I write to you, O prince," said the young Englishman, "or shall I not? Observing in you the certain symptoms of the most dangerous malady, and assured as I am that I possess the remedies suitable to cure you, how can I refrain from pronouncing the word which alone can preserve your life? I love you, sire, as son never loved his father, and God perhaps will make my voice to be like that of His own Son, *whose voice even the dead hear.* O prince, you are dealing the most deadly blow against the Church that it can possibly receive; you rob it of the chief whom it possesses upon earth. Why should a king, who is the supreme head of the State, occupy a similar place in the Church? If we may trust the arguments of your doctors, we must conclude that Nero was the head of the Church. We should laugh, if the laughter were not to be followed by tears. There is as great a distance between the ecclesiastical and the civil power, as there is between heaven and earth. There are three estates in human society: first, the people; then the king, who is the son of the people; and lastly, the priest, who being the *spouse of the people* is consequently the *father of the king.* But you, in imitation of the pride of Lucifer, set yourself above the vicar of Jesus Christ. . . .

"What! you have rent the Church, as it was never before rent in that island, you have plundered and cruelly tormented it, and you claim, in virtue of such merits, to be called its supreme head. There are two Churches: if you are at the head of one, it is not the Church of Christ; if you are, it is like Satan, who is the prince of the world, which he oppresses under his tyranny. . . . You reign, but after the fashion of the Turks. A simple nod of your head has more power than ancient laws and rights. Sword in hand you decide religious controversies. Is not that thoroughly Turkish and barbarian? . . .

"O England! if you have not forgotten your ancient liberty, what indignation ought to possess you, when you see your king plunder, condemn, murder, squander all your wealth, and leave you nothing but tears. Beware, for if you let your grievances be heard, you will be afflicted with still deeper wounds. O my country! it is in your power to change your great sorrow into greater joy. Neither Nero nor Domitian, nor —I dare affirm—Luther himself, if he had been king of England, would have wished to avenge himself by putting to death such men as Fisher and Sir Thomas More! . . .

"What king has ever given more numerous signs of respect to the supreme pontiff than that Francis I who spoke of you, O Henry, in words received with applause by the whole Christian world: 'your friend even to the altar' (i.e. to the last extremity)?—The Emperor Charles has just subdued the pirates; but is there any pirate that is worse than you? Have you not plundered the wealth of the Church, thrown the bodies of the saints into prison, and reduced men's souls to slavery? If I heard that the Emperor with all his fleet was sailing for Constantinople, I would fall at his feet, and say—were it even in the straits of the Hellespont—'O Emperor, what are you thinking of? Do you not see that a much greater danger than the Turks threatens the Christian republic? Change your route. What would be the use of expelling the Turks from Europe, when new Turks are hatched among us?' Certainly the English for slighter causes have forced their kings to put off their crowns."

After the apostrophe addressed to Charles V, Reginald Pole returns to Henry VIII, and imagining himself to be the prophet Elijah before king Ahab, he says with great boldness: "O king, the Lord hath commanded me to curse you; but if you will patiently listen to me, he will return you good for evil. Why delay to confess your sin? Do not say that you have done everything according to the rules of Holy Scripture. Does not the Church, which gives it authority, know what is to be received and what rejected? You have forsaken the fountain of wisdom. Return to the Church, O prince! and all that you have lost you shall regain with more splendour and glory.

"But if anyone hears the sound of the trumpet and does not heed it, the sword is drawn from the scabbard, the guilty is smitten, and his blood is upon his own head."

We have hardly given the flower of this long tirade, written in the style of the 16th century, which, divided into four books, fills one hundred and ninety-two folio pages. It reached England at the moment of the condemnation of the innocent Anne, which Pole unconsciously protested against as unjust, more unjust even than the sentences of Fisher and More. Henry did not at first read his "pupil's" philippic through. He saw enough, however, to regard it as an insult, a divorce which Italy had sent him. He ordered Pole to return to England; but the latter remembered too well the fate of Fisher and Sir Thomas More to run the risk. Bishop Tunstall, one of the enemies of the Reformation, wrote, however, to Pole, that as Christ was the head of the Church, to separate it from the pope was not to separate from its head. This refutation was short but complete.

The king was resolved to maintain his independence of the pope. Some have ascribed this determination to Pole's treatise, and others to the influence of Jane Seymour. Both these circumstances may have had some weight in Henry's mind; but the great cause, we repeat, is that he would not suffer any master but himself in England. Gardiner replied to Pole in a treatise which he entitled: *On True Obedience*, to which Bonner wrote the preface.

Paul III was not the only one who descried the signal of triumph in Anne's death: the princess Mary believed that she would now become heiress-presumptive to the crown. Lady Kingston, having discharged Anne Boleyn's Christian commission, Catherine's daughter, but slightly affected by this touching conduct, took advantage of it for her own interest, and charged that lady with a letter addressed to Cromwell, in which she begged him to intercede for her with the king, so that the rank which belonged to her should be restored. Henry consented to receive his daughter into favour, but not without conditions: "Madam," said Norfolk, who had been sent to her by the king, "here are the articles which require your signature."

The daughter of the proud Catherine of Aragon was to acknowledge four points: the supremacy of the king, the imposture of the pope, the incest of her own mother, and her own illegitimacy. She refused, but as Norfolk was not to be shaken, she signed the two first articles; then laying down the pen, she exclaimed: "As for my own shame and my mother's —never!" Cromwell threatened her, called her obstinate and unnatural, and told her that her father would abandon her: the unhappy princess signed everything. She was restored to favour, and given the means to maintain a household suitable to her rank; but she was deceived in thinking that the misfortune of her little half-sister Elizabeth would replace her on the steps of the throne.

Parliament met on the 8th of June, when the chancellor announced to them that the king, notwithstanding his mishaps in matrimony, *had yielded to the humble solicitations of the nobility*, and formed a new union. The two houses ratified the accomplished facts. No man desired to stir the ashes from which sparks might issue and kindle a great conflagration. At no price would they compromise the most exalted persons in the kingdom, and especially the king. All the allegations, even the most absurd, were admitted: Parliament wanted to have done with the matter. It even went further: the king was thanked for the *most excellent goodness* which had induced him to marry a lady whose brilliant youth, remarkable beauty, and purity of blood were the sure pledges of the happy issue which a marriage with her could not fail to produce; and his most respectful subjects, determined to bury the faults of their prince under flowers, compared him for beauty to Absalom, for strength to Samson, and for wisdom to Solomon. Parliament added that as the daughters of Catherine and Anne were both illegitimate, the succession had devolved upon the children of Jane Seymour. As, however, it was possible that she might not have any issue, parliament granted Henry the privilege of naming his successor in his will: an enormous prerogative, conferred upon the most capricious of monarchs. Those who refused to take the oath required by the statute were to be declared guilty of high treason.

Parliament, having thus arranged the king's business, set about the business of the country. "My lords," said ministers on the 4th of July to the upper house, "the bishop of Rome, whom some persons call *pope*, wishing to have the means of satisfying his love of luxury and tyranny, has obscured the Word of God, excluded Jesus Christ from the soul, banished princes from their kingdoms, monopolized the mind, body, and goods of all Christians, and, in particular, extorted great sums of money from England by his worthless superstitions." Parliament decided that the penalties of *præmunire* should be inflicted on everybody who recognized the authority of the Roman pontiff, and that every student, ecclesiastic, and civil functionary should be bound to renounce the pope in an oath made in the name of God and all his saints.[1]

This bill was the cause of great joy in England; the protestant spirit was stirred; there was a great outburst of sarcasms, and one could see that the citizens of the capital naturally were not friends to the papacy. Man is inclined to laugh at what he has respected when he finds that he has been deceived, and then readily classes among human follies what he had once taken for the wisdom of heaven. A contest of epigrams was begun in London, similar to that which had so often taken place at Rome between Pasquin and Marforio: perhaps, however, the jokes were occasionally a little heavy. "Do you see the stole round the priest's neck?" said one wit; "it is nothing else but the bishop of Rome's rope"—"Matins, masses, and evensong are nothing but a roaring, howling, whistling, murmuring, tomring, and juggling."—"It is as lawful to christen a child in a tub of water at home or in a ditch by the way, as in a font-stone in the church."—Gradually this jesting spirit made its way to the lower classes of society—"Holy water is very useful," said one who haunted the London taverns; "for as it is already salted, you have only to put an onion in it to make sauce for a gibbet of mutton."—"What is that you say?"

[1] "So help me God, all saints, and the Holy Evangelists."—Act of Parliament, 28 Henry VIII, Cap. 7.

replied some blacksmith; "it is a very good medicine for a
horse with a galled back." But while frivolity and a desire to
show one's wit, however coarse it might be, gave birth to silly
jests merely provocative of laughter, the love of truth inspired
the evangelical Christians with serious words which irritated
the priests more than the raillery of the jesters. "The Church,"
they said, "is not the clergy, the Church is the congregation of
good men only. All ceremonies accustomed in the Church and
not clearly expressed in Scripture ought to be done away.
When the sinner is converted, all the sins over which he sheds
tears are remitted freely by the Father who is in heaven."

Along with the words of the profane and of the pious came
the words of the priests. A convocation of the clergy was
summoned to meet at St. Paul's on the 9th June. The bishops
came and took their places, and anyone might count the
votes which Rome and the Reformation had on the episcopal
bench. For the latter there were: Archbishop Cranmer;
Goodrich, bishop of Ely; Shaxton, bishop of Salisbury; Fox,
bishop of Hereford; Latimer, bishop of Worcester; Hilsey,
bishop of Rochester; Barlow, bishop of St. David's; Warton,
bishop of St. Asaph; and Sampson, bishop of Chichester—
nine votes in all. For Rome there were: Lee, archbishop of
York; Stokesley, bishop of London; Tunstall, bishop of
Durham; Longland, bishop of Lincoln; Vesey, bishop of
Exeter; Clerk, bishop of Bath; Lee, bishop of Lichfield;
Salcot, bishop of Bangor; and Rugge, bishop of Norwich—
nine against nine. If Gardiner had not been in France there
would have been a majority against the Reformation. A
numerous company of priors and mitred abbots, members of
the upper house, seemed to assure victory to the partisans of
tradition. The clergy, who assembled under their respective
banners, were divided not by shades but by glaring colours,
and people asked, as they looked on this chequered group,
which of the colours would carry the day. Cranmer had taken
precautions that they should not leave the church without
being enlightened on that point.

The bishop of London having sung the mass of the Holy
Ghost, Latimer, who had been selected by the primate to edify
the assembly, went up into the pulpit. Being a man of bold and
independent character, and penetrating, practical mind which

would discover and point out every subterfuge, he wanted a Reform more complete even than Cranmer desired. He took for his text the parable of the unjust steward (St. Luke 16, 1–8). "Brethren," he said, "ye have come here to-day to hear of great and weighty matters. Ye look, I am assured, to hear of me such things as shall be meet for this assembly." Then, having introduced his subject Latimer continued: "A faithful steward coineth no new money, but taketh it ready coined of the good man of the house. Now, what numbers of our bishops, abbots, prelates, and curates, despising the money of the Lord as copper and not current, teach that now redemption purchased by money, and devised by men is of efficacy, and not redemption purchased by Christ."

The whole of Latimer's sermon was in this strain. He did not stop here; in the afternoon he preached again. "You know the proverb," he said—" 'An evil crow, an evil egg.' The devil has begotten the world, and the world in its turn has many children. There is my Lady Pride, Dame Gluttony, Mistress Avarice, Lady Lechery, Dame Subtlety, and others, that now hard and scant ye may find any corner, any kind of life, where many of his children be not. In court, in cowls, in cloisters, yea, where shall ye not find them? Howbeit, they that be secular are not children of the world, nor they children of light that are called spiritual and of the clergy. No, no; as ye find among the laity many children of light, so among the clergy ye shall find many children of the world. They do execrate and detest the world (though indeed the world is their father) in words and outward signs; but in heart and works they coll[1] and kiss him. They ever say one thing and think another, and live every day as if all their life were a shroving time (a carnival). I see many such among the bishops, abbots, priors, archdeacons, deans, and others of that sort, who are met together in this convocation, to take into consideration all that concerns the glory of Christ and the wealth of the people of England. But it is to be feared lest, as light hath many of her children here, so the world hath sent some of his whelps hither; amongst the which I know there can be no concord nor unity, albeit they be in one place, in one congregation. What have you been doing these seven years

[1] [To hang round the neck.]

and more? Show us what the English have gained by your long and great assemblies. Have they become even a hair's breadth better? In God's name, what have you done?—so great fathers, so many, so long a season, so oft assembled together—what have you done? Two things: the one that you have burnt a dead man;[1] the other, that ye went about to burn one being alive.[2] Ye have oft sat in consultation, but what have ye done? Ye have had many things in deliberation, but what one is put forth whereby either Christ is more glorified, or else Christ's people made more holy? I appeal to your own conscience."

Here Latimer began, as Luther had done in his *Appeal to the German Nobility*, to pass in review the abuses and errors of the clergy—the Court of Arches,[3] the episcopal consistories, saints' days, images, vows, pilgrimages, certain vigils which he called "bacchanalia," marriage, baptism, the mass, and relics.

After this severe catalogue, the bishop exclaimed: "If there be nothing to be amended or redressed, my lords, be ye of good cheer, be merry; and at the least, because we have nothing else to do, let us reason the matter how we may be richer. Let us fall to some pleasant communication; afterwards let us go home, even as good as we came hither, that is, right-begotten children of the world, and utterly worldlings. . . . If there be nothing to be changed in our fashions, let us say as the evil servant said, 'It will be long ere my master come.' This is pleasant. Let us beat our fellows; let us eat and drink with drunkards. Surely, as oft as we do not take away the abuse of things, so oft we beat our fellows. As oft as we give not the people their true food, so oft we beat our fellows. As oft as we let them die in superstition, so oft we beat them. To be short, as oft as we blind lead them blind, so oft we beat and grievously beat our fellows. When we welter in pleasures and idleness, then we eat and drink with drunkards. But God will come, God will come. He will not tarry long away. He will come upon such a day as we nothing look for Him and at

---

[1] [William Tracy, in the year 1532. See p. 69.]
[2] Referring to himself.
[3] [The chief and most ancient consistory court belonging to the archbishop of Canterbury.]

such hour as we know not. He will come and cut us in pieces. He will reward us as He doth the hypocrites. He will set us where wailing shall be, my brethren; where gnashing of teeth shall be, my brethren. And let here be the end of our tragedy, if ye will. These be the delicate dishes prepared for the world's beloved children. These be the wafers and junkets provided for worldly prelates—wailing and gnashing of teeth.

"If you will not die eternally, live not worldly. Preach truly the Word of God. Feed ye tenderly the flock of Christ. Love the light. Walk in the light, and so be the children of light while you are in the world, that you may shine in the world to come bright as the sun, with the Father, the Son, and the Holy Ghost. Amen."[1]

An action full of simplicity and warmth had accompanied the firm and courageous words of the Reformer. The reverend members of convocation had found their man, and his sermon appeared to them more bitter than wormwood. They dared not, however, show their anger, for behind Latimer was Cranmer, and they feared lest they should find the king behind Cranmer.

Ere long the clergy received another mortification which they dared not complain of. A rumour got abroad that Cromwell would be the representative of Henry VIII in the assembly. "What!" they cried out, "a layman, a man who has never taken a degree in any university!" But what was the astonishment of the prelates, when they saw not Cromwell enter, but Dr. William Petre, the proctor of the vicar-general, whom the primate seated by his side—a delegate of a delegate! On the 21st of June, Cromwell himself came down, and took his seat above all the prelates. The lay element took, with a bold step, a position from which it had been so long banished.

It was to be expected that the champions of the middle ages would not submit to such affronts, and particularly to such a terrible fire as Latimer's, without unmasking their batteries in return, and striving to dismantle those of the enemy. They saw that they could not maintain the supremacy of the pope and attack that of the king; but they knew that Henry adhered to transubstantiation and other superstitious doctrines of the dark ages; and accordingly they determined to attack by this breach, not only Latimer, but all the supporters

[1] Latimer, *Sermons* (Parker Society), pp. 33–57.

of the Reformation. Roman-catholicism did not intend to
perish without a struggle; it resolved—in order that it might
hold its ground in England—to make a vigorous onslaught.
The lower house having chosen for its prolocutor one Richard
Gwent, archdeacon of Bishop Stokesley and a zealous upholder
of Romish doctrine, the cabal set to work, and the words of
Wycliffe, of the Lollards, of the Reformers, and even of the
jesting citizens having been carefully recorded, Gwent proposed that the lower house should lay before the upper house
sixty-seven evil doctrines (*mala dogmata*). Nothing was forgotten,
not even *the horse with the galled back*. To no purpose were they
reminded that what was blamable in this catalogue were
only "the indiscreet expressions of illiterate persons"; and
that the rudeness of their imagination alone had caused them
to utter these pointed sarcasms. In vain were they reminded
that, even in horse races, the riders to be sure of reaching their
goal pass beyond it. The enumeration of the *mala dogmata*
was carried, without omitting a single article.

On the 23rd of June, the prolocutor appeared with his
long list before the upper house of convocation. "There are
certain errors," he said, "which cause disturbance in the
kingdom," and then he read the sixty-seven *mala dogmata*.
"They affirm," he continued, "that no doctrine must be
believed unless it be proved by Holy Scripture; that Christ,
having shed His blood, has fully redeemed us, so that now we
have only to say, O God, I entreat Thy Majesty to blot out
my iniquity. They say that the sacrifice of the mass is nothing
but a piece of bread; that auricular confession was invented
by the priests to learn the secrets of the heart, and to put
money in their purse; that purgatory is a cheat; that what is
usually called the Church is merely the old synagogue, and
that the true Church is the assembly of the just; that prayer
is just as effectual in the open air as in a temple; that priests
may marry. And these heresies are not only preached, but
are printed in books stamped *cum privilegio* (with privilege) and
the ignorant imagine that those words indicate the king's
approbation."

The two armies stood face to face, and the scholastic party
had no sooner read their lengthy manifesto than the combat
began. "Oh, what tugging was here betwixt these opposite

sides," says honest Fuller. They separated without coming to any decision. Men began to discuss which side they should take: "Neither one nor the other," said those who fancied themselves the cleverest. "When two stout and sturdy travellers meet together and both desire the way, yet neither is willing to fight for it, in their passage they so shove and shoulder one another, that they divide the way between them, and yet neither gets the same. So these two opposite parties in the convocation were fain at last in a drawn battle to part the prize between them, neither of them being conquering or conquered."[1] Thus the Church, *the pillar of truth*, was required to admit both black and white—to say Yes and No. "A medley religion," exclaims Fuller; "an expedient, to salve (if not the consciences) at least the credits of both sides."

Cranmer and Cromwell determined to use the opportunity to make the balance incline to the evangelical side. They went down to convocation. While passing along the street Cromwell noticed a stranger—one Alesius, a Scotsman, who had been compelled to seek refuge in Germany for having professed the pure Gospel, and there had formed a close intimacy with Melanchthon. Cranmer, as well as Cromwell, desirous of having such an evangelical man in England—one who was in perfect harmony with the Protestants of Germany, and whose native tongue was English—had invited him over to London.[2] Melanchthon had given him a letter for the king, along with which he sent a copy of his commentary on the Epistle to the Romans. Henry was so charmed with the Scotsman, that he gave him the title of "King's Scholar." Alesius was living at the archbishop's palace in Lambeth. Cromwell, observing him so seasonably, called him and invited him to accompany them to Westminster. He thought that a man of such power might be useful to him; and it is even possible that the meeting had been prearranged. Together the Englishman and the Scotsman entered the chamber in which the bishops were sitting round a table, with a number of priests standing behind them. When the vicar-general and Alesius, who was unknown to most of them, appeared, they all rose and bowed to the king's representative. Cromwell

---

[1] Fuller's *Church History* (1655), p. 213.
[2] Preface to Alesius' treatise *On the Authority of the Word of God*.

returned the salutation, and, after seating the exile in the highest place, opposite the two archbishops, he addressed them as follows: "His Majesty will not rest until, in harmony with convocation and parliament, he has put an end to the controversies which have taken place, not only in this kingdom but in every country. Discuss these questions, therefore, with charity, without brawling or scolding, and decide all things by the Word of God. Establish the divine and perfect truth as it is found in Scripture."

Cromwell wanted the submission of *all* to the divine revelation; the traditional party answered him by putting forward human doctrines and human authorities. Stokesley, bishop of London, endeavoured to prove, by certain glosses and passages, that there were seven sacraments: the archbishop of York and others supported him by their sophistry and their shouts. "Such disputes about words, and such cries," said Cranmer, "are unbecoming serious men. Let us seek Christ's glory, the peace of the Church, and the means by which sins are forgiven. Let us enquire how we may bring consolation to uneasy souls; how we may give the assurance of God's love to consciences troubled by the remembrance of their sins. Let us acknowledge that it is not the outward use of the sacraments that justifies a man, and that our justification proceeds solely from faith in the Saviour." The prelate spoke admirably and in accordance with Scripture: it was necessary to back up this noble confession. Cromwell, who kept his Scotsman in reserve, now introduced him to the clergy, as the "king's scholar," and asked him what he thought of the discussion. Alesius, speaking in the assembly of bishops, showed that there were only *two* sacraments—Baptism and the Lord's Supper, and that no ceremony ought to be put in the same rank with them. The bishop of London chafed with anger in his seat. Shall a mere Scotsman, driven from his country and entertained by German Protestants, presume to teach the prelates of England? He shouted out indignantly, "All that is false!" Alesius declared himself ready to prove what he had said out of Scripture and the old fathers. Then Fox, bishop of Hereford, who had just returned from Wittenberg, whither he had been sent by the king, and where he had been enlightened by conversing with Luther and

Melanchthon, rose up and uttered these noble sentiments: "Christ hath so lightened the world at this time," he said, "that the light of the Gospel hath put to flight all misty darkness; and the world will no longer endure to be led astray by all that fantastic rubbish with which the priests formerly filled their imaginations and their sermons." This was pointed at Bishop Stokesley and his friends: "It is vain to resist the Lord; His hand drives away the clouds. The laity know the Holy Scriptures now better than many of us. The Germans have made the text of the Bible so easy, by the Hebrew and Greek tongue, that even women and children wonder at the blindness and falsehood that hath been hitherto. Consider that you make not yourselves to be laughed to scorn of all the world. If you resist the voice of God, you will give cause for belief that there is not one spark of learning or godliness in you. All things consist not in painted eloquence and strength of authority. For truth is of so great power, strength, and efficacy, that it can neither be defended with words nor be overcome with any strength; but after she hath hidden herself long, at length she pusheth up her head and appeareth." Such was the eloquent and Christian language with which even bishops endeavoured to bring about the triumph of that English Reformation which some have been pleased to represent as "the product of an amorous caprice." Moved by such Christian remarks, Alesius exclaimed, "Yes, it is the Word of God that bringeth life; the Word of God is the very substance and body of the Sacrament. It makes us certain and sure of the will of God to save our souls: the outward ceremony is but a token of that lively inflammation which we receive through faith in the Word and promise of the Lord." At these words the bishop of London could not contain himself. "The Word of God," he cried; "Yes, granted! But you are far deceived if you think there is no *other* Word of God but that which every souter (shoemaker) and cobbler may read in his mother-tongue." Stokesley believed in another Word of God besides the Bible; he thought, as the council of Trent did a little later, "That we must receive *with similar respect and equal piety the Holy Scriptures and* TRADITION."[1] As it was noon, Cromwell broke up the meeting.

[1] Council of Trent, 4th sitting, 8th of April, 1546.

The debate had been sharp. The sacerdotal, sacramental, ritualist party had been beaten; the evangelicals desired to secure their victory.

Alesius, after his return to Lambeth, began to compose a treatise; Stokesley, on the other hand, prepared to get up a conspiracy against Alesius. Next day the bishops, who arrived first at Westminster, entered into conversation about the last sitting, and were very indignant that a stranger, a Scotsman, should have been allowed to sit and speak among them. Stokesley called upon Cranmer to resist such an irregularity. The archbishop, who was always rather weak, consented, and Cromwell entering shortly after with his protégé, an archdeacon went up to the latter and told him that his presence was disagreeable to the bishops. "It is better to give way," said Cromwell to Alesius; "I do not want to expose you to the hatred of the prelates. When once they take a dislike to a man, they never rest until they have got him out of the way. They have already put to death many Christians for whom the king felt great esteem." Alesius withdrew and the debate opened. "Are there seven sacraments or only two," was the question. It was impossible to come to an understanding.

Convocation, an old clerical body, in which were assembled the most resolute partisans of the abuses, superstitions, and doctrines of the Middle Ages, was the real stronghold of Rome in England. To undertake to introduce the light and life of the Gospel into it was a rash and impracticable enterprise. The divine Head of the Church Himself has declared that *"no man putteth new cloth to an old garment, neither do men put new wine into old bottles."* There was but one thing to be done: Suppress the assembly and form a new one, composed of members and ministers of the Church, who acknowledge no other foundation, no other rule, than the Word of God. *"New wine must be put into new bottles."* Such a step as this would have helped powerfully to reform the Church of England really and completely. But it was not taken.

CHAPTER TWELVE

Henry Enforces "Catholicism minus the Pope"

(Autumn 1536)

AFTER Anne Boleyn's death, the men of the Reformation had taken the initiative, and Cranmer, Cromwell, Latimer, and Alesius seemed on the point of winning the prize of the contest. The intervention of a greater personage was about to affect the situation profoundly.

Anne's disgrace and the wedding with Jane Seymour had occupied the king with far other matters than theology. Cranmer had the field free to advance the Reformation. This was not what Henry intended; and as soon as he noticed it, he roused himself, as if from slumber, and hastened to put things in order. Though rejecting the authority of the pope, he remained faithful to his doctrines. He proceeded to act in his character as head of the Church, and resolved to fulminate a bull, as the pontiffs had done. Reginald Pole, in the book which he had addressed to him, observed that in matters touching the pope, we must not regard either his character or his life, but only his authority; and that the lapses of a pope in morals detract nothing from his infallibility in faith. Henry understood this distinction very clearly, and showed himself a pope in every way. He did not believe that there was any incompatibility between the right he claimed of taking a new wife whenever he pleased, by means of divorce or the scaffold, and that of declaring the oracles of God on contrition, justification, and ecclesiastical rites and ceremonies. The rupture of the negotiations with the obstinate German Protestants gave him more liberty, and even caused him a little vexation. His chagrin was not unmingled with anger, and he was not grieved to show them what they stood to lose by not accepting him. In this respect Henry was like a woman who, annoyed at being rejected by the man she prefers, gives her hand to his rival in bravado. He returned, therefore, to his

theological labours. The doctors of the scholastic party spared
him the pains of drawing up for himself the required articles; but
he revised them and was elated at the importance of his work.
"We have in our own person taken great pain, study, labours,
and travails," he said, "over certain articles which will establish
concord in our Church." Cromwell, always submissive to his
master and well knowing the cost of resistance, laid this royal
labour before the upper house of convocation. In religious
matters Henry had never done anything so important. The
doctrine of the authority of the prince over the dogmas of the
Church now became a *fact*. The king's dogmatic paper,
entitled *Articles about religion set out by the Convocation, and
published by the King's authority*, bears a strong resemblance to
the *Exposition* and the *Type of Faith*, published in the seventh
century, during the monothelite controversy, by the emperors
of Constantinople—Heraclius and Constans II. That prince,
who in a political sense gave England a new impulse, sought
his models as an ecclesiastical ruler in the Lower Empire.
Everybody was eager to know what doctrines the new head
of the Church was going to proclaim. The partisans of Rome
were doubtless quite as much surprised as the Reformers, but
their astonishment was that of joy; the surprise of the evangelicals
was that of fear. The vicar-general read the royal oracles
aloud: "All the words contained in the whole canon of the
Bible," he said, "and in the three creeds—the Apostles', the
Nicene, and the Athanasian—*according to the interpretation which
the holy approved doctors in the Church do defend*, shall be received
and observed as the infallible words of God, so that whosoever
rejects them is not a member of Christ but a member of the
devil, and eternally damned."

That was the Romish doctrine, and Bossuet, in his examination of the royal document, appears much satisfied with the
article.

"The sacrament of baptism should be administered to infants,
in order that they may receive the Holy Ghost and be purified
of sin by its secret virtue and operation. If a man falls after
baptism the sacrament of penance is necessary to his salvation;
he must go to confession, ask absolution at the priest's hands,
and look upon the words uttered by the confessor as the *voice
of God* speaking out of heaven."

——"That is the whole substance of the catholic doctrine," the partisans of Rome might urge.

"Under the form of the bread and the wine are verily, substantially, and really contained the body and very blood of the Saviour which was born of the Virgin."

——"That indicates most precisely the real presence of the body," say the Romish doctors.[1]

"The merits of the Saviour's passion are the only and worthy causes of our justification; but, before giving it to us, God requires of us inward contrition, perfect faith, hope, and charity, and all the other spiritual motions which must necessarily concur in the remission of our sins."

——The council of Trent declared the same doctrine not long after.[2]

"Images ought to be preserved in the churches. Only let those who kneel before them and adore them know that such honour is not paid to the images, but to God."

——"To use such language," Roman-catholics have said, "is to approve of image-worship to the extreme."[3]

"It is praiseworthy," continued Cromwell, "to address prayers to our Blessed Lady, to St. John the Baptist, to each of the apostles, or to any other saint, in order that they may pray for us and with us; but without believing there is more mercy in them than in Christ."

——"If the king looks upon this as a kind of Reformation," said a Romish doctor, "he is only making game of the word; for no catholic addresses the saints except to have their prayers."[4]

"As for the ceremonies, such as sprinkling with holy water, distributing the consecrated bread, prostration before the cross and kissing it, exorcisms, etc., these rites and others equally praiseworthy ought to be maintained as putting us in remembrance of spiritual things."

——"That is precisely our idea," said the partisans of Romish tradition.[5]

"Finally, as to purgatory, the people shall be taught that

[1] Bossuet, *Histoire des Variations*, liv. vii. § 25.
[2] Council of Trent, sixth session, canons 9 & 11.
[3] Bossuet, *Variations*, liv. vii. § 26.
[4] *Ibid.*
[5] Bossuet, *Variations*, liv. vii. § 27.

Christians ought to pray for the souls of the dead, and give alms, in order that others may pray for them, so that their souls may be relieved of some part of their pain."

——"All that we teach is here approved of," said the great opponent of Protestantism.[1]

Such was the religion which the prince whom some writers call the father of the Reformation desired to establish in England. If England became Protestant, it was certainly in spite of Henry VIII.

A long debate ensued in convocation and elsewhere. The decided evangelicals could see nothing in these articles but an abandonment of Scripture, a "political daubing," in which the object was only to please certain persons and to attain certain ends. The men of the moderate party said, on the other hand, "Ought we not to rejoice that the Scriptures and ancient creeds are re-established as rules of faith, without considering the pope?" But above these opposite opinions rose the terrible voice of the king: *Sic volo, sic jubeo:* Such is my pleasure, such are my orders. If the primate and his friends resisted, they would be set aside and the Reformation lost.

It does not appear that Cranmer had any share in drawing up these articles, but he signed them. It has been said, to excuse him, that neither he, nor many of his colleagues, had at that time a distinct knowledge of such matters, and that they intended to make amendments in the articles; but these allegations are insufficient. Two facts alone explain the concessions of this pious man: the king's despotic will and the archbishop's characteristic weakness. He always bent his head; but, we must also acknowledge, it was in order to raise it again. Archbishop Lee, sixteen bishops, forty abbots or priors, and fifty archdeacons or proctors signed after Cromwell and the primate. The articles passed through convocation, because— like Anne's condemnation—*it was the king's will.* Nothing can better explain the concessions of Cranmer, Cromwell, and others in the case of Anne Boleyn, than their support of these articles, which were precisely the opposite of the Scriptural doctrine whose triumph they had at heart. In both cases they had yielded slavishly to those magic words: *Le roi le veut*, the king wills it. Those four words were sufficient: that man was

[1] Bossuet, *Variations*, liv. vii. § 28.

loyal who sacrificed his own will to the will of the sovereign. It was only by degrees that the free principles of Protestantism were to penetrate among the people, and give England liberty along with order. Still, that excuse is not sufficient: Cranmer would have left a more glorious name if he had suffered martyrdom under Henry VIII, and not waited for the reign of Mary.

When the king's articles were known, discontent broke out in the opposite parties. "Be silent, you contentious preachers and you factious schoolmen," said the politicians: "you would sooner disturb the peace of the world, than relinquish or retract one particle!" The articles were sent all over England, with orders that everyone should conform to them or incur the wrath of the king and the Church.

Cranmer did not look upon the game as lost. To bend before the blast, and then rise up again and guide the Reform to a good end, was his system. He first strove to prevent the evil by suggesting measures calculated to remedy it. Convocation resolved that a petition should be addressed to the king, praying him to permit his lay subjects to read the Bible in *English*, and to order a new translation of it to be made; moreover, a great number of feast-days were abolished as favouring "sloth, idleness, thieves, excesses, vagabonds, and riots"; and finally, on the last day of the session (20th of July), convocation declared—to show clearly that there was no question of returning to popery—that there was nothing more pernicious than a general council; and that, consequently, they must decline to attend that which the pope intended to hold in the city of Mantua. Thereupon parliament and convocation were dissolved, and the king did without them for three years.

Henry VIII was satisfied with his minister. Cromwell was created Lord Privy-Seal, the 2nd of July, 1536, baron, and a few days later vicegerent in ecclesiastical matters (*in rebus ecclesiasticis*). Wishing to tone down what savoured too much of the schools in the king's articles, he circulated among all the priests some instructions which were passably evangelical. "I enjoin you," he said, "to make your parishioners understand that they do rather apply themselves to the keeping of God's commandments and fulfilling of His works of charity, and providing for their families, than if they went about to pilgrimages. Advise parents and masters to teach their children and their servants the Lord's Prayer, the Apostles' Creed, and the Ten Commandments, in their mother-tongue." He even undertook to reform the clergy. "Deans, parsons, vicars, curates, and priests," he said, "are forbidden to haunt taverns, to drink or brawl after dinner or supper, to play at cards day or night. If they have any leisure, they should read the Scriptures, or occupy themselves with some honest exercise."

But Cranmer and Cromwell went further than this. They wished to circulate the Holy Scriptures. Tyndale's version was, in Cromwell's opinion, too far compromised to be officially circulated; he had, therefore, patronized another translation. Coverdale, who was born in 1488, in the North Riding of Yorkshire, had undertaken (as we have seen) to translate the Bible, and had applied to Cromwell to procure him the necessary books.[1] Tyndale was more independent, a man of firmer and bolder character than Coverdale. He did not seek the aid of men, and finished his work (so to say) alone with God. Coverdale, pious no doubt like his rival, felt the need of being supported, and said, in his letter to Cromwell, that he implored his help, "prostrate on the knees of his heart."

Coverdale knew Greek and Hebrew. He began his task about 1530; on the 4th of October, 1535, the book appeared, probably at Zurich, under the title: BIBLIA, *the Bible, that is to say, the Holy Scriptures of the Old and New Testament;* and reached England in the early part of 1536. At the beginning of the volume was a dedication to Henry VIII, which ended by imploring the divine blessing on the king and on his "dearest just wife, and most virtuous princess, queen Anne." Cromwell was to present this translation to the king, and circulate it throughout the country; but this *dearest wife*, this *most virtuous princess* had just been accused by Henry, dragged before the tribunals, and beheaded. It was impossible to distribute a single copy of this version without arousing the monarch's anger. Those who desired that the ship which had come so far should not be wrecked in the harbour had recourse to several expedients. The decapitated queen's name

---

[1] Coverdale's *Remains* (Parker Society), p. 490. The letter is dated the 1st of May, but has no year: it appears to me to be 1530: [but it may be as early as 1527].

was *Anne*, that of the queen-regnant was *Jeanne:* there was a resemblance between them. Some copies corrected with a pen have instead of *queen Anne,—queen JAne;* in others the name of the queen is simply scratched out.[1] These expedients were not sufficient: a new title-page was printed and dated 1536, the current year.

It seems probable that the king gave his verbal approval to the new translation, but that he showed no appreciation of its merits and no enthusiasm for its circulation. Nevertheless, the Reformation, taught by pious ministers, was spreading more and more. The priests murmured in vain: "Not long ago," they said, "the Lollards were put to death for reading the Gospel in English, and now we are ordered to teach it in that language. We are robbed of our privileges, and our labours are increased."

The king had proclaimed and laid down his Ten Articles to little purpose: faith gave pious ministers and Christians a courage which the great ones of the earth did not possess. John Gale, pastor of Thwaite, in Suffolk, a quick, decided, but rather imprudent man, attacked the royal articles from his pulpit. But he did not stop there. His church was ornamented with images of the Virgin and Saints, before which the devout used to stick up tapers. "Austin," said he one day to a parishioner, "follow me;" and the two men, with great exertions, took away the iron rods on which the worshippers used to set their tapers, and turned the images to the wall.— "Listen," said Dr. Barret to his parishioners, "the lifting up of the host betokens simply that the Father has sent his Son to suffer death for man, and the lifting up of the chalice that *the Son has shed his blood for our salvation.*"—"Christ," said the prior of Dorchester, "does not dwell in churches of stone, but in heaven above and in the hearts of men on earth."— The minister of Hothfield declared that: "Our Lady is not the queen of heaven, and has no more power than another woman." "Pull him out of the pulpit," said the exasperated bailiff to the vicar. "I dare not," answered the latter. In fact, the congregation were delighted at hearing their minister say of Jesus, as Peter did: *Neither is there salvation in any other,* and

[1] Such copies may be found at the British Museum, and in the library at Lambeth.

that very day more than a hundred embraced their pastor's doctrines. Jerome, vicar of Stepney, endeavoured to plant the pure truth of Christ in the conscience, and root out all vain traditions, dreams and fantasies. Being invited to preach at St. Paul's Cross, on the fourth Sunday in Lent, he said: "There are two sorts of people among you: the free, who are freely justified without the penance of the law and without meritorious works; and the slaves, who are still under the yoke of the law."—Even a bishop, Barlow of St. David's, said in a stately cathedral: "If two or three cobblers or weavers, elect of God, meet together in the name of the Lord, they form a true Church of God."

Proceedings were commenced against those who had thus braved the king's articles. Jerome appeared before Henry VIII at Westminster. The poor fellow, intimidated by the royal majesty, tremblingly acknowledged that the sacraments were necessary for salvation; but he was burnt five years after in the cause of the Gospel. Gale and others were accused of heresy and treason before the criminal court. The books were not spared. There were some, indeed, that went beyond all bounds. One, entitled *The little garden of the souls*, contained a passage in which the beheading of John the Baptist and of Anne Boleyn were ascribed to the same motive—the reproach of a criminal love uttered against two princes: one by Anne, and the other by John. Henry compared to Herod! Anne Boleyn to Saint John the Baptist! Tunstall denounced this audacious publication to Cromwell.

The crown-officers were to see that the doctrines of the pope were taught everywhere; but, without the pope and his authority, this system has no solid foundation. The Holy Scriptures, to which evangelical Christians appeal, is a firm foundation. The authority of the pope—a vicious principle— at least puts those who admit it in a position to know what they believe. But catholicism with Romish doctrine and without the pope has no ground to stand on. Non-Roman catholicism has but a treacherous support. Another system had already, in the sixteenth century, set up reason as the supreme rule; but it presents a thousand different opinions, and no absolute truth. There is but one real foundation: *Thy Word is truth*, says Jesus Christ, and Jesus Christ is Lord.

CHAPTER THIRTEEN

The Pilgrimage of Grace
(October 1536)

THE bastard system of a catholicism without a pope, put forward by the king, did not enjoy great favour, and the evangelical Reform gained fresh adherents every day. The more consistent popish system endeavoured to stand against it. There were still many partisans of Rome in the aristocracy and among the populations of the north. A mighty effort was about to be made to expel both Cranmer's Protestantism and the king's Catholicism, and restore the papacy to its privileges. A great revolution is rarely accomplished without the friends of the old order of things combining to resist it.

Many members of the House of Lords saw with alarm the House of Commons gaining an influence which it had never possessed before, and taking the initiative in reforms which were not (as they thought) within its sphere. Trained in the hatred of heresy, those noble lords were indignant at seeing heretics invested with the episcopal dignity, and a layman, Cromwell, presuming to direct the convocation of the clergy. Some of them formed a league, and Lord Darcy, who was at their head, had a conference on the subject with the ambassador of Charles V. That prince assured him that he would be supported. The English partisans of the pope, aided by the imperialists, would be amply sufficient, they thought, to re-establish the authority of the Roman pontiff.

There was great agitation especially among the inhabitants of the towns and villages of the North. Those of the counties of York and Lincoln, too remote from London to feel its influence, besides being ignorant and superstitious, were submissive to the priests as to the very representatives of God. The names of the Reformers Luther, Melanchthon, Œcolampadius, and Tyndale were known by the priests, who taught

327

their flocks to detest them. Everything they saw exasperated them. If they went a journey, the monasteries which were their ordinary hostelries existed no longer. If they worked in the fields, they saw approaching them some ragged monk, with tangled hair and beard, with haggard eye, without bread to support him, or roof to shelter him, to whom hatred still gave strength to complain and to curse. These unhappy wretches went roaming up and down the country, knocking at every door; the peasants received them like saints, seated them at their table, and starved themselves for their nourishment. "See," said the monks, showing their rags to the people about them, "see to what a condition the members of Jesus Christ are reduced! A schismatic and heretical prince has expelled us from the houses of the Lord. But the Holy Father has excommunicated and dethroned him: no one should henceforth obey him." Such words produced their effect.

In the autumn of 1536, the ferment increased among the inhabitants of the rural districts who had no longer their field labours to divert them. They assembled in great numbers round the monasteries to see what the king meant to do with them. They looked on at a distance, and with angry eyes watched the commissioners who at times behaved violently, indulged in exactions, or threw down, one after another, the stones of the building which had been held for so long in reverence. Another day they saw the agent of some lord settle in the monastery with his wife, children, and servants; they heard those profane lay-folks laugh and chatter as they entered the sacred doors, whose thresholds had until now been trodden only by the sandals of the silent monks. A report spread abroad that the monasteries still surviving were also about to be suppressed. Dr. Makerel, formerly prior of Barlings, disguised as a labourer, and a monk (some writers say a shoemaker) named Nicholas Melton, who received the name of "Captain Cobbler," endeavoured to inflame men's minds and drive them to revolt. Everywhere the people listened to the agitators; and ere long the superior clergy appeared in the line of battle. "Neither the king's Highness nor any temporal man," they said, "may be supreme head of the Church. The Pope of Rome is Christ's vicar, and must alone be acknowledged as supreme head of Christendom."

On Monday, 2nd of October, 1536, the ecclesiastical commission was to visit the parish of Louth in Lincolnshire, and the clergy of the district were ordered to be present. Only a few days before, a neighbouring monastery had been suppressed and two of Cromwell's agents placed in it to see to the closing. The evening before the inspection (it was a Sunday) a number of the townspeople brought out a large silver cross which belonged to the parish, and shouting out, "Follow the cross! All follow the cross! God knows if we can do so for long," marched in procession through the town, with Melton leading the way. Some went to the church, took possession of the consecrated jewels, and remained under arms all night to guard them for fear the royal commissioners should carry them off. On Monday morning one of the commissioners, who had no suspicions, quietly rode into the town, followed by a single servant. All of a sudden the alarm-bell was rung, and a crowd of armed men filled the streets. The terrified commissioner ran into the church, hoping to find it an inviolable asylum; but the mob laid hold of him, dragged him out into the market-place, and pointing a sword at his breast, said to him, "Swear fidelity to the commons or you are a dead man." All the town took an oath to be faithful "to God, the King, and the commons, for the wealth of Holy Church." On Tuesday morning the alarm-bell was rung again; the cobbler and a tailor named Big Jack marched out, followed by a crowd of men, some on foot and some on horseback. Whole parishes, headed by their priests, joined them and marched with the rest. The monks prayed aloud for the pope, and cried out that if the gentry did not join them they should all be hanged; but gentlemen and even sheriffs united with the tumultuous troops. Twenty thousand men of Lincolnshire were in arms. England, like Germany, had its peasants' revolt; but while Luther was opposed to it, the archbishop of York, with many abbots and priests, encouraged it in England.

The insurgents did not delay proclaiming their grievances. They declared that if the monasteries were restored, men of mean birth dismissed from the Council, and heretic bishops deprived, they would acknowledge the king as head of the Church. The movement was instigated by the monks more than by the pope. Great disorders were committed.

The court was plunged into consternation by this revolt.
The king, who had no standing army, felt his weakness, and
his anger knew no bounds. "What!" he said to the *traitors* (for
such was the name he gave them) "what! do you, the rude
commons of one shire, and that one of the most *brute and
beastly* (stupid) of the whole realm, presume to find fault
with your king? Return to your homes, surrender to our
lieutenants a hundred of your leaders, and prepare to submit
to such condign punishment as we shall think you worthy of;
otherwise you will expose yourselves, your wives and children,
your lands and goods, not only to the indignation of God,
but to utter destruction by force and violence of the sword."

Such threats as these only served to increase the commotion.
"Christianity is going to be abolished," said the priests; "you
will soon find yourselves under the sword of *Turks*! But
whoever sheds his blood with us shall inherit eternal glory."
The people crowded to them from all quarters. Lord Shrewsbury, sent by the king against the rebellion, being unable to
collect more than 3,000 men, and having to contend against
ten times as many, had halted at Nottingham. London already
imagined the rebels were at its gates, and mighty exertions
were made. Sir John Russell and the duke of Suffolk were
sent forward with forces hurriedly equipped.

The insurgents were numerically strong, but with no
efficient leader or store of provisions. Two opinions arose
among them: the gentlemen and farmers cried, "Home,
home!" the priests and the people shouted, "To arms!" The
party of the friends of order continued increasing, and at last
prevailed. The duke of Suffolk entered Lincoln on October 17,
and the rebels dispersed.

A still greater danger threatened the established order of
things. The men of the North were more extreme than those of
Lincoln. On October 8 there was a riot at Beverley, in
Yorkshire. A Westminster lawyer, Robert Aske, who had
passed his vacation in field-sports, was returning to London,
when he was stopped by the rebels and proclaimed their
leader. On October 15 he marched to York and replaced the
monks in possession of their monasteries. Lord Darcy, an old
soldier of Ferdinand of Spain and Louis XII and a warm papal
partisan, quitted his castle of Pontefract to join the insurrection.

The priests stirred up the people, and ere long, the army, which amounted to at least 30,000 men, formed a long procession, "the *Pilgrimage of Grace*," which marched through the county of York. Each parish paraded under a captain, priests carrying the church cross in front by way of flag. A large banner, which floated in the midst of this multitude, represented on one side Christ with the five wounds on a cross, and on the other a plough, a chalice, a pix, and a hunting-horn. Every pilgrim wore embroidered on his sleeve the five wounds of Christ with the name of Jesus in the midst. The insurgents had a thousand bows and as many bills, besides other arms,[1] but hardly one poor copy of the Testament of Christ. "Ah!" said Latimer, preaching in Lincolnshire, "I will tell you what is the true Christian man's pilgrimage. There are, the Saviour tells us, eight days' journeys." Then he described the eight beatitudes in the most evangelical manner: the poor in spirit, those who mourn, those who are meek, those who hunger and thirst after righteousness, and the rest.[2]

Aske's pilgrimage was of another sort. Addressing the people of those parts, he said to them: "Lords, knights, masters, and friends, evil-disposed persons have filled the king's mind with new inventions: the holy body of the Church has been despoiled. We have therefore undertaken this *pilgrimage* for the reformation of what is amiss and the punishment of heretics.[3] If you will not come with us we will fight and die against you." Bonfires were lighted on all the hills to call the people to arms. Wherever these new crusaders appeared the monks were replaced in their monasteries and the peasants constrained to join the pilgrimage, under pain of seeing their houses pulled down, their goods seized, and their bodies handed over to the mercy of the captains.

There was this notable difference between the revolt in Germany and that in the North of England. In Germany, a few nobles only joined the people and were compelled to do so. In England, almost all the nobility of the North rallied to it of their own accord. The earls of Westmorland, Rutland,

---

[1] Bale, *Works* (Parker Society), p. 327.

[2] Latimer, *Sermons* (Parker Society), p. 476.

[3] Lingard says that this expedition was named jestingly "the Pilgrimage of Grace." He is mistaken: the rebels themselves seriously call it by this name six times in their proclamation.

and Huntingdon, Lords Latimer, Lumley, Scrope, Conyers, and the representatives of several other great families followed the example of old Lord Darcy. One single nobleman, Percy, earl of Northumberland, remained faithful to the king. He had been ill since the unjust sentence which had struck the loyal wife of Henry VIII—a sentence in which he had refused to join—and was now at his castle lying on a bed of pain which was soon to be the bed of death. The rebels surrounded his dwelling and summoned him to join the insurrection. He might now have avenged the crime committed by Henry VIII against Anne Boleyn, but he refused. Savage voices shouted out, "Cut off his head, and make Sir Thomas Percy earl in his stead." But the noble and courageous man said calmly to those around him, "I can die but once; let them kill me, and so put an end to my sorrows."

The king, more alarmed at this revolt than at the former one, asked with terror whether his people desired to force him to replace his neck under the detested yoke of the pope. In this crisis he displayed great activity. Being at Windsor, he wrote letter after letter to Cromwell. "I will sell all my plate," he said. "Go to the Tower, take as much plate as you may want, and coin it into money." Henry displayed no less intelligence than decision. He named as commander of his little army a devoted servant, who was also the chief of the papal party at the court—the duke of Norfolk. Once already, for the condemnation of the protestant Anne Boleyn, Henry had selected this chief of the Romish party. This clever policy succeeded equally well for the king in both affairs.

London, Windsor, and all the south of England were in great commotion. People imagined that the papacy, borne on the lusty arms of the northern men, was about to return in triumph into the capital; that perhaps the Catholic king of the Scots, Henry's nephew, would enter with it and place England once more under the papal sceptre. The friends of the Gospel were deeply agitated. "That great captain the devil," said Latimer in the London pulpits, "has all sorts of ordnance to shoot at Christian men. These men of the North, who wear the cross and the wounds before and behind, are marching against Him who bare the cross and suffered those wounds. They have risen (they say) to support the king, and they are fighting against him. They come forward in the name of the Church, and fight against the Church, which is the congregation of faithful men. Let us fight with the sword of the Spirit, which is the Word of God.''

The rebels, far from being calmed, showed—part of them at least—that they were animated by the vilest sentiments. A body of insurgents had invested the castle of Skipton, the only place in the county of York which still held for the king. The wife and daughters of Lord Clifford, and other ladies who inhabited it, happened to be at an abbey not far off, just when the castle was beleaguered. The insurgents caused Lord Clifford to be informed that if he did not surrender, his wife and daughters would be brought next day to the foot of the walls and be given up to the camp-followers. In the middle of the night, Christopher Aske, brother of Robert, who had remained faithful, crept through the camp of the besiegers, and by unfrequented roads succeeded in bringing into the castle all those ladies, whom he thus saved from the most infamous outrages.[1]

Robert Aske, Lord Darcy, the archbishop of York, and several other leaders had their headquarters at Pontefract castle, where Lancaster Herald, despatched by the king, presented himself on the 21st of October. After passing through many troops of armed men—"very cruel fellows," he says—he was at last introduced to the great captain. Seeing Lord Darcy and the archbishop before him—persons more important than the Westminster lawyer—the Herald began to address them. Aske was offended, and rising from his seat told him haughtily that he was the person to be addressed. The messenger discharged his mission. He represented to the leaders of the rebellion that they were but a handful before the great power of his Majesty, and that the king had done nothing in regard to religion but what the clergy of York and Canterbury had acknowledged to be in conformity with the Word of God. When the speech was ended, Aske, as if he did not care for the Herald's words, said rudely to him, "Show me your proclamation." "He behaved," wrote the envoy, "as though he had been some great prince, with great rigour and like a tyrant." "Herald," said Aske, "this proclamation

---

[1] This fact is mentioned in one of the depositions of the trial which followed the revolt. See Christopher Aske's Examination.

shall neither be read at the market-cross nor elsewhere amongst my people. We want the redress of our grievances, and we will die fighting to obtain them." The Herald asked what were their grievances. "My followers and I," replied the chief, "will walk in pilgrimage to London, to his Majesty, to expel from the council all the vile blood in it, and set up all the noble blood again; and also to obtain the full restitution of Christ's Church." "Will you give me that in writing?" said the Herald. Aske gave him the oath which the rebels took, and at the same time putting his hand on the paper, he said with a loud voice, "This is my act; I will die in its defence, and all my followers will die with me." The Herald, intimidated by the authoritative tone of the chief, bent his knee before the rebel captain, for which he was brought to trial and executed in the following year. "Give him a guard of forty men, and see him out of town," said Aske.

Forthwith thirty thousand well-armed men, of whom twelve thousand were mounted, set out under the orders of Aske, Lord Darcy, and other noblemen of the country. Norfolk had only a small force, which he could not trust; accordingly the rebels were convinced that when they appeared, the king's soldiers and perhaps the duke himself would join them. The rebel army arrived on the banks of the Don, on the other side of which (at Doncaster) the king's forces were stationed. Those ardent men, who were six against one, inflamed by monks who were impatient to return to their nests, proposed to pass the Don, overthrow Norfolk, enter London, dictate to the king the execution of all the partisans of the Reformation, and restore the papal power in England. The rising of the water, increased by heavy rains, did not permit them to cross the river. Every hour's delay was a gain to the royal cause; the insurgents, having brought no provisions with them, were forced to disband to go in search of them elsewhere. Norfolk took advantage of this to circulate an address among the rebels. "Unhappy men!" it said, "what folly hath led you to make this most shameful rebellion against our most righteous king, who hath kept you in peace against all your enemies? Fye, for shame! How can you do this to one who loves you more than all his subjects? If you do not return, every man to his house, we will show you the hardest

courtesy that ever was shown to men, that have loved you so
well as we have done. But if you go to your homes, you shall
have us most humble suitors to his Highness for you." This
proclamation was signed by Lords Norfolk, Shrewsbury,
Exeter, Rutland, and Huntingdon, all catholics, and the
greatest names in England.

The insurgents thus found themselves in the most difficult
position. They must attack the supporters of their own cause.
If the lords who had signed the proclamation were slain,
England would lose her best councillors, and her greatest
generals, and the Church would be deprived of the most
zealous catholics. The strength of England would be sacrificed
and the country opened to her enemies. Old Lord Darcy
was for attacking; young Robert Aske for negotiation. On
the 27th of October, commissioners from both parties met on
the bridge leading to Doncaster. The rebel commissioners
consented to lay down their arms, provided the heresies of
Luther, Wycliffe, Huss, Melanchthon, Œcolampadius, and the
works of Tyndale were destroyed and nullified; that the
supremacy was restored to the see of Rome; that the suppressed
abbeys were re-established; that heretical bishops and lords
were punished by fire or otherwise; and that a parliament
was held promptly at Nottingham or York.

There could no longer be any doubt that the object of the
insurrection was to crush the Reformation. The names of
most of the reformers were mentioned in the articles, and fire
or sword were to do justice to the most illustrious of their
adherents. The same evening they handed in a letter addressed:
*To the King's Royal Highness. From Doncaster, this Saturday, at
eleven of the clock at night. Haste, post, haste, haste, haste!* The
rebels themselves were in such haste that they waited no
longer. The next day (28th of October) the king's lieutenant
announced at one in the afternoon that the insurgents had
dispersed and were returning to their homes. Two of the
rebel leaders were to carry the stipulated conditions to the
king, and Norfolk was to accompany them. That zealous
catholic was not perhaps without a hope that the petition
would induce Henry to become reconciled to the pope. He
was greatly deceived.

It was clear that the king was rapidly gaining the upper

hand. Norfolk caused the rebels to believe that their demands would be met. In the outcome, however, this was not the case. The king benefited by delay. He was able to build up his forces in the North, and early in December, in consequence of threats and promises, the rebel army finally broke up. The one formidable insurrection of Henry's reign was over.

Thus God had scattered the forces of those who had stood up against Wycliffe, Huss, and Luther. The kingdom resumed its usual tranquillity. A little later the men of the North, excited by the intrigues of the pope and Reginald Pole, now a cardinal, again took up arms; but they were defeated; seventy of them were hanged on the walls of Carlisle, and Lords Darcy and Hussey, with sundry barons, abbots, priors, and a great number of priests, were executed in different places. The scheming archbishop of York alone escaped, it is not known how. The cottages, parsonages, and castles of the North were filled with anguish and terror. Henry, who cut off the heads of his most intimate friends and of his queen, did not think of sparing rebels. It was a terrible lesson, but not very effectual. The priests did not lose their courage; they still kept asking for the re-establishment of the pope, the death of the Lutherans, and the annihilation of the Reform. An event which occurred at this time seemed likely to favour their desires. A great blow was about to be dealt against the Reformation. But the ways of God are not as our ways, and from what seems destined to compromise His cause, He often makes His triumph proceed.

CHAPTER FOURTEEN

The Martyrdom of Tyndale

(From 1535 to October 1536)

MOST of the reformers, Luther, Zwingli, Calvin, Knox, and others, have acquired that name by their preachings, their writings, their struggles, and their actions. It is not so with the principal reformer of England: all his activity was concentred in the Holy Scriptures. Tyndale was less prominent than the other instruments of God who were awakened to upraise the Church. We might say that, knowing the weakness of man, he had retired and hidden himself to allow the Word from Heaven to act by itself. He had studied it, translated it, and sent it over the sea: it must now do its own work. Is it not written: *The field is the world, and the seed is the Word?* But there is another characteristic, or rather another fact, which distinguishes him from them, and this we have to describe.

While Pole and the papistical party, the new adversaries of Henry VIII, were agitating on the continent, Tyndale, the man whom the king had pursued so long without being able to catch, was in prison at Vilvorde, near Brussels. In vain was he girt around with the thick walls of that huge fortress. Tyndale was free. "There is the captivity and bondage," he could say, "whence Christ delivered us, redeemed and loosed us. His blood, His death, His patience in suffering rebukes and wrongs, His prayers and fastings, His meekness and fulfilling of the uttermost point of the law . . . broke the bonds of Satan, wherein we were so strait bound." Thus Tyndale was as truly free at Vilvorde, as Paul had been at Rome.

For some years before his arrest, Tyndale had been labouring hard to produce a translation of the Old Testament worthy to take its place beside his English New Testament of 1525, and in the task he had realized his need of a skilled and

337

sympathetic assistant. At that time there lived at Antwerp, as chaplain to the English merchants in that city, a young man from the county of Warwick, named John Rogers, who had been educated at Pembroke Hall, Cambridge, and was a little more than thirty years old. Rogers was learned, but submissive to the Romish traditions. Tyndale having made his acquaintance, asked him to help in translating the Holy Scriptures, and Rogers caught joyfully at the opportunity of employing his Greek and Hebrew. Close and constant contact with the Word of God gradually effected in him that great transformation, that total renewal of the man which is the object of redemption. "I have found the true light in the Gospel," he said one day to Tyndale; "I now see the filthiness of Rome, and I cast from my shoulders the heavy yoke it has imposed upon me." From that hour Tyndale received from Rogers the help which he had formerly received from John Fryth, that pious martyr, whose example Rogers was to follow by enduring the punishment of fire—the first to do so under Mary. The Holy Scriptures have been written in English with the blood of martyrs—if we may so speak—the blood of Fryth, Tyndale, and Rogers: it is a crown of glory for that translation.

It is highly probable that Tyndale, before his imprisonment, had completed his Old Testament translation as far as the end of the Books of Chronicles. The manuscript was left by him in the capable hands of Rogers, who pressed on so diligently with the work of printing, that a few months before Tyndale was burned, an English version of the entire Bible was in circulation in his native land. Rogers did not himself undertake the translation of the remainder of the Old Testament but made use of the version which Myles Coverdale had already published.

Doubtless, Tyndale took pleasure in his gloomy dungeon in following with his mind's eye the divine Scripture from city to city and from cottage to cottage; his imagination pictured to him the struggles it would have to go through, and also its victories. "The Word of God," he said, "never was without persecution—no more than the sun can be without his light. By what right doth the pope forbid God to speak in the English tongue? Why should not the sermons of the apostles, preached no doubt in the mother-tongue of those who heard them, be now written in the mother-tongue of those who read them?"[1] Tyndale did not think of proving the divinity of the Bible by learned dissertations. "Scripture derives its authority from Him who sent it," he said. "Would you know the reason why men believe in Scripture?—It is *Scripture.*—It is itself the instrument which outwardly leads men to believe, whilst inwardly, the Spirit of God Himself, speaking through Scripture, gives faith to His children."[2] We do not know for certain in what city Rogers printed the great English folio Bible but it was probably Antwerp. Extraordinary precautions were required to prevent the persecutors from entering the house where men had the boldness to print the Word of God, and from breaking the printing-presses. Tyndale had the great comfort of knowing that the whole Bible was going to be published, and that prophets, apostles, and Christ Himself would speak by it after his death.

This man, so active, so learned, and so truly great, whose works circulated far and wide with so much power, had at the same time within him a pure and beneficent light—the love of God and of man—which shed its mild rays on all around him. The depth of his faith, the charm of his conversation, the uprightness of his conduct touched those who came near him. The gaoler liked to bring him his food, in order to talk with him, and his daughter often accompanied him and listened eagerly to the words of the pious Englishman. Tyndale spoke of Jesus Christ; it seemed to him that the riches of the divine Spirit were about to transform Christendom; that the children of God were about to be manifested, and that the Lord was about *to gather together his elect.* "Summer is nigh," he was wont to say, "for the trees blossom." In truth, young shoots and even old trees, long barren, flourished within the very walls of the castle. The gaoler, his daughter, and other members of their house were converted to the Gospel by Tyndale's life and doctrine. However dark the machinations of his enemies, they could not obscure the divine light kindled in his heart, and which *shone before men.* There was an invincible power in this Christian man. Full of hope in the final victory

---

[1] Tyndale, *Doctrinal Treatises* (Parker Society), pp. 131, 161, 148.
[2] Tyndale, *Answer to More* (Parker Society), pp. 136, 139.

of Jesus Christ, he courageously trampled under foot tribulations, trials, and death itself. He believed in the victory of the Word. "I am bound like a malefactor," he said, "but the Word of God is not bound." The bitterness of his last days was changed into great peace and divine sweetness.

His friends did not forget him. Among the English merchants at Antwerp was one whose affection had often reminded him that "friendship is the assemblage of every virtue," as a wise man of antiquity styles it. Thomas Poyntz, one of whose ancestors had come over from Normandy with William the Conqueror, had perhaps known the reformer in the house of Lady Walsh, who also belonged to this ancient family. For nearly a year the merchant had entertained the translator of the Scriptures beneath his roof, and a mutual and unlimited confidence was established between them. When Poyntz saw his friend in prison, he resolved to do everything possible to save him. Poyntz's elder brother, John, who had retired to his estate at North Ockenden, in Essex, had accompanied the king in 1520 to the Field of Cloth of Gold, and although no longer at court, he still enjoyed the favour of Henry VIII. Thomas determined to write to John. "Brother," he said, "William Tyndale is in prison, and likely to suffer death, unless the king should extend his gracious help to him. He has lain in my house three quarters of a year, and I know that the king has never a truer-hearted subject.[1] When the pope gave his Majesty the title of Defender of the Faith, he prophesied like Caiaphas. The papists thought our prince should be a great maintainer of their abominations; but God has entered his Grace into the right battle. The king should know that the death of this man will be one of the highest pleasures to the enemies of the Gospel. If it might please his Majesty to send for this man, it might, by the means thereof, be opened to the court and council of this country (Brabant) that they would be at another point with the bishop of Rome within a short space."

The letter is dated the 25th August, and was forwarded by John Poyntz to the vicar-general on the 21st September. Meanwhile, however, having received information from other sources, Cromwell had, with the king's approval, already

[1] Robert Demaus, *William Tyndale*, pp. 401–4.

taken action, for by the 4th September he had prepared
letters to be sent to two leading members of the Council of
Brabant. On the 10th of September, 1535, a messenger arrived
in Antwerp with two letters from the vicar-general—one for
the marquis of Bergen-op-Zoom, and the other for Carondolet,
archbishop of Palermo and president of the council of Brabant.
Alas! the marquis had started two days before for Germany,
whither he was conducting the princess of Denmark. Thomas
Poyntz mounted his horse, and caught up the escort about
fifteen miles from Maestricht. The marquis hurriedly glanced
over Cromwell's despatch. "I have no leisure to write," he
said; "the princess is making ready to depart." "I will follow
you to the next baiting-place," answered Tyndale's indefatigable
friend. "Be it so," replied Bergen-op-Zoom.

On arriving at Maestricht, the marquis wrote to the
Company of Merchant Adventurers, to Cromwell, and to his
friend the archbishop, president of the council of Brabant,
and gave the three letters to Poyntz. The latter presented the
letters of Cromwell and of the marquis to the president, but
the archbishop and the council of Brabant were opposed to
Tyndale. Poyntz immediately started for London, and laid
the answer of the council before Cromwell, entreating him
to insist that Tyndale should be immediately set at liberty,
for the danger was great. The answer was delayed a month.
Poyntz handed it to the Emperor's Council at Brussels, and
every day this true and generous friend went to the office to
learn the result. "Your request will be granted," said one of
the clerks on the fourth day. Poyntz was transported with joy.
Tyndale was saved.

The traitor Philips, however, who had delivered Tyndale to
his enemies, was then at Louvain. He had run away from Antwerp, knowing that the English merchants were angry with
him, and had sold his books with the intent of escaping to Paris.
But the Louvain priests, who still needed him, reassured him,
and remaining in that stronghold of Romanism, he began to
translate into Latin such passages in Tyndale's writings as
he thought best calculated to offend the catholics. He was
thus occupied when the news of Tyndale's approaching
deliverance filled him and his friends with alarm. What was
to be done? He thought the only means of preventing the

liberation of the prisoner was to shut up the liberator himself. Philips went straight to the procurator-general. "That man, Poyntz," he said, "is as much a heretic as Tyndale." Two sergeants-of-arms were sent to keep watch over Poyntz at his house, and for six days in succession he was examined upon a hundred different articles. At the beginning of February 1536, he learnt that he was about to be sent to prison, and knowing what would follow, he formed a prompt resolution. One night, when the sergeants-of-arms were asleep, he escaped and left the city early, just as the gates were opened. Horsemen were sent in search of him; but as Poyntz knew the country well, he escaped them, got on board a ship, and arrived safe and sound at his brother's house at North Ockenden.[1]

When Tyndale heard of this escape, he knew what it indicated; but he was not overwhelmed, and almost at the foot of the scaffold, he bravely fought many a tough battle. The Louvain doctors undertook to make him abjure his faith, and represented to him that he was condemned by the Church. "The authority of Jesus Christ," answered Tyndale, "is independent of the authority of the Church." They called upon him to make submission to the successor of the Apostle Peter. "Holy Scripture," he said, "is the first of the Apostles, and the *ruler* in the kingdom of Christ."[2] The Romish doctors ineffectually attacked him in his prison: he showed them that they were entangled in vain traditions and miserable superstitions, and overthrew all their pretences.

A most interesting memento of Tyndale's confinement at Vilvorde, and the only surviving document in the reformer's own hand, has come to light in the archives of the Council

---

[1] [Poyntz's efforts to obtain the release of his friend Tyndale proved very costly to him, and are worthy of the grateful remembrance of his fellow-countrymen. His goods in the Netherlands he lost; his wife, Anna van Calva, a native of Antwerp, refused to join him in England; for many years he was separated from his children. After eleven years he succeeded, on his brother's death, to the family estates in Essex, but financial embarrassment, dating from his losses in 1536, seems to have been his lot until his death in 1562. His epitaph in North Ockenden Church reads as follows: "He, for faithful service to his prince and warm-hearted profession of Gospel truth, suffered bonds and imprisonment beyond the sea, and would plainly have been destined to death, had he not, trusting in divine providence, saved himself in a striking manner by escaping from his prison. In this chapel he now sleeps peacefully in the Lord, 1562."]

[2] Tyndale's *Expositions* (Parker Society), pp. 195, 251.

of Brabant. It is a letter, written in Latin, which Tyndale addressed in all probability to the governor of the prison, and is worthy of being quoted in full:—

"I believe, right worshipful, that you are not ignorant of what has been determined concerning me (by the Council of Brabant); therefore I entreat your lordship and that by the Lord Jesus, that if I am to remain here (in Vilvorde) during the winter, you will request the Commissary to be kind enough to send me from my goods which he has in his possession, a warmer cap, for I suffer extremely from cold in the head, being afflicted with a perpetual catarrh, which is considerably increased in this cell. A warmer coat also, for that which I have is very thin: also a piece of cloth to patch my leggings; my overcoat is worn out; my shirts are also worn out. He has a woollen shirt of mine, if he will be kind enough to send it. I have also with him leggings of thicker cloth for putting on above; he has also warmer night caps. I wish also his permission to have a lamp in the evening, for it is wearisome to sit alone in the dark. But above all I entreat and beseech your clemency to be urgent with the Commissary that he may kindly permit me to have my Hebrew Bible, Hebrew Grammar, and Hebrew Dictionary, that I may spend my time with that study. And in return, may you obtain your dearest wish, provided always it be consistent with the salvation of your soul. But if, before the close of the winter, a different decision be reached concerning me, I shall be patient, abiding the will of God to the glory of the grace of my Lord Jesus Christ, whose Spirit, I pray, may ever direct your heart. Amen. W. TYNDALE."

What reception this letter met with we do not know, but the noble dignity which marks its style is a tribute to the continued power of the word of the truth of the Gospel in the life and witness of the illustrious prisoner. In season and out of season he bore faithful testimony to the word of divine grace, until "death God's endless mercies sealed, and made the sacrifice complete."

During this time Poyntz was working with all his might in England to ward off the blow by which his friend was about to be struck. John assisted Thomas, but all was useless. The king cared very little for these evangelicals. His religion

consisted in rejecting the Roman pontiff and making himself
pope; as for those reformers, let them be burnt in Brabant,
it will save him the trouble.

All hope was not, however, lost. They had confidence in
the vice-gerent, the *hammer* of the monks. On the 13th of April
Stephen Vaughan wrote to Cromwell from Antwerp: "If you
will send me a letter for the privy-council, I can still save
Tyndale from the fire; only make haste, for if you are slack
about it, it will be too late." But there were cases in which
Cromwell could do nothing without the king, and Henry was
deaf. He had special motives at that time for sacrificing
Tyndale: the discontent which broke out in the North of
England made him desirous of conciliating the Low Countries.
Charles V also, who was vigorously attacked by Francis I,
prayed *his very good brother* (Henry VIII) to unite with him
for the public good of Christendom. Queen Mary, regent of the
Netherlands, wrote from Brussels to her uncle, entreating
him to yield to this prayer, and the king was quite ready to
abandon Tyndale to such powerful allies. Mary, a woman
of upright heart but feeble character, easily yielded to outward
impressions, and had at that time bad counsellors about her.
"Those animals (the monks) are all powerful at the Court of
Brussels," said Erasmus. "Mary is only a puppet placed there
by our nation; Montigny is the play-thing of the Franciscans;
the cardinal-archbishop of Liége is a domineering person, and
full of violence; and as for the archbishop of Palermo, he is a
mere giver of words and nothing else."[1]

Among such personages, and under their influence, the
court was formed, and the trial of the English reformer began.
Tyndale refused to be represented by counsel. "I will answer
my accusers myself," he said. The doctrine for which he was
tried was this: "The man who throws off the worldly existence
which he has lived far from God, and receives by a living
faith the complete remission of his sins, which the death of
Christ has purchased for him, is introduced by a glorious
adoption into the very family of God." This was certainly a
crime for which a reformer could joyfully suffer. In August
1536, Tyndale appeared before the ecclesiastical court. "You

[1] Letter to Cholerus. Erasmus died shortly after, on the 12th of July,
1536.

are charged," said his judges, "with having infringed the imperial decree which forbids anyone to teach that faith alone justifies." The accusation was not without truth. A new edition of Tyndale's *Wicked Mammon* had just appeared in London under the title: *Treatise of Justification by Faith only.* Every man could read in it the crime with which he was charged.

Tyndale had his reasons when he declared he would defend himself. It was not his own cause that he undertook to defend, but the cause of the Bible: a Brabant lawyer would have supported it very poorly. It was in his heart to proclaim solemnly, before he died, that while all human religions make salvation proceed from the works of man, the divine religion makes it proceed from a work of God. "A man, whom the sense of his sins has confounded," said Tyndale, "loses all confidence and joy. The first thing to be done to save him is, therefore, to lighten him of the heavy burden under which his conscience is bowed down. He must believe in the perfect work of Christ which reconciles him completely with God; then he has peace, and Christ imparts to him, by His Spirit, a holy regeneration.—Yes," he exclaimed, "we believe and are at peace in our consciences, because that God who cannot lie, hath promised to forgive us for Christ's sake. . . . As a child, when his father threateneth him for his fault, hath never rest till he hear the word of mercy and forgiveness of his father's mouth again; but as soon as he heareth his father say, 'Go thy way, do me no more so; I forgive thee this fault!' then is his heart at rest; then runneth he to no man to make intercession for him; neither, though there come any false merchant, saying: 'What wilt thou give me and I will obtain pardon of thy father for thee?' will he suffer himself to be beguiled. No, he will not buy of a *wily fox* what his father hath given him freely."[1]

Tyndale had spoken to the consciences of his hearers, and some of them were beginning to believe that his cause was the cause of the Gospel. "Truly," exclaimed the procurator-general, as did formerly the centurion near the cross; "truly this was a good, learned, and pious man."[2] But the priests

[1] Tyndale, *Doctrinal Treatises* (Parker Society), p. 294.
[2] Foxe, *Acts*, v. p. 127.

would not allow so costly a prey to be snatched from them. Tyndale was declared guilty of erroneous, captious, rash, ill-sounding, dangerous, scandalous, and heretical propositions, and was condemned to be solemnly degraded and then handed over to the secular power. They were eager to make him go through the ceremonial, even all the mummeries, used on such occasions: it was too good a case to allow of any curtailment. The reformer was dressed in his sacerdotal robes, the sacred vessels were placed in his hands, and he was taken before the bishop. The latter, having been informed of the *crime* of the accused man, stripped him of the ornaments of his order, and after a barber had shaved the whole of his head, the bishop declared him deprived of the crown of the priesthood, and expelled, like an undutiful child, from the inheritance of the Lord.

One day would have been sufficient to cut off from this world the man who was its ornament, and those who walked in the darkness of fanaticism waited impatiently for the fatal hour; but the secular power hesitated for awhile, and the reformer stayed nearly two months longer in prison, always full of faith, peace, and joy. "Well," said those who came near him in the castle of Vilvorde, "if that man is not a good Christian, we do not know of one upon earth." Religious courage was personified in Tyndale. He had never suffered himself to be stopped by any difficulty, privation, or suffering; he had resolutely followed the call he had received, which was to give England the Word of God. Nothing had terrified him, nothing had dispirited him; with admirable perseverance he had continued his work, and now he was going to give his life for it. Firm in his convictions, he had never sacrificed the least truth to prudence or to fear; firm in his hope, he had never doubted that the labour of his life would bear fruit, for that labour had the promises of God. A pious and intrepid man, he is one of the noblest examples of Christian heroism.

The faint hope which some of Tyndale's friends had entertained, on seeing the delay of "justice," was soon destroyed. The imperial government prepared at last to complete the wishes of the priests. Friday, the 6th of October, 1536, was the day that terminated the miserable but glorious life of the reformer.

The gates of the prison rolled back, a procession crossed the foss and the bridge under which slept the waters of the Senne, passed the outer walls, and halted without the fortifications. Before leaving the castle, Tyndale, a grateful friend, had entrusted the gaoler with a letter intended for Poyntz; the gaoler took it himself to Antwerp not long after, but it has not come down to us. On arriving at the scene of punishment, the reformer found a numerous crowd assembled. The government had wished to show the people the punishment of a heretic, but they only witnessed the triumph of a martyr. Tyndale was calm. "I call God to record," he could say, "that I have never altered, against the voice of my conscience, one syllable of His Word. Nor would do this day, if all the pleasures, honours, and riches of the earth might be given me."[1] The joy of hope filled his heart: yet one painful idea took possession of him. Dying far from his country, abandoned by his king, he felt saddened at the thought of that prince, who had already persecuted so many of God's servants, and who remained obstinately rebellious against that divine light which everywhere shone around him. Tyndale would not have that soul perish through carelessness. His charity buried all the faults of the monarch: he prayed that those sins might be blotted out from before the face of God; he would have saved Henry VIII at any cost. While the executioner was fastening him to the post, the reformer exclaimed in a loud and suppliant voice: "Lord, open the king of England's eyes!"[2] They were his last words. Instantly afterwards he was strangled, and flames consumed the martyr's body. His last cry was wafted to the British isles, and repeated in every assembly of Christians. A great death had crowned a great life. "Such," says the old chronicler, John Foxe, "such is the story of that true servant and martyr of God, William Tyndale, who, for his notable pains and travail, may well be called *the Apostle of England in this our later age*."[3]

His fellow-countrymen profited by the work of his life. After the arrival in England of the first copies of Tyndale's New Testament early in 1526, edition followed rapidly upon

---

[1] Foxe, *Acts*, v. p. 134.
[2] *Ibid.*, p. 127.
[3] *Ibid.*, p. 114.

edition. It was like a mighty river continually bearing new waters to the sea. Did the reformer's death dry them up suddenly? No. A greater work still was to be accomplished: the entire Bible (Matthew's Bible) was already circulating privately. The king had refused his consent to the circulation of Coverdale's Bible; would he not do the same with this, and with greater reason? A powerful protector alone could secure the free circulation of Scripture. Richard Grafton, the printer, went to London to ask permission openly to sell the precious volume, and with the intention of applying to Cranmer.

Would Cranmer protect it? The king and Cromwell had declared against Tyndale, and the primate had looked on: that was too much his custom. His essentially prudent mind, the conviction he felt that he could do no good to the Church unless he kept the place he occupied, and perhaps his love of life inclined him to yield to his master's despotic will. So long as Henry VIII was on the throne of England, Cranmer was (humanly speaking) the only possible reformer. A John the Baptist, a Knox would have been dashed to pieces at the first shock. The sceptre was then an axe; to save the head, it was necessary to bend it. The primate, therefore, bent his head frequently. He hid himself during the royal anger, but when the storm had passed he appeared again. The primate was the victim of an error. He had said that the king ought to command the Church, and every time the tyrant's order was heard, he appeared to believe that God Himself enjoined him to obey. Cranmer was the image of his Church which, under the weight of its greatness and with many weaknesses hidden beneath its robes, has notwithstanding always had within it a mighty principle of truth and life.

Grafton, the printer, had an audience of the archbishop at Forde, in Kent: he presented the martyr's Bible, and asked him to procure its free circulation. The archbishop took the book, examined it, and was delighted with it. Fidelity, clearness, strength, simplicity, unction—all were combined in this admirable translation. Cranmer had much eagerness in proposing what he thought useful. He sent the volume to Cromwell, begging him to present it to his Majesty and obtain permission for it to be sold, "until such time that we (the bishops)," he added, "shall put forth a better translation—which, I think, will not be till a day after doomsday."[1]

Henry ran over the book: Tyndale's name was not in it, and the dedication to his Majesty was very well written. The king regarding (and not without reason) Holy Scripture as the most powerful engine to destroy the papal system, and believing that this translation would help him to emancipate England from the Romish domination, came to an unexpected resolution: he authorized the sale and the reading of the Bible throughout the kingdom. The book carried the words at the foot of its title page, "Set forth with the Kinges most gracyous lycence." All Englishmen might safely buy and read it. Inconsistent and whimsical prince! at one and the same time he published and imposed all over his realm the doctrines of Romanism, and circulated without obstacle the Divine Word that overthrew them! We may well say that the blood of a martyr, precious in the eyes of the Supreme King, opened the gates of England to the Holy Scriptures. Cromwell having informed the archbishop of the royal decision, the latter exclaimed, "What you have just done gives me more pleasure than if you had given me a thousand pounds. I doubt not but that hereby such fruit of good knowledge shall ensue, that it shall well appear hereafter, what high and acceptable service you have done unto God and the king, which shall so much redound to your honour that (besides God's reward) you shall obtain perpetual memory for the same."[2]

For centuries the English people had been waiting for such a permission, even from before the time of Wycliffe; and accordingly the Bible circulated rapidly. The impetuosity with which the living waters rushed forth, carrying with them everything they met in their course, was like the sudden opening of a huge floodgate. This great event, more important than divorces, treaties, and wars, was the conquest of England by the Reformation. "It was a wonderful thing to see," says an old historian. Whoever possessed the means bought the book and read it or had it read to him by others. Aged persons learnt their letters in order to study the Holy Scriptures of

[1] Cranmer, *Letters and Remains* (Parker Society) (4th August, 1537), p. 344.
[2] *Ibid.*, p. 346.

God. In many places there were meetings for reading; poor people clubbed their savings together and purchased a Bible, and then in some remote corner of the church, they modestly formed a circle, and read the Holy Book between them. A crowd of men, women, and young folks, disgusted with the barren pomp of the altars, and with the worship of dumb images, would gather round them to taste the precious promises of the Gospel. God Himself spoke under the arched roofs of those old chapels or time-worn cathedrals, where for generations nothing had been heard but masses and litanies. The people wished, instead of the noisy chants of the priests, to hear the voice of Jesus Christ, of Paul and of John, of Peter and of James. The Christianity of the apostles reappeared in the Church.

But with it came persecution, according to the words of the Master: *The brother shall deliver up the brother to death, and the father the child.* A father, exasperated because his son, a mere boy, had taken part in these holy readings, caught him by the hair, and put a cord round his neck to hang him. In all the towns and villages of Tyndale's country the holy pages were opened, and the delighted readers found therein those treasures of peace and joy which the martyr had known. Many cried out with him, "We know that this Word is from God, as we know that fire burns; not because anyone has told us, but because a Divine fire consumes our hearts. O the brightness of the face of Moses! O the splendour of the glory of Jesus Christ, which no veil conceals! O the inward power of the Divine word, which compels us, with so much sweetness, to love and to do! O the temple of God within us, in which the Son of God dwells!" Tyndale had desired to set the world on fire by his Master's Word, and that fire was kindled. The general dissemination of the Holy Scriptures forms an important epoch in the Reformation of England. It is like one of those pillars which separate one territory from another.

Jane Seymour, third wife of Henry VIII. Drawing by Holbein. "About the middle of October 1537 an event occurred which was of great importance for the triumph of the Gospel. There was at that time great rejoicing in the palace of the Tudors and in all England, for Queen Jane (Seymour) on October 12th presented to Henry VIII the son which he had so much desired." (Page 353.)

Hugh Latimer, Bishop of Worcester. The boldest preacher during the reign of Henry VIII, Latimer never forgot two sayings which were impressed upon his heart when he was chaplain to the King: "He who for fear of any power *hides the truth*, provokes the wrath of God to come to him, for he fears man more than God" (Augustine). And, "He is not only a traitor to the truth who openly for truth reads a lie; but he also who *does not freely pronounce and show the truth* that he knoweth" (Chrysostom).

West Kington church, Wiltshire, scene of
Latimer's labours between 1531 and 1535.
Latimer was one of the first to show that, by
exposition of Scripture and earnest prayer,
not only London but all England might be
won for the Gospel. The pulpit is believed
to be the one from which Latimer preached.

Martyrs at Smithfield. The old engravings recapture the vivid impression these tragic events made upon the popular mind. The drawing shown above depicts the burning of Anne Askew, a lady of gentle birth, the friend of Queen Catherine Parr and one of the last martyrs of Henry VIII's reign.

Modern Smithfield. Only a small plaque on the rear wall of St. Bartholomew's Hospital remains to perpetuate the memory of the many who suffered for their faith in Tudor times. A further link with this heroic era is provided by a small bookshop a few yards away in Little Britain at which Merle d'Aubigné's History of the Reformation in England may be bought

John Foxe (1516–87) who following Tyndale was one of the first to have the vision of flooding England with the printed Word, and whose famous *Acts and Monuments* were in Elizabethan times to carry the story of the Reformation into every parish in the land. Foxe's writings, the authenticity of which has survived repeated assaults, have lost none of their power, but modern Protestants have lost the vision of this faithful writer who once exclaimed, "The Pope must abolish printing, or he must seek a new world to reign over, for by this printing the doctrine of the Gospel soundeth to all nations and countries under heaven."

"Matthew's Bible", generally considered to be the real primary version of our English Bible. The New Testament and the Old as far as the Second Book of Chronicles were the work of Tyndale; the remainder was completed by John Rogers under the pseudonym of Thomas Matthew. The royal favour being temporarily procured for it by Cromwell and Cranmer, it was published in 1537 with the King's licence, and "God Himself spoke under the arched roofs of those old chapels or time-worn cathedrals, where for generations nothing had been heard but masses and litanies". In 1543 Parliament ordered the removal or obliteration of all marginal notes, an indication that they recognized the tremendous influence exerted by Tyndale's notes.

The death-bed scene of Henry VIII. This contemporary drawing depicts the downfall of the Papal hierarchy and the coming triumphs of the Gospel. The dying king points to his youthful successor, Edward VI, whose uncle, the Duke of Somerset, Lord Protector 1547–9, stands at his side. Seated on the right are the Council, among them Cranmer, who in February 1548 ordered the removal of all images from churches, as is depicted (top right). It is presumed therefore that the picture was drawn at some time between February 1548 and October 1549, the date of Somerset's fall.

BOOK THREE

Reformation, Reaction, Relief

CHAPTER ONE

Three Parties Divide England
(1536–1540)

THERE were in 1536 three distinct parties in England, the papists, the evangelicals, and the Anglican Catholics who were halting between the two extremes. It was a question which of the three would gain the upper hand.

The Reformation in England was born of the power of the Word of God, and did not encounter there such obstacles as were raised against it in France by a powerful clergy and by princes hostile to evangelical faith and morality. The English prelates, weakened by various circumstances, were unable to withstand an energetic attack; and the sovereign was "the mad Henry," as Luther had called him. His whims opened the doors to religious freedom, of which the Reformation was to take advantage. Thus England, which had remained in a state of rudeness and ignorance much longer than France, was early enlightened by the Reformation; and the nation awakened by the Gospel gave birth in the sixteenth century to such masterminds as France, though more highly civilized, failed to produce so early. Shakespeare was born in 1564, one month before the death of Calvin. The Reformation placed England a century ahead of the rest of Europe. The final triumph, however, of the Reformation was not reached without many conflicts; and the two adversaries more than once engaged hand to hand, before one overthrew the other.

About the middle of October 1537 an event occurred which was of great importance for the triumph of the Gospel. There was at that time great rejoicing in the palace of the Tudors and in all England, for Queen Jane (Seymour), on October 12, presented to Henry VIII the son which he had so much desired. Letters written beforehand, in the name of the Queen, announced it in every place, and congratulations arrived from all quarters. This birth was called "the most joyful news

which for many years had been announced in England."
Bishop Latimer wrote: "Here is no less joying and rejoicing
in these parts for the birth of our prince, whom we hungered
so long, than there was, I trow, among the neighbours at the
birth of St. John Baptist." (Luke 1. 58.) A prince born to
reign! exclaimed the politicians. "God grant him long life
and abundant honours!" they wrote from the Continent.
"Our prince," Cromwell sent word to the ambassadors of
England, "our Lord be thanked, is in good health, and
sucketh like a child of his puissance, which you my lord
William can declare." It was all the more important to declare
this, because the very contrary was asserted. It was even
reported by some that the child was dead. As Henry feared
that some attempt might be made on his son's life, he forbade
that anyone should approach the cradle without an order
signed by his own hand. Everything brought into the child's
room was to be perfumed, and measures of precaution against
poison were taken. The infant was named Edward; Archbishop Cranmer baptized him, and was one of his godfathers.
A fortnight after his birth Sir Edward Seymour, his uncle by
the mother's side, was created Earl of Hertford. It was alleged
that a spell had been thrown upon the king to prevent his
having a male child; and behold, he had now an heir in spite
of the spell. His dynasty was strengthened. Henry VIII became
more powerful at home, more respected abroad.

This great rejoicing was followed by a great mourning.
The queen developed puerperal fever and died twelve days
after the birth of her son. "Divine Providence," wrote Henry
to his fellow monarch of France, "has mingled my joy with
the bitterness of the death of her who brought me this
happiness." Certainly Henry lamented her untimely death
with all sincerity.

With the birth of the young prince the hopes of the partisans of the Catholic Mary disappeared, and the friends of the
Reformation rejoiced at the thought that the young prince
was godson of the archbishop. Many circumstances contributed
to their encouragement. They witnessed the formation of
unlooked-for ties between the evangelicals of England and
those of Switzerland; and the pure Gospel as professed by
the latter began to exercise a real influence over England.

Edward, during his very short reign, was to fulfil the best hopes to which his birth had given rise, and the triumph to which his reign seemed destined was already visibly in preparation.

Simon Grynaeus, the friend of Erasmus and Melanchthon, and professor at the university of Basel, had as early as 1531 held intercourse with Henry VIII and Cranmer.[1] Afterwards Cranmer and Henry Bullinger, successor of Zwingli at Zurich, had also become acquainted with each other; and, as early as 1536, some young Englishmen of good family had betaken themselves to Zurich, that they might drink at the full fountain of Christian knowledge and life which sprang forth there. Some of them lived in the house of Pellican, others with Bullinger himself. These young men were John Butler, who had a rich patrimony in England—a sagacious man and a Christian who persevered in prayer; Nicholas Partridge, from Kent, a man of active and devoted character; Bartholomew Traheron, who had already (1527 and 1528) declared at Oxford for the Reformation, and had been persecuted by Doctor London; Nicholas Eliot, who had studied law in England, and who afterwards held some government office; and others besides.[2] Bullinger was strongly attached to these young Englishmen. He directed their studies and, in addition to his public teaching, he explained to them in his own house the prophet Isaiah.

There was much talk at Zurich at this time about a young French theologian, Calvin by name, who was settled at Geneva, and had published a profound and eloquent exposition of Christian doctrines. The young Englishmen eagerly longed to make his acquaintance. Butler, Partridge, Eliot, and Traheron set out for Geneva in November 1537, bearing letters of introduction from Bullinger to the reformer. The latter received them in the most kindly manner. It was more than common courtesy, they wrote to Bullinger.[3] They were delighted with his appearance and with his conversation, at once so simple and so fruitful. They felt a charm which

---

[1] See his letter to Henry VIII, *Original Letters relative to the English Reformation* (Parker Society), ii. p. 554.
[2] *Original Letters*, &c. (Parker Society), ii, pp. 621, 316, 608, 225, 226.
[3] *Ibid.*, p. 623.

drew them to his presence again and again. The master taught well, and the disciples listened well. The four Englishmen, being called elsewhere, took their departure deeply saddened by the painful separation. A letter written by Butler and Traheron shortly afterwards is the first communication addressed by England to the reformer of Geneva. It runs as follows:—"We wish you the true joy in Christ. May as much happiness be appointed to us from henceforth as our going away from you has occasioned us sorrow! For although our absence, as we hope, will not be of very long continuance, yet we cannot but grieve at being deprived even for a few hours of so much suavity of disposition and delightful conversation. And this also distresses us in no small measure, lest there should be any persons who may regard us as resembling flies, which swarm everywhere in the summer, but disappear on the approach of winter. You may be assured that, if we had been able to assist you in any way, no pleasure should have called us away from you, nor should any peril have withdrawn us. This distress, indeed, which the disordered tempers of certain individuals have brought upon you, is far beyond our power to alleviate. But you have one, Christ Jesus, who can easily dispel by the beams of his consolation whatever cloud may arise upon your mind. He will restore to you a joyful tranquillity; he will scatter and put to flight your enemies; he will make you gloriously to triumph over your conquered adversaries; and we will entreat him, as earnestly as we can, to do this as speedily as possible. We have written these few lines at present, most amiable and learned Master Calvin, that you may receive a memorial of our regard towards you. Salute in our names that individual of a truly heroic spirit and singular learning and godliness, Master Farel. Salute, too, our sincere friends Master Olivetan and your brother Fontaine. Our countrymen send abundant salutations. Farewell, very dear friend."[1]

England at this time did justice to the Genevan reformer.

Much admiration was likewise felt for Bullinger. "We confess ourselves to be entirely yours," wrote to him the four Englishmen, "as long as we can be our own." The works of

[1] *Original Letters relative to the English Reformation* (Parker Society), ii. p. 621.

the Zurich doctor were much read in England, and diffused there the spirit of the gospel. Nicholas Eliot wrote to him:—
"And how great weight all persons attribute to your commentaries, how greedily they embrace and admire them (to pass over numberless other arguments), the booksellers are most ample witnesses whom by the sale of your writings alone ... you see suddenly become as rich as Crœsus. May God, therefore, give you the disposition to publish all your writings as speedily as possible, whereby you will not only fill the coffers of the booksellers, but will gain over very many souls to Christ, and adorn his church with most precious jewels."[1]

At the news that the king of England had separated from the pope, the Swiss theologians were filled with hope, and they vied with each other in speeding his progress towards the truth. Bullinger composed two works in Latin which he dedicated to Henry VIII; the first of them on *The Authority, the Certitude, the Stability and the Absolute Perfection of Holy Scripture;* the second on *The Institution and the Function of Bishops.* He forwarded copies of these works to Partridge and Eliot for presentation to the king, to Cranmer, and to Cromwell. The two young Englishmen went first to the archbishop and delivered to him the volumes intended for the king and for himself. The archbishop consented to present the book to the prince, but not till after he had read it himself, and on condition that Eliot and Partridge should be present, that they might answer any questions asked by the king. Then going to Cromwell, they gave him the copy intended for him; and the vicegerent, more prompt than the archbishop, showed it the same day to Henry VIII, to whom Cranmer then hastened to present his own copy. The king expressed a wish that the work should be translated into English. "Your books are wonderfully well received," wrote Eliot to Bullinger, "not only by our king, but equally so by the lord Cromwell, who is keeper of the king's privy seal and vicar-general of the church of England."

Other Continental divines who held the same views as the Swiss likewise dedicated some theological writings both to the king and to Cranmer. Wolfgang Capito, who was at the time at Strasburg, dedicated to Henry VIII a book in which he treated, among other subjects, of the mass (*Responsum de Missa,*

[1] *Original Letters,* &c., ii. p. 620.

&c.). The king, as usual, handed it to two persons belonging to the two opposing parties, in order to get their opinions. He then examined their verdict, and announced his own. Cranmer wrote to Capito that the king "could by no means digest" his piece on the mass,[1] although at the same time he approved some of the other pieces. Martin Bucer, a colleague of Capito, having written a commentary on the Epistle to the Romans, dedicated it to Cranmer, and wrote to him as follows:—"It is not enough to have shaken off the yoke of the pope, and to be unwilling to take upon us the yoke of Christ; but if God be for us who can be against us? and Christianity is a warfare."[2]

While the Swiss and the Strasburgers were seeking to enlighten England, the Roman party on the Continent and the Catholic party in England itself were striving to keep her in darkness. The pope, in sorrow and in anger, saw England lost to Rome. Nevertheless the Catholic rising in the northern counties in October, 1536, allowed him still to cherish hope. The king of France and the Emperor, both near neighbours of England, could if necessary strike with the sword. The pope must therefore stir up to action not only the English Catholics, but also the courts of Paris and Brussels. Whom should he select for the mission? Reginald Pole, an Englishman, a zealous Roman Catholic, and a kinsman of Henry VIII, seemed to be the man made for the occasion. It was he who had lately written these words—"There was never a greater matter entreated, of more importance to the wealth of the realm and the whole church than this (the re-establishment of papal authority). And this same that you go about to take away, the authority of one head in the church, was a more principal and groundle cause of the loss of the Orient, to be in infidels' hands, and all true religion degenerate, than ever was the Turk's sword, as most wisest men have judged. For if they had agreed all with the Occidental Church, they had never come to that misery; and like misery, if God have not mercy on us to return to the church, is most to be feared in our realm. . . . Your sweet liberty you have got, since you were delivered from the obedience papal, speaketh for itself.

[1] Cranmer to Capito, *Original Letters* (Parker Society), p. 16.
[2] Bucer to Cranmer, *Ibid.*, p. 525.

Whereof the rest of the realm hath such part that you be without envy of other countries, that no nation wisheth the same to have such liberty granted them." This last assertion was doubtful.

Pole was at this time at Padua, where he had studied, and where he was resident by permission of the king. He avoided going to Rome lest he should offend Henry. But he received one day an invitation from Paul III, who summoned him to the Vatican to take part in a consultation about the general council. To comply with this summons would be to cross the Rubicon; it would make Henry VIII his irreconcilable enemy, and would expose to great danger not only himself but all his family. Pole therefore hesitated. The advice, however, of the pious Contarini, the command of the pope, and his own enthusiasm for the cause, brought him to a decision. On his arrival at Rome he gave himself up entirely; and when Christmas was drawing near, on December 20, 1536, the pope created him cardinal, together with del Monte, afterwards Julius III; Caraffa, afterwards Paul IV; Sadoleto, Borgia, Cajetan, and four others. These proceedings were very seriously criticized in England. For the vainglory of a red hat, said Tunstall and Stokesley, Pole is, in fact, an instrument of the pope to set forth his malice, to depose the king from his kingdom, and to stir his subjects against him. There, was, however, something more in his case than a cardinal's hat; there was, we must acknowledge, a faith, doubtless fanatical but sincere, in the papacy. Not long afterwards the pope nominated him the new cardinal legate beyond the Alps; the object of this measure being to excite men's minds. He was to induce the king of France and the Emperor to enter into the views of the Roman court, to inflame the Catholics of England, and, if he should be unable to go there himself, to take up his residence in the Netherlands, and thence conspire for the overthrow of Protestantism in England.

At the beginning of Lent 1537, Pole, attended by a numerous suite, set out from Rome. The pope, who was not thoroughly sure of his new legate, had appointed as his adviser the bishop of Verona, who was to make up for any deficiency of experience on the part of the legate, and to put him on his guard against pride. Henry VIII, on learning the nature of his young cousin's mission, was exceedingly angry. He declared Pole a rebel, set a price on his head, and promised fifty thousand crowns to anyone who should kill him. Cromwell, following his master's example, exclaimed, "I will make him eat his own heart." This was only a figure of speech, but it was rather a strong one. No sooner had Henry VIII heard of the arrival of Pole in France than he demanded that Francis I should deliver him up, as a subject in rebellion against his king. Pole had not been long at Paris before he heard of this demand. It aroused in his heart more pride than fear. It revealed to him his own importance; and turning to his attendants he said, "This news makes me glad; I know now that I am a cardinal." Francis I did not concede the demand of the angry Tudor; but he did consider the mission of Pole as one of those attacks on the power of kings in which the papacy from time to time indulged. When Pole, therefore, made his appearance at the palace he was refused admission. While still only at the door, and even before he had had time to knock, he himself tells us, he was sent away. "I am ready to weep," he added, "to find that a king does not receive a legate of Rome." Francis I having sent him an order to leave France, he fled to Cambrai, which at that time formed part of the Netherlands.

No sooner was he there than, under great excitement about what had occurred to him at Paris, he wrote to Cromwell, complaining bitterly that Henry VIII, in order to get him into his power, did not scruple to violate both God's law and man's, and even "to disturb all commerce between country and country." "I was ashamed to hear that . . . a prince of honour should desire of another prince of like honour, Betray thine own ambassador, betray the legate, and give him into my ambassador's hands to be brought to me." The like, he says, was never heard of in Christendom. Pole had more hope of the Emperor than of Francis I; but he was soon undeceived. He was not permitted to go out of the town; and a courier entrusted with his despatches was arrested by the Imperialists at Valenciennes and sent back to him. He now resolved on taking a step towards opening communication with the English government; and as he did not venture to present

himself to the ambassadors of Henry VIII in France, he sent
to them the bishop of Verona. But this prelate, likewise, was
not received, and he was only allowed to speak to one of the
secretaries. He endeavoured to convince him of the perfect
innocence of Pole and of his mission. "The cardinal-legate,"
he said, "is solely charged by the pope to treat of the safety of
Christendom." This was true in the sense intended by Rome;
but it is well known what this safety, in her view, required.

Fresh movements in the north of England tended to increase
the anger of Henry VIII. It was not enough that Pole had been
driven from France. The king himself now wrote to Hutton,
his envoy at Brussels—"You shall deliver unto the regent
(Margaret) our letters for the stay of his entry into the
Emperor's dominions; . . . you shall press them . . . neither
to admit him to her presence, nor to suffer unto him to have
any other entertainment than beseemeth the traitor and rebel
of their friend and ally. . . . You shall in any wise cause good
secret and substantial espial to be made upon him from place
to place where he shall be." Pole, on his part, spoke as a Roman
legate. He summoned the queen to prove her submission to
the apostolic see, and to grant him an audience; and he made
use of serious menaces. "If traitors, conspirators, rebels, and
other offenders," said the English ambassador, "might under
the shadow of legacie have sure access into all places, and
thereby to trouble and espy all things, that were overmuch
dangerous." This was no question of rebellion, Pole sent word
to the regent by the bishop of Verona, but of the Reformation;
and he was sent to refute the errors which it was spreading in
England. Her opinion was that he should return, "for that
she had no commission of the Emperor to intermeddle in any
point of his legacy."

Hereupon Pole went from Cambrai to Liége; but in consequence of the advice of the bishop of Liége, he only ventured
to go there in disguise. He was received into the bishop's
palace, but his stay there was "not without great fear." He
set out again on August 22, and went to Rome. Never had
any mission of a Roman pontiff so entirely failed. The
ambitious projects of the pope against the Reformation in
England had proved abortive. But one of the secrets of Roman
policy is to put a good face on a bad case. The less successful

Pole had been the more necessary it was to assume an air of satisfaction with him and his embassy. In any case, was it not a victory for him to have returned safe and sound after having to do with Francis I, Henry VIII, and Charles V? It was November when he reached Rome; and he was received as generals used to be received by the ancient Romans after great victories. They carried him, so to speak, on their arms; everyone heaped upon him demonstrations of respect and joy; and his secretary, on the last day of the year 1537, wrote to the Catholics of England, to describe to them *the great triumph that was made at Rome for the safe arrival of his master*. Rome may win or lose, she always celebrates a triumph.

This mission of Reginald Pole had fatal consequences. In the following year, his brother, Henry lord Montague, and his kinsmen, Henry the marquis of Exeter, and Sir Edward Nevil, were arrested and committed to the Tower. Some time afterwards his mother, Margaret countess of Salisbury, the last of the Plantagenets, a woman of remarkable spirit, was likewise arrested. They were charged with aiming at the deposition of Henry and at placing Reginald on the throne. "I do perceive," it was said, "it should be for my lord Montague's brother, which is beyond the sea with the bishop of Rome, and is an arrant traitor to the king's Highness." They were condemned and executed in January 1539. The countess was not executed till May 1541.

Paul III had been mistaken is selecting the cousin of the king to stir up Catholic Europe against him. But some other legate might have a chance of success. Henry felt the necessity of securing allies upon the Continent. Cranmer promptly availed himself of this feeling to persuade Henry to unite with the Protestants of Germany. The elector of Saxony, the landgrave of Hesse, and the other Protestant princes, finding that the king had resolutely broken with the pope, had suppressed the monasteries and begun other reforms, consented to send a deputation. On May 12, 1538, Francis Burkhardt, vice-chancellor of Saxony, George von Boyneburg, doctor of law, and Frederick Myconius, superintendent of the church of Gotha—a diplomatist, a jurist, and a theologian—set out for London. The princes wished to be worthily represented, and the envoys were to live in magnificent style and keep a liberal table. The king received them with much goodwill. He thanked them that, laying aside their own affairs, they had undertaken so laborious a journey; and he especially spoke of Melanchthon in the most loving terms. But the delegates, whilst they were so honourably treated by their own princes and by the king of England, were much less so by inferior agents. They were hardly settled in the house assigned to them than they were attacked by the inhabitants, "a multitude of rats daily and nightly running in their chambers." In addition to this annoyance, the kitchen was adjacent to the parlour in which they were to dine, so that the house was full of smells, and all who came in were offended.

But certain bishops were to give them more trouble than the rats. Cranmer received them as friends and brethren, and endeavoured to take advantage of their presence to promote the triumph of the Gospel in England; but Tunstall, Stokesley, and others left no stone unturned to render their mission abortive. The discussion took place in the archbishop's palace at Lambeth, and they did their best to protract it, obstinately defending the doctrines and the customs of the Middle Ages. They were willing, indeed, to separate from Rome; but this was in order to unite with the Greek church, not with the evangelicals. Each of the two conflicting parties endeavoured to gain over to itself those English doctors who were still wavering. One day, Richard Sampson, bishop of Chichester, who usually went with the Scholastic party, having come to Lambeth at an early hour, Cranmer took him aside and so forcibly urged on him the necessity of abandoning tradition that the bishop, a weak man, was convinced. But Stokesley, who had doubtless noticed something in the course of the discussion, in his turn took Sampson aside into the gallery, just when the meeting was breaking up, and spoke to him very earnestly in behalf of the practices of the church. These customs are essential, said Stokesley, for they are found in the Greek church. The bishop of Chichester, driven in one direction by the bishop of London and in the opposite by the archbishop of Canterbury, was much embarrassed, and did not know which way to turn. His decision was for the last speaker. The semi-Roman doctors at this period, who sacrificed to the king the Roman rite, felt it incumbent upon them to cross all Europe for the purpose of finding in the Turkish empire the Greek rite, which was for them the Gospel. England must be dressed in a Grecian garb. But Cranmer would not hear of it; and he presented his countrymen the wedding garment of which the Saviour speaks.

The summer was now drawing to an end. The German delegates had been in London for some three months without having made any progress. Wearied with fruitless discussions, they began to think of their departure. But before setting out, about the middle of August, they forwarded to the king a document in which they argued from Holy Scripture, from the testimony of the most ancient of the Fathers, and from the practice of the primitive church, against the withdrawal of the cup from the laity, private masses, and the celibacy of priests, three errors which they looked upon as having essentially contributed to the deformation of Christendom. When Cranmer heard of their intention to leave England, he was much affected. Their departure dissipated all his hopes. Must he then renounce the hope of seeing the Word of God prevail in England as it was prevailing in evangelical Germany? He summoned them to Lambeth, and entreated them earnestly and with much kindliness for the king's sake to remain. They replied "that at the king's request they would be very well content to tarry during his pleasure, not only a month or two, but a year or two, if they were at their own liberty. But forasmuch they had been so long from their princes, and had not all this season any letters from them, it was not to be doubted but that they were daily looked for at home, and therefore they durst not tarry." However, after renewed entreaties, they said, "We will consult together." They discussed with one another the question whether they ought to leave England just at the time when she was perhaps on the point of siding with the truth. Shall we refuse to sacrifice our private convenience to interests so great? They adopted the least convenient but most useful course. We will tarry, they said, for a month, "upon hope that their tarrying should grow into some good success concerning the points of their commission," and "trusting that the king's Majesty would write unto their princes for their excuse in thus long tarrying." The evangelicals

of Germany believed it to be their duty to tolerate certain
secondary differences, but frankly to renounce those errors and
abuses which were contrary to the essential doctrines of the
Gospel, and to unite in the great truths of the faith. This was
precisely what the Catholic party and the king himself had
no intention of doing. When Cranmer urged the bishops to
apply themselves to the task of answering the Germans, they
replied "that the king's grace hath taken upon himself to
answer the said orators in that behalf . . . and therefore they
will not meddle with the abuses, lest they should write therein
contrary to that the king shall write." It was, indeed, neither
pleasant nor safe to contradict Henry VIII. But in this case
the king's opinion was only a convenient veil, behind which
the bishops sought to conceal their ill-will and their evil
doctrines. Their reply was nothing but an evasion. The book
was written, not by the king, but by one of themselves, Tunstall
bishop of Durham. He ran no risk of contradicting himself.
In spite of this ill-will, the Germans remained not only one
month but two. Their conduct, like that of Cranmer, was
upright, devoted, noble, and Christian; while the bishops of
London and Durham and their friends, clever men no doubt,
were souls of a lower cast, who strove to escape by chicanery
from the free discussion proposed to them, and passed off their
knavery as prudence.

The German doctors had now nothing more to do. They
had offered the hand and it had been rejected. The vessel
which was to convey them was waiting. They were exhausted
with fatigue; and one of them, Myconius, whom the English
climate appeared not to suit, was very ill. They set out at
the beginning of October, and gave an account of their
mission to their sovereigns and to Melanchthon. The latter
thought that, considering the affection which the king displayed towards him, he might, if he intervened at this time,
do something to incline the balance the right way. He therefore
wrote to Henry VIII a remarkable letter, in which, after
expressing his warm gratitude for the king's goodwill, he
added:—"I commend to you, Sire, the cause of the Christian
religion. Your Majesty knows that the principal duty of
sovereigns is to protect and propagate the heavenly doctrine,
and for this reason God gives them the same name as his own,

saying to them, *Ye are gods* (Ps. 82. 6). My earnest desire is to
see a true agreement, so far as regards the doctrine of piety,
established between all the churches which condemn Roman
tyranny, an agreement which should cause the glory of God
to shine forth, should induce the other nations to unite with
us and maintain peace in the churches." Melanchthon was
right as to the last point; but was he right as to the office he
assigned to kings? In his view it was a heroic action to take
up arms for the church. But what church was it necessary to
protect and extend sword in hand? Catholic princes, assuredly,
drew the sword against the Protestants rather than the Protestants against the Catholics. The most heroic kings, by this
rule, would be Philip II and Louis XIV. Melanchthon's
principle leads by a straight road to the Inquisition. To
express our whole thought on the matter—what descendant of
the Huguenots could possibly acknowledge as true, as divine,
a principle by virtue of which his forefathers, men of whom
the world was not worthy, were stripped of everything,
afflicted, tormented, scattered in the deserts, mountains, and
caves of the earth, cast into prison, tortured, banished, and
put to death? Conscience, which is the voice of God, is higher
than all the voices of men.

CHAPTER TWO

An "*Appeal to Caesar*" and its Outcome
(1538)

THE Romish party in England did not confine itself to preventing the union of Henry with the Protestants of Germany; but contended at all points against evangelical reformation, and strove to gain over the king by a display of enthusiastic devotion to his person and his ecclesiastical supremacy. This was especially the policy of Bishop Stephen Gardiner. Endowed with great acuteness of intellect, he had studied the king's character, and he put forth all his powers to secure his adoption of his own views. Henry did not esteem his character, but highly appreciated his talents, and on this account employed him. Now Gardiner was the mainstay of the Scholastic doctrines and the most inflexible opponent of the Reformation. He had been employed by the King and Wolsey in numerous diplomatic missions on the continent, where his extensive knowledge of canon law gave him great advantages. He had visited the court of the Emperor, and had had interviews with the Roman legate. One day, at Ratisbon, an Italian named Ludovico, a servant of the legate, while talking with one of the attendants of Sir Henry Knyvet, who was a member of the English embassy, had confided to him the statement that Gardiner had secretly been reconciled with the pope, and had entered into correspondence with him. Knyvet, exceedingly anxious to know what to think of it, had had a conference with Ludovico, and had come away convinced of the reality of the fact. No sooner did Gardiner get wind of these things, than he betook himself to Granvella, chancellor of the Empire, and sharply complained to him of the calumnies of Ludovico. The chancellor ordered the Italian to be put in prison; but in spite of this measure many continued to believe that he had spoken truth. We are inclined to think that Ludovico said more than he knew. The story,

however, indicates from which quarter the wind was blowing
in the sphere in which Gardiner moved. He had set out for
Paris on October 1, 1535; and on September 28, 1538, there
was to be seen entering London a brilliant and numerous
band, mules and chariots hung with draperies on which were
embroidered the arms of the master, lackeys, gentlemen
dressed in velvet, with many ushers and soldiers. This was
Gardiner and his suite.

The three years' absence of this formidable adversary of the
Gospel had been marked by a slackening of the persecution,
and by a more active propagation of the Holy Scriptures.
His return was to be distinguished by a vigorous renewal of
the struggle against the Gospel. This was the main business
of Gardiner. To this he consecrated all the resources of the
most acute understanding and the most persistent character.
He began immediately to lay snares round the king, whom
in this respect it was not very hard to entrap. Two difficulties,
however, arose. At first Henry VIII, by the influence of the
deceased queen as some have supposed, had been somewhat
softened towards the Reformation. Then the rumours of the
reconciliation of Gardiner with the pope might have alienated
the king from him. The crafty man proceeded cleverly and
killed two birds with one stone. "The pope," he said to the
king, "is doing all he can to ruin you." Henry, provoked at
the mission of Pole, had no doubt of that. "You ought then,
Sire," continued the bishop, "to do all that is possible to
conciliate the Continental powers, and to place yourself in
security from the treacherous designs of Rome. Now the
surest means of conciliating Francis I, Charles V, and other
potentates, is to proceed rigorously against heretics." Henry
agreed to the means proposed with the more readiness because
he had always been a fanatic for the corporal presence, and
because the Lutherans, in his view, could not take offence at
seeing him burn some who denied it.

A beginning was made with the Anabaptists. These wretched
people were persecuted in all European countries. Some of
them had taken refuge in England. In October 1538 the king
appointed a commission to examine certain people "lately
come into the kingdom, who are keeping themselves in con-
cealment in various nooks and corners." The commission

was authorized to proceed, even supposing this should be in contravention of any statutes of the realm.

Four Anabaptists bore the faggots at Paul's church, and two others, a man and a woman, originally from the Netherlands, were burnt in Smithfield. Cranmer and Bonner sat on this commission, side by side with Stokesley and Sampson. This fact shows what astonishing error prevailed at the time in the minds of men. Gardiner wanted to go further; and while associating, when persecution was in hand, with such men as Cranmer, he had secret conferences with Stokesley, bishop of London, Tunstall of Durham, Sampson of Chichester, and others who were devoted to the doctrines of the Middle Ages. They talked over the means of resisting the reforms of Cranmer and Cromwell, and of restoring Catholicism.

Bishop Sampson, one of Gardiner's allies, was a staunch friend of ancient superstitions, and attached especial importance to the requirement that God should not be addressed in a language understood by the common people. "In all places," he said, "both with the Latins and the Greeks, the ministers of the church sung or said their offices or prayers in the Latin or Greek grammatical tongue, and not in the vulgar. That the people prayed apart in such tongues as they would . . . and he wished that all the ministers were so well learned that they understood their offices, service, or prayers which they said in the Latin tongue." In his view, it was not lawful to speak to God except *grammatically*.

Sampson, a weak and narrow-minded man, was swayed by prejudices and ruled by stronger men; and he had introduced in his diocese customs contrary to the orders of the king. Weak minds are often in the van when important movements are beginning; the strong ones are in the rear and urge them on. This was the case with Sampson and Gardiner. Cromwell, who had a keen and penetrating intellect, and whose glance easily searched the depths of men's hearts and pierced to the core of facts, perceived that some project was hatching against the Reformation; and as he did not dare to attack the real leaders, he had Sampson arrested and committed to the Tower. The bishop was not strong-minded and trembled for a slight cause; it may, therefore, be imagined how it was with him when he found himself in the state prison. He fell into great trouble and extraordinary dejection of mind. His imagination was filled with fatal presentiments, and his soul was assailed by great terrors. To have displeased the king and Cromwell, what a crime! One might have thought that he would die of it, says a historian. He saw himself already on the scaffold of Bishop Fisher and Sir Thomas More. At this time the powerful minister summoned him to his presence. Sampson admitted the formation of an alliance between Gardiner, Stokesley, Tunstall, and himself to maintain the old religion, its traditions and rites, and to resist any innovation. He avowed the fact that his colleagues and himself stood pledged to put forth all their efforts for the restoration of degenerated Catholicism. In their opinion, nothing which the Greeks had preserved ought to be rejected in England. One day when Bishop Sampson was passing over the Thames in a barge, in company with the bishop of Durham, to Lambeth Palace, the latter produced an old Greek book which he used to carry in his pocket, and showed Sampson several places in that book wherein matters that were then in controversy were ordained by the Greek Church. These bishops, who spoke so courageously to each other, did not speak so with the king. They feigned complete accordance with him; and for him they had nothing but flatteries. Cranmer was not strong, but at least he was never a hypocrite. Sampson, however, exhibited so much penitence and promised so much submission that he was liberated. But Cromwell now knew what to think of the matter. A conspiracy was threatening the work which he had been at so much pains to accomplish. He observed that the archbishop's influence was declining at court, and he began to have secret forebodings of calamity in which he would be himself involved.

Gardiner, in fact, energetically urged the king to re-establish all the ancient usages. Thus, although but a little while before orders had been given to place Bibles in the churches, and to preach against pilgrimages, tapers, kissing of relics, and other like practices, it was now forbidden to translate, publish, and circulate any religious works without the king's permission; and injunctions were issued for the use of holy water, for processions, for kneeling down and crawling before the cross, and for lighting of tapers before the *Corpus Christi*. Discussions about the sacrament of the Eucharist were prohibited. It was Gardiner's wish to seal these ordinances with the blood of martyrs. He proceeded therefore to strike a blow at an evangelical and esteemed Englishman, and to invest his death with a certain importance.

We have previously mentioned a certain young minister, John Nicholson, surnamed Lambert, who had been arrested and imprisoned in 1532, but afterwards released. The passing of the years only deepened his firm evangelical convictions.

In 1538, being informed one day that Doctor Taylor was to preach at St. Peter's Church, Cornhill, Lambert went to hear him, not only because of his well-known gifts, but also because he was not far from the Gospel. He was later appointed bishop of Lincoln under pious King Edward, and was deprived of that office under the fanatical Mary. Taylor preached that day on the real presence of Christ in the bread and the wine. Lambert also believed, indeed, in the presence of the Lord in the Supper, but this presence, he believed, was in the hearts of the faithful. After the service he went to see Taylor, and with modesty and kindliness urged various arguments against the doctrines which he had been setting forth. "I have not time just now," said the doctor, "to discuss the point with you, as other matters demand my attention; but oblige me by putting your thoughts in writing and call again when I am more at leisure." Lambert applied himself to the task of writing, and against the doctrine of the presence in the *bread* he adduced ten arguments, which were, says Foxe, very powerful. It does not appear that Taylor replied to them. He was an upright man, who gave impartial consideration to these questions, and by Lambert's reasoning he seems to have been somewhat shaken. As Taylor was anxious to be enlightened himself and to try to satisfy his friendly opponent, he communicated the document to Dr. Barnes. The latter, a truly evangelical Christian, was nevertheless of opinion that to put forward the doctrine of this little work would seriously injure the cause of the Reformation. He therefore advised Taylor to speak to Archbishop Cranmer on the subject. Cranmer, who was of the same opinion, invited Lambert to a conference, at which Barnes, Taylor, and Latimer were also present. These four divines had not at this time abandoned the view which the ex-chaplain of Antwerp opposed; and considering the fresh revival of sacramental Catholicism, they were not inclined to do so. They strove therefore to change the opinion of the pious minister, but in vain. Finding that they unanimously condemned his views, he exclaimed: "Well then, I appeal to the king." This was a foolish and fatal appeal.

Gardiner did not lose a minute, but promptly took the business in hand, because he saw in it an opportunity of striking a heavy blow; and, what was an inestimable advantage, he would have on his side, he thought, Cranmer and the other three evangelical divines. He therefore "went straight to the king," and requesting a private audience, addressed him in the most flattering terms. Then, as if the interests of the king were dearer to him than to the king himself, he respectfully pointed out that he had everywhere excited by various recent proceedings suspicion and hatred; but that at this moment a way was open for pacifying men's minds, "if only in this matter of John Lambert, he would manifest unto the people how strictly he would resist heretics; and by this new rumour he would bring to pass not only to extinguish all other former rumours, and as it were with one nail to drive out another, but also should discharge himself of all suspicion, in that he now began to be reported to be a favourer of new sects and opinions."

The vanity as well as the interests of Henry VIII dictated to him the same course as Gardiner advised. He determined to avail himself of this opportunity to make an ostentatious display of his own knowledge and zeal. He would make arrangements of an imposing character; it would not be enough to hold a mere conversation, but there must be a grand show. He therefore ordered invitations to be sent to a great number of nobles and bishops to attend the solemn trial at which he would appear as head of the church. He was not content with the title alone, he would show that he acted the part. One of the principal characteristics of Henry VIII was a fondness for showing off what he conceived himself to be or what he supposed himself to know, without ever suspecting that display is often the ruin of those who wish to seem more than they are.

Meanwhile Lambert, confined at Lambeth, wrote an apology for his faith which he dedicated to the king, and in which he solidly established the doctrine which he had professed.[1] He rejoiced that his request to be heard before Henry VIII had been granted. He desired that his trial might be blessed, and he indulged in the pleasing illusion that the king, once set in the presence of the truth, must needs be enlightened and would publicly proclaim it. These pleasant fancies gave him courage, and he lived and hoped.

On the appointed day, Friday, November 16, 1538, the assembly was constituted in Westminster Hall. The king, in his robes of state, sat upon the throne. On his right were the bishops, judges, and jurisconsults; on his left the lords temporal of the realm and the officers of the royal house. The guards, attired in white, were near their master, and a crowd of spectators filled the hall. The prisoner was placed at the bar. The bishop of Chichester spoke to the following effect: That the king in this session would have all states, degrees, bishops, and all others to be admonished of his will and pleasure, that no man should conceive any sinister opinion of him, as that now, the authority and name of the bishop of Rome being utterly abolished, he would also extinguish all religion, or give liberty unto heretics to perturb and trouble, without punishment, the churches of England, whereof he is the head. And moreover that they should not think that they were assembled at that present to make any disputation upon the heretical doctrine; but only for this purpose, that by the industry of him and other bishops the heresies of this man here present (meaning Lambert), and the heresies of all such like, should be refuted or openly condemned in the presence of them all. Henry's part then began. His look was sternly fixed on Lambert, who stood facing him; his features were contracted, his brows were knit. His whole aspect was adapted to inspire terror, and indicated a violence of anger unbecoming in a judge, and still more so in a sovereign. He rose, stood leaning on a white cushion, and looking Lambert full in the face, he said to him in a disdainful tone: "Ho! good fellow, what is thy name?" The accused, humbly kneeling

---

[1] This apology, entitled *A Treatise of John Lambert upon the sacrament, addressed to the king*, is given in Foxe, *Acts*, v, pp. 237–50.

down, replied: "My name is John Nicholson, although of many I be called Lambert." "What!" said the king, "have you two names? I would not trust you, having two names, although you were my brother." "O most noble prince," replied the accused, "your bishops forced me of necessity to change my name." Thereupon the king, interrupting him, commanded him to declare what he thought as touching the sacrament of the altar. "Sire," said Lambert, "first of all I give God thanks that you do not disdain to hear me. Many good men, in many places, are put to death, without your knowledge. But now, forasmuch as that high and eternal King of kings, in whose hands are the hearts of all princes, hath inspired and stirred up the king's mind to understand the causes of his subjects, specially whom God of His divine goodness hath so abundantly endued with so great gifts of judgment and knowledge, I do not mistrust but that God will bring some great thing to pass through him, to the setting forth of the glory of His Name." Henry, who could not bear to be praised by a heretic, rudely interrupted Lambert, and said to him in an angry tone: "I came not hither to hear mine own praises thus painted out in my presence; but briefly go to the matter, without any more circumstance." There was so much harshness in the king's voice that Lambert was agitated and confused. He had dreamed of something very different. He had conceived a sovereign just and elevated above the reach of clerical passions, whose noble understanding would be struck with the beauty of the Gospel. But he saw a passionate man, a servant of the priests. In astonishment and confusion he kept silence for a few minutes, questioning within himself what he ought to do in the extremity to which he was reduced.

Lambert was especially attached to the great verities of the Christian religion, and during his previous trial he made unreserved confession of them. "Our Saviour would not have us greatly esteem our merits," said he, "when we have done what is commanded by God, but rather reckon ourselves to be but servants unprofitable to God . . . not regarding our merit, but His grace and benefit. Woe be to the life of men, said St. Augustine, be they ever so holy, if Thou shalt examine them, setting Thy mercy aside. . . . Again he says, Doth any man

give what he oweth not unto Thee, that Thou should'st be in
his debt? and hath any man aught that is not Thine? . . .
All my hope is in the Lord's death. His death is my merit, my
refuge, my health, and my resurrection. And thus," adds
Lambert, "we should serve God with hearty love as children,
and not for need or dread, as unloving thralls and servants."[1]

On this occasion the king wanted to localize the attack and
to limit the examination of Lambert to the subject of the
sacrament. Finding that the accused stood silent, the king
said to him in a hasty manner with anger and vehemency:[2]
"Why standest thou still? Answer as touching the sacrament
of the altar, whether dost thou say that it is the body of
Christ or wilt deny it?" After uttering these words, the king
lifted up his cap adorned with pearls and feathers, probably as
a token of reverence for the subject under discussion. "I
answer with St. Augustine," said Lambert, "that it is the body
of Christ after a certain manner." The king replied: "Answer
me neither out of St. Augustine, nor by the authority of any
other; but tell me plainly whether thou sayest it is the body
of Christ or no." Lambert felt what might be the consequences
of his answer, but without hesitation he said: "Then I deny
it to be the body of Christ." "Mark well!" exclaimed the
king; "for now thou shalt be condemned even by Christ's own
word, *Hoc est corpus meum* (this is my body)."

The king then turning to Cranmer commanded him to
refute the opinion of the accused. The archbishop spoke with
modesty, calling Lambert "brother," and although opposing
his arguments he told him that if he proved his opinion from
Holy Scripture, he (Cranmer) would willingly embrace it.
Gardiner, finding that Cranmer was too weak, began to
speak. Tunstall and Stokesley followed. Lambert had put
forward ten arguments, and ten doctors were appointed to
deal with them, each doctor to impugn one of them. Of the
whole disputation the passage which made the deepest impression on the assembly was Stokesley's argument. "It is
the doctrine of the philosophers," he said, "that a substance
cannot be changed but into a substance." Then, by the
example of water boiling on the fire, he affirmed the substance

[1] Foxe, *Acts,* v. pp. 188–89.
[2] *Ibid.,* p. 230.

of the water to pass into the substance of the air.[1] On hearing this argument, the aspect of the bishops, hitherto somewhat uneasy, suddenly changed. They were transported with joy, and considered this transmutation of the elements as giving them the victory, and they cast their looks over the whole assembly with an air of triumph. Loud shouts of applause for some time interrupted the sitting. When silence was at length restored, Lambert replied that the moistness of the water, its real essence, remained even after this transformation; that nothing was changed but the form; while in their system of the *corpus domini* (the body of the Lord) the substance itself was changed; and that it is impossible that the qualities and accidents of things should remain in their own nature apart from their own subject. But Lambert was not allowed to finish his refutation. The king and the bishops, indignant that he ventured to impugn an argument which had transported them with admiration, gave vent to their rage against him, so that he was forced to silence, and had to endure patiently all their insults.

The sitting had lasted from noon till five o'clock. It had been a real martyrdom for Lambert. Loaded with rebukes and insults, intimidated by the solemnity of the proceedings and by the authority of the persons with whom he had to do, alarmed by the presence of the king and by the terrible threats which were uttered against him, his body too, which was weak before, giving way under the fatigue of a session of five hours, during which, standing all the time, he had been compelled to fight a fierce battle, convinced that the clearest and most irresistible demonstrations would be smothered amidst the outcries of the bystanders, he called to mind these words of Scripture, "Be still," and was silent. This self-restraint was regarded as defeat. Where is the knowledge so much boasted of? they said; where is his power of argumentation? The assembly had looked for great bursts of eloquence, but the accused was silent. The palm of victory was awarded to the king and the bishops by noisy and universal shouts of applause.

It was now night. The servants of the royal house appeared in the hall and lighted the torches. Henry began to find his part as head of the church somewhat wearisome. He deter-

[1] Foxe, *Acts*, v. pp. 232–33.

mined to bring the business to a conclusion, and by his severity to give to the pope and to Christendom a brilliant proof of his orthodoxy. "What sayest thou now," he said to Lambert, "after all these great labours which thou hast taken upon thee, and all the reasons and instructions of these learned men? Art thou not yet satisfied? Wilt thou live or die? What sayest thou? Thou hast yet free choice." Lambert answered, "I commend my soul into the hands of God, but my body I wholly yield and submit unto your clemency." Then said the king, "In that case you must die, for I will not be a patron unto heretics." Unhappy Lambert! He had committed himself to the mercy of a prince who never spared a man who offended him, were it even his closest friend. The monarch turned to his vicar-general and said, "Cromwell, read the sentence of condemnation." This was a cruel task to impose upon a man universally considered to be the friend of the evangelicals. But Cromwell felt the ground already trembling under his feet. He took the sentence and read it. Lambert was condemned to be burnt.

Four days afterwards, on Tuesday, November 20, the evangelist was taken out of the prison at eight o'clock in the morning and brought to Cromwell's house. Cromwell summoned him to his room and announced that the hour of his death was come. The tidings greatly consoled and gladdened Lambert. It is stated that Cromwell added some words by way of excuse for the part which he had taken in his condemnation, and sent him into the room where the gentlemen of his household were at breakfast. He sat down and at their invitation partook of the meal with them, with all the composure of a Christian. Immediately after breakfast he was taken to Smithfield, and was there placed on the pile, which was not raised high. His legs only were burnt, and nothing remained but the stumps. He was, however, still alive; and two of the soldiers, observing that his whole body could not be consumed, thrust into him their halberds, one on each side, and raised him above the fire. The martyr, stretching towards the people his hands now burning, said, "None but Christ! None but Christ!" At this moment the soldiers withdrew their weapons and let the pious Lambert drop into the fire, which speedily consumed him.

Henry VIII, however, was not satisfied. The hope which he had entertained of inducing Lambert to recant had been disappointed. The Anglo-Catholic party made up for this by everywhere extolling his learning and his eloquence. They praised his sayings to the skies—every one of them was an oracle; he was in very deed the defender of the faith. There was one, not belonging to that party, who wrote to Sir Thomas Wyatt, then foreign minister to the king, as follows:—"It was marvellous to see the gravity and the majestic air with which his Majesty discharged the functions of *Supreme Head of the Anglican Church;* the mildness with which he tried to convert that unhappy man; the force of reasoning with which he opposed him. Would that the princes and potentates of Christendom could have been present at the spectacle; they would certainly have admired the wisdom and judgment of his Majesty, and would have said *that the king is the most excellent prince in the Christian world.*"

This writer was Cromwell himself. He suppressed at this time all the best aspirations of his nature, believing that, as is generally thought, if one means to retain the favour of princes, it is necessary to adapt one's self to all their wishes. A mournful fall, which was not to be the only one of the kind! It has been said, "Every flatterer, whoever he may be, is always a treacherous and hateful creature."

CHAPTER THREE

The "Whip of Six Strings"

(1538–1540)

WHILE the English Catholic party were recovering their former influence over Henry's mind, some members of the Roman Catholic party were labouring to re-establish the influence of the pope. They supposed that they had found a clue by means of which the king might be brought back to the obedience of Rome. Henry who, while busy in preparing fires for the martyrs, did not forget the marriage altar, was very desirous of obtaining the hand of Christina of Denmark, duchess of Milan and a widow. Now, it was this princess, a niece of Charles V, of whom it was thought possible to make use for gaining over the king to the pope. She was now at the court of Brussels; and it is related that to the first offer of Henry VIII she had replied with a smile—"I have but one head; if I had two, one of them should be at the service of his Majesty." If she did not say this, as some friends of Henry VIII have maintained, something like it was doubtless said by one of the courtiers. However this may be, the king did not meet with a refusal. Francis I, alarmed at the prospect of an alliance between Henry VIII and Charles V, sent word to Henry that the Emperor was deceiving him. The king did not believe it. The queen regent of the Netherlands endeavoured to bring about this union; Spanish commissioners arrived to conduct the negotiation, and Wriothesley, the English envoy at Brussels, devoted himself zealously to the business. One of the principal officers of the court, taking supper with the latter, in June 1538, inquired of him for news about the negotiation. Wriothesley expressed his surprise "that the Emperor had been so slack therein." His companion remarked that the only difficulty in the matter was that Henry VIII had "married the lady Katherine, to whom the duchess is near

kinswoman," so that the marriage could not be solemnized
without a dispensation from the pope.

The Emperor spoke more clearly still. Wyatt was instructed
to tell the king that the hand of the duchess of Milan would
be given to him, with a dowry of one hundred thousand
crowns, and an annuity of fifteen thousand, secured on the
duchy; and that for the gift of this beautiful and accomplished
young widow all they required of him was that *he should be
reconciled with the bishop of Rome*. This was fixing a high price
on the hand of Christina. The princess, considering perhaps
that it was a glorious task to bring back Henry VIII to the
bosom of the papacy, declared her readiness to obey the
Emperor. The pope, on his part, was willing to grant the
necessary dispensation; but the king must first make his
submission. To the great regret of the Roman party nothing
came of these proposals. One circumstance might have influenced the king's decision. Before the negotiations were closed,
in December 1538, the pope published the bull of 1535,
in which he excommunicated Henry VIII. Had the pontiff
no hope of good from the matrimonial intrigue, or did he
intend to catch the king by fear?

During the late summer of 1538, while these mundane
negotiations were continuing, a remarkable decision had
been taken on a totally different matter. It had been strangely
resolved by the king's Majesty that the Bible in an English
translation should be made available to all his Majesty's
subjects. "Strangely" in respect of the king's character and
religious inclinations, but perhaps not so when looked at in
the light of the dying Tyndale's prayer, "Lord, open the king
of England's eyes." The royal sanction was transmitted to the
nation through Injunctions issued by Thomas Cromwell to
all the clergy, and dated the 5th September:—

"In the name of God, Amen. By the authority and commission of . . .
Henry . . . I, Thomas lord Cromwell, lord privy seal, vicegerent to the
king's said highness, for all his jurisdiction ecclesiastical within this realm,
do for the advancement of the true honour of Almighty God, increase of
virtue, and discharge of the king's majesty, give and exhibit unto you
(Parson So and so) these injunctions following:

ITEM, That ye shall provide . . . one book of the whole Bible of the
largest volume in English, and the same shall be set up in some

convenient place within the . . . church . . . whereas your parishioners may most commodiously resort to the same and read it; the charge of which book shall be ratably borne between you the parson and the parishioners aforesaid, the onehalf by you and the otherhalf by them.

ITEM, That you shall discourage no man privily or apertly from the reading and hearing of the said Bible, but shall expressly provoke, stir, and exhort every person to read the same, as that which is the very lively Word of God, that every Christian person is bound to embrace, believe and follow, if they look to be saved; admonishing them nevertheless to avoid all contention and altercation therein, but to use an honest sobriety in the inquisition of the true sense of the same, and to refer the explication of obscure places to men of higher judgment in Scripture. . . ."

Other Items deal with the memorizing of the Pater Noster, the Creed, and the Ten Commandments; the turning away from objects of superstition and idolatry; a warning not to repose trust in works devised by men, such as pilgrimages, and the offering of money to images and at the shrines of relics; and the necessity for keeping a parish register of weddings, christenings and burials.

A truly momentous series of Injunctions! the first official recognition of the authority, necessity, and availability of the Holy Book of God! the first clear declaration of the infinite value to men's souls of God's Word written!

It is remarkable that another king than Henry played a part in introducing the Bible into the churches. The Emperor and Francis I, king of France, occasionally coquetted with the king of England, whom each of them was anxious to win over to his own side. Francis, knowing how sensitive Henry was on the subject of marriage, offered him his son Henry of Orleans for the princess Mary. Cromwell, who was now giving way to the Anglo-Catholic party on many points essential to reform, was all the more desirous of holding by those which his master would really permit. Amongst these was the translation of the Bible. He saw in the offer made by Francis I an opening of which he might avail himself. An edition of the Bible, extending to 2,500 copies, published the year before by the eminent printer Richard Grafton in conjunction with Whitchurch, was now exhausted. Cromwell determined to issue a new one; and as printing was better

executed at Paris than in London, the French paper also being
superior, he begged the king to request permission of Francis I
to have the edition printed at Paris. Francis addressed a royal
letter to his beloved Grafton and Whitchurch, saying that
having received credible testimonies to the effect that his very
dear brother, the king of the English, whose subjects they were,
had granted full and lawful liberty to print, both in Latin
and in English, the Holy Bible, and to import it into his
kingdom, he gave them himself his authorization so to do.
Francis comforted himself with the thought that his own
subjects spoke neither English nor Latin; and, besides, this
book so much dreaded would be immediately exported from
France.

Grafton and the pious and learned Coverdale arrived at
Paris, at the end of spring 1538, to undertake this new edition
of Tyndale's translation. They lodged in the house of the
printer Francis Regnault, who had for some time printed
missals for England. As the sale of these had very much fallen
off, Regnault changed his course, and determined to print
the Bible. The two Englishmen selected a fine type and the
best paper to be had in France. But these were expensive, and
as early as June 23 they were obliged to apply to Cromwell
to furnish them with the means for carrying on *his* edition of
the Bible. They were moreover beset with other difficulties.
They could not make their appearance out of doors in Paris
without being exposed to threats; and they were in daily
expectation that their work would be interrupted. Francis I,
their reputed protector, was gone to Nice. By December 13,
after six months' labour, their fears had become so serious
that when Bonner, who had succeeded Gardiner as English
ambassador in France, was setting out from Paris on his way
to London, they begged him to take with him the portion
already printed and deliver it to Cromwell. The hypocritical
Bonner, not satisfied with all the benefices he now held, was
grasping at the bishopric of Hereford, which he called *a
great good fortune*, and which he succeeded in getting. He was
at this time bent on currying favour with Cromwell, on whose
influence the election depended, and therefore, hiding his
face under a gracious mask, which he was ere long impudently
to throw off, he had most eagerly complied with the request.

Four days later, December 17, the officers of the French inquisitor-general entered the printing-office and presented a document signed by Le Tellier, summoning Regnault and all whom it concerned to appear and make answer touching the printing of the Bible. He was at the same time enjoined to suspend the work, and forbidden to take away what was already printed. Are we to suppose that the Inquisition did not trouble itself about the royal letters of Francis I, or that the prince had changed his mind? Either of these suppositions might be entertained. In consequence of the despatch of the packet to London, there were but a few sheets to be seized, and these were condemned to be burnt in the Place Maubert. But the officer was even more greedy of gain than fanatical; and gold being offered him by the Englishmen for the property, almost all the sheets were restored to them. His compliance is perhaps partly to be explained by the consideration that this was not a common case. The proprietors of the sheets seized were the lord Cromwell, first secretary of state, and the king of England. The matter did not rest here; the bold Cromwell was not to be baffled. Agents sent by him to Paris got possession of the presses, the types, and even the *printers*, and took the whole away with them to London. In two months from the time of their arrival the printing was completed. On the last page appeared the statement: *The whole Bible finished in 1539*; and the grateful editors added, *To the Lord the achievement is due.* The violent proceeding of the Inquisition turned to a great gain for England. Many French printers and a large stock of type had been imported; and henceforward many and more beautiful editions of the Bible were printed in England. "The wicked diggeth a pit and falleth into it."

Two parties therefore existed in England, and these frequently concerned themselves more with the points on which they differed than with the great facts of their religion. In one pulpit a preacher would call for reformation of the abuses of Rome; in a neighbouring church, another preacher would advocate their maintenance at any cost. One monk of York preached against purgatory, while some of his colleagues defended the doctrine. All this gave rise to most exciting discussion amongst the hearers. In addition to the two chief

N(II)

parties, there were the profane, animated by a spirit of unbelief and without reverence for sacred things. While pious men were peacefully assembled for the reading of the Holy Scriptures these mockers sat in public-houses over their pots of beer, uttering their sarcasms against everybody, and especially against the priests. If they spoke of those who gave only the wafer, and not the wine, they would say:—"That is because he has drunk the whole of it; the bottle is empty." At times they undertook even to discuss, as in old times was done at Byzantium, the most difficult points in theology, and this was still worse. The king, anxious to play his part as head of the church, was desirous of bringing about a union of the two chief parties, and had no doubt that the party of the profane would then disappear. His favourite notion, like that of princes in general, was to have but one single religious opinion in his kingdom. In a royal proclamation he required that the party of reformation and the party of tradition should "draw in one yoke," like a pair of good oxen at the plough. He did not omit, however, to read the priests a lesson. He rebuked them for busying themselves far more with the distribution of the consecrated wafer and with the sprinkling of their flocks with holy water than with teaching them what these acts meant.

When the parliament met on April 28, 1539, the lord chancellor announced that the king was very anxious to see all his subjects holding one and the same opinion in religion, and required that a committee should be nominated to examine the various opinions, and to draw up articles of agreement to which everyone might give his consent. On May 5 nine commissioners were named, five of whom were rigid Catholics, and at their head was Lee, archbishop of York. A project was presented "for extirpating heresies among the people." A catalogue of heresies was to be drawn up and read at all the services. The commissioners held discussion for one day, but neither of the two parties would make any concession. As the vicegerent Cromwell and the archbishop of Canterbury were in the ranks of the reformation party, the majority was unable to gain the ascendancy, and the commission arrived at no decision.

The king was very much dissatisfied with this result. He

had been willing to leave the work of conciliation in the hands
of the bishops, and now the bishops did not agree. His patience,
of which he had no large stock, was exhausted. The Catholic
party took advantage of his dissatisfaction, and hinted to him
that if he really aimed at unity he would have to take the
matter into his own hands, and settle the doctrine to which
all must assent. Why should he allow his subjects the liberty
of thinking for themselves? Was he not in England master
and ruler of everything?

Another circumstance, of an entirely different kind, acted
powerfully, about this time, upon the king's mind. The pope
had just entered into an alliance with the Emperor and the
king of France. Invasion threatened. A fact of such importance
could not fail to make a great noise in England. "Methinks,"
said one of the foreign diplomatists now in England, "that if
the pope sent an interdict and excommunications, with an
injunction that no merchant should trade in any way with
the English, the nation would, without further trouble, bestir
itself and compel the king to return to the church." Henry,
in alarm, adopted two measures of defence against this triple
alliance. He gave orders for the fortification of the ports,
examination of the condition of various landing-places, and
reviewing of the troops; and at the same time, instead of
endeavouring after a union of the two parties, he determined
to throw himself entirely on the Scholastic and Catholic side.
He hoped thereby to satisfy the majority of his subjects, who
still adhered to the Roman church, and perhaps also to
appease the powers. "The king is determined on grounds
of policy," it was said, "that these articles should pass."

Six articles were therefore drawn up of a reactionary
character, and the duke of Norfolk was selected to bring
them forward. He did not pride himself on scriptural knowledge. "I have never read the Holy Scriptures and I never
will read them," he said; "all that I want is that everything
should be as it was of old." But if Norfolk was not a great
theologian, he was the most powerful and the most Catholic
lord of the Privy Council and of the kingdom. On the 16th of
May, the duke rose in the upper house and spoke to the
following effect:—"The commission which you had named
has done nothing, and this we had clearly foreseen. We

come, therefore, to present to you six articles, which, after your examination and approval, are to become binding. They are the following: 1st, if anyone allege that after consecration there remains any other substance in the sacrament of the altar than the natural body of Christ conceived of the Virgin Mary, he shall be adjudged a heretic and suffer death by burning, and shall forfeit to the king all his lands and goods, as in the case of high treason; 2nd, if anyone teach that the sacrament is to be given to laymen under both kinds; or 3rd, that any man who has taken holy orders may nevertheless marry; 4th, that any man or woman who has vowed chastity may marry; 5th, that private masses are not lawful and should not be used; or 6th, that auricular confession is not according to the law of God—any such person shall be adjudged to suffer death, and forfeit lands and goods as a felon."

Cromwell had been obliged to sanction, and perhaps even to prepare, this document. When once the king energetically announced his will the minister bowed his head, knowing well that if he raised it in opposition he would certainly lose it. Nevertheless, that he might to some extent be justified in his own sight, he had resolved that the weapon should be two-edged, and had added an article purporting that any priest giving himself up to uncleanness should for the first offence be deprived of his benefices, his goods, and his liberty, and for the second should be *punished with death* like the others.

These articles which have been called *the Whip with six strings* and *the Bloody Statute*, were submitted to the parliament. But none of the lords temporal, or of the commons, aware that the king was fully resolved, ventured to assail them. One man, however, rose, and this was Cranmer. "Like a constant patron of God's cause," says the chronicler, "he took upon him the earnest defence of the truth, oppressed in the parliament; three days together disputing against those six wicked articles; bringing forth such allegations and authorities as might easily have helped the cause, if the majority, as is often the case, had not overthrown the better." Cranmer spoke temperately, with respect for the sovereign, but also with fidelity and courage. "It is not my own cause that I defend," he said, "it is that of God Almighty."

The archbishop of Canterbury was not, however, alone.

The bishops who belonged to the evangelical party, Latimer of Worcester, Hilsey of Rochester, Barlow of St. David's, Goodrich of Ely, and Shaxton of Salisbury, likewise spoke against the articles. But the king insisted, and the act passed. These articles, said Cranmer at a later time, were "in some things so enforced by the evil counsel of certain papists against the truth and common judgment both of divines and lawyers, that if the king's Majesty himself had not come personally into the parliament house, those laws had never passed." Cranmer never signed nor consented to the Six Articles.

The parliament at the same time conferred on the king unlimited powers. A bill was carried purporting that some having by their disobedience shown that they did not well understand what a king can do by virtue of his royal power, it was decreed that every proclamation of his Majesty, even when inflicting fines and penalties, should have the same force as an Act of parliament. The Act was not passed without difficulty and as soon as Henry died it was repealed. But the fact was clearly shown in 1539 that when truth was sacrificed, liberty became the next victim.

Latimer, bishop of Worcester, immediately after the close of the Parliamentary session, received word from Cromwell that the king requested him to resign his office. His heart leaped for joy as he laid aside his episcopal vestments. "Now I am rid of a heavy burden," he said, "and never did my shoulders feel so light." One of his former colleagues having expressed his surprise, he replied: "I am resolved to be guided only by the Book of God, and sooner than depart one jot from that, let me be trampled under the feet of wild horses!" It seems highly probable that, although the king must have been offended at Latimer's resistance to the Six Articles, he had not himself actually informed Cromwell that Latimer must be removed from his post. But the resignation having been tendered ("freely" says the subsequent 'writ to elect' a successor), Henry allowed it to stand, and, to show his royal displeasure, he ordered the ex-bishop to be kept in custody in the house of Sampson, bishop of Chichester, near Chancery Lane. It seems probable that after several months he was allowed his liberty. The fact is, however, that his activities between 1540 and 1547 when the king died, are very obscure. He certainly ended this period as a prisoner in the Tower of London. Shaxton, bishop of Salisbury, likewise resigned his see, after the Six Articles were passed. Under queen Mary he became a violent persecutor. Many evangelical Christians quitted England, and among them especially to be noted are John Hooper, John Rogers, and John Butler. Cranmer remained in his archiepiscopal palace at Lambeth. Historians have generally stated that he sent away his wife and children to his wife's relations in Germany, but there is no strong evidence for such a belief. Cranmer, during his trial in Mary's reign, admitted that he had kept his wife secretly during the latter years of Henry's reign and had brought her out during the reign of Edward, but no suggestion was made that her years of hiding were spent with her relations in Germany.

That Cranmer did not resign is only explicable on the ground of the efforts made by Henry VIII to retain him. On the day of the prorogation of parliament, June 28, 1539, Henry, fearing lest the archbishop, disheartened and distrusted, should offer to him his resignation, sent for him, and, receiving him with all the graciousness of manner which he knew so well how to assume when he wished, said: "I have heard with what force and learning you opposed the Six Articles. Pray state your arguments in writing, and deliver the statement to me." Nor was this all that Henry did. Desirous that all men, and particularly the adherents of English Catholicism, should know the esteem which he felt for the primate, he commanded the leader of this party, the duke of Norfolk, his brother-in-law, the duke of Suffolk, Norfolk's rival, lord Cromwell, and several other lords to dine the next day with the archbishop at Lambeth. You will assure him, he said, of my sincere affection, and you will add that although his arguments did not convince the parliament, they displayed much wisdom and learning.

The company, according to the king's request, arrived at the archbishop's palace, and Cranmer gave his guests an honourable reception. The latter executed the king's commission, adding that he must not be disheartened although the parliament had come to a decision contrary to his opinion. Cranmer replied that "he was obliged to his Majesty for his good affection, and to the lords for the pains they had taken."

Then he added resolutely: "I have hope in God that hereafter my allegations and authorities will take place, to the glory of God and commodity of the realm." They sat down to table. Every guest apparently did his best to make himself agreeable to the primate. "My lord of Canterbury," said Cromwell, "you are most happy of all men; for you may do and speak what you list, and, say what all men can against you, the king will never believe one word to detriment or hindrance." The meal, however, did not pass altogether so smoothly. The king had brought together, in Cromwell and Norfolk, the most heterogeneous elements; and the feast of peace was disturbed by a sudden explosion. Cromwell, continuing his praises, instituted a parallel between cardinal Wolsey and the archbishop of Canterbury. "The cardinal," he said, "lost his friends by his haughtiness and pride; while you gain over your enemies by your kindliness and your meekness." "You must be well aware of that, my lord Cromwell," said the duke of Norfolk, "for the cardinal was *your master*." Cromwell, stung by these words, acknowledged the obligations under which he lay to the cardinal, but added: "I was never so far in love with him as to have waited upon him to Rome if he had been chosen pope, as I understand, my lord duke, that you would have done." Norfolk denied this. But Cromwell persisted in his assertion, and even specified a considerable sum which the duke was to receive for his services as admiral to the new pope, and for conducting him to Rome. The duke, no longer restraining himself, swore with great oaths that Cromwell was a liar. The two speakers, forgetting that they were attending a feast of peace, became more and more excited and did not spare hard words. Cranmer interposed to pacify them. But from this time these two powerful ministers of the king swore deadly hatred to each other. One or other of them must needs fall.

The king's course with respect to Cranmer is not so strange as it appears. Without Cranmer, he would have been under the necessity of choosing another primate, and what a task would that have been. Gardiner, indeed, was quite ready to take the post; but the king, although he listened to him, did not place complete confidence in him. Not only did it seem to Henry difficult to find any other man than Cranmer; but there was a further difficulty of appointing an archbishop in due form. Could it be done by the aid of the pope? Impossible. Without the pope? This too was very difficult. The priesthood would not concede such a power to the king, nor was it probable that they would accept his choice. The king foresaw troubles and conflicts without end. The best course was to keep the present primate, and this was the course adopted. Herein lay the security of the archbishop in the midst of the misfortunes and scenes of blood around him. He had made a declaration of his faith, and he did not withdraw from it. He hoped for better things, according to the advances which were made him. He believed that by keeping his post he might prevent many calamities. The Six Articles were a storm which must be allowed to blow over; and, in accordance with his character, he bowed his head while the wind blew in that direction.

It should further be remembered that, in the sixteenth century, the idea of the overriding obligation of duty to the State and the Sovereign normally held the rights of the individual conscience in abeyance, whenever the two came into conflict. In modern times men feel free to resign public posts which begin to trouble their consciences. In the time of the Tudors this was rarely the case: the martyrs were exceptions. Men in office esteemed the royal power and prerogative to be so great that most of them would have considered opposition to the king's will almost tantamount to rebellion against God.

Moreover, Henry's absolutism was in practice modified by a spasmodic consideration and understanding which he showed towards servants he favoured. In certain circumstances he was prepared to permit the exercise of their private consciences. Thus, Sir Thomas More, Chancellor though he was, disapproved of the king's desire for a divorce from Catherine of Aragon. Accordingly, Henry was careful not to require him to put his hand to the business. Similarly, the king exempted Archbishop Cranmer from the awful work of enforcing the penalties imposed by the "whip of six strings." Cranmer, therefore, continued to hold office. Never had he passed through a sadder term of years.

The "bloody statute" was the cause of profound sorrow among the evangelical Christians. Some of them, more hasty than others, making use of the strong language of the time, asserted that the Six Articles had been written, not with Gardiner's ink, as people said, "but with the blood of a dragon, or rather the claws of the devil."[1] They have been spoken of, by Roman Catholics of a later age, as "the enactments of this severe and barbarous statute."[2] But the Catholics of that age rejoiced in them, and believed that it was all over with the Reformation. Commissioners were immediately named to execute this cruel law, and there was always a bishop among them. These commissioners, who sat in London in Mercer's Chapel, formerly a dwelling house and reputed to be the place of Becket's birth, even exaggerated the harshness of the Six Articles. Fifteen days had not elapsed before five hundred persons were imprisoned, some for having read the Bible, others for their posture at church. The greatest zeal was displayed by Norfolk among the lords temporal, and by Stokesley, Gardiner, and Tunstall among the lords spiritual. Their aim was to get a *Book of Ceremonies*, a strange farrago of Romish superstitions, adopted as the rule of worship.

The violent thunder-clap which had suddenly pealed over England, and occasioned so much trouble, was nowhere on the Continent more unexpected, nowhere excited a greater commotion than at Wittenberg. Bucer on one side, and several refugees arriving at Hamburg on the other had made known this barbarous statute to the reformers, and had entreated the Protestants of Germany to interpose with Henry in behalf of their fellow-religionists. Luther, Melanchthon, Jonas, and Bugenhagen met together, and were unanimous in their indignation. "The king," they said, "knows perfectly well that our doctrine concerning the sacrament, the marriage of priests, and other analogous subjects, is true. How many books he has read on the subject! How many reports have been made to him by the most competent judges! He has even had a book translated, in which the whole matter is explained, and he makes use of this book every day in his prayers. Has he not heard and approved Latimer, Cranmer, and other pious divines? He has even censured the king of France for condemning this doctrine.

---

[1] Foxe, *Acts*, v. p. 359.
[2] Lingard, *Hist. of England*, v. p. 131.

And now he condemns it himself more harshly than the king
or the pope. He makes laws like Nebuchadnezzar, and declares
that he will put to death anyone who does not observe them.
Great sovereigns of our day are taking it into their heads to
fashion for themselves religions which may turn to their own
advantage, like Antiochus Epiphanes of old. I have power,
says the king of England, to require that any one of my
courtiers shall not marry so long as he intends to remain at
court; for the same reason I have also power to forbid the
marriage of priests. We are now entreated to address re-
monstrances to this prince. The Scripture certainly teaches us
to endeavour to bring back the weak; but it requires that the
proud who compound with their conscience should be left
to go in their own way. It is clear that the king of England
makes terms with conscience. He has already been warned,
and has paid no attention; there is, therefore, no hope that he
will listen to reason if he be warned anew. Consider, besides,
what kind of men those are in whose hands he places himself.
Look at Gardiner, who while exposing before all the nation
his scandalous connexions (*liaisons*) dares to assert that it is
contrary to the law of God for a minister of God to have a
lawful wife."

Thus did the theologians of Wittenberg talk of the matter.
Calvin thought with them, and he wrote, almost on the same
day, that the king of England had distinctly shown his disposition by the impious edict which he had published. On
behalf of the theologians, Melanchthon wrote to Henry; and
after an exordium in which he endeavoured to prepare the
king's mind, he said, "What affects and afflicts me is not only
the danger of those who hold the same faith as we do; but it
is to see you making yourself the instrument of the impiety
and cruelty of others; the doctrine of Christ is set aside in
your kingdom, superstitious rites are perpetuated, and debauchery is sanctioned; in a word, the Roman antichrist
is rejoicing in his heart because you take up arms on his
side and against us, and is hoping, by means of your bishops,
easily to recover what by wise counsel has been taken from
him." Melanchthon then combats the several articles and
refutes the sophisms of the Catholic party on the subject.
"Illustrious king," he continued, "I am grieved at heart that

you, while condemning the tyranny of the bishop of Rome, should undertake the defence of institutions which are the very sinews of his power. You are threatening the members of Jesus Christ with the most atrocious punishments, and you are putting out the light of evangelical truth which was beginning to shine in your churches. Sire, this is not the way to put away antichrist, this is establishing him . . . this is confirmation of his idolatry, his errors, his cruelty, and his debaucheries.

"I implore you, therefore, to alter the decree of your bishops. Let the prayers offered up to God by so many pious souls throughout the world for the true reformation of the Church, for the suppression of impious rites, and for the propagation of the Gospel, move you. Do justice to those pious men who are now in prison for the Lord's sake. If you do this, your great clemency will be praised by posterity as long as learning exists. Behold how Jesus Christ wandered about from place to place. He was hungry, He was thirsty, naked and bound; He complained of the raging of the priests, of the unjust cruelty of kings; He commands that the members of His body should not be torn in pieces, and that His Gospel should be honoured. It is the duty of a pious king to receive this Gospel and to watch over it. By doing so, you will be rendering to God acceptable worship."

Had these eloquent exhortations any influence on Henry VIII? On a former occasion he had shown himself provoked rather than pleased by letters of the reformer. However, after the loud peal of thunder which had alarmed evangelical Christians in every part of Europe, the horizon cleared a little, and the future looked less threatening.

About this time a bill was passed withdrawing heretics from the jurisdiction of the bishops, and subjecting them to the secular courts. The chancellor, supported by Cranmer, Cromwell, and Suffolk, and with the sanction of the king, set at liberty the five hundred persons who had been committed to prison. The thunderbolt had indeed trenched the seas, but nobody was hurt—at least for the moment.

Henry resorted to other means for the purpose of reassuring those who imagined that the pope was already re-established in England. He exhibited to the citizens of London the spectacle of one of those sea-fights on which the ancient Romans used to lavish such enormous sums. Two galleys, one of them decorated with the royal ensigns, the other with the papal arms, appeared on the Thames, and a naval combat began. The two crews attacked each other; the struggle was sharp and obstinate; at length the soldiers of the king boarded the enemy and threw into the water amidst the shouts of the people an effigy of the pope and images of several cardinals. The pontifical phantom, seized by bold hands, was dragged through the streets; it was then hanged and burnt. It would have been better for the king to let alone such puerile and vulgar sports, which pleased none but the mob, and to give more serious proofs of his attachment to the Gospel.

A Bitter Cup for Henry VIII

(1539–1540)

AT the period which we have now reached, Henry VIII displayed to an increasingly marked degree that autocratic disposition which submits to no control. He lifted up or cast down; he crowned men with honours or sent them to the scaffold. He pronounced things white or black as suited him, and there was no other rule but his own absolute and arbitrary power. A simple and modest princess was one of the first to learn by experience that he was a despot in his family as well as in church and state.

Henry had now been a widower for two years—a widower against his will; for shortly after the death of Jane Seymour he had sought in almost all quarters for a wife, but he had failed. The two great Continental sovereigns had just been reconciled with each other, and the Emperor had even cast a slight upon the king of England in the affair of the duchess of Milan. Henry was therefore now desirous of contracting a marriage which should give offence to Charles, and should at the same time win for himself allies among the enemies of that potentate. Cromwell, for his part, felt the ground tremble under his feet; Norfolk and Gardiner had confirmed their triumph by getting the Six Articles passed. The vice-gerent was therefore aiming to strengthen at once his own position and that of the Reformation, both of them impaired. Some have supposed it possible that his scheme was to unite the nations of the Germanic race, England, Germany, and the North, in support of the Reformation against the nations of the Latin race. We do not think that Cromwell went so far as this. A young Protestant princess, Anne, daughter of the duke of Cleves and sister-in-law of the elector of Saxony, who consequently possessed both the religious and the political qualifications looked for by the king and his minister, was proposed to Henry by his ambassadors on the Continent, and Cromwell immediately took the matter in hand. This union would bring the king of England into intimate relations with the Protestant princes, and would ensure, he thought, the triumph of the Reformation in England, for Henry's wives appeared to have great influence over him, at least so long as they were in favour. Henry was, however, seeking something more in his betrothed than diplomatic advantages. Cromwell knew this, and did not fail to make use of that argument. "Everyone praises the beauty of this lady," he wrote to the king (March 18, 1539), "and it is said that she surpasses all other women, even the duchess of Milan. She excels the latter both in the features of her countenance and in her whole figure as much as the golden sun excelleth the silver moon. Her portrait shall be sent you. At the same time, everyone speaks of her virtue, her chastity, her modesty, and the seriousness of her aspect." The portrait of Anne, painted by Hans Holbein, was presented to the king, and it gave him the idea of a lady not only very beautiful, but of tall and majestic stature. He was charmed and hesitated no longer. On September 16, the Count Palatine of the Rhine and other ambassadors of the elector of Saxony and the duke of Cleves arrived at Windsor. Cromwell having announced them to the king, the latter desired his minister to put all other matters out of his head, saving this only. The affair was arranged, the marriage contract signed on October 4th at Hampton Court, and the ambassadors on their departure received magnificent presents.

The princess, whose father was dead and had been succeeded by his son, left Germany towards the close of the year 1539. Her suite numbered two hundred and sixty-three persons, among them a great many *seigneurs*, thirteen trumpeters, and two hundred and twenty-eight horses. The earl of Southampton, lord Howard, and four hundred other noblemen and gentlemen, arrayed in damask, satin, and velvet, went a mile out of Calais to escort her. The superb cortège entered the town, and came in sight of the English vessels decorated with a hundred banners of silk and gold, and the marines all under arms. As soon as the princess appeared the trumpets sounded, volleys of cannon succeeded each other, and so dense was the smoke that the members of the suite could no longer see each other. Everyone was in admiration. After a repast provided by Southampton, there were jousts and tourneys. The progress of the princess being delayed by rough weather, Southampton, aware of the impatience of his master, felt it necessary to write to him to remember "that neither the winds nor the seas obey the commands of men." He added that "the surpassing beauty of the princess did not fall short of what had been told him." Anne was of simple character and timid disposition, and very desirous of pleasing the king; and she dreaded making her appearance at the famous and sumptuous court of Henry VIII. Southampton having called the next day to pay his respects to her, she invited him to play with her some game at cards which the king liked, with a view to her learning it and being able to play with his Majesty. The earl took his seat at the card-table in company with Anne and lord William Howard, while other courtiers stood behind the princess and taught her the game. "I can assure your Majesty," wrote the courtier, "that she plays with as much grace and dignity as any noble lady that I ever saw in my life." Anne, resolved on serving her apprenticeship to the manners of the court, begged Southampton to return to sup with her, bringing with him some of the nobles, because she was "much desirous to see the manner and fashion of Englishmen sitting at their meat." The earl replied that this would be contrary to English custom; but at length he yielded to her wish.

As soon as the weather appeared more promising, the princess and her suite crossed the Channel and reached Dover, whence, in the midst of a violent storm, they proceeded to Canterbury. The archbishop, accompanied by several other bishops, received Anne in his episcopal town, in a high wind and heavy rain; the princess appearing as if she might be the sun which was to disperse the fogs and the darkness of England, and to bring about there the triumph of evangelical light. Anne went on to Rochester, about half way between Canterbury and London. The king, unable to rest, eagerly longing to see his intended spouse, set out accompanied by his grand equerry, Sir Anthony Brown, and went incognito to Rochester. He was announced, and entered the room in which the princess was; but no sooner had he crossed the threshold and seen Anne, than he stopped confused and troubled. Never had any man been more deceived in his expectation. His imagination—that mistress of error and of falsehood, as it has been called—had depicted to him a beauty full of majesty and grace; and one glance had dispersed all his dreams. Anne was good and well-meaning, but rather weak-minded. Her features were coarse; her brown complexion was not at all like roses and lilies; she was very corpulent, and her manners were awkward. Henry had exquisite good taste; he could appreciate beauties and defects, especially in the figure, the bearing, and the attire of a woman. Taste is not without its corresponding distaste. Instead of love, the king felt for Anne only repugnance and aversion. Struck with astonishment and alarm, he stood before her, amazed and silent. Moreover, any conversation would have been impossible, for Anne was not acquainted with English nor Henry with German. The betrothed couple could not even speak to each other. Henry left the room, not having courage even to offer to the princess the handsome present which he brought for her. He threw himself into his bark, and returned gloomy and pensive to Greenwich. "He was woe," he said to himself, "that ever she came unto England." He deliberated with himself how to break it off. How could men in their senses have made him reports so false? He was glad, he said, that "he had kept himself from making any pact of bond with her." He thought, however, that the matter was too far gone for him to break it off. "It would drive the duke her brother into the Emperor or French king's hands." The inconvenience of a flattering portrait had never been so deeply felt. It is not to be doubted that if at this very moment the Emperor and the king of France had not been together at Paris, Henry would have immediately sent back the unfortunate young lady.

Shortly after the king's arrival at Greenwich, Cromwell, the promoter of this unfortunate affair, presented himself to his Majesty, not without fear, and inquired how he liked the lady Anne. The king replied,—"Nothing so well as she was spoken of. Had I known as much before as I do now, she should not have come within this realm." Then, with a deep sigh, he exclaimed, "What remedy?" "I know none," said Cromwell, "and I am very sorry therefor." The agents of the king had given proof neither of intelligence nor of integrity in the matter. Southampton, who had had a good view of her at Calais, had spoken to the king only of her beauty. On the following day Anne arrived at Greenwich; the king conducted her to the apartment assigned to her, and then retired to his own, very melancholy and in an ill humour. Cromwell again presented himself. "My lord," said the king, "say what they will, she is nothing so fair as she hath been reported . . . howbeit, she is well and seemly." "By my faith, sir," replied Cromwell, "ye say truth; but I think she has a queenly manner." "Call together the council," said Henry.

The princess made her entry into London in great pomp, and appeared at the palace. The court had heard of Henry's disappointment and was in consternation. "Our king," they said, "could never marry such a queen." In default of speech, music would have been a means of communication; it speaks and moves. Henry and his courtiers were passionately fond of it; but Anne did not know a single note. She knew nothing but the ordinary occupations of women. In vain did Cromwell venture to say to his master that she had, nevertheless, a portly and fine person. Henry's only thought was how to get rid of her. The marriage ceremony was deferred for a few days. The council took into consideration the question whether certain projects of union between Anne and the son of the duke of Lorraine did not form an obstacle to her marriage with Henry. But they found here no adequate ground of objection. "I am not well treated," the king said to Cromwell. Many were afraid of a rupture. The divorce between Henry and Catherine, the cruelty with which he had treated the innocent Anne Boleyn, had already given rise to so much discontent in Europe that people dreaded a fresh outbreak. The cup was bitter, but he must drink it. The 6th of January was positively fixed for the fatal nuptials. The king was heard the day before murmuring in a low tone with an accent of despair,—"It must be; it must be," and presently after, "I will put my neck under the yoke." He determined to live in a becoming way with the queen. An insuperable antipathy filled his heart, but courteous words were on his lips. In the morning the king said to Cromwell,—"If it were not for the great preparations that my states and people have made for her, and for fear of making a ruffle in the world, and of driving her brother into the hands of the Emperor and the French king's hands, being now together, I would never have married her." Cromwell's position had been first shaken by his quarrel with Norfolk; it sustained a second shock from the king's disappointment. Henry blamed him for his misfortune, and Cromwell in vain laid the blame on Southampton.

On January 6 the marriage ceremony was performed at Greenwich by the archbishop, with much solemnity but also with great mournfulness. Henry comforted himself for his misfortune by the thought that he should be allied with the Protestant princes against the Emperor, if only they would consent somewhat to modify their doctrine. On the morrow Cromwell again asked him how he liked the queen. Worse than ever, replied the king. He continued, however, to testify to his wife the respect due to her.

It was generally anticipated that this union would be favourable to the Reformation. Butler, in a letter to Bullinger at Zurich, wrote: "The state and condition of that kingdom is much more sound and healthy since the marriage of the queen than it was before. She is an excellent woman, and one who fears God; great hopes are entertained of a very extensive propagation of the Gospel by her influence." And in another letter he says: "There is great hope that it [the kingdom] will ere long be in a much more healthy state; and this every good man is striving for in persevering prayer to God."[1] Religious books were publicly offered for sale, and many faithful ministers, particularly Barnes, freely preached the truth with much power, and no one troubled them.[2] These good people were under a delusion. "The king," they said, "who is exceedingly merciful, would willingly desire the promotion of the truth."[3]

But the Protestantism of the king of England was displayed not so much in matters of faith as in public affairs. He showed much irritation against the Emperor; and this gave rise to a

[1] *Original Letters relative to the English Reformation* (Parker Society), ii. pp. 627–28, Feb. 24 and March 29, 1540.
[2] "The word is powerfully preached by Barnes and his fellow-ministers." —*Ibid.*
[3] Partridge to Bullinger, Feb. 26, 1540.—*Original Letters*, &c., ii. p. 614.

characteristic conversation. Henry having instructed (January 1540) his ambassador in the Netherlands, Sir Thomas Wyatt, to make certain representations and demands on various subjects which concerned his government, "*I shall not interfere,*" Charles drily replied. Wyatt having further made complaint that the English merchants in Spain were interfered with by the Inquisition, the Emperor laconically answered that he knew nothing about it, and referred him to Granvella. Wyatt then having been so bold as to remark that the monarch answered him in an ungracious manner, Charles interrupted him and said that he "abused his words toward him." But the ambassador, who meant exactly to carry out his master's orders, did not stop, but uttered the word ingratitude. Henry considered Charles ungrateful on the ground that he had greatly obliged him on one important occasion. In fact, the Emperor Maximilian having offered to secure the Empire for the king of England, the thought of encircling his brows with the crown of the Roman emperors inflamed the ardent imagination of the young prince, who was an enthusiast for the romantic traditions of the Middle Ages. But, after the death of Maximilian, the Germans decided in favour of Charles. The latter then came to England, and the two kings met. Not very much is known of what they said in their interview; but whatever it might be, Henry yielded, and he believed that to his generosity Charles was indebted for the Empire. "*Ingratitude–*" replied the Emperor to the ambassador. "From whom mean you to proceed that ingratitude? . . . I would ye knew I am not ingrate, and if the king your master hath done me a good turn I have done him as good or better. And I take it so, that I cannot be toward him ingrate; the inferior may be ingrate to the greater. But peradventure because the language is not your natural tongue, ye may mistake the term." "Sir," replied Wyatt, "I do not know that I misdo in using the term that I am commanded." The Emperor was much moved. "Monsieur l'ambassadeur," he said, "the king's opinions be not always the best." "My master," Wyatt answered, "is a prince to give reason to God and to the world sufficient in his opinions." "It may be," Charles said coolly. His intentions were evidently becoming more and more aggressive. Henry VIII clearly perceived what his projects were. "Remember," said the king the same month to the duke of Norfolk, whom he had sent as envoy extraordinary to France, "that Charles has it in his head to bring Christendom to a monarchy. For if he be persuaded that he is a superior to all kings, then it is not to be doubted that he will by all ways and means . . . cause all those whom he so reputeth for his inferiors to acknowledge his superiority in such sort as their estates should easily be altered at his will." These words show that Henry possessed more political good sense than was usually attributed to him; but they are not exactly a proof of his *evangelical* zeal.

He did something, however, in this direction. Representatives of the elector of Saxony and the landgrave of Hesse had accompanied Anne of Cleves to England. Henry received them kindly and entertained them magnificently; he succeeded so well in dazzling them by his converse and his manners, that these grave ambassadors sent word to their masters how the nuptials of his Majesty had been celebrated under joyful and sacred auspices. Nevertheless, they did not conceal from Henry VIII that the elector and the landgrave "had been thrown into consternation, as well as many others, by an atrocious decree, the result of the artifices of certain bishops, partisans of Roman impiety." Thereupon the king, who wished by all means to gain over the evangelical princes, declared to their representatives "that his wisdom should soften the harshness of the decree, that he would even suspend its execution, and that there was nothing in the world that he more desired than to see the true doctrine of Christ shine in all churches, and that he was determined always to set heavenly truth before the tradition of men." In consequence of these statements of the king the Wittenberg theologians sent to him some evangelical articles, to which they requested his adherence, and which were entirely opposed to those of Gardiner. We shall presently see how Henry proceeded to fulfil his promises.

Cromwell was anxious to take advantage of these declarations to get the Gospel preached, and he knew men capable of preaching it. He relied most of all on Barnes, who had returned to England with the most flattering testimonials from the Wittenberg reformers, and even from the elector of

Saxony and the king of Denmark. Barnes had been employed by Henry in the negotiation of his marriage with Anne of Cleves, and had thus contributed to this union, a circumstance which did not greatly recommend him to the king. There were, besides, Thomas Garret, curate of All Saints' Church, in Honey-lane, of whom we have elsewhere spoken; William Jerome, vicar of Stepney, and others. Bonner, who on his return from France was elected bishop of London, and who was afterwards a zealous persecutor, designated these three evangelical ministers to preach at Paul's Cross during Lent in 1540. Bonner, perhaps, still wished to curry favour with Cromwell; or perhaps these preachers had been complained of, and the king wished to put them to the test. Barnes was to preach the first Sunday (Feb. 14); but Gardiner, foreboding danger, wished to prevent him, and consequently sent word to Bonner that he would himself preach that day. Barnes resigned the pulpit to this powerful prelate, who, well aware what doctrine the three evangelicals would proclaim at St. Paul's, was determined to prevent them, and craftily to stir up prejudices against the innovators and their innovations. Confutation beforehand, he thought, is more useful than afterwards. It is better to be first than second; better to prevent evils than to cure them. He displayed some ingenuity and wit. Many persons were attracted by the notion that the Reformation was a progress and advance. He alleged that it was the contrary; and, taking for his text the words addressed to Jesus by the tempter on the pinnacle of the temple, *Cast thyself down*, he said: "Now-a-days the devil tempteth the world and biddeth them to cast themselves backward. There is no 'forward' in the new teaching, but all backward. Now the devil teacheth, Come back from fasting, come back from praying, come back from confession, come back from weeping for thy sins; and all is backward, insomuch that men must now learn to say their Pater-Noster backward."[1] The bishop of Winchester censured with especial severity the evangelical preachers, on the ground that they taught the remission of sins through faith and not by works. Of old, he said, heaven was sold at Rome for a little money; now that we have done with all that trumpery the devil hath invented

[1] Gardiner's Sermon, Foxe, *Acts*, v. p. 430.

another—he offers us heaven for nothing! A living faith which unites us to the Saviour was counted as nothing by Gardiner.

On a subsequent Sunday Barnes preached. The lord mayor and Gardiner, side by side, and many other *reporters*, says the chronicle, were present at the service. The preacher vigorously defended the doctrine attacked by the bishop; but unfortunately, he indulged, like him, in attempts at wit, and even in a play upon his name, complaining of the *gardener* who "had planted such evil herbs in the garden of God's Scripture." This punning would anywhere have been offensive; it was doubly offensive in the pulpit in the presence of the bishop himself. "Punning," says one "is the poorest kind of would-be wit." Garret preached energetically the next Sunday; but he studiously avoided offending anyone. Lastly, Jerome preached, and taking up the passage relating to Sarah and Hagar in the epistle of St. Paul to the Galatians, maintained that all those who are born of Sarah, the lawful wife, that is, who have been regenerated by faith, are fully and positively justified.

Bishop Gardiner and his friends lost no time in complaining to the king of the "intolerable arrogance of Barnes." "A prelate of the kingdom to be thus insulted at Paul's Cross!" said the former ambassador to France. Henry sent for the culprit to his cabinet. Barnes confessed that he had forgotten himself, and promised to be on his guard against such rash speeches in future. Jerome and Garret likewise were reprimanded; and the king commanded the three evangelists to read in public on the following Sunday, at the solemn Easter service celebrated in the church of St. Mary's Hospital, a retractation which was delivered to them in writing. They felt bound to submit unreservedly to the commands of the king. Barnes, therefore, when the 4th of April was come, ascended the pulpit and read word for word the official paper which he had received. After this, turning to the bishop of Winchester, who was present by order of the king, he earnestly and respectfully begged his pardon, asking him twice to lift up his hand, if he forgave him. Gardiner "with much ado, wagged his finger a little." Having thus discharged, as he believed, his duty, first as a subject, then as a Christian, Barnes felt bound to discharge also that of a minister of God. He therefore preached powerfully the doctrine of salvation by grace, the very doctrine for which he was persecuted. The lord mayor, who was sitting by Gardiner's side, turned to the bishop and asked him whether he should send him from the pulpit to prison for preaching so boldly contrary to his retractation. Garret and Jerome having followed the example of Barnes, the king gave orders that the three evangelists should be taken and confined in the Tower. "Three of our best ministers," wrote Butler to Bullinger, "are confined in the Tower of London. You may judge from this of our misfortunes."

At the same time that Henry VIII was imprisoning the ministers of God's Word, he was giving more liberty to the Word itself. It must be confessed that In his conflict with the pope he did make use of the Bible. He interpreted it, indeed, in his own way; but still he used it and helped to circulate it. This was a fact of importance for the Reformation in England.

The edition of the Bible sometimes called "Cranmer's Bible" appeared at this time (April 1540). Actually it was the second edition of the Great Bible already mentioned, but as the archbishop supplied a preface to it, his name has thus been honourably linked with the Word. The preface commends to the subjects of Henry the widespread reading of the Holy Scriptures, and appeals to the authority of the ancient fathers of the church in support of the claim that the Word is the sufficient rule of faith and life.

"Here may all manner of persons: men, women, young, old; learned, unlearned; rich, poor; priests, laymen; lords, ladies; officers, tenants, and mean men; virgins, wives, widows; lawyers, merchants, artificers, husbandmen; and all manner of persons, of what estate or condition soever they be; may in This Book learn all things, what they ought to believe, what they ought to do, and what they should not do, as well concerning Almighty God, as also concerning themselves, and all others . . . to the reading of Scripture none can be enemy. . . . I would advise you all, that come to the reading or hearing of This Book, which is the Word of God, the most precious jewel and most holy relic that remaineth upon earth, that ye bring with you the fear of God . . . and use not your knowledge thereof to vain glory of frivolous disputation, but to the honour of God, increase of virtue, and edification both of yourselves and of others."

Thus ran Cranmer's preface. In the fourth and sixth editions the title includes mention of the fact that Cuthbert Tunstall was one of the two bishops made responsible for the oversight of the work of printing and publishing. We may well conjecture whether Tunstall did this work with a willing mind: he was the bishop of London who had refused help and permission to Tyndale to translate the Word into English, and who had previously bought up copies of the Testaments in order to burn them at Paul's Cross: and the book he now helped to bring before the people was based, in part, on the work he had so vigorously opposed!

A magnificent copy on vellum was presented to the king. In the same month appeared another Bible, printed in smaller type; in July another great Bible; in November a third in folio, authorized by Henry VIII, "supreme head of his church." It would seem even that there was one more edition this year. The enemies of the Bible were in power. Nevertheless the Bible was gaining the victory; and the luminary which was to enlighten the world was beginning to shed abroad its light everywhere.

CHAPTER FIVE

The Disgrace and Death of Thomas Cromwell
(1540)

EIGHT days after the imprisonment of Barnes and his two friends (April 12, 1540), parliament opened for the first time without abbots or priors. Cromwell was thoughtful and uneasy; he saw everywhere occasions of alarm; he felt his position insecure. The statute of the Six Articles, the conviction which possessed his mind that the doctrines of the Middle Ages were regaining an indisputable ascendancy over the king, the wrath of Norfolk, and Henry's ill will on account of the queen whom Cromwell had chosen for him—these were the dark points which threatened his future. His friends were scattered or persecuted; his enemies were gathered about the throne. Henry, however, made no sign, but secretly meditated a violent blow. He concealed the game he was playing so that others, and especially Cromwell himself, should have no perception of it. The powerful minister, therefore, appeared in parliament, assuming a confident air, as the ever-powerful organ of the supreme will of the king. Henry VIII, the man of extremes, thought proper at this time to exhibit himself as an advocate of a middle course. The country is agitated by religious dissensions, said the vicegerent, his representative; and in his speech to the House he set forth on the one hand the rooted superstition and obstinate clinging to popery, and on the other thoughtless and impertinent and culpable rashness (referring doubtless to Barnes). He said that the king desired a union of the two parties; that he leaned to neither side; that he would equally repress the licence of heretics and that of the papists, and that he "set the pure and sincere doctrine of Christ before his eyes." These words of Cromwell were wise. Union in the truth is the great want of all ages. But Henry added his comment. He refused to turn to the right or to the left. He would not himself hold, nor did he intend to permit England to hold, any other doctrine than that prescribed by his own sovereign authority, sword in hand. Cromwell did not fail to let it be known by what method the king meant to bring about this union; he insisted on penalties against all who did not submit to the Bible and against those who put upon it a wrong interpretation. Henry intended to strike right and left with his vigorous hand. To carry out the scheme of union a commission was appointed, the result of which, after two years' labours, was a confused medley of truths and errors.

Strange to say, although Cromwell was now on the brink of an abyss, the king still heaped favours upon him. He was already chancellor of the exchequer, first secretary of state, vicegerent and vicar-general of England in spiritual affairs, lord privy seal, and knight of the Garter; but he was now to see fresh honours added to all these. The earl of Essex had just died, and a week later died William, lord Sandys of "The Vyne," who had been lord chamberlain. Hereupon Henry made Cromwell, "the blacksmith's son," whom Norfolk and the other nobles despised so heartily, earl of Essex and lord chamberlain, and had his name placed at the head of the roll of peers. Wealth was no more wanting to him than honours. He received a large portion of the property of the deceased lord Essex; the king conferred on him numerous manors taken from the suppressed monasteries; he owned great estates in eight counties; and he still continued to superintend the business of the crown. We might well ask how it came to pass that such a profusion of favours fell to his lot just at the time when the king was angry with him as the man who had given him Anne of Cleves for a wife; when the imprisonment of Barnes, his friend and confidential agent, greatly compromised him, and when, in addition to these things, Norfolk, Gardiner, and the whole Catholic party were striving to put down this *parvenu*, who offended them and stood in their way. Two answers may be given to this question. Henry was desirous that Cromwell should make a great effort to secure the assent of parliament to bills of a very extraordinary character but very advantageous to the king; and it was his hope that the titles under which Cromwell would appear before the houses would make success easier. Several contemporaries, however, assigned a different cause for these royal favours. "Some persons now suspect," wrote Hilles to Bullinger, "that this was all an artifice, to make people conclude that he [Cromwell] must have been a most wicked traitor, and guilty of treason in every possible way; or else the king would never have executed one who was so dear to him, as was made manifest by the presents he had bestowed upon him." Besides, was it not the custom of the ancients to crown their victims with flowers before sacrificing them?

Henry was greedy of money, and was in want of it, for he spent it prodigally. He applied to Cromwell for it. The latter was aware that in making himself the king's instrument in this matter he was estranging from himself the mind of the nation; but he considered that a great sovereign must have great resources, and he was always willing to sacrifice himself for the king, for to him he owed everything, and he loved him in spite of his faults. On April 23, four days after receiving from the king such extraordinary favours, Cromwell proposed to the House to suppress the Knights of St. John of Jerusalem, and urged that their estates, which were considerable, should be given to the king. This was agreed to by Parliament. On May 3 he demanded for his Majesty a subsidy of unparalleled character, namely, four tenths and fifteenths, in addition to ten per cent. on the rents of lands and five per cent. on the value of merchandise. This also he obtained. Next he went to the convocation of the clergy, and claimed from them two tenths and twenty per cent. on ecclesiastical revenues for two years. Again he succeeded. By May 8 the king had obtained through Cromwell's energy all that he wished for.

On the very next day, Sunday, May 9, Cromwell received in his palace a note from the king thus worded:—

"HENRY R. By the King.

"Right trusty and well beloved cousin,—We greet you well; signifying unto you our pleasure and commandment is that forthwith, and upon the receipt of these our letters, setting all other affairs apart, ye do repair unto us, for the treaty of such great and weighty matters as whereupon doth consist the surety of our person, the preservation of our honour, and the tranquillity and quietness of you, and all other our loving and faithful subjects, like as at your arrival here ye shall more plainly perceive and understand. And that ye fail not hereof, as we specially trust you.

"Given under our signet, at our manor of Westminster, the 9th day of May."

What could this urgent and mysterious note mean? Cromwell could not rest after reading it. "The surety of our person, the preservation of our honour" are in question, said the king. We may imagine the agitation of his mind, his fears as to the result of the visit, and the state of perplexity in which, without losing a minute, he went in obedience to the king's command. We have no information as to what passed at this interview. Probably the minister supposed that he had justified himself in his master's sight. On the following day, Monday, the earl of Essex was present as usual in the House of Lords and introduced a bill. The day after, parliament was prorogued till May 25. What could be the reason for this? It has been supposed that Cromwell's enemies wished to gain the time needful for collecting evidence in support of the charges which they intended to bring against him. When the fifteen days had elapsed, parliament met again, and the earl of Essex was in his place on the first and following days. He was still in the assembly as minister of the king on June 10, on which day, at three o'clock, there was a meeting of the Privy Council. The duke of Norfolk, the earl of Essex, and the other members were quietly seated round the table, when the duke rose and accused Cromwell of high treason. Cromwell understood that Norfolk was acting under the sanction of the king, and he recollected the note of May 9. The lord chancellor arrested him and had him conducted to the Tower.

Norfolk was more than ever in favour, for Henry, husband of Anne of Cleves, was at this time enamoured of Norfolk's niece. He believed—and Gardiner, doubtless, did not fail to encourage the belief—that he must promptly take advantage of the extraordinary goodwill which the king testified to him to overthrow the adversary of English Catholicism, the powerful protector of the Bible and the Reformation. In the judgment of this party, Cromwell was a heretic and a chief of heretics. This was the principal motive, and substantially the only motive of the attack made on the earl of Essex. In a letter addressed at this time by the Council to Sir John Wallop, ambassador at the court of France, a circular letter sent also to the principal officers and representatives of the king, the crime of which Cromwell was accused is distinctly set forth. "The lord privy seal," it was therein said, "to whom the king's said Majesty hath been so special good and gracious lord, neither remembering his duty herein to God, nor yet to his Highness . . . hath not only wrought clean contrary to this his Grace's most godly intent, secretly and indirectly advancing the one of the extremes, and leaving the mean indifferent true and virtuous way which his Majesty sought and so entirely desired; but also hath showed himself so fervently bent to the maintenance of that his outrage that he hath not spared most privily, most traitorously, to devise how to continue the same, and plainly in terms to say, as it hath been justified to his face by good witness, that if the king and all his realm would turn and vary from his opinions, he would fight in the field in his own person, with his sword in his hand, against him and all other; adding that if he lived a year or two he trusted to bring things to that frame that it should not lie in the king's power to resist or let it, if he would; binding his words with such oaths and making such gesture and demonstration with his arms, that it might well appear he had no less fixed in his heart than was uttered with his mouth. For the which apparent and most detestable treasons, and also for . . . other enormities . . . he is committed to the Tower of London, there to remain till it shall please his Majesty to have him thereupon tried according to the order of his laws." It was added that the king, remembering how men wanting the knowledge of the truth would speak diversely of the matter, desired them to declare and open the whole truth.

Nothing could be more at variance with the character and the whole life of Cromwell than the foolish sayings attributed to him. Every intelligent man might see that they were mere falsehoods invented by the Catholic party to hide its own criminal conduct. But at the same time it most clearly pointed out in this letter the real motive of the blow aimed at Cromwell, the first, true, efficient cause of his fall, the object which his enemies had in view and towards which they were working.

They fancied that the overthrow of Cromwell would be the overthrow of the Reformation. Wallop did not fail to impart the information to the court to which he was accredited; and Henry VIII was delighted to hear of "the friendly rejoyce of our good brother the French king, the constable and others there," on learning of the arrest of the lord privy seal. This rejoicing was very natural on the part of Francis I, Montmorency, and the rest of them.

As soon as the arrest of June 10 was known, the majority of those who had most eagerly sought after the favour of Cromwell, and especially Bonner, bishop of London, immediately turned round and declared against him. He had gained no popularity by promoting the last bills passed to the king's advantage; and the news of his imprisonment was therefore received with shouts of joy. In the midst of the general dejection, one man alone remained faithful to the prisoner—this was Cranmer. The man who had formerly undertaken the defence of Anne Boleyn now came forward in defence of Cromwell. The archbishop did not attend the Privy Council on Thursday, June 10; but being in his place on the Friday, he heard that the earl of Essex had been arrested as a traitor. The tidings astonished and affected him deeply. He saw in Cromwell at this time not only his personal friend, not only the prudent and devoted supporter of the Reformation, but also the ablest minister and the most faithful servant of the king. He saw the danger to which he exposed himself by undertaking the defence of the prisoner; and he felt that it was his duty not recklessly to offend the king. He therefore wrote to him in a prudent manner, reminding him, nevertheless, energetically of all that Cromwell had been. His letter to the king was written the day after he heard of the fall of the minister. "I heard yesterday in your Grace's council," he says, "that he [Cromwell] is a traitor; yet who cannot be sorrowful and amazed that he should be a traitor against your Majesty, he that was so advanced by your Majesty; he whose surety was only by your Majesty; he who loved your Majesty (as I ever thought) no less than God; he who studied always to set forwards whatsoever was your Majesty's will and pleasure; he that cared for no man's displeasure to serve your Majesty; he that was such a servant, in my judgment, in wisdom, diligence, faithfulness, and experience, as no prince in this realm ever had; he that was so vigilant to preserve your Majesty from all treasons that few could be so secretly conceived but he detected the same in the beginning? If the noble princes of memory, king John, Henry II, and Richard II had had such a counsellor about them, I suppose that they should never have been so traitorously abandoned and overthrown as those good princes were. . . . I loved him as my friend, for so I took him to be; but I chiefly loved him for the love which I thought I saw him bear ever towards your Grace, singularly above all other. But now, if he be a traitor, I am sorry that ever I loved him or trusted him, and I am very glad that his treason is discovered in time. But yet again I am very sorrowful, for who shall your Grace trust hereafter, if you might not trust him? Alas! I bewail and lament your Grace's chance herein, I wot not whom your Grace may trust. But I pray God continually night and day to send such a counsellor in his place whom your Grace may trust, and who for all his qualities can and will serve your Grace like to him, and that will have so much solicitude and care to preserve your Grace from all dangers as I ever thought he had."

Cranmer was doubtless a weak man; but assuredly it was a proof of some devotion to truth and justice, and of some boldness too, thus to plead the cause of the prisoner before a prince so absolute as Henry VIII, and even to express the wish that some efficient successor might be found. Cranmer wrote to the king *boldly*. The prince being intolerant of contradiction, this step of the archbishop was more than was needed to ruin him as well as Cromwell.

Meanwhile, the enemies of the prisoner were trying to find other grounds of accusation besides that which they had first brought forward. Indeed, it seemed to some persons a strange thing that he who, under Henry VIII, was head of the church, vicegerent in spiritual affairs, should be a heretic and a patron of heretics; and many found in this charge an "occasion of merriment." They set to work, therefore, after the blow, to discover offences on the part of the accused. After taking great pains, this is what they discovered and set forth in the bill of attainder: 1. That he had set at liberty some prisoners suspected of treason; a crime indeed in the eyes of a gloomy despot, but in the judgment of righteous men an act of justice and virtue. 2. That he had granted freedom of export of corn, horses, and other articles of commerce; the crime of free trade which would be no crime now. Not a single instance can be specified in which Cromwell had received a present for such licence. 3. That he had, though a low-born man, given places and orders, saying only that he was sure that the king would approve them. On this point Cromwell might reasonably allege the multiplicity of matters entrusted to his care, and the annoyance to which it must have subjected the king, had he continually troubled him to decide the most trifling questions. 4. That he had given permission, both to the king's subjects and to foreigners, to cross the sea "without any search." This intelligent minister appears to have aimed at an order of things less vexatious and more liberal than that established under Henry VIII, and in this respect he stood ahead of his age. 5. That he had made a large fortune, that he had lived in great state, and had not duly honoured the nobility. There were not a few of the nobles who were far from being honourable, and this great worker had no liking for drones and idlers. With respect to his fortune, Cromwell incurred heavy expenses for the affairs of the realm. In many countries he kept well-paid agents, and the money which he had in his hands was spent more in state affairs than in satisfying his personal wishes. In all this there was evidently more to praise than to blame. But Cromwell had enemies who went further than his official accusers. The Roman Catholics gave out that he had aspired to the hand of the king's daughter, the princess Mary.

These groundless charges were followed by the true motives for his disgrace. It was alleged that he had adopted heretical (that is to say, evangelical) opinions; that he had promoted the circulation of heretical works; that he had settled in the realm many heretical ministers; and that he had caused men accused of heresy to be set at liberty. That when anyone went to him to make complaint of detestable errors, he defended the heretics and severely censured the informers; and that in March last, persons having complained to him of the new preachers, he answered that "their preaching was good." For these *crimes*, the acts of a Christian, honest and beneficent man, condemnation must be pronounced. Cromwell indeed was guilty.

The conduct of the prosecution was entrusted to Richard Rich, formerly speaker of the House of Commons, now solicitor-general and chancellor of the court of augmentations. He had already rendered service to the king in the trials of Bishop Fisher and Sir Thomas More; the same might be expected of him in the trial of Cromwell. It appears that he accused Cromwell of being connected with Throgmorton, the friend and agent of Cardinal Pole. Now the mere mention of Pole's name would put Henry out of temper. Cromwell's alliance with this friend of the pope was the pendant of his scheme of marriage with the lady Mary; the one was as probable as the other. Cromwell wrote from his prison to the king on the subject, and stoutly denied the fable. It was not introduced into the formal pleadings; but the charge was left vaguely impending over him, and it was reasserted that he was guilty of treason. Cromwell was certainly not faultless. He was above all a politician, and political interests had too much weight with him. He was the advocate of some vexatious and unjust measures, and he acted sometimes in opposition to his own principles. But his main fault was a too servile devotion to the prince who pretended that he had been betrayed by him. His fall, in certain respects, resembles that of his earlier master, Cardinal Wolsey.

His enemies were afraid that, if the trial were conducted openly before his peers according to law, he would make his voice heard and clear himself of all their imputations. They resolved therefore to proceed against him without trial and without discussion, by the parliamentary method, by bill of attainder; a course pronounced by Roman Catholics themselves "a most iniquitous measure."[1] He ought to have been tried, and he was not tried. He was, however, confronted on Friday, June 11, the day after his arrest, with one of his accusers, and thus learnt what were the charges brought against him. Conducted again to the Tower, he became fully aware of the danger which was impending over him. The power of his enemies, Gardiner and Norfolk, the increasing disfavour of Anne of Cleves, which seemed inevitably to

[1] Lingard, *Hist. of England*, v. p. 143.

O(II)

involve his own ruin, the proceedings instituted against
Barnes and other evangelists, the anger of the king—all these
things alarmed him and produced the conviction in his mind
that the issue was doubtful, and that the danger was certain.
He was in a state of great distress and deep melancholy;
gloomy thoughts oppressed him, and his limbs trembled. The
prison has been called the porch of the grave, and Cromwell
indeed looked upon it as a grave. On June 30 he wrote to the
king from his gloomy abode an affecting letter, "with heavy
heart and trembling hand," as he himself said.

About the end of June, the duke of Norfolk, the lord
chancellor, and the lord high admiral went to the Tower,
instructed to examine Cromwell and to make various declarations to him on the part of the king. The most important of
these related to the marriage of Henry VIII with Anne of
Cleves. They called upon him to state all that he knew
touching this marriage, "as he might do before God on the
dread day of judgment." On June 30 Cromwell wrote to the
king a letter in which he set forth what he knew on the
subject; and he added: "And this is all that I know, most
gracious and most merciful sovereign lord, beseeching Almighty
God . . . to counsel you, preserve you, maintain you, remedy
you, relieve and defend you, as may be most to your honour,
with prosperity, health and comfort of your heart's desire
. . . [giving you] continuance of Nestor's years. . . . I am a
most woeful prisoner, ready to take the death, when it shall
please God and your Majesty; and yet the frail flesh inciteth
me continually to call to your Grace for mercy and grace for
mine offences: and thus Christ save, preserve, and keep you.

"Written at the Tower this Wednesday, the last day of
June, with the heavy heart and trembling hand of your
Highness' most heavy and most miserable prisoner and poor
slave,

"THOMAS CRUMWELL."

After having signed the letter, Cromwell, overpowered
with terror at his future prospects, added:—

"Most gracious prince, I cry for mercy, mercy, mercy."[1]

The heads of the clerical party, impatient to be rid of an

[1] Cromwell's Letter to Henry VIII. Burnet, *Records*, i. p. 301.

enemy whom they hated, hurried on the fatal decree. The parliament met on Thursday, June 17, seven days after Cromwell's imprisonment; and Cranmer, who had attended the sittings of the House of Lords on the previous days, was not present on this occasion. The earl of Southampton, who had become lord keeper of the privy seal in Cromwell's place, entered and presented the bill of attainder against his predecessor. It was read a first time. The second and third readings followed on Saturday the 19th. Cranmer, whose absence had probably been noticed, was present; and, according to his lamentable system, adapted to the despotism of his master, after having complied with the dictate of his conscience by calling to mind the merits of Cromwell, he complied with the will of the king, and by his silence acquiesced in the proceedings of the House. The bill was sent to the lower House. It appears that the commons raised some scruples or objections, for the bill remained under consideration for ten days. It was not until June 29 that the commons sent the bill back to the peers, with some amendments; and the peers, ever in haste, ordered that the three readings should take place at the same sitting. They then sent it to the king, who gave his assent to it. The man who was prosecuted had been so powerful that it was feared lest he should regain his strength and begin to advance with fresh energy.

The king, meanwhile, seems to have hesitated. He was less decided than those who at this time enjoyed his favour.

Although the lord chancellor, the duke of Norfolk, and lord Russell had come to announce to Cromwell that the Bill of Attainder had passed, he remained still a whole month in the Tower. The royal commissioners interrogated him at intervals on various subjects. It seems even that the king sent him relief, probably to mitigate the severities of his imprisonment. Cromwell habitually received the king's commissioners with dignity, and answered them with discretion. Whether the questions touched on temporal or ecclesiastical affairs, he ever showed himself better informed than his questioners.[1]

Henry sent word to him that he might write anything that he thought meet under his present circumstances. From this, Cromwell appears to have conceived a hope that the king

---

[1] Foxe, *Acts*, v. p. 401.

would not permit his sentence to be executed. He took courage and wrote to the king. "Most gracious king," he said, "your most lamentable servant and prisoner, prostrate at the feet of your most excellent Majesty, have heard your pleasure . . . that I should write. . . . First, where I have been accused to your Majesty of treason, to that I say, I never in all my life thought willingly to do that thing that might or should displease your Majesty. . . . What labours, pains, and travails I have taken, according to my most bounden duty God also knoweth. . . . If it had been or were in my power, to make your Majesty so puissant, as all the world should be compelled to obey you, Christ He knoweth I would, . . . for your Majesty hath been . . . more like a dear father . . . than a master. Should any faction or any affection to any point make me a traitor to your Majesty, then all the devils in hell confound me, and the vengeance of God light upon me. . . . Yet our Lord, if it be His will, can do with me as he did with Susan, who was falsely accused. . . . Other hope than in God and your Majesty I have not. . . . Amongst other things, most gracious Sovereign, master comptroller shewed me that your Grace shewed him that within these fourteen days ye committed a matter of great secrecy, which I did reveal. . . . This I did. . . . I spake privily with her [the queen's] lord chamberlain . . . desiring him . . . to find some mean that the queen might be induced to order your Grace pleasantly in her behaviour towards you. . . . If I have offended your Majesty therein, prostrate at your Majesty's feet I most lowly ask mercy and pardon of your Highness. . . . Written with the quaking hand and most sorrowful heart of your most sorrowful subject and most humble servant and prisoner, this Saturday at the Tower of London.

"THOMAS CRUMWELL."[1]

Cromwell was resigned to death; and the principal object of his concern was the fate of his son, his grandchildren, and likewise of his domestic servants. His son was in a good position, having married a sister of the queen Jane Seymour. "Sir, upon my knees," he said, "I most humbly beseech your gracious Majesty to be a good and gracious lord to my poor

[1] Burnet, *Records*, ii. p. 214.

son, the good and virtuous woman his wife, and their poor children, and also to my servants. And this I desire of your Grace for Christ's sake." The unhappy father, returning to his own case, finished by saying, "Most gracious prince, mercy, mercy, mercy!" Cromwell wrote twice in this manner; and the king was so much affected by the second of these letters that he "commanded it thrice to be read to him."

Would Cromwell then, after all, escape? Those who were ignorant of what was passing at court looked upon it as impossible that he should be sacrificed so long as Anne of Cleves was queen of England. But the very circumstances which seemed to them the guarantee of his safety were to be instead the occasion of his ruin.

Henry's dislike to his wife was ever increasing, and he was determined to get rid of her. But, as usual, he concealed beneath flowers the weapon with which he was about to strike her. In the month of March, the king gave, in honour of the queen, a grand fête with a tournament, as he had done for Anne Boleyn; and amongst the numerous combatants who took part in the jousting were Sir Thomas Seymour, the earl of Sussex, Harry Howard, and Richard Cromwell, nephew of the earl of Essex, and ancestor of the great Protector Oliver.

One circumstance contributed to hasten the decision of the king. There was at the court a young lady, small of stature, of a good figure and beautiful countenance, of ladylike manners, coquettish and forward, who at this time made a deep impression on Henry. This was Catherine Howard, a niece of the duke of Norfolk, now residing with her grandmother, the duchess dowager, who allowed her great liberty. Catherine was in every respect a contrast to Anne of Cleves. Henry resolved to marry her, and for this purpose to get rid forthwith of his present wife. As he was desirous of being provisionally relieved of her presence, he persuaded her that a change of air would be very beneficial to her, and that it was necessary that she should make a stay in the country. On June 24 he sent the good princess, who felt grateful for his attentions, to Richmond. At the same time he despatched the bishop of Bath to her brother, the duke of Cleves, with a view to prepare him for the very unexpected decision which was impending over his sister, and to avert any vexatious consequences.

Cromwell, then, had no aid to look for at the hands of a queen already forsaken and ere long repudiated. He could not hope to escape death. His enemies were urgent for the execution of the bill. They professed to have discovered a correspondence which he had carried on with the Protestant princes of Germany.

Cromwell's determination to offer no opposition to the king led him to commit serious mistakes, unworthy of a Christian. Nevertheless, according to documents still extant, he died like a Christian. He was not the first, nor the last, who in the presence of death, of capital punishment, has examined himself, and confessed himself a sinner. While he spurned the accusations made by his enemies, he humbled himself before the weightier and more solemn accusations of his own conscience. How often had his own will been opposed to the commandments of the divine will! But at the same time he discovered in the Gospel the grace which he had but imperfectly known; and the doctrines which the Catholic church of the first ages had professed became dear to him.

On July 28, 1540, Cromwell was taken to Tower Hill, the place of execution. On reaching the scaffold he said: "I am come hither to die, and not to purge myself. . . . For since the time that I have had years of discretion, I have lived a sinner and offended my Lord God, for the which I ask Him heartily forgiveness. And it is not unknown to many of you that I have been a great travailler in this world, and being but of a base degree, was called to high estate; and since the time I came thereunto I have offended my prince, for the which I ask him heartily forgiveness, and beseech you all to pray to God with me, that He will forgive me. O Father, forgive me! O Son, forgive me! O Holy Ghost, forgive me! O Three Persons in one God, forgive me! . . . I die in the Catholic faith. . . . I heartily desire you to pray for the king's grace, that he may long live with you in health and prosperity."

By insisting in so marked a manner on the doctrine of the Trinity, professed in the fourth century by the councils of Nicæa and Constantinople, Cromwell doubtless intended to show that this was the Catholic doctrine in which he asserted that he died. But he did not omit to give evidence that his faith was that of the Scriptures.

After his confession, he knelt down, and at this solemn hour he uttered this Christian and fervent prayer: "O Lord Jesu! which art the only health of all men living and the everlasting life of them which die in Thee, I, wretched sinner, do submit myself wholly unto Thy most blessed will, and being sure that the thing cannot perish which is committed unto Thy mercy, willingly now I leave this frail and wicked flesh, in sure hope that Thou wilt, in better wise, restore it to me again at the last day in the resurrection of the just. I beseech Thee, most merciful Lord Jesus Christ! that Thou wilt by Thy grace make strong my soul against all temptations, and defend me with the buckler of Thy mercy against all the assaults of the devil. I see and acknowledge that there is in myself no hope of salvation, but all my confidence, hope, and trust is in Thy most merciful goodness. I have no merits nor good works which I may allege before Thee. Of sins and evil works, alas! I see a great heap; but yet through Thy mercy I trust to be in the number of them to whom Thou wilt not impute their sins; but wilt take and accept me for righteous and just, and to be the inheritor of everlasting life. Thou, merciful Lord! wast born for my sake; Thou didst suffer both hunger and thirst for my sake; Thou didst teach, pray, and fast for my sake; all Thy holy actions and works Thou wroughtest for my sake; Thou sufferedst most grievous pains and torments for my sake; finally, Thou gavest Thy most precious body and Thy blood to be shed on the cross for my sake. Now, most merciful Saviour! let all these things profit me, that Thou freely hast done for me, which hast given Thyself also for me. Let Thy blood cleanse and wash away the spots and foulness of my sins. Let Thy righteousness hide and cover my unrighteousness. Let the merits of Thy passion and blood-shedding be satisfaction for my sins. Give me, Lord! Thy grace, that the faith of my salvation in Thy blood waver not in me, but may ever be firm and constant; that the hope of Thy mercy and life everlasting never decay in me: that love wax not cold in me. Finally, that the weakness of my flesh be not overcome with the fear of death. Grant me, merciful Saviour! that when death hath shut up the eyes of my body, yet the eyes of my soul may still behold and look upon Thee; and when death hath taken away the use of my tongue, yet my heart may cry and say unto Thee, 'Lord! into Thy hands I commend my soul; Lord Jesu! receive my spirit!' Amen."[1]

This is one of the most beautiful prayers handed down to us in Christian times.

Cromwell having finished his prayer and being now ready, a stroke of the axe severed his head from his body.

Thus died a man who, although he had risen from the lowliest to the loftiest estate, never allowed himself to be seduced by pride, nor made giddy by the pomps of the world, who continued attached to his old acquaintances, and was eager to honour the meanest who had rendered him any service; a man who powerfully contributed to the establishment of Protestantism in England, although his enemies, unaware of the very different meanings of the words "Catholicism" and "Popery," took pleasure in circulating the report in Europe, after his death, that he died a Roman Catholic; a man who for eight years governed his country, the king, the parliament, and convocation, who had the direction of all domestic as well as foreign affairs; who executed what he had advised, and who, in spite of the blots which he himself lamented, was one of the most intelligent, most active, and most influential of English ministers. It is said that the king ere long regretted him. However this may be, he protected his son and gave him proofs of his favours, doubtless in remembrance of his father.

Another nobleman, Walter, lord Hungerford, was beheaded at the same time with Cromwell, for having endeavoured to ascertain, by "conjuring," how long the king would live.

[1] Foxe, v. p. 403. It is possible that the prayer may have been written in the prison.

CHAPTER SIX

The Divorce of Anne of Cleves
(1540)

THE Catholic party was triumphant. It had set aside the Protestant queen and sacrificed the Protestant minister; and it now proceeded to take measures of a less startling character, but which were a more direct attack on the very work of the Reformation. It thought proper to put to death some of those zealous men who were boldly preaching the pure Gospel, not only for the sake of getting rid of them, but even more for the purpose of terrifying those who were imitating them or who were willing to do so.

Of these men, Barnes, Garret, and Jerome were best known. They were in prison; but Henry had hitherto scrupled about sacrificing men who preached a doctrine opposed to the pope. The party, moreover, united all their forces to bring about the fall of Cromwell, who had been confined within the same walls. After his death, the death of the preachers followed as a matter of course; it was merely the corollary; it was a natural consequence, and needed no special demonstration; the sentence, according to the Romish party, had only to be pronounced to be evidently justified. On these principles the king's council and the parliament proceeded; and two days after the execution of Cromwell, these three evangelists, without any public hearing, without knowing any cause of their condemnation, without receiving any communication whatsoever, were taken out of prison, July 30, 1540, to be conducted to Smithfield, where they were to be deprived, not only of their ministry, but of their lives.

Henry, however, was not free from uneasiness. He had openly asserted that he leaned neither to one side nor to the other; that he weighed both parties in a just balance; and now, while he is boasting of his impartiality, everybody persists in saying that he gives all the advantage to the papists. What

is he to do in order to be just and impartial? Three papists
must be found to be put to death at the same time with the
evangelicals. Then nobody will venture to assert that the
king does not hold the balance even. The measure shall be
faultless and one of the glories of his reign. The three papists
selected to be placed in the other scale bore the names of
Abel, Powel, and Fetherstone. The first two were political
pamphleteers who had supported the cause of Catherine of
Aragon; and the third was, like them, an opponent of royal
supremacy. It seems that in this matter the king also made
allowance for the composition of his own council, which
comprised both friends and enemies of the Reformation.
Amongst the former were the archbishop of Canterbury, the
duke of Suffolk, viscounts Beauchamp and Lisle, Russell,
Paget, Sadler, and Audley. Amongst the latter were the
bishops of Winchester and Durham, the duke of Norfolk, the
earl of Southampton, Sir Anthony Browne, Paulet, Baker,
Richard, and Wingfield. There was therefore a majority of
one against the Reformation, just enough to turn the scale.
Henry, with a show of impartiality, assigned three victims
to each of these parties. Preparations were made at the Tower
for carrying out this equitable sentence. In the courtyard
were three hurdles, of oblong shape, formed of branches of
trees closely intertwined, on which the culprits were to be
drawn to the place of execution. Why three only, as there
were six condemned? The reason was soon to be seen. When
the three prisoners of each side were brought out, they
proceeded to lay one evangelical on the first hurdle, and by
his side a papist, binding them properly to each other to
keep them in this strange coupling. The same process was
gone through with the second and the third hurdles; they
then set out, and the six prisoners were drawn two and two
to Smithfield. Thus, in every street through which the
procession passed, Henry VIII proclaimed by this strange
spectacle that his government was impartial, and condemned
alike the two classes of divines and of doctrines.

The three hurdles reached Smithfield. Two and two, the
prisoners were unbound, and the three evangelicals were
conducted to the stake. No trial having been allowed them
by the court, these upright and pious men felt it their duty

to supply its place at the foot of the scaffold. The day of their death thus became for them the day of hearing. The tribunal was sitting and the assembly was large. Barnes was the first speaker. He said: "I am come hither to be burned as a heretic. . . . God I take to record, I never (to my knowledge) taught any erroneous doctrine . . . and I neither moved nor gave occasion of any insurrection. . . . I believe in the Holy and Blessed Trinity; . . . and that this blessed Trinity sent down the second person, Jesus Christ, into the womb of the most blessed and purest Virgin Mary. . . . I believe that through His death he overcame sin, death and hell; and that there is none other satisfaction to the Father, but this His death and passion only." At these words Barnes, deeply moved, raised his hands to heaven, and prayed God to forgive him his sins. This profession of faith did not satisfy the sheriff. Then some one asked him what he thought of praying to the saints. "I believe," answered Barnes, "that they are worthy of all the honour that Scripture willeth them to have. But, I say, throughout all Scripture we are not commanded to pray to any saints. . . . If saints do pray for us, then I trust to pray for you within the next half-hour." He was silent, and the sheriff said to him: "Well, have you anything more to say?" He answered: "Have ye any articles against me for the which I am condemned?" The sheriff answered: "No." Barnes then put the question to the people whether any knew wherefore he died. No one answered. Then he resumed: "They that have been the occasion of it, I pray God forgive them, as I would be forgiven myself. And Doctor Stephen, bishop of Winchester that now is, if he have sought or wrought this my death, either by word or deed, I pray God forgive him. . . . I pray that God may give [the king] prosperity, and that he may long reign among you; and after him that godly prince Edward may so reign that he may finish those things that his father hath begun."[1] Then collecting himself, Barnes addressed three requests to the sheriff, the prayer of a dying man. The first was that the king might employ the wealth of the abbeys which had been poured into the treasury in relieving his poor subjects who were in great need of it. The second was that marriage might be respected, and that men

[1] Foxe, *Acts*, v. p. 435.

might not live in uncleanness. The third, that the name of God might not be taken in vain in abominable oaths. These prayers of a dying man, who was sent to the scaffold by Henry himself, ought to have produced some impression on the heart of the king. Jerome and Garret likewise addressed affecting exhortations to the people. After this, these three Christians uttered together their last prayer, shook hands with and embraced one another, and then meekly gave themselves up to the executioner. They were bound to the same stake, and breathed their last in patience and in faith.

On the same day, at the same hour, and at the same place where the three friends of the Gospel were burnt, the three followers of the pope, Abel, Fetherstone, and Powel were hanged. A foreigner who was present exclaimed: "What strange people live here? Here they hang papists, there they burn anti-papists!" The simple-minded and ignorant asked what kind of religion people should have in England, seeing that both Romanism and Protestantism led to death. A courtier exclaimed: "Verily, henceforth I will be of the king's religion, that is to say, of none at all!"

Cromwell and these six men were not to be the only objects of the king's displeasure. Even before they had undergone their sentence, the king had caused his divorce to be pronounced. In marrying Anne of Cleves, his chief object had been to form an alliance with the Protestants against the Emperor. Now these two opponents were by this time reconciled with each other. Henry, therefore, deeply irritated, no longer hesitated to rid himself of the new queen. He was influenced, moreover, by another motive. He was smitten with the charms of another woman. However, as he dreaded the raillery, the censures, and even the calamities which the divorce might bring upon him, he was anxious not to appear as the originator of it, and should the accusation be made, to be able to repel it as a foul imposture without shadow of reality. He resolved, therefore, to adopt such a course that this strange proceeding should seem to have been imposed upon him. This intention he hinted to one of the lords in whom he had full confidence; and the latter made some communications about it, on July 3, to the Privy Council. On the 6th his Majesty's ministers pointed out to the upper house the propriety of their humbly requesting the king, in conjunction with the lower house, that the convocation of the clergy might examine into his marriage with Anne of Cleves, and see whether it were valid. The lords adopted the proposal; and a commission consisting of the lord chancellor, the archbishop of Canterbury, and the dukes of Norfolk and Suffolk, presented it to the commons, who gave their assent to it. Consequently the whole house of lords and a commission of twenty members of the lower house appeared before the king, and stated that the matter about which they had to confer with him was of such an important character that they must first request his permission to lay it before them. Henry, feigning utter ignorance of what they meant, commanded them to speak. They then said,—"We humbly pray your Majesty to allow the validity of your marriage to be investigated by the convocation of the clergy; we attach all the more importance to this proceeding because the question bears upon the succession to the throne of your Majesty." It was well known that the king did not love Anne, and that he was even in love with another. This is a striking instance of the degree of meanness to which Henry VIII had reduced his parliament; for an assembly, even if some mean souls are to be found in it, undertakes not to be despicable, and what is noblest in it usually comes to the surface. But if the shameful compliances of the parliament astonish us, the audacious hypocrisy of Henry VIII surprises us still more. He stood up to answer as if in the presence of the Deity; and concealing his real motives he said,—"There is nothing in the world more dear to me than the glory of God, the good of England, and the declaration of the truth." All the actors in this comedy played their parts to perfection. The king immediately sent to Richmond some of his councillors, amongst them Suffolk and Gardiner, to communicate to the queen the demand of the parliament and to ascertain her opinion with respect to it. Without delay, Anne gave her consent to the proposal.

The next day, July 7, the matter was brought before convocation by Gardiner, bishop of Winchester, who was very anxious to see a Roman Catholic queen upon the throne of England. A committee was nominated for the purpose of examining the witnesses; and of this committee the bishop was a member. An autograph declaration of the king was produced, in which he dwelt strongly on the fact that he took such a dislike to Anne as soon as he saw her that he thought instantly of breaking off the match; that he never inwardly consented to the marriage, and that in fact it had never been consummated. Within two days all the witnesses were heard. Henry was impatient; and the Roman party urgently appealed to the assembly to deliver a judgment which would rid England of a Protestant queen. Cranmer, out of fear or feebleness (he had just seen Cromwell lose his head), went with the rest of them.

On July 9, convocation, relying upon the two reasons given by the king, and upon the fact that there was something ambiguous in Anne's engagement with the son of the duke of Lorraine, decided that his Majesty "was at liberty to contract another marriage for the good of the realm." None of these reasons had any validity. Nor did Henry escape the condemnation and the raillery which he had so much feared. "It appears," said Francis I, "that over there they are pleased to do with their women as with their geldings,—bring a number of them together and make them trot, and then take the one which goes easiest."

The archbishop of Canterbury on July 10 reported to the upper house that convocation had declared the marriage null and void by virtue both of the law of God and of the law of England. The bishop of Winchester read the judgment and explained at length the grounds of it, and the house declared itself satisfied. The archbishop and the bishop made the same report to the commons. On the following day— Henry did not intend that any time should be lost—the lord chancellor, the duke of Norfolk, the earl of Southampton, and the bishop of Winchester betook themselves to Richmond again, and informed Anne, on the king's behalf, of the proceedings of parliament and of convocation. Anne was distressed by the communication. She had supposed that the clergy would acknowledge, as it was their duty to do, the validity of her marriage. However it may be, so sharp was the stroke that she fainted away. The necessary care was bestowed on her, and she recovered, and gradually reconciled herself to the thought of submission to Henry's will. The

delegates told her that the king, while requiring her to renounce the title of queen, conferred on her that of his adopted
sister, and gave her precedence in rank of all the ladies of the
court, immediately after the queen and the daughters of the
king. Anne was modest; she did not think highly of herself,
and had often felt that she was not made to be queen of
England. She therefore submitted, and the same day, July 11,
wrote to the king,—"Though this case must needs be most
hard and sorrowful unto me, for the great love which I bear
to your most noble person, yet having more regard to God
and His truth than to any worldly affection, as it beseemed
me. . . . I knowledge myself hereby to accept and approve
the same [determination of the clergy] wholly and entirely
putting myself, for my state and condition, to your Highness's
goodness and pleasure; most humbly beseeching your Majesty
. . . to take me for one of your most humble servants." She
subscribed herself "Your Majesty's most humble sister and
servant, Anne of Cleves."

The king sent word to her that he conferred on her a
pension of four thousand pounds a year, and the palace at
Richmond. Anne wrote to him again, July 16, to thank him
for his great kindness, and at the same time sent him her ring.
She preferred—and herein she showed some pride—to remain
in England, rather than to go home after such a disgrace had
fallen upon her. "I account God pleased," she wrote to her
brother, "with what is done, and know myself to have suffered
no wrong or injury. . . . I find the king's Highness . . . to be as
a most kind, loving and friendly father and brother. . . . I
am so well content and satisfied, that I much desire my
mother, you, and other mine allies so to understand it, accept
and take it." Seldom has a woman carried self-renunciation to
such a length.

CHAPTER SEVEN

Catherine Howard, the Fifth Queen

(1540)

WHO should take the place of the repudiated queen? This was the question discussed at court and in the town. The Anglican Catholics, delighted at the dismissal of the Protestant queen, were determined to do all they possibly could to place on the throne a woman of their own party. Such a one was already found. The bishop of Winchester, for some time past, had frequently been holding feasts and entertainments for the king. To these he invited a young lady, who though of small stature was of elegant carriage, and had handsome features and a graceful figure and manners. She was the fifth child and second daughter of Lord Edmund Howard, and niece of the duke of Norfolk, the leader of the Catholic party. She very soon attracted the attention of the king, who took increasing pleasure in her society. This occurred before the divorce of Anne. "It is a certain fact," says a contemporary, "that about the same time many citizens of London saw the king very frequently in the daytime, and sometimes at midnight, pass over to her on the river Thames in a little boat. . . . The citizens regarded all this not as a sign of divorcing the queen, but of adultery."[1] Whether this supposition was well founded or not we cannot say. The king, when once he had decided on a separation from Anne of Cleves, had thought of her successor. He was quite determined, after his mischance, to be guided neither by his ministers, nor by his ambassadors, nor by political considerations, but solely by his own eyes, his own tastes, and the happiness he might hope for. Catherine pleased him very much; and his union with Anne was no sooner annulled than he proceeded to his fifth marriage. The nuptials were celebrated

[1] *Original Letters relative to the English Reformation* (Parker Society), i, p. 202.

430

on the 8th of August, eleven days after the execution of Cromwell; and on the same day Catherine was presented at court as queen. The king was charmed with Catherine Howard, his pretty young wife; she was so amiable, her intercourse was so pleasant, that he believed he had, after so many more or less unfortunate attempts, found his ideal at last. Her virtuous sentiments, the good behaviour which she resolved to maintain filled him with delight; and he was ever expressing his happiness in "having obtained such a jewel of womanhood." He had no foreboding of the terrible blow which was soon to shatter all this happiness.

The new queen was distinguished from the former chiefly by the difference in religion, with a corresponding difference in morality. The niece of the duke of Norfolk, Gardiner's friend, was of course an adherent of the Catholic faith; and the Catholic party hailed her as at once the symbol and the instrument of reaction. They had had plenty of Protestant queens, Anne Boleyn, Jane Seymour, and Anne of Cleves. Now that they had a Catholic queen, Catholicism—many said popery—would recover its power. Henry was so much enamoured of his new spouse that, in honour of her, he once more became a fervent Catholic. He celebrated all the Saints' days, frequently received the holy sacrament, and publicly offered thanksgiving to God for this happy union which he hoped to enjoy for a long time. The conversion of Henry, for the change was nothing less, brought with it a change of policy. He now abandoned France and the German Protestants in order to ally himself with the Empire; and we find him ere long busily engaged in a project for the marriage of his daughter Mary to the Emperor Charles V. This project, however, came to nothing. Gardiner, Norfolk, and the other leaders of the Catholic party, rejoicing in the breeze which bore their vessel onward, set all sails to the wind. Just after the divorce of Anne of Cleves, and by way of a first boon to the Romish party, the penalties for impure living imposed on the priests and nuns were mitigated. In contempt of the authority of Holy Scripture as well as of that of parliament itself, Henry got an Act passed by virtue of which every determination concerning faith, worship, and ceremonies, adopted with the sanction of the king by a commission of archbishops, bishops, and other ecclesiastics nominated by him, was to be received, believed, and observed by the whole nation, just as if parliament had approved every one of these articles, even if this decree were contrary to former usages and ordinances. This was a proclamation of infallibility in England, for the benefit of the pope-king, under cover of which he might found a religion to his own taste. Cranmer had established in all cathedral churches professors entrusted with the teaching of Hebrew and Greek, in order that students might become well acquainted with sacred literature, and that the church might never want ministers capable of edifying it. But the enemies of the Reformation, who now enjoyed royal favour, fettered or abolished this institution and other similar ones, to the great damage both of religion and the country. On the other hand, the Catholic ceremonies, abrogated by Cranmer and Cromwell —the consecration of bread and of water, the embers with which the priest marked the foreheads of the faithful, the palm-branches blessed on Palm-Sunday, the tapers carried at Candlemas, and other like customs—were re-established; and penalties were imposed on those who should neglect them. A new edition of the *Institution of a Christian Man* explained to the people the king's doctrine. It treated of the seven sacraments, the mass, transubstantiation, the salutation of the Virgin, and other doctrines of the kind to which conformity was required. At length, as if with a view to ensure the permanence of this system, Bonner was made bishop of London; and this man, who had been the most abject flatterer and servant of Cromwell during his life, turned about after his death and became the persecutor of those whom Cromwell had protected.

At the spectacle of this reaction, so marvellous in their eyes, the Anglican Catholics and even the papists broke out with joy, and awaited with impatience "the crowning of the edifice." England, in their view, was saved. The church was triumphant. But while there was rejoicing on the one side, there was mourning on the other. The establishment of superstitious practices, the prospect of the penalties contained in the statute of the Six Articles, penalties which had not yet been enforced but were on the point of being so, spread distress and alarm among the evangelicals. Those who did not add to their faith manly energy shut up their convictions in their own breasts, carefully abstained from conversation on religious subjects, and looked with suspicion upon every stranger, fearing that he might be one of Gardiner's spies.

Bonner was active and eager, going forward in pursuit of his object and allowing nothing to check him. Cromwell and Cranmer, to whom he used to make fair professions, believed that he was capable of being of service to the Reformation, and therefore gave him promotion in ecclesiastical offices. But no sooner had Cromwell been put in prison than his signal deceitfulness showed itself. Grafton, who printed the Bible under the patronage of the vicegerent, having met Bonner, to whom Cromwell had introduced him, exclaimed, "How grieved I am to hear that lord Cromwell has been sent to the Tower!" "It would have been much better," replied Bonner, "if he had been sent there long ago." Shortly after, Grafton was cited before the council, and was accused of having printed, by Cromwell's order, certain suspected verses; and Bonner, for the purpose of aggravating his criminality, did not fail to report what the accused had said to him about the man who had been his own personal benefactor. The chancellor, however, a friend of Grafton, succeeded in saving the printer of the Bible. Bonner indemnified himself for this disappointment by persecuting a great many citizens of London. He vented his rage especially on a poor youth of fifteen, ignorant and uncultivated, named Richard Mekins, whom he accused of having spoken against the Eucharist and in favour of Barnes; but the grand jury found him "not guilty." Hereupon Bonner became furious. "You are perjured," he said to the jury. "The witnesses do not agree," they replied. "The one deposed that Mekins had said the sacrament was nothing but a *ceremony;* and the other that it was nothing but a *signification.*" "But did he not say," exclaimed the bishop, "that Barnes died holy?" "But we cannot find these words," said the jury, "to be against the statute." Upon which Bonner cursed and was in a great rage. "Retire again," he said, "consult together, and bring in the bill." Mekins was condemned to die. In vain was it shown that he was a poor ignorant creature and that he had done nothing worse than repeat what he had heard, and this without even understanding it. In vain, too, did his father and mother, who were in great distress, attempt to mitigate the harsh treatment to which he was subjected in prison. The poor lad was ready to say or do anything to escape being burnt. They made him speak well of Bonner and of his great charity towards him; they made him declare that he hated all heretics, and then they burnt him. This was only the beginning, and Bonner hoped by such proceedings to prepare the way for greater triumphs.

The persecution became more general. Two hundred and two persons were prosecuted in thirty-nine London parishes. The offences were such as the following—having read the Holy Scriptures aloud in the churches; having refused to carry palm-branches on Palm Sunday; having had one or other of their kinsfolk buried without the masses for the dead; having received Latimer, Barnes, Garret, or other evangelicals; having held religious meetings in their houses of an evening; having said that the holy sacrament was a good thing, but was not, as some asserted, God Himself; having spoken much about the Holy Scriptures; having declared that they liked better to hear a sermon than a mass; and other the like offences. Among the delinquents were some of the priests. One of these was accused of having caused suspected persons to be invited to his sermons by his beadle, without having the bells rung; another of having preached without the orders of his superior; others, of not making use of holy water, of not going in procession, and so on.[1]

The inquisition which was made at this time was so rigorous that all the prisons of London would not hold the accused. They had to place some of them in the halls of various buildings. The case was embarrassing. The Catholics of the court were not alone in instigating the king to persecution. Francis I sent word to him by Wallop, "that it had well liked him to hear that his Majesty *was reforming* the Lutheran sect, for that he was ever of opinion that no good could come of them but much evil." But there were other influences at court besides that of Francis I, Norfolk, and Gardiner. Lord Audley obtained the king's sanction for the release of the prisoners, who, however, had to give their promise to appear at the Star Chamber on All Souls' Day. Ultimately they were let alone.

---

[1] Foxe, in his *Acts*, v. pp. 443–49, gives the names of all these persons, naming also their parishes and their offences.

But this does not mean that all the evangelicals were spared. Two ministers were at this time distinguished both for their high connexions and for their faith and eloquence. One of these was the Scotsman, Alexander Seaton, chaplain to the duke of Suffolk. Preaching powerfully at St. Antholin's church, in London, he said,—"*Of ourselves we can do nothing*, says St. Paul; *I pray thee, then, where is thy will? Art thou better than Paul, James, Peter, and all the apostles?* Hast thou any more grace than they? Tell me now if thy will be anything or nothing? . . . Paul said he could do nothing. . . . If you ask me when we will leave preaching only Christ, even when they do leave to preach that works do merit, and suffer Christ to be a whole satisfier and only mean to our justification." Seaton was condemned to bear a faggot at Paul's Cross. Another minister, Dr. Crome, was a learned man and a favourite of the archbishop. This did not prevent the king from commanding him to preach that the sacrifice of the mass is useful both for the living and the dead. Crome preached the Gospel in its simplicity at St. Paul's on the appointed day, and contented himself with reading the king's order after the sermon. He was immediately forbidden to preach.

Laymen were treated with greater severity. Bibles, it is known, had been placed in all the churches, and were fastened by chains to the pillars. A crowd of people used to gather about one of these pillars. On one occasion a young man of fine figure, possessed of great zeal, and gifted with a powerful voice, stood near the pillar holding the Bible in his hands, and reading it aloud so that all might hear him. His name was John Porter. Bonner sharply rebuked him. "I trust I have done nothing against the law," said Porter; and this was true. But the bishop committed him to Newgate. There this young Christian was put in irons; his legs, his arms, and his head were attached to the wall by means of an iron collar. One of his kinsmen, by a gift of money, induced the gaoler to deliver him from this punishment; and the favour they accorded him was to place him in the company of thieves and murderers. Porter exhorted them to repent, and taught them the way of salvation. The unhappy man was then cast into the deepest dungeon, was cruelly treated, and loaded with irons. Eight days afterwards he died. Cries and groans had been heard in the night. Some said that he had been subjected to the torture called "the devil on the neck," a horrible instrument by which, in three or four hours, the back and the whole body were torn in pieces.

Meanwhile, a far more formidable blow was preparing. Cromwell, the lay protector of the Reformation, had already been sacrificed; its ecclesiastical protector, Cranmer, must now fall in the same way. This second blow seemed easier than the first. Since the fall of Cromwell, men of the utmost moderation thought "there was no hope that reformed religion should any one week longer stand." All those of feeble character sided with the opposite party. Cranmer alone, amongst the bishops and the ecclesiastical commissioners of the king, still upheld evangelical truth. This obstacle in the way of the extension of English catholicism must be utterly overthrown.

Plot after plot was formed against him, but Cranmer's foes retired baffled. New plans were concocted. Doctor London and other agents of the party which looked up to Gardiner as its head took in hand to go over the diocese of the archbishop with a view to collecting all the sayings and all the facts, true or false, which they might turn to account as weapons against him. In one place a conversation was reported to them; in another a sermon was denounced; elsewhere neglected ritual was talked about. "Three of the preachers of the cathedral church," they were told, namely, Ridley, Drum and Scory, "are attacking the ceremonies of the church." Some of the canons, opponents of the primate, brought various charges against him, and strove to depict his marriage in the most repulsive colours. Sir John Gostwick, whose accounts as treasurer of war and of the court were not correct, accused Cranmer before the parliament of being the pastor of heretics.[1] All these grievances were set forth in a memorial which was presented to the king. At the same time, the most influential members of the privy council declared to the king that the realm was infested with heresies; that thereby "horrible commotions and uproars" might spring up, as had been the case in Germany; and that these calamities must be chiefly imputed to the archbishop of Canterbury, who both by his own preaching and that of his chaplains had filled England

[1] [Probably the Parliament of 1544–45]

with pernicious doctrines. "Who is his accuser?" said the king. The lords replied: "Forasmuch as Cranmer is a councillor, no man durst take upon him to accuse him. But if it please your Highness to commit him to the Tower for a time, there would be accusations and proofs enough against him." "Well then," said the king, "I grant you leave to commit him to-morrow to the Tower for his trial." The enemies of the archbishop and of the Reformation went away well content.

Meanwhile, Henry VIII began to reflect on the answer which he had given to his councillors. There is nothing to show that it was not made in earnest; but he foresaw that Cranmer's death would leave an awkward void. When Cranmer was gone, how should he maintain the conflict with the pope and the papists, with whom he had no mind to be reconciled? The primate's character and services came back to his memory. Time was passing. At midnight the king, unable to sleep, sent for Sir Antony Denny and said to him, "Go to Lambeth and command the archbishop to come forthwith to the court." Henry then, in a state of excitement, began to walk about in one of the corridors of the palace, awaiting the arrival of Cranmer. At length the primate entered and the king said to him: "Ah, my lord of Canterbury, I can tell you news. . . . It is determined by me and the council, that you to-morrow at nine o'clock shall be committed to the Tower, for that you and your chaplains (as information is given us) have taught and preached, and thereby sown within the realm such a number of execrable heresies, that it is feared the whole realm being infected with them no small contentions and commotions will rise thereby amongst my subjects, . . . and therefore the council have requested me, for the trial of this matter, to suffer them to commit you to the Tower."

The story of Cromwell was to be repeated, and this was the first step. Nevertheless, Cranmer did not utter a word of opposition or supplication. Kneeling down before the king, according to his custom, he said: "I am content, if it please your Grace, with all my heart to go thither at your Highness' commandment, and I most humbly thank your Majesty that I may come to my trial, for there be that have many ways slandered me, and now this way I hope to show myself not worthy of such a report." The king, touched by his uprightness, said: "Oh Lord, what manner of man be you! What simplicity is in you! . . . Do you not know . . . how many great enemies you have? Do you consider what an easy thing it is to procure three or four false knaves to witness against you? Think you to have better luck that way than Christ your master had? I see it, you will run headlong to your undoing, if I would suffer you. Your enemies shall not so prevail against you, for I have otherwise devised with myself to keep you out of their hands. Yet, notwithstanding, to-morrow when the council shall sit and send for you, resort unto them; and if in charging you with this matter they do commit you to the Tower, require of them . . . that you may have your accusers brought before them and that you may answer their accusations. . . . If no entreaty or reasonable request will serve, then deliver unto them this ring"—the king at the same time delivered his ring to the archbishop— "and say unto them: If there be no remedy, my lords, but that I must needs go to the Tower, then I revoke my cause from you and appeal to the king's own person by this his token to you all. So soon as they shall see this my ring, they know it so well, that they shall understand that I have resumed the whole cause into mine own hands." The archbishop was so much moved by the king's kindness that he "had much ado to forbear tears." "Well," said the king, "go your ways, my lord, and do as I have bidden you." The archbishop bent his knee in expression of his gratitude, and taking leave of the king returned to Lambeth before day.

On the morrow, about eight o'clock, the council sent an usher of the palace to summon the archbishop. He set out forthwith and presented himself at the door of the council chamber. But his colleagues, glad to complete the work which they had begun by putting the vicegerent to death, were not content with sending the primate to the scaffold; but were determined to subject Cranmer to various humiliations before the final catastrophe. The archbishop could not be let in, but was compelled to wait there among the pages, lackeys, and other servingmen. Doctor Butts, the king's physician, happening to pass through the room, and observing how the archbishop was treated, went to the king and said: "My lord of Canterbury, if it please your Grace, is well promoted; for now he is become a lackey or a serving-man, for yonder he standeth this halfhour without the council-chamber door amongst them." "It is not so," said the king, "I trow, nor the council hath not so little discretion as to use the metropolitan of the realm in that sort, specially being one of their own number; but let them alone, and we shall hear more soon."

At length the archbishop was admitted. He did as the king had bidden him; and when he saw that none of his statements or reasons were of any avail with the council, he presented the king's ring, appealing at the same time to his Majesty. Here-upon, the whole council was struck with astonishment; and the earl of Bedford, who was not one of Gardiner's party, with a solemn oath exclaimed: "When you first began this matter, my lords, I told you what would come of it. Do you think that the king will suffer this man's finger to ache? Much more, I warrant you, will he defend his life against brabbling varlets. You do but cumber yourselves to hear tales and fables against him." The members of the council immediately rose and carried the king's ring to him, thus surrendering the matter, according to the usage of the time, into his hands.

When they had all come into the presence of the king, he said to them with a severe countenance: "Ah, my lords, I thought I had had wiser men of my council than now I find you. What discretion was this in you, thus to make the primate of the realm, and one of you in office, to wait at the council-chamber door amongst serving-men? . . . You had no such commission of me to handle him. I was content that you should try him as a councillor, and not as a mean subject. But now I well perceive that things be done against him maliciously; and if some of you might have had your minds, you would have tried him to the uttermost. But I do you all to wit, and protest, that if a prince may be beholding unto his subject" and (here Henry laid his hand solemnly upon his breast), "by the faith I owe to God, I take this man here, my lord of Canterbury, to be of all other a most faithful subject unto us, and one to whom we are much beholding." The Catholic members of the council were disconcerted, confused, and unable to make any answer. One or two of them, however, took courage, made excuses, and assured the king that their object in trying the primate was to clear him of the calumnies of the world, and not to proceed against him maliciously. The king, who was not to be imposed upon by these hypocritical assertions, said: "Well, well, my lords, take him and well use him, as he is worthy to be, and make no more ado." All the lords then went up to Cranmer, and took him by the hand as if they had been his dearest friends. The archbishop, who was of a conciliatory disposition, forgave them. But the king sent to prison for a certain time some of the archbishop's accusers; and he sent a message to Sir John Gostwick, to the effect that he was a wicked varlet, and that unless he made his apologies to the metropolitan, he would make of him an example which should be a warning to all false accusers. These facts are creditable to Henry VIII. It was doubtless his aim to keep a certain middle course; and like many other despots he had happy intervals.

At the end of August 1541, Henry went to York, for the purpose of holding an interview with his nephew, the king of Scotland, whom he was anxious to persuade to declare himself independent of the pope. Henry made magnificent preparations for his reception; but Cardinal Beaton prevented the young prince from going. This excited the bitterest discontent in Henry's mind, and became afterwards the cause of a breach. The queen, who accompanied him, endeavoured to divert him from his vexation; and the king, more and more pleased with his marriage, after his return to London, made public thanksgiving on All Saints Day (October 24) that God had given him so amiable and excellent a wife, and even requested the bishop of Lincoln to join in his commendations of her. This excessive satisfaction was ere long to be interrupted.

During the king's journey, one John Lascelles, who had a married sister living in the county of Sussex, paid her a visit. This woman had formerly been in the service of the old duchess of Norfolk, grandmother to the queen, and by whom Catherine had been brought up. In the course of conversation the brother and sister talked about this young lady, whom the sister had known well, and who had now become wife to the king. The brother, ambitious for his sister's advancement, said to her: "You ought to ask the queen to place

you among her attendants." "I shall certainly not do
so," she answered; "I cannot think of the queen but with
sadness." "Why?" "She is so frivolous in character and
in life." "How so?" Then the woman related that Catherine
had had improper intercourse with one of the officers of the
ducal house of Norfolk, named Francis Derham; and that she
had been very familiar with another whose name was Manox.
Lascelles perceived the importance of these statements; and
as he could not take upon himself the responsibility of concealing them, he determined to report them to the archbishop.
The communication greatly embarrassed Cranmer. If he
should keep the matter secret and it should afterwards become
known, he would be ruined. Nor would he less certainly be
ruined if he should divulge it, and then no proof be forth-
coming. But what chiefly weighed upon his mind was the
thought of the agitation which would be excited. To think of
another wife of the king executed at the Tower! To think
of this prince, his country, and perhaps also the work which
was in process of accomplishment in England, becoming the
objects of ridicule and perhaps of abhorrence! As he was
unwilling to assume alone the responsibility imposed by so
grave a communication, he opened his mind on the subject
to the lord chancellor and to other members of the privy
council, to whom the king had entrusted the despatch of
business during his absence. "They were greatly troubled and
inquieted." After having well weighed the reasons for and
against, they came to the conclusion that, as this matter
mainly concerned the king, Cranmer should inform him of it.
This was a hard task to undertake; and the archbishop, who
was deeply affected, durst not venture to make *viva voce* so
frightful a communication. He therefore put down in writing
the report which had been made to him, and had it laid
before the king. The latter was terribly shocked; but as he
tenderly loved his wife and had a high opinion of her virtue,
he said that it was a calumny. However, he privately assembled
in his cabinet the lord privy seal, the lord admiral, Sir Anthony
Browne, and Sir Thomas Wriothesley, a friend of the duke of
Norfolk, who had taken a leading part in the divorce of Anne
of Cleves, and laid the case before them, declaring at the same
time that he did not believe in it. These lords privately

examined Lascelles and his sister, who persisted in their depositions; next Manox and Derham, who asserted the truth of their statements; the latter, moreover, mentioning three of the duchess of Norfolk's women who likewise had knowledge of the facts. The members of the council made their report to the king, who, pierced with grief, remained silent for some time. At length he burst into tears, and commanded the duke of Norfolk, the queen's uncle, the archbishop of Canterbury, the high chamberlain, and the bishop of Winchester, who had promoted the marriage, to go to Catherine and examine her. At first she denied everything. But when Cranmer was sent to her, on the evening of the first inquisition, the words of the primate, his admonitions, the reports which he made to her, which proved that her conduct was perfectly well known, convinced her of the uselessness of her denials, and she then made full confession, and even added some strange details. It does not appear that the queen felt it her duty to confess her offences to God, but she resolved at least to confess them to men. While making her confession she was in a state of so great agitation that the archbishop was in dread every moment of her losing her reason. He thought, according to her confessions, that she had been seduced by the infamous Derham, with the privity even of his own wife. The household of the duchess dowager of Norfolk appears to have been very disorderly. Cranmer wrote down or caused to be written this confession, and Catherine signed it.[1] He had scarcely left the unhappy woman, when she fell into a state of raving delirium.

The king was thrown into great excitement by the news of Catherine's confession of the reality of his misfortune. The very intensity of his love served to increase his trouble and his wrath; but, for all this, some feeling of pity remained in his heart. "Return to her," he said to Cranmer, "and first make use of the strongest expressions to give her a sense of the greatness of her offences; second, state to her what the law provides in such cases, and what she must suffer for her crime; and lastly express to her my feelings of pity and forgiveness." Cranmer returned to Catherine and found her in a fit of agitation so violent that he never remembered—so he wrote to the king—seeing any creature in such a state. The keepers

[1] The confession is given by Burnet, *Hist. Reform.*, iii, p. 224.

told him that this had continued from his departure from her. "It would have pitied," said the good archbishop, "any man's heart in the world to have looked upon her." Indeed, she was almost in a frenzy; she was not without strength, but her strength was that of a frantic person. The archbishop had had too much experience in the cure of souls to adopt the order prescribed by the king. He saw that if he spoke first to her of the crime and its punishment, he might throw her into some dangerous ecstasy, from which she could not be rescued. He therefore began with the last part of the royal message, and told the queen that his Majesty's mercy extended to her, and that he had compassion on her misfortune. Catherine hereupon lifted up her hands, became quiet, and gave utterance to the humblest thanksgivings to the king who showed her so much mercy. She became more self-possessed; continuing, however, to sob and weep. But "after a little pausing, she suddenly fell into a new state of agony, much worse than she was before."[1]

Cranmer, desirous of delivering her from this frightful delirium, said to her: "Some new fantasy has come into your head, madam; pray open it to me." After a time, when her passion subsided and she was capable of speech, she wept freely and said: "Alas, my lord, that I am alive! The fear of death grieved me not so much before, as doth now the remembrance of the king's goodness. For when I remember how gracious and loving a prince I had, I cannot but sorrow; but this sudden mercy, and more than I could have looked for, showed unto me so unworthy at this time, maketh mine offences to appear before mine eyes much more heinous than they did before; and the more I consider the greatness of his mercy, the more I do sorrow in my heart that I should so misorder myself against his Majesty." The fact that the compassion of the king touched Catherine more than the fear of a trial and of death, seemed to indicate a state of mind less wayward than one might have expected. But in vain Cranmer said to her everything calculated to pacify her; she remained for a long time "in a great pang;" and even fell soon into another fearful state of agitation. At length, in the afternoon she came gradually to herself, and was in a quiet state till

[1] Cranmer, *Works* (Parker Society), ii. p. 408.

night. Cranmer, during this interval of relief, had "good communications with her." He rejoiced at having brought her into some quiet. She told him that there had been a marriage contract between her and Derham, only verbal indeed, she said; but that nevertheless, though never announced and acknowledged, it had been consummated. She added that she had acted under compulsion of that man. At six o'clock, she had another fit of frenzy. "Ah," she said afterwards to Cranmer, "when the clock struck, I remembered the time when Master Heneage was wont to bring me knowledge of his Grace." In consequence of Cranmer's report, Henry commanded that the queen should be conducted to Sion House, where two apartments were to be assigned to her and attendants nominated by the king.

Charges against Catherine were accumulating. She had taken into her service, as queen, the wretched Derham and, employing him as secretary, had often admitted him into her private apartments; and this the council regarded as evidence of adultery. She had also again attached to herself one of the women implicated in her first irregularities. At length it was proved that another gentleman, one Culpepper, a kinsman of her mother, had been introduced, in the king's absence on a journey, into the queen's private apartments by Lady Rochford, at a suspicious hour and under circumstances which usually indicate crime. Culpepper confessed it.

Now began the condemnations and the executions; and Henry VIII included in the trial not only those who were guilty but also the near relatives and servants of the queen, who, though well knowing her offences, had not reported them to the king. On the 7th, the council determined that the duchess-dowager of Norfolk, grandmother to the queen, her uncle, Lord William Howard, her aunts Lady Howard and Lady Bridgewater, together with Alice Wilks, Catherine Tylney, Damport, Walgrave, Malin Tilney, Mary Lascelles, Bulmer, Ashby, Anne Haward and Margaret Benet were all guilty of not having revealed the crime of high treason, and that they should be prosecuted. On the 8th the king ordered that all these persons, Mary Lascelles excepted, should be committed to the Tower; and this was done. Lord William Howard was imprisoned on December 9; the Duchess of

Norfolk on the 10th, and Lady Bridgewater on the 13th. All of them stoutly protested their ignorance and their innocence. On December 10, 1541, Culpepper was beheaded at Tyburn; and the same day Derham was hanged, drawn and quartered.

Meanwhile, the Duke of Norfolk had taken refuge at Kenninghall, about ninety miles from London. On December 15, he wrote to the king, saying that by reason of the offences committed by his family he found himself in the utmost perplexity. Twice in his letter he "prostrates himself at the king's feet;" and he expresses "some hope that your Highness will not conceive any displeasure in your most gentle heart against me; that, God knoweth, never did think thought which might be to your discontentation." There did, however, remain something in the "most gentle heart" of Henry VIII.

Parliament met, by the king's command, on January 16, 1542, to give its attention to this business. Thus it was to the highest national assembly that the king entrusted the regulation of his domestic interests. On January 21, the chancellor introduced in the upper house a bill in which the king was requested not to trouble himself about the matter, considering that it might shorten his life; to declare guilty of high treason the queen and all her accomplices; and to condemn the queen and Lady Rochford to death. The bill passed both houses and received the royal assent.

On February 12, the queen—she was only about twenty years of age—and Lady Rochford, her accomplice, were taken to Tower Hill and beheaded. The queen, while she confessed the offences which had preceded her marriage, protested to the last before God and His holy angels that she had never violated her faith to the king. But her previous offences gave credibility to those which were subsequent to her marriage. With regard to Lady Rochford, the confidant of the queen, she was universally hated. People called to mind the fact that her calumnies had been the principal cause of the death of the innocent Anne Boleyn and of her own husband; and nobody was sorry for her. The king pardoned the old duchess of Norfolk and some others who had been prosecuted for not disclosing the crime.

These events did not call forth within the realm many remarks of a painful kind for Henry VIII; but the great example of immorality presented by the English court lessened the esteem in which it was held in Europe. There was no lack of similar licentiousness in France and elsewhere; but there a veil was thrown over it, while in England it was public talk. Opinion afterwards became severe with regard to the king; and when his conduct to three of his former wives was remembered, people said of the disgrace cast on him by Catherine Howard, that he well deserved it. As for the Catholic party, which had given Catherine to Henry and had cherished the hope that by her influence it should achieve its final triumph, it was greatly mortified. Some Catholics, referring to these offences, have since tried to lessen the abhorrence and the shame of them by saying "that a conspiracy was hatched to bring the queen to the scaffold." But the evidence produced against Catherine is so clear that they have been obliged to alter their tone. Catholicism assuredly has had its virtuous princesses in abundance, but it must be acknowledged that she who became its patroness in England in 1541 did not do it much honour.

The elevation of Catherine Howard to the throne had been followed by an elevation of Catholicism in England; and the fall of this unhappy woman was followed by a depression of the party to which she belonged. This is our reason for dwelling on her history. These last events appear to have given offence at Rome. Pope Paul III displayed more irritation than ever against Henry VIII. One of the king's ambassadors at Venice wrote to him at this time,—"The bishop of Rome is earnestly at work to bring about a union of the Emperor and the king of France for the ruin of your Majesty." The zeal and the caution of Cranmer in the affair of Catherine had greatly increased the king's liking for him. Cranmer, however, was in no haste to take advantage of this to get any bold measures passed in favour of the Reformation. He knew that any such attempt would have had a contrary result. But he lost no opportunity of diffusing in England the principles of the Reformation.

The convocation of the clergy met on 20th of January. On Friday, February 17, the translation of the Holy Scriptures was on the order of the day. The suppression of the English Bible was desired by the majority of the bishops, most of all by Gardiner, who, since the fall of Catherine Howard, felt more than ever the necessity of resisting reformation. As he was unable to re-establish at once the Vulgate as a whole, he endeavoured to retain what he could of it in the translation, so that the people might not understand what they read and might abandon it altogether. He proposed therefore to keep in the English translation one hundred and two Latin words "for the sake of their native meaning and their dignity." Among these words were *Ecclesia, pœnitentia, pontifex, holocaustum, simulacrum, episcopus, confessio, hostia,* and others. In addition to the design which he entertained of preventing the people from understanding what they read, he had still another in regard to such as might understand any part of it. If he was desirous of retaining certain words, this was for the purpose of retaining certain dogmas. "Witness," says Fuller, "the word *Penance*, which according to *vulgar sound*, contrary to the *original sense* thereof, was a *magazine of will-worship*, and brought in much *gain* to the *Priests* who were desirous to *keep* that *word*, because that *word kept them*."[1] Cranmer gave the king warning of the matter; and it was agreed that the bishops should have nothing to do with the translation of the Bible. On March 10 the archbishop informed convocation that it was the king's intention to have the translation examined by the universities of Oxford and Cambridge. The bishops were greatly annoyed; but Cranmer assured them that the king's determination was to be carried out. All the prelates but two protested against this course. This decree, however, had no other object than to get rid of the bishops, for the universities were never consulted. This was obviously a blow struck at the convocation of the clergy.

The change which resulted from the disgrace of the Howards was apparent even in the case of the enemies of the Reformation. Bonner, bishop of London, a man at once violent and fickle, who after the death of Cromwell had suddenly turned against the Reformation, after the death of Catherine made a show of turning in the contrary direction. He published various admonitions and injunctions for the guidance of his diocese. "It is very expedient," he said to the laity, "that whosoever repaireth hither [to the church] to read this book, or any

[1] Fuller, *Church History* (1655), Book v. p. 239.

P(II)

such like, in any other place, he prepare himself chiefly and principally with all devotion, humility and quietness to be edified and made the better thereby." To the clergy he said: "Every parson, vicar and curate shall read over and diligently study every week one chapter of the Bible, . . . proceeding from chapter to chapter, from the beginning of the Gospel of Matthew, to the end of the New Testament. . . . You are to instruct, teach and bring up in learning the best ye can all such children of your parishioners as shall come to you for the same; or at the least to teach them to read English, . . . so that they may thereby the better learn and know how to believe, how to pray, how to live to God's pleasure."

CHAPTER EIGHT

Cranmer Pursues his Task

(1542)

THE principles of the Reformation were spreading more and more, and especially among the London merchants; doubtless because they held more intercourse than other classes with foreigners. These men of business were much better informed than we in our days would suppose. One of them, Richard Hilles, had large business transactions with Strasburg and the rest of Germany; and while engaged in these he paid some attention to theological literature. He not merely read, but formed an opinion of the works which he read, and was thus at the same time merchant and critic. He read the *Ecclesiastical History* of Eusebius, as well as his *Preparation* and *Demonstration;* but he was not satisfied with *Eusebius.* He found in his writings false notions on free will and on the marriage of ministers. On the other hand he was exceedingly pleased with this author's comments on Daniel's seventy weeks. Tertullian charmed him by his simplicity, his piety, and likewise by the soundness of his judgment on the Eucharist; but he found much fault with his work on *Prescriptions against Heretics.*[1] Cyprian edified him by the fulness of his piety; but he was shocked by his overmuch severity, and by his opinions on satisfaction, which in his view were derogatory to the righteousness of Christ. Lactantius he loved as the defender of the cause of God; but he sharply criticized his opinions on the virtue of almsgiving, on the necessity of abstinence from the use of flowers and perfumes, on the method of making up for evil works by good ones, on the millennium, and many other subjects. Origen, Augustine, and

---

[1] Letter from Hilles to Bullinger, of December 18, 1542, the date of Catherine's trial.—*Original Letters relative to the English Reformation* (Parker Society), i. pp. 228, 229.

Jerome were also included in the cycle of his studious labours.[1] Hilles considered it a great loss, even to a merchant, to pursue no studies. He found in them a remedy against the too strong influences of worldly affairs.

For him, however, the essential matter was the study of the Word of God. He used frequently to read and expound it in the houses of evangelical Christians in London. Bishop Gardiner, when examining one of Hilles' neighbours, said to him: "Has not Richard Hilles been every day in your house, teaching you and others like you, and poisoning my flock?" Some ecclesiastics one day called upon him, while making a collection for placing tapers before the crucifix and the sepulchre of Christ in the parish church. He refused to contribute. The priests entreated his kinsmen and friends to urge him not to set himself against a practice which had existed for five centuries. No custom, said he, can prevail against the word of Christ—*They that worship him must worship him in spirit and in truth.* The priests now increased their threatenings, and Hilles left London and went to Strasburg, keeping up at the same time his house of business in London. The reader of Tertullian, Cyprian, Origen, and Augustine, on leaving the banks of the Rhine, went to Frankfort and to Nüremberg to sell his cloth. Moreover he made a good use of the money which he received. "I send herewith to your piety," he wrote to Bullinger, "ten Italian crowns, which I desire to be laid out according to your pleasure, as occasion may offer, upon the poor exiles (rich, however, in Christ), and those especially, if such there be, who are in distress among you."

While laymen thus joined knowledge with faith, and business with teaching, Cranmer was slowly pursuing his task. When parliament met, January 22, 1543, the archbishop introduced *a Bill for the advancement of true religion.* This Act at once prohibited and enjoined the reading of the Bible. Was this intentional or accidental? We are disposed to think it accidental. There were two currents of opinion in England, and both of them reappeared in the laws. Only it is to be noted that the better current was the stronger; it was the good cause which seemed ultimately to gain the ascendancy on this occasion. It was ordered that the Bibles bearing Tyndale's

---

[1] *Original Letters relative to the English Reformation*, pp. 234–35.

name should be suppressed; but the printers still issued his translation with hardly any alteration, shielding it under the names of Matthew, Taverner, Cranmer, and even Tunstall and Heath. It was therefore read everywhere. The Act forbade that anyone should read the Bible to others, either in any church or elsewhere, without the sanction of the king or of some bishop. But at the same time the chancellor of England, officers of the army, the king's judges, the magistrates of any town or borough, and the Speaker of the House of Commons, who were accustomed to take a passage of Scripture as the text of their discourses, were empowered to read it. Further, every person of noble rank, male or female, being head of a family, was permitted to read the Bible or to cause it to be read by one of their domestics, in their own house, their garden or orchard, to their own family. Likewise, every trader or other person being head of a household was allowed to read it in private; but apprentices, workpeople and such like, were to abstain. This enactment, thus interdicting the Bible to the common people, was both impious and absurd; impious in its prohibition, but also absurd, because reading in the family was recommended, and this might be done even by the domestics. The knowledge of the Scriptures might thus reach those to whom they were proscribed.

At the same time, on the demand of Cranmer, the Act of Six Articles was somewhat modified. Those who had infringed its clauses were no longer to be punished with death, if they were laymen; and priests were to incur this penalty only after the third offence. This was certainly no great gain, but the primate obtained what he could.

He also endeavoured to render as harmless as possible the book, *The necessary doctrine and erudition of any Christian Man*, which was published in 1543, and was called *The King's Book*, to distinguish it from *The Institution of a Christian Man* of 1537, which was called *The Bishops' Book*. This book of the king held a middle course between the doctrine of the pope and that of the Reformation, leaning, however, towards the latter. The grace and the mercy of God were established as the principle of our justification. Some reforms were introduced with respect to the worship of images and of the saints; the article on purgatory was omitted; large rights were granted to the church of every country; the vulgar tongue was recognized as necessary to meet the religious wants of the people. Still, many obscurities and errors were to be found in this book.

An event was approaching which would draw the king more decisively to the side of the Reformation. Although he had now made five successive marriages, and had experienced, undoubtedly by his own fault, only a long series of disappointments and vexations, he was once more looking for a wife. A law which had been passed after the discovery of the misconduct of Catherine Howard terrified the maidens of England, even the most innocent among them; they would have been afraid of falling victims to the unjust suspicions of Henry VIII. The new law stated that any unchaste woman marrying a king of England without informing him of her unchastity would be guilty of high treason. Henry now determined to marry a widow.

Catherine Parr, a lady of some thirty years of age, already twice widowed, was now at the court. She was a woman of good sense, of virtuous and amiable character, beautiful, and agreeable in manners. But she was wanting in that human prudence, so necessary at the court, and particularly to the wife of Henry VIII; and hereby she was exposed to great danger. The king was now in a declining state; and his bodily infirmities as well as his irritable temper made it a necessity that some gentle and very considerate wife should take care of him. He married the noble dowager on July 12, 1543; and he found in her the affection and the kind attentions of a virtuous lady. The crown was to Catherine but a poor compensation; but she discharged her duty devotedly, and shed some rays of sunshine over the last years of the king. The queen was favourable to the Reformation, as was likewise her brother, who was created earl of Essex, and her uncle, made Lord Parr of Horton. Cranmer and all those who wished for a real reformation were on the side of the new queen; while Gardiner and his party, including the new chancellor, Wriothesley (now created Baron), taking alarm at this influence which was opposed to them, became more zealous than ever in the maintenance of the old doctrine. These men felt that the power which they had possessed under Catherine Howard might slip out of their hands; and they resolved to spread terror among the friends of the Reformation, not excepting the queen herself, by attacking Cranmer. It was always this man at whom they aimed and struck their blows, nor was this the last time they did so.

The prebendaries of Canterbury and other priests of the same diocese, strongly attached to the Catholic doctrine, and disquieted and shocked by the reforming principles of the archbishop, came to an understanding with Gardiner, held a great many meetings among themselves, and collected a large number of reports hostile to the archbishop. They accused him of having removed images and prohibited the partisans of the old doctrines from preaching; and the rumour was soon everywhere current that "the bishop of Winchester had bent his bow to shoot at some of the head deer." The long list of charges brought against the primate was forwarded to the king. Amongst the accusers were found some members of Cranmer's church, magistrates whom he had laid under obligation to him, and men who almost daily sat at his table. Henry was pained and irritated; he loved Cranmer, but these numerous accusations disturbed him. Taking the document with him, he went out, as if going to take a walk alone on the banks of the Thames. He entered his bark. "To Lambeth," he said to his boatmen. Some of the domestics of the archbishop saw the boat approaching; they recognized the king, and gave information to their master, who immediately came down to pay his respects to his Majesty. Henry invited him to enter the bark; and when they were seated together, the boatmen being at a distance, the king began to lament the growth of heresy, and the debates which would inevitably result from it, and declared that he was determined to find out who was the principal promoter of these false doctrines and to make an example of him. "What think you of it?" he added. "Sir," replied Cranmer, "it is a good resolution; but I entreat you to consider well what heresy is, and not to condemn those as heretics who stand for the Word of God against human inventions." After further explanations, the king said to him: "You are the man who, as I am informed, is the chief encourager of heresy." The king then handed to him the articles of accusation collected by his opponents. Cranmer took the papers and read them. When he had finished, he begged the king to appoint a commission to investigate these grievances, and frankly explained to him his own view of the case. The king, touched by his simplicity and candour, disclosed to him the conspiracy, and promised to nominate a commission; insisting, however, that the primate should be the chief member and that he should proceed against his accusers. Cranmer refused to do this. The commission was nominated, but as some of its members secretly favoured the cause of Cranmer's opponents, it made little progress during the six long weeks of its sittings. At this point the king's favourite physician, and an influential gentleman of the chamber intervened. In consequence, Sir (Dr.) Thomas Legh, a layman of York, who had acquired a reputation for energy and thoroughness during the visitation of the monasteries was introduced into the commission. He made diligent inquiry, and found that men to whom Cranmer had rendered great services were in the number of the conspirators. Cranmer bore himself with great meekness towards them. He declined to confound and put them to shame as the king had required him to do; and the result was that, instead of condemning Cranmer, every one of them acknowledged that he was the first to practise the virtues which he preached to others, and thus showed himself to be a true bishop and a worthy reformer.

As Gardiner and his colleagues had failed in their attempt to bring down the head deer, they determined to indemnify themselves by attacking lesser game. A society of friends of the Gospel had been formed at Oxford, the members of which were leading lowly and quiet lives, but at the same time were making courageous confession of the truth. Fourteen of them were apprehended by Doctor London, supported by the bishop of Winchester. The persecutors chiefly directed their attack against three of these men. Robert Testwood, famed for his musical attainments and attached as a "singing-man" to the chapel of Windsor College, used to speak with respect of Luther, ventured to read the Holy Scriptures, and exhorted his acquaintances not to bow down before dumb images, but to worship only the true and living God. Henry Filmer, a churchwarden, could not endure the fooleries which the priests retailed in the pulpit; and the latter, greatly stung by his criticism, accused him of being so thoroughly corrupted

by heresy that he alone would suffice to poison the whole
nation. Antony Peerson, a priest, preached with so much faith
and eloquence, that the people flocked in crowds to hear him,
both at Oxford and in the surrounding country places.

A fourth culprit at length appeared before the council.
He was a poor man, simple-minded, and of mean appearance.
Some loose sheets of a book lay upon the table in front of the
bishop of Winchester. "John Marbeck," said the bishop,
"dost thou know wherefore thou art sent for?" "No, my lord,"
he replied. The bishop, taking up some of the sheets said
to him: "Understandest thou the Latin tongue?" "No,
my lord," he answered, "but simply." Gardiner then stated to
the council that the book he held in his hand was a Concordance, and that it was translated word for word from
the original compiled for the use of preachers. He asserted
"that if such a book should go forth in English, it would
destroy the Latin tongue." Two days later Gardiner again
sent for Marbeck. "Marbeck," said the bishop, "what a
devil made thee to meddle with the Scriptures?[1] Thy vocation
was another way . . . why the devil didst thou not hold thee
there? . . . What helpers hadst thou in setting forth thy book?"
"Forsooth, my lord," answered Marbeck, "none." "It is not
possible that thou should'st do it without help," exclaimed the
bishop. Then addressing one of his chaplains: "Here is a
marvellous thing; this fellow hath taken upon him to set out
the Concordance in English, which book, when it was set out
in Latin, was not done without the help and diligence of a
dozen learned men at least, and yet will he bear me in hand
that he hath done it alone." Then, addressing Marbeck, he
said: "Say what thou wilt, except God himself would come
down from heaven and tell me so, I will not believe it." Marbeck
was taken back to prison, and was placed in close confinement,
with irons on his hands and feet. He was five times examined;
and on the fifth occasion a new charge was brought against
him;—he had written out with his own hand a letter of John
Calvin. This was worse than spending his time over the
Bible.

---

[1] Foxe, who relates these circumstances, adds in a note,—"Christ saith—
Search the Scriptures; and Winchester saith—The devil makes men to
meddle with the Scriptures." *Acts*, v. p. 478.

Gardiner exerted himself to the utmost to secure the condemnation of this man to death, in company with Testwood, Filmer, and Peerson. His efforts met with success. These three Christians were burnt alive; and they met death with so much humility, patience, and devotion to Jesus, their only refuge, that some of the bystanders declared that they would willingly have died with them and like them. But the persecutors failed in their attempt with respect to Marbeck. Cranmer was able to convince the king that the making of a Concordance to the Bible ought not to be visited with death. It is well known that Henry VIII attached much importance to the Holy Scriptures, which he considered the most powerful weapon against the pope. Marbeck, therefore, was spared.

It is, moreover, no wonder that there should still have been martyrs. The queen, indeed, was friendly to their cause; but political circumstances were not favourable. After forty years' intermittent friendship with France, Henry VIII was about to declare war against that kingdom. The pretexts for this course were many. The first was the alliance of the king of France with the Turks, "who are daily advancing to destroy and ruin our holy faith and religion, to the great regret of all good Christians," said the Privy Council. A second pretext was that the sums of money which France was bound to pay annually to the king had fallen into arrear for nine years; there was also the question of the subsidies granted by France to Scotland during the war between Henry VIII and the Scots in 1542; the reception and protection of English rebels by Francis I; and the detention in French ports of faithful subjects of the king, merchants and others, with their ships and merchandise. In the despatch which we have just cited, the king also declared that, if within twenty days the grievances set forth were not redressed, he should claim the kingdom of France unjustly held by Francis I. The French ambassador replied in a conciliatory manner. Diplomacy made no reference to other grounds of complaint of a more private character, which perhaps throw light upon those which occasioned the rupture. Francis I had jested about the way in which Henry VIII dealt with his wives. Henry had sought the hand of French princesses, and they had no mind for this foreign husband; and lastly, Francis did not fulfil the promise which he had made to separate from Rome. There were many other pretexts besides, more or less reasonable, which determined the king to invade France.

While withdrawing from alliance with Francis I, Henry could not but at the same time enter into closer relation with Charles V. This reconciliation seemed natural, for the king of England was really, in respect to religion, more in harmony with the Emperor than with the Protestants of Germany, whose alliance he had for some time desired. But Charles required first of all that the legitimacy and the rights of his cousin, the princess Mary, should be acknowledged; and this Henry refused to do, because it would have involved an acknowledgment of his injustice to Catherine of Aragon. A solution which satisfied the Emperor was ultimately devised. It was provided by Act of Parliament that if Prince Edward should die without children, "the crown should go to the lady Mary."[1] But in this Act no mention was made of her legitimacy. The result of the concession of this point to Charles V was to bring on England a five years' bloody persecution, and to give her people Philip II of Spain for their king. In default of any issue of Mary, Elizabeth was to succeed to the throne. This matter being arranged, the Emperor Charles V and Henry concluded a treaty of alliance in February 1543, agreeing to attack France jointly within the next two years.

The war which Henry VIII, "king of England, *France*, and Ireland," said the parliament, now carried on against Francis I has little to do with the history of the Reformation. The king, having named the queen regent of his kingdom, embarked for Calais on July 14, 1544, on a vessel hung with cloth of gold. He was now feeble and corpulent and he suffered from an open ulcer in his leg, but his vanity and love of display were always conspicuous, even when setting out for a war. He arrived on the frontier of France at the head of a considerable force, but he himself did not take active control. The Emperor, who had got the start of him, was already within two days' march of Paris; and the city was in alarm at the approach of the Germans. "I cannot prevent my people of Paris from being afraid," said Francis, "but I will prevent them from suffering injury." Charles paid little respect to his

[1] Act of Succession, 35 Henry VIII, c. 1.

engagement with Henry VIII, and now treated separately with Francis at Crêpy, near Laon, September 19, and left the king of England to get out of the affair as well as he could. Henry captured Boulogne, but this was all that he had of his kingdom of France. On September 30 he returned to London.

The war, however, continued until 1546. England, abandoned by the Emperor, found sympathy in a quarter where it might least have been expected—in Italy. Some of the Italians, who were conscious of the evils brought on their own land by the papacy, were filled with admiration for the prince and the nation which had cast off its yoke. Edmund Harvel, ambassador of Henry VIII in Italy, being at this time at Venice, was continually receiving visits from captains of high reputation, who came to offer their services. Among these was Ercole Visconti of Milan, a man of high birth, a great captain, and one who, having extensive connexions in Italy, might render great service to the king. The French were now making an attempt to retake Boulogne; but the Italian soldiers who were serving in their army were constantly going over to the English, at the rate of thirty per day. The Italian companies were thus so largely reduced that the captains requested permission to leave the camp for want of soldiers to command; and permission was given them. In this matter the pope was involved in difficulty. He had undertaken to furnish Francis I with a body of four thousand men; but as the king was afraid that these Roman soldiers would pass over to the English army, he requested Paul III to substitute for these auxiliaries a monthly subsidy of 16,000 crowns. "As the Italian nation," added the English ambassador optimistically in his letter to Henry VIII, "is alienate from the French king, so the same is more and more inclined to your Majesty."

But if in Italy there were many supporters of Protestantism, in England its opponents were still more numerous. The fanatical party had attempted in 1543 to expel the reformed party from the town of Windsor by means of martyrdom. But the account was not settled; it still remained to purify the castle. It was known that Testwood, Filmer, Peerson, and Marbeck himself had had patrons in Sir Thomas and Lady Cardine, Sir Philip and Lady Hobby, Dr. Haynes, dean of

Exeter, and other persons at the court. Dr. London, who was always on the look-out for heretics, and a pleader named Simons, sent to Gardiner one Robert Ockam, a secretary, with letters, accusations, and secret documents as to the way in which they intended to proceed. But one of the queen's servants reached the court before him and gave notice of the scheme. Ockam, on his arrival, was arrested, all the papers were examined, and evidence was discovered in them of an actual conspiracy against many persons at the court. This aroused great indignation in the king's mind. It is highly probable that these gentlemen and their wives owed their safety to the influence of the queen and of Cranmer. London and Simons, unaware that their letters and documents had fallen into the hands of their judges, denied the plot, and this even upon oath. Their own writings were now produced, it was proved that they were guilty of perjury, and they were condemned to ignominious punishment. London, that great slayer of heretics, and his colleague were conducted on horseback, facing backwards, with the name of perjurer on their foreheads, through the streets of Windsor, Reading, and Newbury, the king being now at the last-named town. They were afterwards set in the pillory, and then taken back to prison. London died there of distress caused by this public disgrace. It was well that the wind should change, and that persecutors should be punished instead of the persecuted; but the manners of the time subjected these wretches to shocking sufferings which it would have been better to spare them.

CHAPTER NINE

The Last Martyrs of Henry's Reign

(1545)

HENRY VIII, sick and fretful, was easily drawn first to one side, then to the other. He was a victim of indecision, of violent excitement and of irresolution. His brother-in-law, the duke of Suffolk, who of all the members of the Privy Council was the most determined supporter of the Reformation, had died in August 1545, and that body was thenceforward impelled in an opposite direction, and carried the king along with it.

Shaxton, having resigned his see of Salisbury after the publication of the Six Articles, had been put in prison, and had long rejected all proposals of recantation addressed to him. Having aggravated his offence while in prison by asserting that the natural body of Christ was not in the sacrament, he was condemned to be burnt. The bishops of London and Worcester, sent by the king, visited him in the prison and strove to convince him. This weak unfortunate man readily professed himself persuaded, and thanked the king "for that he had delivered him at the same time from the temporal and from the everlasting fire." On July 13, 1546, he was set at liberty. As he grew old his understanding became still weaker; and in Mary's reign the unhappy man was one of the most eager to burn those whom he had called his brethren.

While there were men like Shaxton, whose fall was decisive and final, others were to be met with who, although in their own hearts decided for the truth, were alarmed when they found themselves in danger of death, and subscribed the Catholic declarations which were offered to them. But after having thus plunged into the abyss, they lifted up their heads as soon as possible and again confessed the truth. One of this class was Dr. Edward Crome, who, at this period, gave way on two occasions, but recovered himself.

Many other blemishes were visible in the general state of the Anglican church; and the obstinacy of the king, in particular, in maintaining in his kingdom, side by side, two things in opposition to each other, the Catholic doctrines and the reading of the Bible, subjected the sacred volume to strange honours. The king in person prorogued the parliament on December 24, and on this occasion made his last speech to the highest body in the state. He spoke as *vicar of God*, and gave a lecture to the ministers and the members of the church. It was his taste; he believed that he was born for this position, and there was in his nature as much of the preceptor as of the king. Moreover, there was nothing which offended him so much as the attempt to address a lecture to himself. Anyone who did so risked his own life. But while he was easily hurt, he did not shrink from hurting the feelings of others. He handled the rod more easily than the sceptre. The Speaker of the house of commons having delivered an address to the king in which he extolled his virtues, Henry replied as follows:—"Whereas you . . . have both praised and extolled me for the notable qualities you have conceived to be in me, I most heartily thank you all that you put me in remembrance of my duty, which is to endeavour myself to obtain and get such excellent qualities and necessary virtues. . . . No prince in the world more favoureth his subjects than I do you, nor any subjects or commons more love and obey their sovereign lord than I perceive you do me. Yet, although I with you, and you with me, be in this perfect love and concord, this friendly amity cannot continue except you, my lords temporal, and you, my lords spiritual, and you, my loving subjects, study and take pains to amend one thing, which is surely amiss and far out of order, . . . which is, that charity and concord is not among you; but discord and dissension beareth rule in every place. St. Paul saith to the Corinthians, in the thirteenth chapter, "Charity is gentle, charity is not envious, charity is not proud," and so forth. Behold then what love and charity is amongst you when one calleth the other heretic and anabaptist; and he calleth him again papist, hypocrite, and pharisee. Be these things tokens of charity amongst you? Are these the signs of fraternal love between you? No, no, I assure you that this lack of charity amongst yourselves will be the hindrance and assuaging of the fervent love between us, except this wound be salved and clearly made whole. I must needs judge the fault and occasion of this discord to be partly by the negligence of you, the fathers and preachers of the spiritualty. . . . I see and hear daily that you of the clergy preach one against another, . . . and few or none do preach truly and sincerely the Word of God. . . . Alas! how can the poor souls live in concord when you preachers sow amongst them, in your sermons, debate and discord? Of you they look for light, and you bring them to darkness. Amend these crimes, I exhort you, and set forth God's Word, both by true preaching and good example-giving; or else I, whom God hath appointed His vicar and high minister here, will see these divisions extinct. . . . Although (as I say) the spiritual men be in some fault . . . yet you of the temporalty be not clean and unspotted of malice and envy; for you rail on bishops, speak slanderously of priests, and rebuke and taunt preachers. . . . Although you be permitted to read Holy Scripture, and to have the Word of God in your mother-tongue, you must understand that it is licensed you so to do, only to inform your own conscience, and to instruct your children and family; not to dispute and make Scripture a railing and a taunting stock against priests and preachers, as many light persons do. I am very sorry to know and hear how unreverently that most precious jewel, the Word of God, is disputed, rhymed, sung, and jangled in every alehouse and tavern, contrary to the true meaning and doctrine of the same. . . . Be in charity one with another, . . . to the which I, as your supreme head and sovereign lord, exhort and require you; and then I doubt not but that love and league, which I spake of in the beginning, shall never be dissolved or broken between us."[1]

The schoolmaster had not spoken amiss. The parliament did not make the retort, "Physician, heal thyself," though it might have been applicable. One of the measures by which the king manifested his *sweet charity* proves that, if he were not, like some old schoolmasters, a tyrant of words and syllables, he tyrannized over the peace and the lives of his people.

There were at the court a certain number of ladies of the highest rank who loved the Gospel—the duchess of Suffolk, the

[1] Foxe, *Acts*, v. p. 534.

countess of Sussex, the countess of Hertford, lady Denny, lady Fitzwilliam, and above all the queen. Associated with these was a pious, lively, and beautiful young lady, of great intelligence and amiable disposition, whose fine qualities had been improved by education. Her name was Anne Askew.[1] She was the second daughter of Sir William Askew, member of a very ancient Lincolnshire family. She had two brothers and two sisters. Her brother Edward was a member of the king's bodyguard. The queen frequently received Anne and other Christian women in her private apartments; and there prayer was made and the Word of God expounded by an evangelical minister. The king, indeed, was aware of these secret meetings, but he feigned ignorance. Anne was at this time in great need of the consolations of the Gospel. Her father, Sir William, had a rich neighbour named Thomas Kyme, with whom he was intimate; and being anxious that his eldest daughter, Martha, should marry a rich man, he arranged with Kyme that she should wed his eldest son. The young lady died before the nuptials took place; and Sir William, reluctant to let slip so good a chance, compelled his second daughter Anne to marry the betrothed of her sister, and by him she became the mother of two children. The Holy Scriptures in the English version attracted Anne's attention, and ere long she became so attached to them that she meditated on them day and night. Led by them to a living faith in Jesus Christ, she renounced Romish superstitions. The priests, who were greatly annoyed, stirred up her young husband against her: being a rough man and a staunch papist, he "violently drove her out of his house." Anne said, "Since, according to the Scripture, *if the unbelieving depart, let him depart. A brother or a sister is not under bondage in such cases*— I claim my divorce." She went to London to take the necessary proceedings; and either through her brother, or otherwise, made the acquaintance of the pious ladies of the court and of the queen herself.

It was a great vexation to the enemies of the Reformation to see persons of the highest rank almost openly professing the evangelical faith. As they did not dare to attack them, they determined to make a beginning with Anne Askew, and thereby to terrify the rest. She had said one day, "I would

---

[1] [Sometimes spelt "Ascue."]

sooner read five lines in the Bible than hear five masses in the church." On another occasion she had denied the corporeal presence of the Saviour in the sacrament. She was sent to prison. When she was taken to Sadler's Hall, the judge, Christopher Dare, asked her, "Do you not believe that the sacrament hanging over the altar is the very body of Christ really?" Anne replied, "Wherefore was St. Stephen stoned to death?" Dare, doubtless, remembered that Stephen had said, "I see the Son of Man sitting *at the right hand of God.*" From this it followed that He was not in the sacrament. He preferred to answer, "I cannot tell." It is possible, however, that his ignorance was not feigned. "No more," said Anne, "will I solve your vain question." Anne was afterwards taken before the lord mayor, Sir Martin Bowes, a passionate bigot. He was under-treasurer of the Mint, and in 1550 obtained the king's pardon for all the false money which he had coined. The magistrate gravely asked her whether a mouse, eating the host, received God or no? "I made no answer, but smiled," says Anne. The bishop's chancellor, who was present, sharply said to her, "St. Paul forbade women to speak or to talk of the Word of God." "How many women," said she in reply, "have you seen go into the pulpit and preach?" "Never any," he said. "You ought not to find fault in poor women, except they have offended the law." She was unlawfully committed to prison, and for eleven days no one was allowed to see her. At this time she was about twenty-five years of age.

One of her cousins, named Brittayne, was admitted to see her. He immediately did everything he could to get Anne released on bail. The lord mayor bade him apply to the chancellor of the bishop of London. The chancellor replied to him, "Apply to the bishop." The bishop said, "I will give order for her to appear before me to-morrow at three o'clock in the afternoon." He then subjected her to a long examination. He asked her, amongst other things, "Do you not think that private masses help the souls departed?" "It is great idolatry," she replied, "to believe more in private masses than in the healthsome death of the dear Son of God." "What kind of answer is this?" said the bishop of London. "It is a mean one," replied Anne, "but good enough for your question." After the examination, at which Anne made clear and brief replies,

Bonner wrote down a certain number of articles of faith, and required that Anne should set her hand to them. She wrote, "I believe so much thereof as the Holy Scripture doth agree unto." This was not what Bonner wanted. The bishop pressed the point, and said, "Sign this document." Anne then wrote, "I, Anne Askew, do believe all manner of things contained in the faith of the Catholic Church." The bishop, well knowing what Anne meant by this word, hurried away into an adjoining room in a great rage. Her cousin Brittayne followed him and implored him to treat his kinswoman kindly. "She is a woman," exclaimed the bishop, "and I am nothing deceived in her." "Take her as a woman," said Brittayne, "and do not set her weak woman's wit to your lordship's great wisdom." At length, Anne's two sureties, to wit, Brittayne and Master Spilman of Grays Inn, were on the following day accepted, and she was set at liberty. These events took place in the year 1545.

Anne having continued to profess the Gospel and to have meetings with her friends, she was again arrested three months later, and was brought before the privy council at Greenwich. On the opening of the examination she refused to go into the matter before the council, and said, "If it be the king's pleasure to hear me, I will show him the truth." "It is not meet," they replied, "for the king to be troubled with you." She answered, "Solomon was reckoned the wisest king that ever lived, yet misliked he not to hear two poor common women; much more his Grace a single woman and his faithful subject." "Tell me your opinion on the sacrament," said the Lord Chancellor." "I believe," she said, "that so oft as I, in a Christian congregation, do receive the bread in remembrance of Christ's death, and with thanksgiving . . . I receive therewith the fruits also of His most glorious passion." "Make a direct answer to the question," said Gardiner. "I will not sing a new song of the Lord," she said, "in a strange land." "You speak in parables," said Gardiner. "It is best for you," she answered; "for if I show the open truth, ye will not accept it." "You are a parrot," said the incensed bishop. She replied, "I am ready to suffer all things at your hands, not only your rebukes, but all that shall follow besides, yea, and all that gladly."

The next day Anne once more appeared before the council.

They began the examination on the subject of transubstantiation. Seeing lord Parr, uncle to the queen, and lord Lisle, she said to them, "It is a great shame for you to counsel contrary to your knowledge." "We would gladly," they answered, "all things were well." Gardiner wished to speak privately with her, but this she refused. Wriothesley, the lord chancellor, then began to examine her again. "How long," said Anne, "will you halt on both sides?" "Where do you find that saying?" said he. "In the Scripture," replied Anne. "You shall be burnt," said the bishop of London. She replied, "I have searched all the Scriptures, yet could I never find that either Christ or His apostles put any creature to death."

Anne was sent back to prison. She was very ill, and believed herself to be near death. Never had she had to endure such attacks. She requested leave to see Latimer, friend and comforter of evangelicals; but this consolation was not allowed her. Resting firmly, as she did, on Scriptural grounds, she did not suffer herself to swerve. To her constitutional resolution she added that which was the fruit of communion with God; and she was thus placed by faith above the attacks which she experienced. Having a good foundation, she resolutely defended the freedom of her conscience and her full trust in Christ; and not only did she encounter her enemies without wavering, but she spoke to them with a power sufficient to awe them, and gave home-thrusts which threw them into confusion. Nevertheless she was only a weak woman, and her bodily strength began to fail. In Newgate she said, "In all my life afore I was never in such pain. The Lord strengthen us in the truth. Pray, pray, pray." She composed while in prison some stanzas which have been pronounced extraordinary, not only for simple beauty and sublime sentiment, but also for the noble structure and music of the verse:

> Like as the armèd knight
> Appointed to the field,
> With this world will I fight,
> And faith shall be my shield.
>
> Faith is that weapon strong
> Which will not fail at need;
> My foes therefore among
> Therewith will I proceed.

I now rejoice in heart,
    And hope bids me do so,
For Christ will take my part,
    And ease me of my woe.

Thou saidst, Lord, whoso knock,
    To him wilt Thou attend;
Undo therefore the lock,
    And Thy strong power send.

More enemies now I have
    Than hairs upon my head,
Let them not me deprave
    But fight Thou in my stead.

On Thee my cure I cast,
    For all their cruel spite
I set not by their haste,
    For Thou art my delight.

I am not she that list
    My anchor to let fall
For every drizzling mist;
    My ship 's substantial.

Not oft use I to write
    In prose nor yet in rhyme,
Yet will I shew one sight
    That I saw in my time.

I saw a royal throne
    Where justice should have sit,
But in her stead was one
    Of moody cruel wit;

Absorpt was righteousness,
    As by the raging flood;
Satan, in his excess,
    Suck'd up the guiltless blood.

Then thought I, Jesus Lord!,
    When Thou shalt judge us all,
Hard is it to record
    On these men what will fall.

Yet, Lord, I Thee desire,
    For that they do to me,
Let them not taste the hire
    Of their iniquity.

By law, Anne had a right to be tried by jury; but on June 28, 1546, she was condemned by the lord chancellor and the council, without further process, to be burnt, for having denied the corporeal presence of Christ in the sacrament. "They would needs know," said Anne, "whether the bread in the box were God, or no; I said 'God is a Spirit and will be worshipped in spirit and truth'." They asked her whether she wished for a priest; she smiled and said she would confess her faults unto God, for she was sure that He would hear her with favour. She added: "I think His grace shall well perceive me to be weighed in an uneven pair of balances. . . . Here I take heaven and earth to record that I shall die in mine innocency."

It was proved that Anne had derived her faith from the Holy Scriptures. Gardiner and his partisans therefore prevailed upon the government, eight days before the death of this young Christian, to draw up a proclamation purporting "that from henceforth no man, woman or person of what estate, condition or degree soever he or they be [consequently including the ladies and gentlemen of the court as well as others], shall, after the last day of August next ensuing, receive, have, take or keep in their possession the text of the New Testament, of Tyndale's or Coverdale's translation in English, nor any other than is permitted by the Act of Parliament; . . . nor after the said day shall receive, have, take or keep in his or their possession any manner of books printed or written in the English tongue which be or shall be set forth in the names of Fryth, Tyndale, Wycliffe, . . . Barnes, Coverdale, . . . or by any of them; . . ." and it was required that all such books should be delivered to the mayor, bailiff or chief constable of the town to be openly burned. (Proclamation of July 8, 1546.)

This was a remarkable proceeding on the part of Henry VIII. But events were stronger than the proclamation, and it remained a dead letter.

Anne's sentence was pronounced before the issue of the proclamation. The trial was over, and there was to be no further inquiry. But her death was not enough to satisfy Rich, Wriothesley and their friends. They had other designs, and were about to perpetrate the most shameful and cruel acts. The object which these men now proposed to themselves was to obtain such evidence as would warrant them in taking proceedings against those ladies of the court who were friends of the Gospel. They went (July 13) to the Tower, where Anne was still confined, and questioned her about her accomplices, naming the duchess-dowager of Suffolk, the countess of Sussex and several others. Anne answered, "If I should pronounce anything against them, I should not be able to prove it." They next asked her whether there were no members of the royal council who gave her their support. She said, none. The king is informed, they replied, that if you choose you can name a great many persons who are members of your sect. She answered that "the king was as well deceived in that behalf as dissembled with in other matters." The only effect of these denials was to irritate Wriothesley and his colleague; and, determined at any cost to obtain information against influential persons at the court, they ordered the rack to be applied to the young woman. This torture lasted a long time; but Anne gave no hint, nor even uttered a cry. The lord chancellor, more and more provoked, said to Sir Antony Knyvet, lieutenant of the Tower, "Strain her on the rack again." The latter refused to do this. It was to no purpose that Wriothesley threatened him if he would not obey. Rich, a member of the privy council, had frequently given proof of his baseness. Wriothesley was ambitious, inflated with self-conceit, haughty, and easily angered if his advice was not taken. These two men now forgot themselves, and the spectacle was presented of the lord chancellor of England and a privy councillor of the king turned into executioners. They set their own hands to the horrible instrument, and so severely applied the torture to the innocent young woman, that she was almost broken upon it and quite dislocated. She fainted away and was well-nigh dead.[1] "Then the lieutenant caused me to be loosed; incontinently I swooned, and then they recovered me again. After

---

[1] "My lord chancellor and master Rich took pains to rack me in their own hands, *till I was nigh dead.*" Bale's *Works* (Parker Society), p. 224. Foxe, *Acts*, v. p. 547. Burnet also relates the fact and adds some details:— "The lord chancellor, throwing off his gown, drew the rack so severely that he almost tore her body asunder." But Burnet is inclined to doubt the fact. The evidence of Anne Askew is positive. Burnet's doubt means nothing more than a bishop's respect for a lord chancellor.

that I sat two long hours, reasoning with my lord chancellor on the bare floor, where he, with many flattering words, persuaded me to leave my opinion. But my Lord God (I thank His everlasting goodness) gave me grace to persevere and will do, I hope, to the very end." Henry VIII himself censured Wriothesley for his cruelty, and excused the lieutenant of the Tower. "Then was I brought to a house," says Anne, "and laid in a bed, with as weary and painful bones as ever had patient Job." The chancellor sent word to her that if she renounced her faith she would be pardoned and should want for nothing, but that otherwise she should be burnt. She answered, "I will sooner die than break my faith." At the same time she fell on her knees in the dungeon and said: "O Lord, I have more enemies now than there be hairs on my head; yet, Lord, let them never overcome me with vain words, but fight Thou, Lord, in my stead, for on Thee I cast my care. With all the spite they can imagine, they fall upon me, who am Thy poor creature. Yet, sweet Lord, let me not set by them that are against me; for in Thee is my whole delight. And Lord, I heartily desire of Thee, that Thou wilt of Thy most merciful goodness forgive them that violence which they do, and have done, unto me. Open also Thou their blind hearts, that they may hereafter do that thing in Thy sight, which is only acceptable before Thee, and to set forth Thy verity aright, without all vain fantasies of sinful men. So be it, O Lord, so be it."[1]

The 16th of July, the day fixed for the last scene of this tragedy, had arrived; everything was ready for the burning of Anne at Smithfield. The execution was to take place not in the morning, the usual time, but at nightfall, to make it the more terrible. It was thus, in every sense, a deed of darkness. They were obliged to carry Anne to the place of execution, for in her state at that time she was unable to walk. When she reached the pile, she was bound to the post by her waist, with a chain which prevented her from sinking down. The wretched Shaxton, nominated for the purpose, then completed his apostasy by delivering a sermon on the sacrament of the altar, a sermon abounding in errors. He had visited Anne in prison and advised her to recant as he had done. She had replied that it had been better for him if he had never been born. In

---

[1] Bale's *Works* (Parker Society), p. 238. Foxe, *Acts*, v. p. 549.

reply to his sermon, Anne, who was in full possession of her faculties, contented herself with saying, "He misseth, and speaketh without the Book." Three other evangelical Christians were to die at the same time with her; Nicholas Belenian, a priest of Shropshire; John Lacels (Lascelles), of the king's household, probably the man who had revealed the incontinence of Catherine Howard, a deed for which the Roman party hated him; and one John Adams, a Colchester tailor. "Now, with quietness," said Lacels, "I commit the whole world to their pastor and herdsman Jesus Christ, the only Saviour and true Messias. . . ." The letter from which we quote is subscribed, "John Lacels, late servant to the king, and now I trust to serve the everlasting King, with the testimony of my blood in Smithfield."

There was an immense gathering of the people. On a platform erected in front of St. Bartholomew's church were seated, as presidents at the execution, Wriothesley, lord chancellor of England, the old duke of Norfolk, the old earl of Bedford, the lord mayor Sir Martin Bowes, and various other notables. When the fire was about to be lighted, the chancellor sent a messenger to Anne Askew, instructed to offer her the king's pardon if she would recant. She answered, "I am not come hither to deny my Lord and Master." The same pardon was offered to the other martyrs, but they refused to accept it and turned away their heads. Then stood up the ignorant and fanatical Bowes, and exclaimed with a loud voice, "*Fiat justitia*" (Let justice be done). Anne was soon wrapt in the flames; and this noble victim who freely offered herself a sacrifice to God, gave up her soul in peace. Her companions did likewise.[1]

These four persons were the last victims of the reign of Henry VIII. The enemies of the Reformation were especially annoyed at this time to see women of the first families of England embrace the faith which they hated. On a woman of most superior mind, but young and weak, fell the last blow levelled against the Gospel by *the defender of the faith*. Anne Askew fell; but the great doctrines which she had so courageously professed were soon to be triumphant in the midst of her fellow-countrymen.

[1] Foxe, *Acts*, v. pp. 550–52.

CHAPTER TEN

Death Casts its Shadow over Catherine Parr
(1546)

IT might be asked how it came to pass that the queen did
not put a stop to these cruel executions. The answer is easy
—she was herself in danger. The enemies of the Reformation,
perceiving her influence over the king, bethought themselves
that the execution of Anne Askew and of her companions did
not advance their cause; that to make it triumphant the death
of the queen was necessary; and that if Catherine were ruined,
the Reformation would fall with her. Shortly after the king's
return from France, these men approached him and cautiously
insinuated that the queen had made large use of her liberty
during his absence; that she diligently read and studied the
Holy Scriptures; that she chose to have about her only women
who shared her opinions; that she had engaged certain would-be
wise and pious persons to assist her in attaining a thorough
knowledge of the sacred writings; that she held private conferences with them on spiritual subjects all the year round, and
that "in Lent every day in the afternoon, for the space of an
hour, one of her said chaplains, in her privy chamber,"
expounded the Word of God to the queen, to the ladies of
her court and of her bedchamber and others who were disposed
to hear these expositions; that the minister frequently attacked
what he called the abuses of the existing church; that the
queen read heretical books proscribed by royal ordinances;
further, that she, the queen of England, employed her leisure
hours in translating religious works, and in composing books
of devotion; and that she had turned some of the psalms into
verse, and had made a collection entitled *Prayers or Meditations*.
The king had always ignored these meetings, determined not
to see what was nevertheless clear, that the queen was an
evangelical Christian like Anne Askew who had lately been
burnt.

Catherine was encouraged by this consideration on the part of the king. She professed her faith in the Gospel unreservedly, and boldly took up the cause of the evangelicals. Her one desire was to make known the truth to the king, and to bring him to the feet of Jesus Christ to find forgiveness for the errors of his life. Without regard to consequences she allowed her overflowing zeal to have free and unrestricted course. She longed to transform not the king alone, but England also. She often exhorted the king "that as he had, to the glory of God and his eternal fame, begun a good and a godly work in banishing that monstrous idol of Rome, so he would thoroughly perfect and finish the same, cleansing and purging his church of England clean from the dregs thereof, wherein as yet remained great superstition."

Was the passionate Henry going to act rigorously towards this queen as he had towards the others? Catherine's blameless conduct, the affection which she testified for him, her respectful bearing, her unwearied endeavour to please him, the attentions which she lavished on him had so much endeared her to him that he allowed her the privilege of being freespoken; and had it not been for the active opposition of its enemies, she might have propagated the Gospel throughout the kingdom. As these determined enemies of the Reformation were beginning to fear the total ruin of their party, they strove to rekindle the evil inclinations of Henry VIII, and to excite his anger against Catherine. In their view it seemed that the boldness of her opinions must inevitably involve her ruin.

But the matter was more difficult than they thought. The king not only loved his wife, but he also liked discussion, especially on theological subjects; and he had too much confidence in his own cleverness and knowledge to dread the arguments of the queen. The latter therefore continued her petty warfare, and in respectful terms advanced good scriptural proofs in support of her faith. Henry used to smile and take it all in good part, or at least never appeared to be offended. Gardiner, Wriothesley and others who heard these discussions were alarmed at them. They were almost ready to give up all for lost; and trembling for themselves, they renounced their project. Not one of them ventured to breathe a word against the queen either before the king or in his absence. At length, they found an unexpected auxiliary.

The ulcer burst in the king's leg, and gave him acute pain which constantly increased. Henry had led a sensual life, and had now become so corpulent, that it was exceedingly difficult to move him from one room to another. He insisted that no one should take notice of his failing powers; and those about him hardly dared to speak of the fact in a whisper. His condition made him peevish; he was restless, and thought that his end was not far off. The least thing irritated him; gloomy and passionate, he had frequent fits of rage. To approach and attend to him had become a difficult task; but Catherine, far from avoiding it, was all the more zealous. Since his illness Henry had given up coming into the queen's apartments, but he invited her to come to see him; and she frequently went of her own accord, after dinner, or after supper, or at any other favourable opportunity. The thought that Henry was gradually drawing near to the grave filled her heart with the deepest emotion; and she availed herself of every opportunity of bringing him to a decision in favour of evangelical truth. Her endeavours for this end may some-times have been made with too much urgency. One evening when Wriothesley and Gardiner, the two leaders of the Catholic party, were with the king, Catherine, who ought to have been on her guard, carried away by the ardour of her faith, endeavoured to prevail upon Henry to undertake the reformation of the church. The king was hurt. His notion that the queen was lecturing him as a pupil in the presence of the lord chancellor and the bishop of Winchester, increased his vexation. He roughly "brake off that matter and took occasion to enter into other talk." This he had never before done; and Catherine was surprised and perplexed. Henry, however, did not reproach her, but spoke affectionately, which was certainly on his part the mark of real love. The queen having risen to retire, he said to her as usual, "Farewell! sweet heart." Catherine meanwhile was disquieted, and felt that keen distress of mind which seizes upon a refined and sus-ceptible woman when she has acted imprudently.

The chancellor and the bishop remained with the king. Gardiner had observed the king's breaking off the conversation;

and he thought, says a contemporary, "that he must strike while the iron was hot;" that he must take advantage of Henry's ill humour, and by a skilful effort get rid of Catherine and put an end to her proselytism. It was a beaten track; the king had already in one way or another rid himself of four of his queens, and it would be an easy matter to do as much with a fifth.

Henry furnished them with the wished-for opportunity. Annoyed at having been humiliated in the presence of the two lords, he said to them in an ironical tone: "A good hearing it is when women become such clerks; and a thing much to my comfort, to come in mine old days to be taught by my wife." The bishop adroitly availed himself of this opening, and put forth all his powers and all his malice to increase the anger of the king. He urged that it was lamentable that the queen "should so much forget herself as to take upon her to stand in any argument with his Majesty;" he praised the king to his face "for his rare virtues, and especially for his learned judgment in matters of religion, above not only princes of that and other ages, but also above doctors professed in theology." He said "that it was an unseemly thing for any of his Majesty's subjects to reason and argue with him so malapertly," and that it was "grievous to him (Gardiner) for his part, and other of his Majesty's counsellors and servants to hear the same." He added "that they all by proof knew his wisdom to be such, that it was not needful for any to put him in mind of any such matters; inferring, moreover, how dangerous and perilous a matter it is . . . for a prince to suffer such insolent words at his subjects' hands, who, as they take boldness to contrary their sovereign in words, so want they no will, but only power and strength, to overthwart him in deeds. Besides this, that the religion by the queen so stiffly maintained did not only disallow and dissolve the policy and politic government of princes, but also taught the people that all things ought to be in common." The bishop went on to assert that "whosoever (saving the reverence due to her for his Majesty's sake) should defend the principles maintained by the queen, deserved death." He did not, however, dare, he said, to speak of the queen, unless he were sure that his Majesty would be his buckler. But with his Majesty's consent his faithful counsellors would soon tear off the hypocritical mask of heresy and would disclose treasons so horrible that his Majesty would no longer cherish a serpent in his own bosom.

The lord chancellor spoke in his turn; and the two conspirators did everything they could to stir up the anger of the king against the queen. They filled his head with a variety of tales, both about herself and about some of her lady-attendants; they told him that they had been favourable to Anne Askew; that they had in their possession heretical books; and that they were guilty of treason as well as of heresy. Suspicion and distrust, to which the king's disposition was too naturally inclined, took possession of him, and he required his two councillors to ascertain whether any articles of law could be brought forward against the queen, even at the risk of her life. They quitted the king's presence, promising to make very good use of the commission entrusted to them.

The bishop and the chancellor set to work immediately. They resorted to means of every kind—tricks, intrigues, secret correspondence—for the purpose of making out an appearance of guilt on the part of the queen. By bribing some of her domestics they were enabled to get a catalogue of the books which she had in her cabinet. Taking counsel with some of their accomplices, it occurred to them that if they began by attacking the queen, this step would excite almost universal reprobation. They determined, therefore, to prepare men's minds by making a beginning with the ladies who enjoyed her confidence, and particularly with those of her own kindred—lady Herbert, afterwards countess of Pembroke, the queen's sister, and first lady of her court; lady Lane, her cousin-german; and lady Tyrwhitt, who by her virtues had gained her entire confidence. Their plan was to examine these three ladies on the Six Articles; to institute a rigorous search in their houses with a view to finding some ground of accusation against Queen Catherine; and, in case they should succeed, to arrest the queen herself and carry her off *by night, in a barge*, to the Tower. The further they proceeded with their work of darkness, the more they encouraged and cheered each other on; they considered themselves quite strong enough to strike at once the great blow, and they resolved to make the first attack on the queen. They therefore drew up against her a bill of indictment, which purported especially that she had

contravened the Six Articles, had violated the royal proclamation by reading prohibited books, and, in short, had
openly maintained heretical doctrine. Nothing was wanting
but to get the king's signature to the bill; for if, without the
sanction of this signature, they should cast suspicions on the
queen, they would expose themselves to a charge of high
treason.

Henry VIII was now at Whitehall; and in consequence of
the state of his health he very seldom left his private apartments.
But few of his councillors, and these only by special order, were
allowed to see him. Gardiner and Wriothesley alone came to
the palace more frequently than usual to confer with him on
the mission which he had entrusted to them. Taking with
them their hateful indictment, they went to the palace, were
admitted to the king's presence, and after a suitable introduction they laid before him the fatal document, requesting
him to sign it. Henry read it, and took careful note of its
contents; then asked for writing materials, and notwithstanding his feebleness he signed it. This was a great victory
for the bishop, the chancellor and the Catholic party; and it
was a great defeat for the Reformation party, apparently the
signal for its ruin. Nothing was now wanting but a writ of
arrest, and the chancellor of England would send the queen
to the Tower. Once there, her situation would be hopeless.

So cleverly had the plot been managed, that during the
whole time the queen had neither known nor suspected anything; she paid her usual visits to the king, and had gradually
allowed herself to speak to him on religion as she used to do.
The king permitted this without gainsaying her; he did not
choose to enter into explanations with her. He was, however,
ill at ease. The burden was oppressive; and one evening, just
after the queen left him, he opened his mind to one of his
physicians—his name appears to have been Thomas Wendy—in
whom he placed full confidence, and said: "I do not like the
queen's religion, and I do not intend to be much longer
worried by the discourses of this *doctoress*." He likewise revealed
to the physician the project formed by some of his councillors,
but forbade him, upon pain of death, to say a word about it
to any living soul. Apparently forgetting the wives whom he
had already sacrificed, Henry was thus coolly preparing, at

the very time when he was himself about to go down to the grave, to add another victim to the hecatomb.

The queen, although encompassed with deadly enemies who were contriving her ruin, was in a state of perfect calmness, when suddenly there burst upon her one of those heavy squalls which so unexpectedly dash the most powerful vessels against the rocks. The chancellor, contented with his triumph, but at the same time agitated, snatched up the paper which, now bearing the king's signature, ensured the ruin of the queen. Vehement passions sometimes distract men and produce absence of mind. In this case it appears that Wriothesley carelessly thrust the paper into his bosom, and dropped it while crossing one of the apartments of the palace. A pious woman of the court, happening to pass that way shortly afterwards, saw the paper and picked it up. Perceiving at the first glance its importance she took it immediately to the queen. Catherine opened it, read the articles with fear and trembling, and as soon as she saw Henry's signature, was struck as by a thunderbolt, and fell into a frightful agony. Her features were completely changed: she uttered loud cries, and seemed to be in her death-struggle. She too, then, was to lay down her life on the scaffold. All her attentions, all her devotion to the king had availed nothing; she must undergo the common lot of the wives of Henry VIII. She bewailed her fate, and struggled against it. At other times she had glimpses of her own faults and uttered reproaches against herself, and then her distress and her lamentations increased. Those of her ladies who were present could hardly bear the sight of so woeful a state; and, trembling themselves, and supposing that the queen was about to be put to death, they were unable to offer her consolation. The remembrance of this harrowing scene was never effaced from their minds.[1]

Some one brought word to the king that the queen was in terrible distress, and that her life seemed to be in danger. A feeling of compassion was awakened in him, and he sent to her immediately the physicians who were with him. They, finding Catherine in this extremity, endeavoured to bring her to herself, and gradually she recovered her senses. The physician to whom Henry had revealed Gardiner's project,

[1] Foxe, *Acts*, v. p. 558.

discovering from some words uttered by the queen that the conspiracy was the cause of her anxiety, requested leave to speak to her in private. He told her that he was risking his life by thus speaking to her, but that his conscience would not allow him to take part in the shedding of innocent blood. He therefore confirmed the foreboding of danger which was impending over her; but added that if she henceforward endeavoured to behave with humble submission to his Majesty, she would regain, he did not doubt, his pardon and his favour.

These words were not enough to deliver Catherine from her disquietude. Her danger was not concealed from the king; and, unable to endure the thought that she might die of grief, he had himself carried into her room. At the sight of the king Catherine rallied sufficiently to explain to him the despair into which she was thrown by the belief that he had totally abandoned her. Henry then spoke to her as an affectionate husband, and comforted her with gentle words; and this poor heart, till then agitated like a stormy sea, gradually became calm again.

The king could now forget the faults of the queen; but the queen herself did not forget them. She understood that she had habitually assumed a higher position than belonged to a wife, and that the king was entitled to an assurance that this state of things should be changed. After supper the next evening, therefore, Catherine rose and, taking with her only her sister, lady Herbert, on whom she leaned, and lady Jane Grey, who carried a candle before her, went to the king's bedchamber. When the three ladies were introduced, Henry was seated and speaking with several gentlemen who stood round him. He received the queen very courteously, and of his own accord, contrary to his usual practice, began to talk with her about religion, as if there was one point on which he wished for further information from the queen. She replied discreetly and as the circumstances required. She then added meekly and in a serious and respectful tone,—"Your Majesty doth right well know, neither I myself am ignorant, what great imperfection and weakness by our first creation is allotted unto us women, to be ordained and appointed as inferior and subject unto man as our head; from which head all our direction ought to proceed. And that as God made man in

Q(II)

his own shape and likeness, whereby he being endued with more special gifts of perfection, might rather be stirred to the contemplation of heavenly things and to the earnest endeavour to obey His commandments, even so also made He woman of man, of whom and by whom she is to be governed, commanded and directed. . . . Your Majesty being so excellent in gifts and ornaments of wisdom, and I a silly poor woman, so much inferior in all respects of nature unto you, how then cometh it now to pass that your Majesty in such diffuse causes of religion will seem to require my judgment? Which when I have uttered and said what I can, yet must I, will I, refer my judgment . . . to your Majesty's wisdom, as my only anchor, supreme head and governor here in earth, next under God, to lean unto." "Not so," said the king; "you are become a doctor, Kate, to instruct us (as we take it), and not to be instructed or directed by us." "If your Majesty take it so," replied the queen, "then hath your Majesty very much mistaken me, who have ever been of the opinion, to think it very unseemly and preposterous for the woman to take upon her the office of an instructor or teacher to her lord and husband, but rather to learn of her husband and be taught by him. And whereas I have, with your Majesty's leave, heretofore been bold to hold talk with your Majesty, wherein sometimes in opinions there hath seemed some difference, I have not done it so much to maintain opinion, as I did it rather to minister talk, not only to the end your Majesty might with less grief pass over this painful time of your infirmity, being attentive to our talk, and hoping that your Majesty should reap some ease thereby; but also that I, hearing your Majesty's learned discourse, might receive to myself some profit thereby; wherein I assure your Majesty, I have not missed any part of my desire in that behalf, always referring myself in all such matters unto your Majesty, as by ordinance of nature it is convenient for me to do." "And is it even so, sweet heart?" answered the king; "and tended your arguments to no worse end? Then perfect friends we are now again, as ever at any time heretofore." Then, as if to seal this promise, Henry, who was sitting in his chair, embraced the queen and kissed her. He added: "It does me more good at this time to hear the words of your mouth, than if I had heard present news that a

hundred thousand pounds in money had fallen unto me."
Lavishing on Catherine tokens of his affection and his happiness,
he promised her that such misapprehensions with regard to
her should never arise again. Then, resuming general conversation, he talked on various interesting subjects with the
queen and with the lords who were present, until the night
was advanced; when he gave the signal for their departure.
There may possibly have been somewhat of exaggeration in
Catherine's words. She had not been altogether so submissive
a learner as she said; but she felt the imperative necessity of
entirely dispersing the clouds which the ill will of her enemies
had gathered over the king's mind, and it is not to be doubted
that in saying what she did she uttered her inmost thought.

Meanwhile, the queen's enemies, who had no suspicion of
the turn things were taking, gave their orders and made their
preparations for the great work of the morrow, which was to
confine Catherine in the Tower. The day was fine, and the
king, wishing to take an airing, went in the afternoon into the
park, accompanied only by two of the gentlemen of his
bedchamber. He sent an invitation to the queen to bear him
company; and Catherine immediately arrived, attended by
her three favourite ladies in waiting. Conversation began, but
they did not talk of theology. Never had the king appeared
more amiable; and his good humour inspired the rest with
cheerfulness. In his conversation there was all the liveliness
of a frank communicative disposition, and the mirth, it seems,
was even noisy. Suddenly, forty halberds were seen gleaming
through the park trees. The lord chancellor was at the head
of the men, and forty bodyguards followed him. He was
coming to arrest the queen and her three ladies and to conduct
them to the Tower. The king, breaking off the conversation
which entertained him so pleasantly, glanced sternly at the
chancellor, and stepping a little aside called him to him.
The chancellor knelt down and addressed to the king, in a
low voice, some words which Catherine could not understand.
She heard only that Henry replied to him in insulting terms,
"Fool, beast, arrant knave!" At the same time he commanded
the chancellor to be gone. Wriothesley and his followers disappeared. Such was the end of the conspiracy formed against
the king's Protestant wife by Wriothesley, Gardiner, and their

friends. Henry then rejoined the queen. His features still
reflected his excitement and anger; but as he approached her
he tried to assume an air of serenity. She had not clearly
understood what was the subject of conversation between the
king and the chancellor; but the king's words had startled
her. She received him gracefully and sought to excuse
Wriothesley, saying: "Albeit I know not what just cause your
Majesty has at this time to be offended with him, yet I think
that ignorance, not will, was the cause of his error; and so
I beseech your Majesty (if the cause be not very heinous), at
my humble suit to take it." "Ah, poor soul!" said the king,
"thou little knowest how evil he deserveth this grace at thy
hands. On my word, sweet heart, he hath been to thee a very
knave." Says Foxe: "Thus departed the lord chancellor out
of the king's presence as he came, with all his train: the whole
mould of all his device being utterly broken."

CHAPTER ELEVEN

The Last Days of Henry VIII
(1546–January 1547)

WEIGHTY consequences followed the miscarriage of the conspiracy formed against the queen. It had been aimed at the queen and the Reformation; but it turned against Roman Catholicism and its leaders. The proverb was again fulfilled,—*whoso diggeth a pit shall fall therein*. The wind changed; Romanism suffered an eclipse, it was no longer illumined by the sun of royalty. The first to fall into disgrace with Henry VIII was, as we have seen, Wriothesley. The king displayed his coolness in various ways. The chancellor, disquieted and alarmed for his own pecuniary interests, was annoyed to see preparations for establishing a new Court of Augmentations, by which his privileges and emoluments would be lessened. He earnestly entreated the king that it might not be established in his time. "I shall have cause," he wrote on October 16, "to be sorry in my heart during my life, if the favour of my gracious master shall so fail, that partly in respect of his poor servant he do not somewhat of his clemency temper it. Thus I make an end, praying God long to preserve his Majesty." In spite of all his efforts, he lost the royal favour, and the new court which he so much dreaded was erected.

A still heavier blow fell upon Gardiner. After the reconciliation between Henry and Catherine, he was obliged to abstain from making his appearance at the court. On December 2, he wrote to the king: "I am so bold to molest your Majesty with these very letters, which be only to desire your Highness, of your accustomed goodness and clemency, to be my good and gracious lord, and to continue such opinion of me as I have ever trusted and, by manifold benefits, certainly known your Majesty to have had of me . . . declare mine inward rejoice of your Highness' favour, and that I would not willingly offend your Majesty for no worldly thing." This man, at other times so strong, now saw before him nothing but disgrace and became excessively fearful. He might be overtaken by a long series of penalties. Who could tell whether Henry, like Ahasuerus of old, would not inflict upon the accuser the fate which he had designed for the accused? The bishop, restless, wrote to Paget, secretary of state: "I hear no specialty of the king's Majesty's miscontentment in this matter of lands, but confusedly that my doings should not be well taken." No answer to either of these two letters is extant. Towards the end of December, the king excluded Gardiner from the number of his executors and from the council of regency under his successor, Edward; and this involved a heavy loss of honour, money, and influence. Henry felt that for the guardianship of his son and of his realm, he must make his choice between Cranmer and Gardiner. Cranmer was selected. It was in vain that Sir Anthony Browne appealed to him, and requested him to reinstate the bishop of Winchester in this office. "If he be left among you," said the king, "he would only sow trouble and division. Do not speak of it." The conspiracy against the queen was not the sole, although probably it was the determining cause of Gardiner's disgrace.

This, however, was but the beginning of the storm. The first lord of the realm and his family were about to be attacked. If Henry no longer struck to the right, he struck to the left; but he dealt his blows without intermission; in one thing he was ever consistent, cruelty.

In addition to the suffering caused by his disease, the king was oppressed by anxiety at the thought of the ambition and rebellion which might snatch the crown from his son and create disturbances in the kingdom after his death. The court was at this time divided into two parties. One of these was headed by the duke of Norfolk, who, owing to his position as chief of the ancient family of the Howards, allied even to the blood royal, was next to the king the most influential man in England. He had been lord treasurer for twenty-five years, and had rendered signal services to the crown. Opposed to this party was that of the Seymours, who had not hitherto played any great part, but who now, as uncles to the young prince, found themselves continually advancing in esteem and authority. Norfolk was the chief of the Catholic party; and a great number of evangelical Christians had been burnt while his influence was dominant. His son, Henry, the earl of Surrey, was likewise attached to the doctrines of the Middle Ages, and was even suspected of having associated in Italy with Cardinal Pole. The Seymours, on the other hand, had always shown themselves friendly to the Reformation; and while Norfolk supported Gardiner, they supported Cranmer. It appeared inevitable that, after the king's death, war would break out between these chiefs, and what would happen then? The more Henry's strength declined, the more numerous became the partisans of the Seymours. The sun was rising for the uncles of the young prince, and was setting for Norfolk. The duke, perceiving this, made advances to the Seymours. He would have liked his son to marry the daughter of Edward Seymour, earl of Hertford, and his daughter, widow of the duke of Richmond, the natural son of the king, to marry Sir Thomas Seymour, Hertford's brother. But neither Surrey nor the duchess were disposed to the match. There was therefore nothing to expect but a vigorous conflict; and the king chose that the victory of the one party and the defeat of the other should be determined in his lifetime and through his intervention. To which of the two parties would the king give the preference? He had always leaned for support upon Norfolk, and the religious views of this old servant were his own. Would he separate from him at this critical moment? After having from the first resisted the Reformation, would he, on the brink of the grave, give it the victory? The past had belonged to Roman Catholicism; should the future belong to the Gospel preached by the party of reform? Should his death belie his whole life? The infamous conspiracy formed against the queen by the Catholic party would not have been enough in itself to induce the king to adopt so strange a resolution. A circumstance of another kind occurred to determine his course.

At the beginning of December 1546, Sir Richard Southwell, who had been one of Cromwell's men, and was afterwards a member of the privy council under Queen Mary, gave the king a warning that the powerful family of the Howards would expose his son to great danger. Before the birth of Edward, Norfolk had been designated as one of the claimants of the crown. His eldest son was a young man of great intelligence, high spirit and indomitable courage, and excelled in military exercises. To these qualifications he added the polish of a courtier, fine taste and an ardent love for the fine arts; his contemporaries were charmed by his poems; and he was looked upon as the flower of the English nobility. These brilliant endowments formed a snare for him. "His head," people said to the king, "is filled with ambitious projects." He had borne the arms of Edward the Confessor in the first quarter, which the king alone had the right to do; if, it was added, he has refused the hand of the daughter of the earl of Hertford, it is because he aspires to that of the princess Mary; and if he should marry her after the death of the king, prince Edward will lose the crown.

The king ordered his chancellor to investigate the charges against the duke of Norfolk and his son, the earl of Surrey; and Wriothesley ere long presented to him a paper, in the form of questions, in his (Wriothesley's) own handwriting. The king read it attentively, pen in hand, hardly able to repress his anger, and underlined with a trembling hand those passages which appeared to him the most important. The following sentences are specimens of what he read:—

"If a man coming *of the collateral line to the heir of the crown*, who ought not to bear the arms of England but on the second quarter . . . *do presume* . . . to bear them in the first quarter, . . . *how this man's intent is to be judged.* . . .

"If a man compassing *with himself to govern the realm do actually go about to rule the king*, and should for that purpose advise his daughter or sister to become the king's harlot, thinking thereby to bring it to pass . . . what this importeth.

"If a man say these words,—'If the king die, who should have the rule of the prince but my father or I?' what it importeth."[1]

On Saturday, December 12, the duke and the earl were separately arrested and taken to the Tower, one by land, the other by the river, neither of them being aware that the other was suffering the same fate. The king had often shown himself very hasty in a matter of this kind; but in this case he was more so than usual. He had not long to live, and he desired

[1] The words underlined by the king are here printed in italics.

that these two great lords should go before him to the grave. The same evening the king sent Sir Richard Southwell, Sir John Gate, and Wymound Carew to Kenninghall, in Norfolk, a principal seat of the family, about ninety miles from London. They travelled as swiftly as they could, and arrived at the mansion by daybreak on Tuesday. They had orders to examine the members of the family, and to affix seals to the effects.

The Howard family, unhappily for itself, was deeply divided. Elizabeth, duchess of Norfolk, daughter of the duke of Buckingham, an irritable and passionate woman, had been separated from her husband since 1533, and apparently not without reason. She said of one of the ladies who were in attendance on her, Elizabeth Holland,—"This woman is the cause of all my unhappiness." There was a certain coolness between the earl of Surrey and his sister, the duchess of Richmond, probably because the latter leaned to the side of the Reformation. Surrey had also had a quarrel with his father, and he was hardly yet reconciled to him. A house divided against itself will not stand. The members of the family, therefore, accused one another; the duchess, it may be believed, did not spare her husband, and the duke called his son a fool. When Sir Richard Southwell and his two companions arrived at Kenninghall on Tuesday morning, they caused all the doors to be securely closed so that no one might escape; and after having taken some evidence of the almoner, they requested to see the duchess of Richmond, the only member of the family then at the mansion, and Mistress Elizabeth Holland, who passed for the duke's favourite. These ladies had only just risen from their beds, and were not ready to make their appearance. However, when they heard that the king's envoys requested to see them, they betook themselves as quickly as possible to the dining-room. Sir John Gate and his friends informed them that the duke and the earl had just been committed to the Tower. The duchess, deeply moved at this startling news, trembled and almost fainted away. She gradually recovered herself, and kneeling down humbled herself as though she were in the king's presence. She said: "Although nature constrains me sore to love my father, whom I have ever thought to be a true and faithful subject, and also to desire the well-doing of his son my natural brother, whom I note to be a rash man, yet for my part I would nor will hide or conceal anything from his Majesty's knowledge, specially if it be of weight." The king's agent searched the house of the duchess of Richmond, inspected her cabinets and her coffers, but they found nothing tending to compromise her. They found no jewels, for she had parted with her own to pay her debts. Next, they visited Elizabeth Holland's room, where they found much gold, many pearls, rings and precious stones; and of these they sent a list to the king. They laid aside the books and manuscripts of the duke; and the next day by their direction the duchess of Richmond and Mistress Holland set out for London, where they were to be examined.

Mistress Holland was examined first. She deposed that the duke had said to her "that the king was sickly, and could not long endure; and the realm like to be in an ill case through diversity of opinions." The duchess of Richmond deposed "that the duke her father would have had her marry Sir Thomas Seymour, brother to the earl of Hertford, which her brother also desired, wishing her withal to endear herself so into the king's favour, as she might the better rule here as others had done; and that she refused." The deposition appears to corroborate one of the charges brought against Norfolk by the chancellor. Nevertheless, the supposition that a father, from ambitious motives, could urge his daughter to consent to incestuous intercourse is so revolting, that one can hardly help asking whether there really was anything more in the case than an exercise of the natural influence of a daughter-in-law over her father-in-law. The duchess corroborated the accusation touching the royal arms borne by Surrey, his hatred of the Seymours, and the ill which he meditated doing them after the king's death; and she added that he had urged her not to carry too far the reading of the Holy Scriptures.

Various other depositions having been taken, the duke and his son were declared guilty of high treason (January 7). On the 13th, Surrey was tried before a jury at Guildhall. He defended himself with much spirit; but he was condemned to death, after a special message from the king had settled the mind of the hesitant jury. This young nobleman, only about thirty years of age, the idol of his countrymen, was executed on Tower Hill. Public feeling was shocked by this act of cruelty, and everyone extolled the high qualities of the earl. His sister, the duchess of Richmond, took charge of his five children, and admirably fulfilled her duty as their aunt, appointing as their tutor John Foxe, author of the *Acts and Monuments of the Martyrs*.

The king was now dangerously ill, but he showed no signs of tenderness. People said that he had never hated or ruined anyone by halves; and he was determined, after the death of the eldest son, to sacrifice the father. Norfolk was very much surprised to find himself a prisoner in the Tower, to which he had consigned so many prisoners. He wrote to the lords to let him have some books, for he said that unless he could read he fell asleep. He asked also for a confessor, as he was desirous of receiving his Creator; and for permission to hear mass and to walk outside his apartment in the daytime. At the age of seventy-three, after having taken the lead in the most cruel measures of the reign of Henry VIII, from the death of Anne Boleyn to the death of Anne Askew, he now found that the day of terror was approaching for himself. His heart was agitated, and fear chilled him. He knew the king too well to have any hope that the great and numerous services which he had rendered to him would avail to arrest the sword already suspended over his head. Meanwhile the prospect of death alarmed him; and in his distress he wrote from his prison in the Tower to his royal master:—"Most gracious and merciful sovereign lord, I your most humble subject prostrate at your foot, do most humbly beseech you to be my good and gracious lord. . . . In all my life I never thought one untrue thought against you or your succession, nor can no more judge or cast in my mind what should be laid to my charge than the child that was born this night. . . . I know not that I have offended any man . . . unless it were such as are angry with me for being quick against such as have been accused for sacramentaries." And fancying that he detected the secret motive of his trial, he added: "Let me recover your gracious favour, with taking of me all the lands and goods I have, or as much thereof as pleaseth your Highness."

The charges brought against Norfolk and Surrey were mere

pretexts. No notice having been taken of the letter just cited, the old man, who was anxious by any means to save his life, determined to humble himself still further. On January 12, nine days before the death of Surrey, in the hope of satisfying the king, he made, in the presence of the members of the privy council, the following confession:—"I, Thomas, duke of Norfolk do confess and acknowledge myself . . . to have offended the king's most excellent Majesty, in the disclosing . . . of his privy and secret counsel . . . to the great peril of his Highness. . . . That I have concealed high treason, in keeping secret the false and traitorous act . . . committed by my son . . . against the king's Majesty . . . in the putting and using the arms of Edward the Confessor, . . . in his scutcheon or arms. . . . Also, that to the peril, slander, and disinherison of the king's majesty and his noble son, Prince Edward, I have . . . borne in the first quarter of my arms . . . the arms of England. . . . Although I be not worthy to have . . . the king's clemency and mercy to be extended to me, . . . yet with a most sorrowful and repentant heart do beseech his Highness to have mercy, pity, and compassion on me."

All was fruitless; Norfolk must die like the best servants and friends of the king, like Fisher, Sir Thomas More, and Cromwell. But the duke, the chief nobleman of the land, could not be tried as was his son. The king assembled the parliament; a bill of attainder was presented to the house of lords, and the three readings were hurried through on January 18, 19, 20. The bill, sent down to the commons, was passed by them, and was sent back on the 24th. Although it was customary to reserve the final step to the close of the session, the king, who was in haste, gave his assent on Thursday the 27th, and the execution of Norfolk was fixed for the morning of the next day. All the preparations for this last act were made during the night; and but a few moments were to intervene before this once powerful man was to be led to the scaffold.

Two victims were now awaiting the remorseless scythe of destiny. Death was approaching at the same time the threshold of the palace and that of the prison. Two men who had filled the world with their renown, who during their lifetime had been closely united, and were the foremost personages of the realm, were about to pass the inexorable gates and to be bound with those bonds which God alone can burst. The only question was which of the two would be the first to receive the final stroke. The general expectation was, no doubt, that Norfolk would be the first, for the executioner was already sharpening the axe which was to smite him.

While the duke, still full of vigorous life, was awaiting in his dungeon the cruel death which he had striven so much to avert, Henry VIII was prostrate on his sick bed at Whitehall. Although everything showed that his last hour was at hand, his physicians did not venture to inform him of it, as it was against the law for anyone to speak of the death of the king. One might almost have said that he was determined to have himself declared immortal by act of parliament. At length, however, Sir Antony Denny, chief gentleman of the chamber, who hardly ever left him, took courage and, approaching the bedside of the dying monarch, cautiously told him that all hope, humanly speaking, was lost, and entreated him to prepare for death. The king, conscious of his failing strength, accused himself of various offences, but added that the grace of God could forgive him all his sins. It has been asserted that he did really repent of his errors. "Several English gentlemen," says Thevet, "assured me that he was truly repentant, and among other things, on account of the injury and crime committed against the said queen (Anne Boleyn)." This is not certain; but we know that Denny, glad to hear him speak of his sins, asked him whether he did not wish to see some ecclesiastic. "If I see anyone," said Henry, "it must be Archbishop Cranmer." "Shall I send for him?" said Denny. The king replied: "I will first take a little sleep, and then, as I feel myself, I will advise upon the matter." An hour or two later the king awoke, and finding that he was now weaker, he asked for Cranmer. The archbishop was at Croydon; and when he arrived the dying man was unable to speak, and was almost unconscious. However, when he saw the primate, he stretched out his hand, but could not utter a word. The archbishop exhorted him to put all his trust in Christ and to implore His mercy. "Give some token with your eyes or hand," he said, "that you trust in the Lord." The king wrung Cranmer's hand as hard as he could, and soon after breathed his last. He died at two o'clock in the morning, Friday, January 28, 1547.

By Henry's death Norfolk's life was saved. The new government declined to begin the new reign by putting to death the foremost peer of England. Norfolk lived for eight years longer. He spent, indeed, the greater part of it in prison; but for more than a year he was at liberty, and died at last at Kenninghall.

Henry died at the age of fifty-six years. It is no easy task to sketch the character of a prince whose principal feature was inconsistency. Moreover, as Lord Herbert of Cherbury said, his history is his best portrait. The epoch in which he lived was that of a resurrection of the human mind. Literature and the arts, political liberty, and evangelical faith were now coming forth from the tomb and returning to life. The human mind, since the outburst of bright light which then illumined it, has sometimes given itself up, it must be confessed, to strange errors; but it has never again fallen into its old sleep. There were some kings, such as Henry VIII and Francis I, who took an interest in the revival of letters; but the greater number were alarmed at the revival of freedom and of faith, and instead of welcoming tried to stifle them. Some authors, and particularly Foxe, the martyrologist, have asserted that if death had not prevented him, Henry VIII would have so securely established the Reformation as not to leave a single mass in the kingdom. This is nothing more than a hypothesis, and it appears to us a very doubtful one. The king had made his will some two years before his death, when he was setting out for the war with France. In it, his chief object was to regulate the order of succession and the composition of the council of regency; but at the same time it contains positive signs of scholastic Catholicism. In this document the king says: "We do instantly desire and require the blessed Virgin Mary His mother, with all the holy company of heaven, continually to pray for us and with us while we live in this world, and in time of passing out of the same."

Moreover, he ordained that the dean and canons of the chapel royal, Windsor, and their successors for ever, should have two priests to say masses at the altar. The will was re-written on December 13, 1546; and the members of the Privy Council signed it as witnesses. But the only change which the king introduced was the omission of Gardiner's name among the members of the council of regency. The passages respecting the Virgin and masses for his soul were retained.

Henry had brought into the world with him remarkable capacities, and these had been improved by education. He has been praised for his application to the business of the State, for his wonderful cleverness, his rare eloquence, his high courage. His abilities certainly give him a place above the average of kings. He regularly attended the council, corresponded with his ambassadors, and took much pains. In politics he had some clear views; he caused the Bible to be printed; but the moral sentiment is shocked when he is held up as a model. The two most conspicuous features of his character were pride and sensuality; and by these vices he was driven to most blameworthy actions, and even to crimes. Pride led him to make himself head of the church, to claim the right to regulate the faith of his subjects, and to punish cruelly those who had the audacity to hold any other opinions on matters of religion than his own. The Reformation of which he is assumed to be the author was hardly a pseudo-reform; we might rather see in it another species of *de*formation. Claiming autocracy in matters of faith, he naturally claimed the same in matters of state. All the duties of his subjects were summed up by him in the one word *obedience;* and those who refused to bow the head to his despotic rule were almost sure to lose it. He was covetous, prodigal, capricious, suspicious; not only was he fickle in his friendships, but on many occasions he did not hesitate to take his victims from amongst his best friends. His treatment of his wives, and especially of Anne Boleyn, condemns him as a man; his bloody persecutions of the evangelicals condemn him as a Christian; the scandalous servility which he endeavoured, and not unsuccessfully, to engraft in the nobles, the bishops, the house of commons and the people, condemn him as a king.

Index

The page references for Volume Two are shown in bold type.

494

LECTURES ON REVIVALS

WILLIAM B. SPRAGUE.

The subject of revival has become almost fashionable today. There is general agreement amongst Evangelicals that we need a revival. But there are many views as to what revival really is, how it may be promoted and what are the hindrances to it. Clear, scriptural and spiritual thinking and teaching on the subject is greatly needed.

This in the opinion of competent judges is just what Sprague provides. "I consider Dr. Sprague's volume," wrote John Angell James, the distinguished nonconformist leader of the last century, "as the most important and satisfactory testimony that has yet reached us on the subject of revivals." Charles Simeon, leader of the Evangelical party in the Church of England, inscribed in the flyleaf of his own copy, "A most valuable book. I love the good sense of Dr. Sprague." Sprague's lectures ask and answer the questions which perplex us about revivals, as well as some which we are not, but should be, asking.

The volume is enhanced by the inclusion of letters to the author from twenty eminent American ministers, describing their own experiences of revivals and giving sound practical advice. Sprague, like them, is never dry or merely theoretical, because he lived at a time when the church in North America was being watered by the dew of heaven. The great object of his book was "to vindicate and advance the cause of *genuine* revivals of religion." All who have the same cause at heart may profit by reading this neglected volume.

472 pages   15/-

C. H. SPURGEON: the Early Years

The two most wonderful phenomena of the nineteenth century, it was once claimed, were Spurgeon in his *youth* and Gladstone in his *old age*. And truly, "phenomenal" is the only word to describe the meteoric rise to fame of the youth who at 16 was "the boy-preacher of the Fens," and pastor of the Baptist Chapel, Waterbeach, while still in his teens. Called to New Park Street Chapel in 1854 when he was scarce 20, he took London by storm.

Unconventional in manner, aggressive in evangelism, preaching "the old-fashioned Gospel," Charles Haddon Spurgeon stood out in marked contrast to his contemporaries. The spiritual awakening which attended his preaching was, however, followed by uproar, ridicule and bitter opposition. His name was lampooned in the press and "kicked about the street as a football." Yet up to 10,000 flocked to hear him in the Surrey Gardens Music Hall on Sunday mornings; the circulation of his weekly printed sermons went up by leaps and bounds; he became the topic and theme of remark in all parts of the land, and even the subject of a leading article in *The Times*.

In the pages of Spurgeon's Autobiography these thrilling "early years" are made to live again in a way no biographer could have done. His was no ordinary life and characteristically his own account of it is quite unique. The republication of this classic of spiritual history has long been overdue. Generously illustrated and carefully edited, this new edition of the first half of Spurgeon's Autobiography carries the story to 1859, the year of revival.

584 pages   24 pages illustrations   21/-